新加勒比:转型之地
(1943—2005)

THE NEW CARIBBEAN
A Region in Transition
(1943-2005)

第二版
Second Edition

[巴哈马] 戈弗雷·埃尼亚斯　著

邹卫宁　刘冬萌　谭　敏　译

中国海洋大学出版社
· 青岛 ·

图书在版编目(CIP)数据

新加勒比:转型之地(1943—2005)/(巴哈马)戈弗雷·埃尼亚斯著;邹卫宁,刘冬萌,谭敏译.—青岛:中国海洋大学出版社,2018.9

书名原文:THE NEW CARIBBEAN: A Region in Transition 1943-2005

ISBN 978-7-5670-1914-0

Ⅰ.①新… Ⅱ.①戈… ②邹… ③刘… ④谭… Ⅲ.①经济发展-研究-西印度群岛-1943-2005 Ⅳ.①F175.095

中国版本图书馆 CIP 数据核字(2018)第 187837 号

出版发行	中国海洋大学出版社		
社 址	青岛市香港东路 23 号	邮政编码	266071
出 版 人	杨立敏		
网 址	http://www.ouc-press.com		
电子信箱	yyf_press@sina.cn		
订购电话	0532-82032573(传真)		
责任编辑	杨亦飞	电 话	0532-85902533
印 制	青岛国彩印刷有限公司		
版 次	2018 年 12 月第 1 版		
印 次	2018 年 12 月第 1 次印刷		
成品尺寸	170 mm×240 mm		
印 张	23		
字 数	420 千		
印 数	1—1 000		
定 价	58.00 元		

Preface*

In my position as Prime Minister of the Commonwealth of The Bahamas, I sit and meet with other Prime Ministers of the English speaking Caribbean and the President of Haiti at the Caribbean Community (CARICOM) Heads of Government Meeting. Through the Caribbean Forum, the Dominican Republic becomes a partner with CARICOM.

It is at the Heads of Government level that initiatives are crafted. I see an evolving Caribbean region from this vantage point. Yes, Ambassador Eneas is right. There is a new Caribbean and it stems, in no small part, from the post World War II economic policies of The Bahamas; policies that have not only changed The Bahamas but also the region. I said this new Caribbean unfolding during my stint as Minister of Tourism many years ago.

In the new Caribbean, Ambassador Eneas captures the political essence of a Caribbean region which came into its own in the 1960s and 1970s when gaining freedom as independent states.

The transformation of so many Caribbean states from agriculture-based economies to one of service-based on tourism and finance is highlighted. Its impact has, in most cases, lifted the standard of living of most countries.

In the 21st century, Caribbean countries are confronted with the twin challenges of globalization and climate change. Globalization has an economic implication while climate change engenders an understanding of leading environmental issues like hurricanes. Indeed, the Caribbean is the most vulnerable region in the world to natural disasters. Over the past two years, The Bahamas has paid a heavy price.

This book provides an illuminating insight into The Bahamas and Caribbean. I can not recommend it too highly.

The Rt. Hon. Perry G. Christie, M. P.,
PRIME MINISTER
COMMONWEALTH OF THE BAHAMAS

* 译者注：本序作于 2012 年。

序*

在担任巴哈马总理期间，我与加勒比英语区其他国家的总理及海地总统在加勒比共同体政府首脑会议上会晤。经由加勒比论坛，多米尼加共和国成为加勒比共同体的一位合作伙伴。

正是在政府首脑层面的会议上我们制定了各项举措。从这一有利角度，我看到了一个不断发展的加勒比地区。是的，埃尼亚斯大使没错。新的加勒比已然存在，这在很大程度上源于第二次世界大战后巴哈马的经济政策。这些政策不仅改变了巴哈马，也改变了加勒比地区。多年前，我在担任旅游部部长时就说过新的加勒比正逐渐显现。

20 世纪六七十年代，加勒比各国陆续独立，获得自由，地区格局逐渐形成。埃尼亚斯大使抓住了新加勒比地区这种政治本质。

埃尼亚斯大使在书中强调，许多加勒比国家的经济从以农业为基础转变为以旅游业和金融业为基础。在多数情况下，这种转变提升了大部分国家人民的生活水平。

21 世纪，加勒比国家面临着全球化和气候变化双重挑战。全球化对经济有影响，而气候变化促使人们了解飓风等主要环境问题。事实上，加勒比是世界上最易遭受自然灾害影响的地区。过去两年来，巴哈马为此付出了沉重的代价。

本书对了解巴哈马和加勒比提供了启发性的洞见，值得强烈推荐。

佩里·格拉德斯通·克里斯蒂阁下
巴哈马总理兼议员

---

*译者注：本序作于 2012 年。

中文版序

《巴哈马农业历史沿革：1492—2012》和《新加勒比：转型之地（1943—2005）》两本书由巴哈马农业与海洋学院校长、巴哈马非常驻联合国粮农组织大使戈弗雷·埃尼亚斯先生撰写，将由中国海洋大学出版社翻译出版，这源于中国和巴哈马的教育合作。

巴哈马是加勒比地区一颗璀璨的明珠，拥有 700 多座岛屿和 2 400 多个珊瑚礁，具有得天独厚的自然资源、温暖气候以及丰富多元的历史文化。中巴于 1997 年 5 月 23 日正式建立外交关系，2013 年 12 月 19 日，中巴签订《中华人民共和国政府与巴哈马国政府关于互免签证的协定》。两国关系经历了 20 多年的发展历程，经贸合作和人文交流持续加强，两国人民的友谊不断深化。

2015 年 1 月，中国-拉美和加勒比国家共同体部长级会议在北京举行。习近平主席、李克强总理分别亲切会见加勒比国家共同体轮值主席国、巴哈马时任总理佩里·格拉德斯通·克里斯蒂。两国领导人长远规划了中巴各领域互利合作的方向。彼时，中国海洋大学于志刚校长专程赴京应约拜访佩里·格拉德斯通·克里斯蒂总理，商谈推动双边教育交流与合作，帮助巴哈马更好地保护生态环境并推动巴哈马农业与海洋经济的可持续发展，落实两国领导人达成的共识。

2015 年 7 月，于志刚校长应邀率团访问巴哈马，在佩里·格拉德斯通·克里斯蒂总理和中国驻巴哈马大使苑桂森等中巴代表见证下，与戈弗雷·埃尼亚斯校长签署了中国海洋大学和巴哈马农业与海洋学院合作备忘录，双方将在人才培养、学术交流、合作研究及产业开发等多方面开展务实互利合作，积极为中巴教育交流及中巴友好做出贡献。在中国海洋大学代表团访问巴哈马期间，作为校际合作内容之一,双方商定由中国海洋大学资助在中国出版由戈弗雷·埃尼亚斯校长编写的两本书《巴哈马农业历史沿革:1492—2012》和《新加勒比:转型之地(1943—2005)》的中译本,以加强两校的合作,增进两国的相互了解与友谊。

巴哈马农业与海洋学院成立于2013年11月,位于巴哈马最大的岛屿——安德鲁斯岛。巴哈马时任总理佩里·格拉德斯通·克里斯蒂是该机构的主要推动者。该机构的设置旨在通过教学、培训等形式培养农业与海洋资源领域技术人才,大力发展种植业、畜牧业和现代渔业。2014年9月,学院首个农业与海洋科学班开班,学生毕业后将授予副学士学位及证书。巴哈马农业与海洋学院正在快速建设中,学院计划占地2 400余亩,其中包括1 800余亩的教学实验用商业农场和多功能滨海实验基地。

我们希望通过本次出版,让更多民众认识和了解巴哈马,促进中巴两国人民之间的友谊。相信在中巴各界的共同努力下,中巴友谊之树将更加枝繁叶茂,结出丰硕果实,造福两国人民。

2013年至2016年我出任中国驻巴哈马大使。2015年1月我有幸参加了习近平主席和李克强总理同佩里·格拉德斯通·克里斯蒂总理的会见,受益良多。我也亲历了中国海洋大学于志刚校长拜访佩里·格拉德斯通·克里斯蒂总理以及对巴哈马的访问,目睹了两校扎扎实实地把双边互利合作不断推向深入。谨以此序感谢中国海洋大学领导的信任并祝福两校交流与合作继续迈向前方。

原中国驻巴哈马大使: 花桂森

2018年7月1日

2015年7月，本书作者（前排右二）陪同巴哈马时任总理佩里·格拉德斯通·克里斯蒂（前排中）会见到访的中国海洋大学代表团

中国海洋大学代表团考察巴哈马农业与海洋学院实习基地

巴哈马农场

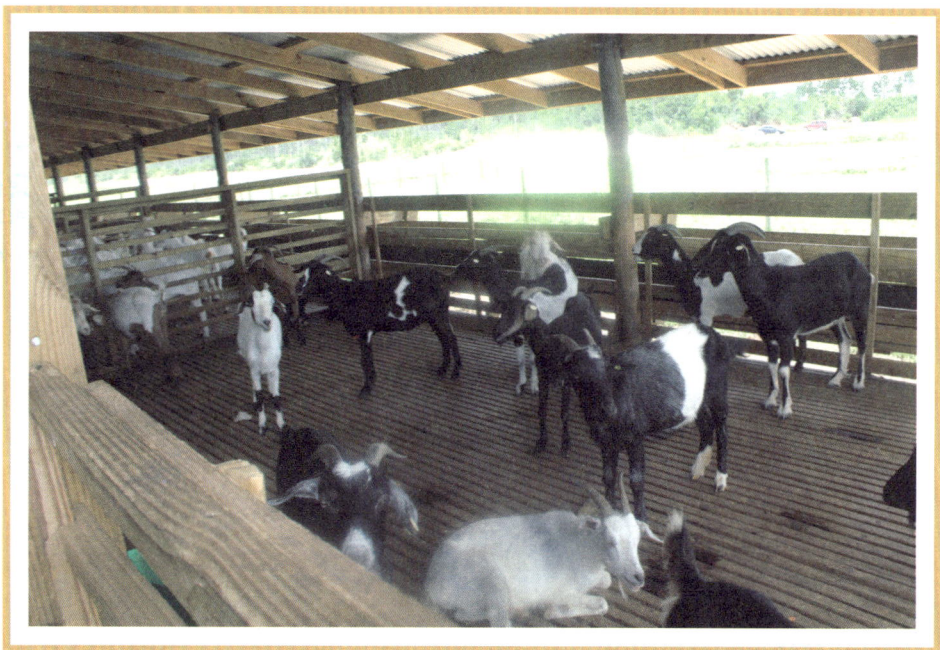

巴哈马养羊场

致　谢

在此感谢单特尔·斯图尔特女士负责打字录入手稿,并准备电子版。她的帮助在此项目中的价值不可估量。

家庭成员提供的帮助往往被视为理所当然。然而,本书的完成离不开我的妻子桑德拉、儿子戈弗雷和蒂莫西以及儿媳瓦妮莎和苏茜的鼓励。他们的校订极其重要,他们对本书的品评也为我提供了宝贵的见解。

感谢《巴哈马日报》及其出版商温德尔·琼斯,让我多年来得以通过《埃尼亚斯文集》进一步了解加勒比。《埃尼亚斯文集》本身就是一个主题论坛。

感谢参与手稿各个准备阶段的拉凯拉·蒂雷利和拉翠霞·马斯格罗夫。他们不得不辨认我的笔迹,以便用电脑录入手稿的几个关键部分。

本书编写过程中的一个要素是利用了信息通信技术,并得到了联合国粮食及农业组织(FAO)及美洲农业合作研究所(IICA)等国际机构的协助。联合国粮食及农业组织办事处(巴巴多斯分区和牙买加办事处、巴哈马联络处)的数据汇编工作极其高效。特在此感谢巴巴多斯的巴巴拉·格雷厄姆博士和西斯戴尔·格拉德先生、巴哈马的格雷格·伯特利先生以及牙买加的邓斯坦·坎贝尔博士。

美洲农业合作研究所的地方代表马利吉斯·阿尔瓦雷斯博士,对该地区农业的意见交流和提供数据方面始终表现出极大的配合。

联合国粮食及农业组织和美洲农业合作研究所通过权力下放政策,为该地区的信息传播提供了有益渠道。为了获得所需的信息和数据,专业人士每次都格外努力。

加勒比家禽协会执行董事罗伯特·贝斯特先生帮忙提供了该地区家禽的有关数据。同该地区其他专业人士建立联系是非常宝贵的,特别是通过互联网上的联合国粮食及农业组织加勒比地区名录。

　　圣公会在海地的工作信息由乔治·洛克伍德先生提供。乔治·洛克伍德先生还帮忙找到了教科书《经济增长理论》和《牙买加小农经济研究》。我在特立尼达圣奥古斯丁的西印度群岛大学学习时用过这些书,但是不知道放在哪儿了。

　　特别感谢巴哈马的艺术家艾比·史密斯女士设计了本书封面。她的作品刻画了"加勒比地区的小农"。小农是奴隶制的遗留物。他们在殖民时期受到剥削,在当今独立时期,仍免不了在经济和社会方面被边缘化。

　　本书的完成离不开上述亲朋好友以及其他人士的支持。

目 录

第8章

加勒比巴哈马:找寻粮食生产的解决之道 // 111

后记:新加勒比 // 144
章节注释 // 147

Chapter 1

A New Era // 161

引　言

我对加勒比地区的迷恋，是从姨妈嫁给一个古巴人后，从巴哈马移居牙买加开始的。姨父的父母是牙买加人。20世纪40年代末，姨妈韦尔涅和姨夫罗伊·约翰逊前往牙买加并在那里定居。

姨父罗伊曾是西印度群岛步兵团的通讯官，驻扎在巴哈马。第二次世界大战结束后，他复员回到父母的家乡牙买加。

姨妈结婚并最终移居牙买加，促成了我们家人到牙买加探亲，也使得我接触到牙买加文化和加勒比的两种语言——古巴的西班牙语和牙买加的克里奥尔英语。有时候，姨父罗伊会根据情况和谈话的主题讲古巴方言或牙买加克里奥尔语。

我对整个加勒比地区兴趣盎然，这主要缘于我对牙买加文化的耳濡目染，加上姨夫罗伊古巴式动作的搞笑滑稽，还有我在牙买加的所见所闻与对加勒比其他岛屿的憧憬，我当时非常渴望能到这些岛屿游览一番。等到姨妈和姨父罗伊回到巴哈马时，我对牙买加的文化已有一定了解。我对加勒比地区的迷恋正始于此。

古巴于我意义重大。20世纪四五十年代，我的外祖父约翰·亨利·桑德斯在当地经营了一家餐厅，就在海湾街旁边。我小的时候每天陪他去市场区（现为拿骚市中心的伍德斯·罗杰斯大道）采购新鲜水果、蔬菜、鱼和本地肉类。

外祖父会到拉吉德岛的船只那儿逛逛。这些船只往返于拉吉德岛和古巴之间采购产品，然后到拿骚市场上出售。正是在那里我接触到了很多古巴商品。其中一种是番石榴干酪，装在约3×12英寸的长方形木箱里，至今都是人们的最爱。当然，还有朗姆酒、利口酒、糖和其他一两种商品。如果我没记错的话，没有雪茄。拉吉德岛的联运是当地与古巴进行稳定贸易的主要途径。

其他一系列事件和场景激起了我深入了解该地区的渴望。西印度人定期涌入巴哈马，这促使我思考加勒比地区人民流动的特性。

几十年来，来自讲英语的殖民地国家的西印度人迁移到巴哈马找工作，有的是业务熟练的商人、警察、家政工、教育工作者、神职人员，还有的担任公务员或在私营部门任专业职位。移民来自牙买加、巴巴多斯、特立尼达和多巴哥及一些东加勒比岛屿，甚至南美大陆，特别是圭亚那和伯利兹（前身为英属洪都拉斯）。他们纷纷前来，加入巴哈马的劳动大军。大多数人通过婚姻融入巴哈马社会，就像我的姨妈和姨夫那样。

这一融入过程根植于共同的语言（英语）、共同的英国教育体系、共同的英国国教、共同的法律制度以及共同的殖民主义和奴隶制遗留问题。融入过程中的另一个重要因素是西印度群岛大学（UWI）。

20世纪60年代，我就读于西印度群岛大学特立尼达圣奥古斯丁校区时，再次接触到了来自各个讲英语的加勒比岛国的当地人。人们觉得巴哈马人与其他西印度人不同，原因是我们说话有明显的鼻音。由于我们靠近美国（US），且经济由旅游带动，所以我们的经济以服务为基础，其他国家的经济则是由庄园或小农产品的出口为驱动。

西印度群岛大学为人们学习辨别语音模式提供了便利，使人们可以辨别每个岛屿人民的口音或方言。作为公职人员，我曾去过大部分岛国，也参加了很多会议、讲座和研讨会。长期接触不同的岛国，加深了我对整个加勒比地区的迷恋。

1980年，联合国粮食及农业组织加勒比和拉丁美洲区域会议在古巴的哈瓦那举行。作为巴哈马代表团的一员，我有幸拜会了古巴总统菲德尔·卡斯特罗。1973年到圭亚那执行另一项实地调研的任务时，我曾与圭亚那已故总统福布斯·伯纳姆有过几次会谈。2000年，作为加勒比家禽协会（CPA）研究小组的一员，我们曾与巴巴多斯总理欧文·亚瑟开会讨论该地区的家禽生产。

林登·奥斯卡·平德林爵士是加勒比共同体的一位著名领导人，他被尊称为"巴哈马独立之父"。从1967到1992年，林登爵士任总理（1967—1973年）和首相（1973—1992年）连续25年领导巴哈马。他享有加勒比共同体任职时间最长的政府首脑这一荣誉。在1997年巴哈马荣誉众议院（本半球第二古老的议会）大选中，我曾有幸与他共同成为他所领导党派的候选人。

我们的地理位置处于美国和伊斯帕尼奥拉岛之间，所以会与海地和多米尼加共和国有所接触。我与多米尼加共和国的接触不多，仅单独访问过罗马尼亚，查看该地区的耕作，还有蓬塔卡纳——该国的一所全包式酒店。

另一方面,海地已发展为巴哈马政府及全体巴哈马人的一个特例。20世纪下半叶之前,巴哈马与海地的联系主要是通过贸易。其中,与海地贸易的最大的交易商之一是威尔弗雷德·图西先生,他是已故图西阁下(我的教父)的兄弟。图西阁下是著名的律师和国会议员。

图西先生的仓库靠近我外祖父的餐厅,临近市场区。他以与海地人做生意谋生,就像拉吉德岛岛民以与古巴人进行贸易一样。

海地弗朗索瓦"老大夫"杜瓦利埃和他的儿子"小大夫"让-克洛德·杜瓦利埃担任总统期间的专制,使海地人开始向巴哈马集体移民。

在杜瓦利埃父子领导海地之前,到巴哈马寻求庇护的海地人是熟练的商人或能工巧匠。在杜瓦利埃政权下,数以千计的海地农村人出逃。这些人没有受过什么教育,非常贫困。农村背景使他们成为巴哈马很多农村公社的农场劳工。

这一类人和我在拿骚圣奥古斯丁学院的那群来自海地的同学形成了鲜明的对比。圣奥古斯丁是一所本笃会修道院学校,由来自明尼苏达州的本笃会修士管理。这些海地同学来自有钱有势的家庭。他们来巴哈马留学是为了参加英国(UK)剑桥海外考试。

2003年,我被任命为巴哈马驻联合国粮食及农业组织大使。联合国粮食及农业组织总干事雅克·迪奥博士在牙买加的加勒比共同体政府首脑会议上就此事致辞。巴哈马总理佩里·格拉德斯通·克里斯蒂阁下将我以大使的身份纳入了巴哈马出席会议代表团队伍。这使我对该地区的政治发展更为赞赏。因为人们可以切实地看到加勒比地区领导人正共同努力,应对21世纪这一关键节点本区域所面临的挑战。

我多次访问该地区,并和住在巴哈马的许多人都有联系,因而与加勒比各国人民进行了广泛的交流。正因如此,加上我本身便是加勒比地区掌握农业发展专业知识的农学家,我同其他人一样认识到加勒比地区的农业处于衰落状态,而旅游业已经在大多数小岛国的经济中占主导地位。由此可见,该地区许多领域正在经历转型。希望本书能够在一定程度上揭示20世纪下半叶及新世纪初加勒比地区已经或正在发生的一些转变。

第 1 章 ››

新时代

> "奴隶制的存在及其后果是加勒比社会历史和发展最根本的因素。如果不考虑奴隶制产生的深远影响，就不可能理解当代加勒比的特性。"
>
> ——牙买加西印度群岛大学费尔南多·恩里克教授

随着第二次世界大战的结束，地缘政治舞台随之改变。欧洲饱受战争蹂躏，西欧各国需要靠美国的马歇尔计划才能得以重建。苏联脱颖而出，成为东方强国，从而随着冷战的开始改变全球范式。这对欧洲国家的殖民地也会产生影响。在第二次世界大战之后的十年内，各殖民前哨的解体陆续开始。

在英帝国，这意味着印度在 1950 年实现独立。七年后的 1957 年，西非殖民地黄金海岸独立为加纳，成为非洲第一个获得独立的英语殖民地。独立运动也席卷了加勒比地区，牙买加在 1962 年成为英属西印度群岛第一个获得独立的殖民地。到 1983 年，几乎所有的前殖民地都脱离英国，获得了独立。只有较小的领地（特克斯和凯科斯群岛、蒙特塞拉特岛、安圭拉岛、英属维尔京群岛、开曼群岛和百慕大群岛）仍然保留为附属地。三个南美国家（伯利兹、圭亚那和苏里南）一致加入加勒比共同体。各国的独立结束了英国对该地区长达约 300 年的控制。

加勒比地区伴随探索、灭绝和剥削而生。在巴哈马这样的英国殖民地，我们作为英国臣民长大，并被教导是欧洲人发现了新大陆，在加勒比的巴哈马群岛第一次登陆。克里斯托弗·哥伦布在瓜纳哈尼岛（他将其改名为圣萨尔瓦多）遇到了阿拉瓦克人，以巴哈马的人口减少告终。上岛后不久，他所遇见的居民被强行带到古巴和伊斯帕尼奥拉岛（今天的海地和多米尼加共和国）工作，最终因此而消亡。为了开采本地区的资源，欧洲人从非洲引入劳力，由此开始了非洲人在新大陆的流散，并将加勒比地区置于这种现象的中心，而这种现象后又演变成不人道的奴隶制。

加勒比地区走向独立的背景是奴隶制。尽管英帝国已于 1834 年废除了奴隶制，但其带来的心理影响已经体现在加勒比的非洲奴隶后裔身上，涉及政治、社会、经济和精神各个方面。随着奴隶制在新大陆的废除，包身工时期迎来了亚洲人的涌入，主要是东印度人、印尼人和中国人，该地区的种族多样性由此得到丰富。正是这些各种各样的人组成了加勒比地区的各个独立国家。

在殖民时期和如今的主权国家期间，地理和政治之间的相互作用对塑造加勒比地区发挥了重要的作用。在殖民时期的鼎盛时期，加勒比地区是三角贸易的重要组成部分。三角贸易促进了朗姆酒和糖从该地区运往英国，而英国又将武器、布料、盐等物品运往西非。在西非，黑人被用来交换这些物品，再卖给加勒比地区的甘蔗种植园园主做奴隶。

如今，加勒比的地理和政治使该地区扮演着与以往不同的角色。经济转型在国家建设中至关重要，而国家建设的复杂性又带来了一系列新的挑战。随着国家独立，国家的统治与治理与殖民时期有所不同。转型在所难免。

由于 20 世纪下半叶获得独立的国家数量较多，讲英语的加勒比国家一直在推动本地区的地缘政治事务。这些于 20 世纪中期获得独立的国家已经能够通过加勒比共同体承担这项任务。加勒比共同体已演变成包容多元文化和不同语言的组织。加勒比共同体中的前英国殖民地国家已经获得独立，拥有较强的民主传统的巴哈马议会和巴巴多斯议会是该半球两个最古老的议会。加勒比地区还有强大的机构基础，特别是真正的区域性高等教育机构——西印度群岛大

图 1.1　加勒比地区领导人：克里斯蒂（左）、卡斯特罗（中）和伯德（右一） [①]

① 古巴共和国总统菲德尔·卡斯特罗先生（该地区任职时间最长的国家元首），巴哈马总理佩里·格拉德斯通·克里斯蒂阁下（巴哈马第三任总理），以及安提瓜和巴布达前总理莱斯特·伯德阁下，摄于 2005 年古巴哈瓦那的加勒比共同体会议。照片由彼得·拉姆齐提供。

学、加勒比开发银行（CDB）、加勒比农业研究与发展研究所（CARDI）、加勒比地区谈判机制（CRNM）和加勒比单一市场和经济（CSME）。加勒比地区独立国家通过加勒比共同体，对推动地区发展、促进地区进步起到了催化作用。此项任务曾经颇具挑战性，未来依然如此。

表 1.1　加勒比共同体——15 个成员国和 5 个准成员

成员国	人口（2006 年估计）	人均收入（2005 年估计）
巴哈马	320 665	17 800 美元
巴巴多斯	279 912	17 000 美元
伯利兹	287 730	6 800 美元
圭亚那	767 245	4 600 美元
海　地	8 308 504	361 美元
牙买加	2 758 124	4 400 美元
苏里南	439 117	4 100 美元
特立尼达和多巴哥	1 065 842	16 700 美元
	小计 14 227 139	

除安圭拉岛和英属维尔京群岛为准成员外，加勒比共同体包括东加勒比国家组织（OECS）的所有成员国。

人口和人均收入数据来自中央情报局（CIA）——世界概况、世界银行（海地）。

分　区

表 1.2　东加勒比国家组织

国　家	人口（2004 年估计）	人均收入（2002 年估计）
安圭拉岛	13 008	8 600 美元
安提瓜和巴布达	68 320	11 000 美元
英属维尔京群岛	22 187	16 000 美元
多米尼克	69 278	5 400 美元
格林纳达	89 357	5 000 美元
蒙特塞拉特岛	9 245	3 400 美元
圣卢西亚	164 213	5 400 美元
圣基茨和尼维斯	38 836	8 800 美元
圣文森特和格林纳丁斯	117 193	2 900 美元
小　计	591 637	

表 1.3　加勒比共同体准成员

国　家	人口（2004 年估计）	人均收入（2002 年估计）
百慕大群岛	65 773	69 900 美元（2004 年）
开曼群岛	45 436	32 300 美元（2004 年）
特克斯和凯科斯群岛	21 152	11 500 美元（2002 年）
小　计	132 361	

续表

国　家	人口（**2004 年估计**）	人均收入（**2002 年估计**）
加勒比共同体合计	14 951 137（2006 年）	
古　巴	11 382 820（2006 年）	3 500 美元（2005 年）
波多黎各	3 927 188（2006 年）	7 000 美元（2005 年）
多米尼加共和国	9 183 984（2006 年）	14 500 美元
美属维尔京群岛	108 605	16 000 美元
荷属安的列斯群岛	221 736	
加勒比地区小计	39 775 470	
马提尼克岛	436 131	14 400 美元（2003 年）
瓜德罗普岛	452 776	7 900 美元（2003 年）
圣马丁岛		
加勒比地区合计	40 664 377	

插曲:《埃尼亚斯文集》《巴哈马日报》 加勒比地缘政治群

无论我们承认与否,巴哈马都是加勒比共同体的一分子。上周,在第 20 届的政府首脑峰会上,加勒比共同体各国接纳了海地。

巴哈马是离海地最近的加勒比共同体国家。相比其他更偏南或加勒比海盆地更深处的加勒比共同体国家,海地可能更让巴哈马担心。

除了加勒比共同体,还有一个名为加勒比论坛(CARIFORUM)的加勒比团体。上周之前,该论坛成员包括加勒比共同体各国以及海地和多米尼加共和国。在可预见的未来,或许在下个世纪初期,古巴将加入其中一个团体。

加勒比共同体内部有一个由七个成员国组成的团体,即东加勒比国家组织。这些国家包括格林纳达、圣文森特和格林纳丁斯、圣卢西亚、多米尼克、安提瓜和巴布达、圣基茨和尼维斯。

随着苏里南加入加勒比共同体,加上现在的海地和即将加入的古巴,三种语言(苏里南的荷兰语、海地的法语以及多米尼加共和国和古巴的西班牙语)将成为加勒比地区各种论坛的用语。

在最近举办的首脑峰会上,委内瑞拉亦严肃提议加入加勒比共同体。委内瑞拉总统亲自向各国元首发表讲话,提出了一些加勒比共同体可能无法忽略的建议。

委内瑞拉是一个石油资源丰富的国家,其民主正处在萌芽阶段;其石油资源带来的资金影响力不容忽视。

这就是加勒比地区目前的地缘情况。加勒比不再局限于位于加勒比海的岛屿。现在,它还包含那些能够感受到加勒比海的温暖的国家,如委内瑞拉。

除去古巴和委内瑞拉,1996年,加勒比论坛成员国的人口约为2 200万人,其中,38%分布在多米尼加共和国,34%在海地。之后,人口分布百分比大幅下落,人口第二多的是牙买加,占12%。

加上古巴的1 100万人口,加勒比论坛成员国的人口增长了50%。如果将委内瑞拉的2 000多万人计算在内,那么加勒比论坛成员国的人口则翻了一番。

全球化加速推进了贸易集团的发展。事实证明,国家能够通过贸易集团的途径扩大出口。这在加勒比共同体已经非常明显,而且随着自由化得到越来越多的重视,贸易将继续增长。

这些国家都拥有着巨大的劳动力市场,但这些地区的失业率居高不下,巴巴多斯和巴哈马除外。通过使劳动力发挥作用,这些国家的出口在加勒比地区以及全球都非常有竞争力。

在本世纪过去的50年里,加勒比地区的政治发生了巨大的变化。古巴卡斯特罗主义的崛起导致古巴被加勒比邻国孤立了近30年的时间;然而,这种情况正在改变。英国、荷兰在该地区实行的非殖民化使该地区产生了许多独立国家,就像加勒比共同体的成员国。

随着独立,这些国家想要构建一种时新的区域认同。这种区域认同能够在加勒比英语区跨越语言差异和文化差异,从而运用民主原则和英国法律体系中所含的共同优势。

三个世纪以来,加勒比地区是英国、法国、西班牙和荷兰这些帝国主义列强争夺最激烈的海外区域。而今天的加勒比地区是世界上政治最稳定的地区之一。如今,加勒比地区面临的主要挑战是如何使本地区经济在全球经济中有效发挥作用。

第 2 章 »

经济转型

创建城市化社会

> "在院子中央,有一团巨火,它为人们提供着光明以及精神上的温暖和欢乐,它也用来调整为舞蹈打节拍的山羊皮小鼓……被此节奏和音乐感动的任何人都可以进这个圈里一起跳舞,在这里他或她的灵魂得到了愉悦。"

> ——巴哈马人克利夫兰·埃尼斯博士,《贝恩小镇》

个案研究:巴哈马

巴哈马的地理位置优势在于其接近美国。毕米尼群岛位于巴哈马群岛北部,距离佛罗里达海岸线只有 48 英里。据说,在晴朗的夜晚从贝利镇可以看到迈阿密耀眼的灯光。

这种近距离正是巴哈马战后经济繁荣的一个重要因素。巴哈马经历了第二次世界大战结束之后以及最近的"9·11"事件后的经济繁荣。

战后繁荣是巴哈马经济转型的催化剂。巴哈马从以农业为基础、季节性旅游型经济向全年型商贸经济转型。同时,它围绕着新普罗维登斯岛的首都拿骚和大巴哈马岛的新建城市弗里波特创建了一个城市化社会。

"9·11"事件后的繁荣将给家庭岛带来前所未有的投资。这是由于克里斯蒂政府鼓励在每一个家庭岛上开发一个支柱型旅游项目的经济发展战略。这个策略将有助于人口从城市中心向家庭岛回迁,通过创造就业机会来扶贫,给巴哈马的东南部带来了可持续的经济活动,促使旅游收入惠及更多人口。

战后繁荣

在第二次世界大战结束之前,大多数巴哈马人居住在外岛,也就是今天我们所说的家庭岛。1943 年,巴哈马的人口不到 7 万,其中,大约有 3 万住在新普罗维登斯岛和首都拿骚附近，剩下的 4 万人分散在 20 个有很多居民的岛上。

20 世纪 40 年代，57% 的人口生活在家庭岛或巴哈马的农村。那时候，巴哈马的大多数岛屿都呈现出一幅古香古色的渔村景象。这体现在社会习俗、饮食、小农（多数情况下为自给农）对土地的依附上，同时，体现在渔民对海的依附上。

英国人迈克尔·克拉通曾经是著名的巴哈马政府中学的历史教师，在他的著作《巴哈马历史》中，克拉通捕捉到了巴哈马在第二次世界大战结束后的氛围。克拉通指出：

> "战争结束了，人们高兴地庆祝，随之而来的并非是一贯的衰落。的确，1945 年后的 25 年是一段无与伦比的时期，扩张和成功几乎毫无间断。旅游业繁荣发展，投资金额和政府收入不断增长，人们生活水平得到巨大提高，教育和政治不断发展。同时，英国政府统治巴哈马的意愿或能力不断降低，促使巴哈马不断进步，走向独立自主。"

20 世纪 40 年代，政治权力掌握在少数白人手中。这些白人包含控制巴哈马贸易的商人团体，他们可以决定巴哈马的经济发展速度。他们的生意在首都拿骚的主要街道——海湾街上，因此，他们被称为海湾街的商业大亨。这种寡头政治控制着巴哈马的政治和经济。

该殖民地有一名皇家总督，他领导着执行委员会和议会机构。海湾街的商业大亨控制着政府部门，操控着殖民地统治管理。

1964 年以前，巴哈马没有部级政府，委员会制度盛行。巴哈马发展委员会是重要的委员会之一。

1949 年，斯塔福德·洛夫特霍斯·桑德斯出任强大的巴哈马发展委员会的主席，并在此职位任职 15 年。1964 年，巴哈马发展委员会演变为旅游部。桑德斯最终被授予爵士爵位，后被称为斯塔福德爵士。在近 18 年里，桑德斯在旅游增长与发展方面有远见卓识，他还负责识别境外银行业务可行的经济活动，最终将成为这一时期巴哈马经济的一个重要部门。

作为发展委员会主席（1949—1964 年）和旅游与金融部部长（1964—1967年），斯塔福德爵士是巴哈马最具影响力的政治人物。他能功成名就，得益于他在法律领域训练有素，且极具商业头脑与政治影响力。

1964 年宪法授予巴哈马内部自治权，部级政府应运而生。在此之前，巴哈马存在选举舞弊行为，使海湾街的商业大亨最终组建了政治基础是少数白人的联合巴哈马人党（UBP）。联合巴哈马人党的政治武器之一便是公司投票。

图 2.1　斯塔福德·洛夫特霍斯·桑德斯爵士 [1]

公司有资格在选举中投票。代表城市选民的斯塔福德爵士大约有 300 家公司在其内庭注册。据说，他会坐在投票间里投自己 300 次票。

斯塔福德爵士出自海湾街商业家族。他曾是肯尼斯·所罗门爵士内庭里的见习律师。他在巴哈马政府中学而非种族隔离的女王学院接受中学教育。

斯塔福德爵士曾接受法律方面的教育，并经培训成为一名律师，他在巴哈马发展了自己的商业头脑和政治技能，是巴哈马成就了他。

1967 年 1 月 10 日，多数裁定原则出现了。林登·O. 平德林带领进步自由党（PLP）击败了联合巴哈马人党，斯塔福德爵士自愿流放到西班牙。1972 年 1 月 25 日，斯塔福德爵士因癌症在伦敦一家医院逝世，享年 59 岁；他再也没有回过巴哈马。然而，他生前曾致力于巴哈马经济转型，即从依赖农业型经济转向以旅游业、金融服务业为主导的经济，他为巴哈马留下的这份遗产使他成为巴哈马有先见之明之人。他为小岛型发展中国家创设的桑德斯模式正在整个地区重复着。

巴哈马是加勒比地区较早开发旅游业的国家。斯塔福德爵士认识到了这一点，巴哈马发展委员会设法改善空运，以便利用巴哈马距美国较近，特别是距离美国东海岸人口稠密的城市中心较近的优势。老拿骚自具魅力，再加上阳光、沙滩、大海，来访游客数量不断增长。

转型过程中的发展成果（1943—2000 年）

20 世纪下半叶，巴哈马生活的方方面面都经历了快速增长和长足发展。巴哈马旅游业蓬勃发展，境外金融中心还处于萌芽期，这些发展促使巴哈马经济

---

[1]　巴哈马开发委员会主席（1949—1964 年）、旅游部部长（1964—1967 年）。

发生了巨大的改变。

巴哈马发展委员会在首任主席哈罗德·格拉德斯通·克里斯蒂的领导下启动了一项促进巴哈马发展的项目。克里斯蒂先生的目标是"将无足轻重的巴哈马变成世界富人的新麦加"。1949 年,斯塔福德爵士成为巴哈马发展委员会主席,巴哈马吸引了约 32 018 名游客。

到 20 世纪 50 年代末,到巴哈马观光的游客达到了 264 758 名。阳光、沙滩和大海成为旅游业宣传项目的核心部分。1949 年引入的《酒店鼓励法案》进一步促进了该计划的实施。

《酒店鼓励法案》是一部激励性的立法法案,在一系列酒店建设项目、设备和材料方面为酒店开发商提供了免税优惠。结合这一法案,据说是当时英帝国最富有的人之一的加拿大百万富翁哈里·奥克斯建造了凯布尔海滩高尔夫球场。利用这种新推力吸引游客,必须为扩建机场做好准备。

1957 年,国家国际机场开始运营,拿骚之外的奥克斯机场关闭了。

开发活动并不局限于新普罗维登斯岛。1955 年,随着《玳瑁湾协议》的签署,大巴哈马岛将经历转型,创建第二个弗里波特。

政治方面有许多骚动。1953 年,年纪轻轻、训练有素的英国律师林登·O.平德林创建了进步自由党,成为该政党领袖。自进步自由党成立以来,该政党就成了白人掌权者的眼中钉,海湾街寡头政治集团最终自己组建了联合巴哈马人党。

政局紧张愈演愈烈,为了抗议旅游公司和酒店利用巴士运送客人,出租车工会发起行动,封锁拿骚国际机场。1958 年,酒店员工与出租车司机联合,该局面演变成为全国性罢工。这一问题直到出租车司机获得运送抵达游客的专有权之后才得以解决。

在这十年间,迁移到新普罗维登斯岛居住的人口比巴哈马其他岛屿的人口加起来还要多。巴哈马已成为一个城市社会。

20 世纪 60 年代是巴哈马旅游业具有里程碑意义的时期。1968 年,巴哈马接纳了 100 万名游客。

这一热潮由很多因素促成。其中,最重要的一点是,拿骚和弗里波特引入了博彩业。

弗里波特将成为旅游目的地,其建有 1 个 18 洞高尔夫球场、2 个微型 9 洞球场,还有卢卡约海滩酒店。在阿巴科岛,特利休阿岛投入开发运行。

霍格岛距新普罗维登斯岛不足 1 英里,后被改名为天堂岛。20 世纪 60 年代末,一座桥将天堂岛与新普罗维登斯岛连接在了一起,从而为新普罗维登斯岛提供了两个景区——凯布尔海滩和天堂岛。

1964 年,政治宪法修正引入部级政府,巴哈马开始内部自治。

1967 年大选见证了海湾街寡头政治团体联合巴哈马人党的消亡,也见证了平德林带领下进步自由党的兴起。

对大多数黑种人来说,1967 年的大选是自 1834 年解放以来最重大的政治事件。

20 世纪五六十年代,巴哈马的社会形态发生了巨大变化。这种变化源于女性不仅可以参与工作,还可以参与巴哈马群岛的政治事务。

女性成为酒店劳动力的一个重要组成部分,成千上万的女性离开新普罗维登斯岛和家庭岛的家到酒店寻求就业,她们主要做服务员。相当数量的女性成为有工资收入的人。对那些单身母亲来说,她们挣取工资,成为家里的顶梁柱。同时,卖纪念品的小商贩中,女性占主要地位;当地的稻草纪念品更是成了巴哈马旅游业的一个重要方面。1960 年,女性获得了投票权,并且取得了立法参与者的席位。

曾经遭受殖民统治的国家摆脱殖民统治后总会发生各种事件,而巴哈马与此相反,享有稳定的发展中国家的声誉。这种稳定为巴哈马的旅游业引来了外国的投资。

到 1970 年年中,游客数量已经上升至 150 万人。高尔夫球场是吸引游客的一个卖点,弗里波特、大巴哈马岛、特利休阿岛、阿巴科岛和新普罗维登斯岛(南大洋和科勒尔港)都在修建新的高尔夫球场。随着旅游业的增长和发展,酒店培训学院和酒店集团应运而生。为了深化游客在社区层面的体验,旅游部实施了人人计划。

人人计划致力于将游客带入普通的巴哈马家庭。

由于美国是巴哈马游客的主要来源市场,巴哈马政府得以与美国政府谈判并达成协议,在拿骚(1974 年)和弗里波特(1976 年)启用预检清关设备。这种设备功能强大,为大量从巴哈马返回美国的美国人提供了便利。

巴哈马在经历了近十年的内部自治和五年的进步自由党的执政后,于 1973 年取得独立,结束了近 300 年的殖民统治,并为其殖民历史画上了句号。

巴哈马现在将开启其国民生活的新篇章。20 世纪 80 年代的巴哈马旅游业发展尤为显著。

克莱门特爵士在三个不同时期对旅游业进行了投资组合:

① 旅游和电信局(1969 年 10 月 14 日—1971 年 11 月 30 日)。

② 外交与旅游部(1984 年 10 月 9 日—1992 年 8 月 19 日)。

③ 旅游与公共人事部(1987 年 10 月 9 日—1990 年 9 月 30 日)。

图 2.2　克莱门特·梅纳德爵士 [①]

总体来说,克莱门特爵士担任巴哈马旅游部部长已有 13 年。在克莱门特爵士的领导下,巴哈马成了加勒比的旅游胜地。

表 2.1　按照性别划分旅游从业人员(旅馆和饭店)1991—2005 年

年　份	合　计	男　性	女　性
1991	21 180	8 800	12 380
1992	21 175	8 950	12 225
1993	18 895	8 385	10 510
1994	18 385	8 850	10 030
1995	19 405	7 625	11 780
1996	20 360	8 655	11 705
1997	21 440	9 240	12 200
1998			
1999	23 300	9 630	13 670
2000			
2001	25 515	10 800	14 715

① 前巴哈马副总理(1985 年 10 月 29 日—1992 年 8 月 18 日)。

续表

年 份	合 计	男 性	女 性
2002	25 690	10 890	14 800
2003	27 920	11 985	15 935
2004	23 765	9 180	14 585
2005	29 095	11 380	17 715

来源:统计局

1980 年初,200 万游客游览了巴哈马。1983 年,这个数字上升到 260 万;三年后(1986 年),这个数字超过了 300 万。在这十年间,乘坐邮轮的乘客多于乘飞机中途停留的乘客。乘坐邮轮是巴哈马游客的首选。

进步自由党作为执政党执政了 25 年,1992 年经历了首次失败。政府的统治落入了由休伯特·A. 英格拉哈姆先生领导的自由民族运动(FNM)手中。

英格拉哈姆政府与南非酒店老板索尔·科兹纳达成了协议。科兹纳收购了天堂岛度假村国际股份有限公司,这使巴哈马旅游业迎来了一个新的局面。科兹纳的收购让巴哈马旅游业重新焕发生机。到 20 世纪 90 年代末,每年到巴哈马旅游的游客数量增长至 400 万。

21 世纪初,由于旅游业增长并发展成为最重要的经济部门,巴哈马的经济、人口和生活方式均发生了变化。55 年来,巴哈马从一个依赖农业的群岛发展成为一个人均收入近 2 万美元的以旅游城市为中心的主权国家。

旅游业和金融服务业一起创建了一个以服务业为基础的经济体。

"9·11"后的繁荣

于美国人而言,"9·11"事件无异于第二个珍珠港事件。对世界其他地区来说,"9·11"事件标志着一个恐怖主义的新时期;"9·11"事件改变了人们出行的方式,也将安全级别提高了一个层次。

"9·11"事件给巴哈马和加勒比地区这些小岛国敲响了警钟。这些小岛国家的经济缺陷被暴露无遗,一切都停了下来——游客不来了;北美领空关闭了,飞机停飞了;邮轮停止航行了;驶往依赖进口地区的集装箱货运船满载着食品、供应物资、饲料,停靠在迈阿密、劳德代尔堡、里维拉海滩、杰克逊维尔和其他地区。

飞机和邮轮是前往巴哈马和加勒比地区旅游的两种重要途径,这两种途径都被暂停了。美国人开始从一个不同的角度审视出国旅游,他们似乎对在美国附近旅游更感兴趣。巴哈马是休闲旅游、构建别居的理想之地。巴哈马距离佛罗里达海岸只有48英里，距离纽约大约1 000英里，巴哈马会意外收获到外国的直接投资。

图2.3　天堂岛上的亚特兰蒂斯——科兹纳国际集团旗舰地产

政府经济发展战略的核心是在各个家庭岛上建立锚固工程，特别是巴哈马东南部那些比北方的松树岛还落后的岛屿（阿巴科岛、安德罗斯岛和大巴哈马岛）。2006年中期，这一战略吸引了约115亿美元的外国直接投资。

该战略的缔造者是2002年5月接替英格拉哈姆政府的克里斯蒂政府。巴哈马首相佩里·格拉德斯通·克里斯蒂阁下非常重视实现这一战略，故在家庭岛实施该战略。

项目已获得批准，并在阿巴科岛、安德罗斯岛、贝里群岛、崎岖岛、伊鲁塞拉岛、伊克祖马斯岛、大巴哈马岛、玛雅古纳岛、新普罗维登斯岛、朗姆屿和圣萨尔瓦多岛等地处于建设或运作阶段，如表2.2所示。

巴哈马政府与一家加拿大公司签署合同，以扩建林登·平德林国际机场，并对机场进行升级。该计划将使机场设施极具现代化，并使林登·平德林国际机场成为该地区继"9·11"事件后最重要的机场。

结合以上所述，政府开始重建拿骚城和拿骚港。"老拿骚"曾是巴哈马发展委员会旅游推广的中心，现在，拿骚城及其港口将基于"老拿骚"进行转型。这一转型将在公共—私营部门的管理下进行。实施转型计划的机构是拿骚经济发展委员会和拿骚旅游发展委员会。

表 2.2 转型过程中的发展成果（1943—2005 年）

年代	年份	游客数量	旅游产品构成	主要国家发展成果/旅游业	人口统计资料（人口增长和变化）			劳动力雇佣/就业按行业门类划分			整个巴哈马的劳动力	就业	
					拿骚	弗里波特、大不列颠岛	家庭岛	农业（小农）	旅游业	金融服务		女性	男性
20世纪40年代	1943				29 391	2 333	37 122						
	1949	32 018	阳光	《酒店鼓励法案》									
	1950	45 371											
20世纪50年代	1951	68 502											
	1952	84 718		凯布尔海滩高尔夫球场									
	1953	90 485	沙滩		46 125	4 095	34 614						
	1954	109 605											
	1955	132 434		《玛瑙湾协议》（弗里波特、大不列颠岛）									
	1956	155 003	大海（邮轮、游艇）	开放拿骚国际机场									
	1957	209 713		大罢工									
	1958	196 658											
	1959	264 758		卡斯特罗推翻巴蒂斯塔									
20世纪60年代	1960	341 977		1个18洞高尔夫球场和2个小型9洞球场（弗里波特、大不列颠岛）									
	1961	368 211											

续表

年代	年份	游客数量	旅游产品构成	主要国家发展成果/旅游业	人口统计资料（人口增长和变化）			劳动力雇佣/就业按行业门类分				就业	
					拿骚	弗里波特、大不列颠岛	家庭岛	农业（小农）	旅游业	金融服务	整个巴哈马的劳动力	女性	男性
20世纪60年代	1962	444 870		霍格岛被重新命名为天堂岛									
	1963	546 404		在位于阿巴科群岛的特利休阿岛上的卢卡约海滩酒店开设赌场	80 907	8 230	41 083						
	1964		赌博、高尔夫球场	天堂岛的开发、内部自治、内阁政府、第一任旅游部部长									
	1965												
	1966			平德林政府									
	1967			天堂岛桥梁建设									
	1968	1 072 213											
	1969												
	1970			引入《克鲁普斯计酒店法案》	101 503	25 859	41 450	3 099					
	1971		高尔夫球场	在位于阿巴科群岛的特利休阿岛上（弗里波特岛）修建5个18洞高尔夫球场和2个小型球场									
	1972												

续表

年代	年份	游客数量	旅游产品构成	主要国家发展成果/旅游业	人口统计资料（人口增长和变化）			劳动力雇佣/就业按行业门类分			整个巴哈马的劳动力	就业	
					拿骚	弗里波特、大不列颠岛	家庭岛	农业（小农）	旅游业	金融服务		女性	男性
20世纪60年代	1973	1 500 010		巴哈马独立/巴哈马酒店培训学院建立				3 320					
	1974		拿骚和美国启用预检清关设施	酒店公司（促进旅游业）；南大洋/科勒尔港；高尔夫球场									
	1975			人人计划				3 797					
20世纪70年代	1976		弗里波特	美国启用预检清关设施									
	1977												
	1978			西印度群岛大学巴哈马东道主计划的酒店和旅游业管理中心				4 214					
	1979				135 437	33 102							
	1980	1 904 560	天堂岛	地中海俱乐部			40 966						
20世纪80年代	1981		家庭岛 弗里波特	伊鲁萨拉岛和圣萨尔瓦多岛多岛 重新开设卢卡约海滩酒店和赌场									

续表

年代	年份	游客数量	旅游产品构成	主要国家发展成果 / 旅游业	人口统计资料（人口增长和变化）			劳动力雇佣 / 就业按行业门类分			整个巴哈马的劳动力	就业	
					拿骚	弗里波特、大不列颠岛	家庭岛	农业（小农）	旅游业	金融服务		女性	男性
20世纪80年代	1982												
	1983	2 631 970		凯布尔海滩酒店									
	1984												
	1985		邮轮	乘客超过 100 万									
	1986	3 007 300		凯布尔海滩的赌场									
	1987												
	1988	3 158 091		邮轮业超过航空业									
	1989												
20世纪90年代	1990				172 196	40 898	41 955						
	1991		邮轮	占 200 万游客，扩建乔治王子码头					21 180	7 955	114 400	55 000	59 400
	1992		邮轮 家庭岛	英格拉哈姆政府 / 伊鲁萨拉岛班纳曼镇公主湾					21 178	7 940	114 700	54 300	60 400
	1993		拿骚国际机场 拿骚	新航站楼（预检清关设施和美国航班）					18 895	11 465	121 800	57 400	64 400
	1994			巴哈马旅游培训中心				1 727	18 880	12 190	124 600	59 100	65 500

续表

年代	年份	游客数量	旅游产品构成	主要国家发展成果/旅游业	人口统计资料（人口增长和变化）			劳动力雇佣/就业按行业门类划分			整个巴哈马的劳动力	就业	
					拿骚	弗里波特、大不列颠岛	家庭岛	农业（小农）	旅游业	金融服务		女性	男性
20世纪90年代	1994		天堂岛主题度假区	阳光国际亚特兰蒂斯（1.4亿美元）第三阶段				1 727	18 880	12 190	124 600	59 100	65 500
			凯布尔海滩	超级俱乐部部微风酒店收购大使海滩酒店									
	1995			桑多兹酒店接管艾美酒店，即从前的巴尔莫勒尔海滩酒店					19 405	10 580	127 440	60 925	66 515
	1996								20 360	11 125	129 765	59 385	70 380
	1997								21 440	12 420	135 255	63 940	71 315
	1998			亚特兰蒂斯第二阶段（6.5亿美元）；重新开放拿骚的英国殖民城市中心；酒店管理和旅游学校的开办；巴哈马大学					22 120	13 970			
	1999								23 300	13 350	145 350	68 105	77 745
21世纪初	2000	4 203 831	弗里波特	我们的卢亚度假村/卢卡亚港	212 432	46 954	45 451						
	2001		"9·11"	卡普里岛/哈勃岛					25 515	16 330	153 310	74 230	79 080

续表

年代	年份	游客数量	旅游产品构成	主要国家发展成果 / 旅游业	人口统计资料（人口增长和变化）			劳动力雇佣 / 就业按行业门类分			整个巴哈马的劳动力	就业	
					拿骚	弗里波特、大不列颠岛	家庭岛	农业（小农）	旅游业	金融服务		女性	男性
21世纪初	2002		圣萨尔瓦多岛联邦航空局认证的国际机场	克里斯蒂新政府新建设施迎接中心、乔治王子码头（280万美元）					25 690	16 475	152 090	74 280	78 410
	2003	4 594 042	伊克祖马斯岛、家庭岛	绿宝石海湾四季酒店					27 920	15 595	154 965	75 825	79 140
	2004	5 000 000	弗里波特	大巴哈马岛国际机场（"9·11"……；飓风（弗朗西斯飓风和珍妮飓风）					23 765	17 575	158 340	76 560	81 780
	2005		天堂岛	科兹纳集团（第三阶段）（10亿美元）				1 242	29 095	16 180	160 530	77 740	82 790

来源：巴哈马统计局

农业包括种植业、渔业和林业。本专栏涉及的是从事种植业的活跃小农数量。

渔业就业人数从1995年的9 300人增加到2004年的12 304人。这些数据由农业和海洋资源部收集。

林业仅限于农用林业，例如，巴哈马东南部的卡蓉树皮。

经济开发区委员会是加拿大的一个先锋机构,在世界 1 500 个城市设有办事处,维持上述进程的机制就是通过这一委员会来进行的。

2005 年,巴哈马迎来了 500 万游客。"9·11"事件后的繁荣,或许会让巴哈马的游客人数在接下来的两到三年内比 2005 年的人数翻一番。

2006 年,巴哈马的人口约为 324 000 人,其中,有 85% 的巴哈马人生活在新普罗维登斯岛和大巴哈马岛之间的城市中心。这些锚固工程为岛屿上完全以种地、打鱼为生的人们创造了新的就业机会。这些岛屿上的年轻人不喜欢务农,在这样一种社会经济环境中,这些锚固工程将阻止女性和年轻人进入城市中心。

此外,锚固工程战略符合联合国千年发展目标:

① 目标 1:根除极端贫穷和饥饿,特别是在农村地区。

② 目标 2:促进两性平等,赋予女性权利。就这一点而言,新普罗维登斯岛和大巴哈马岛的旅游业有所成效。毫无疑问,家庭岛的旅游业也会同样有效。

③ 目标 3:确保环境的可持续性。需要对家庭岛的所有这些项目进行环境影响研究。

关于医疗保健,针对上述岛屿的人口,建有 12 个社区保健区,包括综合性医院、主要医院和卫星医院。在新普罗维登斯岛和大巴哈马岛有大型医院;阿巴科岛、伊鲁萨拉岛和伊克祖马斯岛规划了微型医院。

关于教育,在教育部的支持下建有 13 个教育区,提供从小学到中学的教育。连同教育部的网络,共有 41 所独立的学校,主要由各个不同的基督教派运营。

这些医疗服务和教育服务归属于 21 个行政区,在巴哈马群岛范围内向居民提供地方政府服务。64 个机场(其中 30 个铺设了路面)连同公共码头和私人游船码头共同组成了家庭岛上无数个入境口岸。

通过锚固工程,改革进程正深化至整个巴哈马。

旅游冲击

第二次世界大战结束以来,巴哈马的旅游业一直非常辉煌。从来没有一段时间像这十年一样,旅游业给巴哈马及其人民带来了诸多切实的福利。

该群岛获此福利并非仅仅由于其地理位置——可通往地球上最富有的一个国家,还因为那些居住在巴哈马群岛上的人们心灵手巧。这些福利也带来了许多挑战,如平民在经济上边缘化,发展差距,贫富两极分化以及外国饮食习惯、文化和生活方式所带来的影响。

最近,由巴哈马统计局做出的一份统计分析表明:

① 2003 年，旅游业总的经济贡献为 28 亿美元，占巴哈马国内生产总值（GDP）的 51%。

② 这一经济活动给当地带来了 16 亿美元的工资收入或占全部工资的 61%。

③ 在就业方面，旅游业催生了 97 383 份工作，占就业基数的 63%。

巴哈马的旅游业实际上直接影响了巴哈马经济的九大领域，即旅馆业、餐饮业、娱乐业、交通业、房地产业、政府管理、制造业、农业综合企业及渔业。近年来，初等到高等的教育体系分别以满足蓬勃发展的旅游业对于人力资源的需求为导向。

在小岛屿发展中国家，旅游业从某些方面说可以是救星，而从另一些方面来说则可能完全扰乱经济，就像在"9·11"事件中所看到的那样。

总体来说，巴哈马在过去、现在和将来都会受益于旅游业。预计"9·11"事件后的繁荣所带来的影响可以使经济持续发展几十年。

表 2.3 "9·11"事件后的项目——重要的外国直接投资

岛　屿	已批准但未开始的项目	已批准项目建设／运营阶段
阿巴科岛	尼安德罗斯和齐默尔曼	曲湾的阿巴科俱乐部
		新普利茅斯开发公司
		阿巴科第六股份有限公司
		海洋前沿
		阿巴科的雀形鸟
安德罗斯岛		椰子农场有限公司
毕米尼岛		毕米尼湾度假区
		毕米尼沙滩
贝瑞岛		国际游船码头——白鲑礁
猫岛	水晶山有限公司	
崎岖岛		皮茨敦·普安·兰丁斯有限公司
伊鲁萨拉岛	伊鲁萨拉岛的鲍威尔角	温德米尔开发公司
		总督港度假区
		伊鲁萨拉岛置业有限公司
		两季度假区
		菠萝园

续表

岛　屿	已批准但未开始的项目	已批准项目建设 / 运营阶段
		落跑山俱乐部
		若莫玛海湾
		珊瑚沙酒店
		情人度假区和码头
伊克祖马斯岛	80/50 私人住宅度假区	福尔摩斯蟹礁
	伊克祖马斯岛度假开发商有限公司	绿宝石湾度假区和码头
	小湾（马文·帕克）	绿宝石湾的罗克角
	三姐妹酒店	格兰德岛别墅
	克拉维茨多媒体	L'lle D' 艾格尼丝
		愈疮树有限公司
		霍珀湾村庄
大巴哈马岛	马里奥特国际度假俱乐部	金石溪企业
	大巴哈马岛的临海区	岛屿海洋投资有限公司
	威廉姆和露丝·海米施	法尔玛科技有限公司
茵那瓜岛	火烈鸟巢度假区	
玛雅古纳岛		亚太咨询集团公司
新普罗维登斯岛		亚特兰蒂斯度假区（三期）
		夏洛茨维尔开发公司
		BH RIU 酒店有限公司
		天堂岛公寓合资有限公司
		风轻语公司
		马利自由度假区
		阿祖拉开发公司
		巴哈·马尔开发商有限公司
朗姆屿		蒙塔纳控股有限公司
圣萨尔瓦多岛		地中海俱乐部——哥伦布村

来源：金融服务与投资部（报纸提供）

衰落的农业

巴哈马的农业处于下滑状态。这反映在两个方面——在过去 25 年（1980—2005 年）中，小农的数目锐减以及部门产出停滞不前。

小 农

有过两次农业普查，一次在 1978 年，一次在 1994 年。1978 年有 4 214 个小农；到 2005 年，这一数字下降到 1 242 个。这反映了该部门损失了 2 972 个小农。25 年来，这一部门每年减少 120 个小农，或者说每月减少 10 个小农。

因小农这一群体正面临老化，并鲜有年轻人加入，小农成了濒危行业。多年来，年轻人从家庭岛移居到拿骚和弗里波特的市中心来寻找就业机会并接受高等教育。

在 1994 年的农业普查中，占小农总数（1 727）65% 的 1 176 个农民的年龄为 55—75 岁。男性的平均寿命为 68—69 岁，到 2008 年，几乎所有农民都可能会死亡，尽管有些人会活得久些。小农总数的 30% 为女性，她们的平均寿命要稍长一些（75.3 岁）。

农业产出

农业综合企业和小农的农产品产值在 2002 年达到高峰，约 6 000 万美元。巴哈马的农业部门由三部分构成：

① 小农；

② 农业综合企业；

③ 出口农业综合企业（美国农业综合企业分别经营着冬季蔬菜和柑橘类产品的离岸农产品出口）。

这三个部分均有大幅下跌，反过来又影响着对这个部门的投资、就业、技术转让、人力发展和部门总的增长。

农业综合企业子行业的增长是由家禽业在肉鸡和食用蛋的生产领域引领的。1998 年，家禽业的产值为 2 100 万美元，而肉鸡生产就占 2 100 万美元。然而，2002 年 11 月，最大的肉鸡生产单位格莱斯顿农场进入了破产管理程序并停业，造成了 800 万—1 000 万美元的产品空缺以及 300 多名农民工下岗，其中，60% 为单亲母亲。

格莱斯顿农场倒闭的主要原因是将肉鸡的关税（含印花税）从 70% 调低至 35%。这是巴哈马政府迫于食品进口商的压力做出的决定。这些食品进口商主要向酒店、高档餐厅和快餐业提供食材。

格莱斯顿农场倒闭后，肉鸡市场现在以进口为主，因为市场上的主要产品如鸡腿、鸡翅都以低于生产成本的价格在巴哈马，甚至整个加勒比地区"倾销"。这样的市场环境让目前巴哈马最大的肉鸡生产商——大巴哈马的巴哈马禽业公司生存艰难。

技术驱动的肉鸡生产曾经是巴哈马农业综合企业最主要的经营业务。然而,格莱斯顿农场的倒闭对整个农业部门的发展造成了毁灭性打击。

由于有免税优惠,靠近美国东海岸且海上交通发达,巴哈马是生产及出口冬季蔬菜、柑橘和其他果园作物到美国的理想之地。

美国的农业综合企业在阿巴科岛、北安德罗斯岛和大巴哈马岛上建立了农场。2004/2005 年,阿巴科岛诺曼城堡地区的柑橘园遭受了致命的柑橘溃疡病害,导致 3 000 英亩葡萄柚受灾。这对于巴哈马对美国的柑橘出口来说是一个打击。

反观农业综合企业这一子部门,市场准入问题备受关注。巴哈马的开放经济使其国内的农业综合企业处于竞争劣势。

巴哈马是唯一一个没有加入世界贸易组织(WTO)的加勒比国家,无须遵守《农业协定》(AOA)的规章制度。从很多方面来说,不依附于世界贸易组织,不遵守《农业协定》,抑制了巴哈马农业综合企业的发展,对其竞争性有消极影响。

对国内生产总值贡献

巴哈马的国内生产总值持续增长。2005 年,国内生产总值预计达到 60 亿美元。这得益于旅游业和金融服务业的发展。

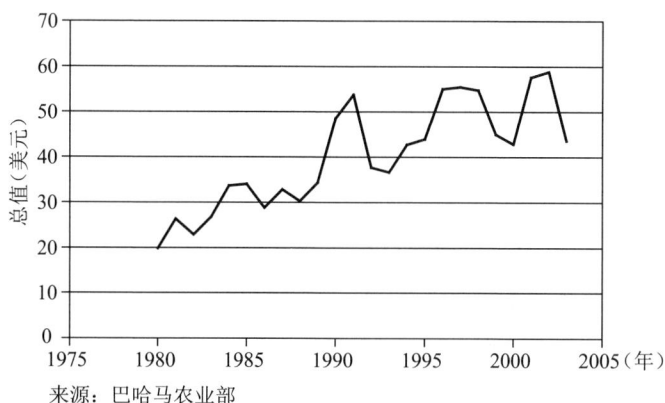

来源:巴哈马农业部

图 2.4　全国产值——农业综合企业和小农子部门(单位:百万美元)

2005 年,渔业对巴哈马的国内生产总值贡献突出,达到 1 亿美元;而农业和林业要么不受重视,要么减产,其对国内生产总值的贡献微乎其微。

20 世纪 50 年代早期,巴哈马在阿巴科的松树岛、安德罗斯岛和大巴哈马岛有兴旺的木材业。然而近年来，这一产业不复存在了。这些地区的松树要么被砍伐后做成篱笆桩，要么被烧制成木炭。

林业专家建议巴哈马出台一项全面的政策来恢复加勒比松，以便对其进行资源化管理。据统计，加勒比松的覆盖面积约为50万英亩（2 023.44平方千米），可实现增收与长期可持续性发展。

在巴哈马东南部，特别是在猫岛、阿克林斯岛和崎岖岛，盛产药用和酒用的卡蓁树皮，收获后主要出口欧洲。

农业对国内生产总值的贡献大幅下降，低至1%。随着禽肉和柑橘出口的减少，观赏苗圃业者和食品加工商又面临市场准入的挑战，农业的贡献率将降至1%以下。

插曲：《埃尼亚斯文集》《巴哈马日报》 经济转型50年

第二次世界大战之后，日本开始经济转型，成为世界上最先进的经济体之一。

1949年，中国的台湾省属农业经济，与古巴竞争，成为世界第一大蔗糖生产地。20世纪80年代，台湾省转型为工业经济，并且成为典范。这证明了农业经济可能转变为工业经济这一经济理论是合乎逻辑的。台湾省为此花费了近40年的时间。

发展经济学家指出，日本和中国的台湾省是经济转型的明证。从广义上说，世界经济在过去50年间经历了两个发展阶段，现在正进入第三个发展阶段。

但是，巴哈马从何处融入这一发展模式？

1950年之前，巴哈马是个宁静的"渔村"式社区。早些时候，一位前内阁大臣说他宁愿巴哈马退回到渔村也不愿看到博彩业的出现。好吧，前大臣离开了我们，而赌场的数量激增。赌场现在是旅游发展的工具。

巴哈马发展委员会主席斯塔福德·洛夫特霍斯·桑德斯爵士意识到一个事实——农业和渔业并不能将巴哈马的经济带到其今天所具有的水平的高度。他修改了这一群岛的经济重心，把全年旅游、房地产开发和离岸银行三个行业合并起来。

20世纪90年代，巴哈马的旅游业产生了10亿美元的外汇收入。巴哈马从一个田园诗般的"渔村"转型为生机勃勃的服务型经济体。

我们没有意识到的是，这一由斯塔福德爵士创造的发展模式正在整个加勒比地区重复出现。除了特立尼达和多巴哥、圭亚那和牙买加以外，其他国家现在依靠旅游业来赚取外汇。像多米尼克和圣卢西亚那些边缘化的经济体则仍然依赖香蕉产业。

巴哈马在过去 45 年里经历了经济转型,随之而来的是一些社会变化——有好有坏。

加勒比教育领域的一位知名学者评论道,巴哈马的专业发展是异常显著的。他指出,要获得这样的专业深度和多样性,牙买加花费了 150 年,特立尼达和多巴哥花费了 100 年,而巴哈马只用了不到 50 年的时间就完成了。

此外,据统计估算,这种经济能够产生的人均收益为 1 万美元,使得这个国家享有较高的生活水平。

社会经济转型不是静态的,而是不断变化的。对于巴哈马人来说幸运的是,斯塔福德爵士很有远见地规划了这一可行的经济模式。进步自由党理智地在此基础之上,建立并通过各种形式的立法基础设施发展、人力培训和发展来加强这一模式,维持一个吸引投资并可持续发展的环境。

除了两三个时期的经济衰退,巴哈马经济在 20 世纪晚期仍然保持着弹性。

如前所述,世界经历了两个发展阶段。战后 30 年的最佳定义为国际阶段。世界从 20 世纪 70 年代开始,在 80 年代加速进入了第二阶段——全球化。20 世纪 90 年代末,世界进入了一个被定义为全球无国界经济的阶段。

巴哈马面临的问题是,我们的国家和人民是否准备好在全球无国界经济所带来的经济氛围中顺利地生存、竞争和运转下去。像我早先所说的,转型并不是静态的。

经济国家主义对全球化

不要把经济国家主义和经济国有化混为一谈。这两个概念有区别,一个意味着经济为国民所拥有,另一个则指国家控制经济活动,特别是收购私有企业。

殖民时期的一个呼求是经济国家主义——其实就是巴哈马人拥有巴哈马,这极大地影响了独立运动。

除了酒店和银行那样的外资企业,巴哈马的国内经济实质上是由海湾街的商人控制的。这其实是联合巴哈马人党统治殖民时期的巴哈马人的生活方式。

进步自由党执政时,对巴哈马人和外国人的合资企业的政策机制是,允许经济扩张但保留某种形式的国家干预和控制,鼓励和允许公民直接参与各种经济活动。

冷战之后,全球经济格局急剧扭转。欧洲经济共同体(EEC)发展为欧盟

（EU）。由加拿大、墨西哥和美国组成的北美自由贸易区（NAFTA）已经形成。在这两个团体中，取消国家关税是为了扩大相关国家的市场。消除国界这一贸易壁垒的概念由此开始。

与此同时，工业国工业企业中的大公司，尤其是那些在殖民化过程中创建的公司，正在完善并使跨国经营商业化，作为其商业和经济统治的手段。

地缘政治环境是建立在资本主义或共产主义意识形态的基础上的，在此背景下，各国不得不选择他们所属"阵营"。随着意识形态同一化的解除，经济发展能够以一种更加直接和开放的方式进行。各国可以更自由地交往，而不必担心它们的政治哲学是资本主义还是马克思主义。

由远程通信和计算机化进步所引领的科技进一步增加了这一氛围。信息经由手机和电脑通过卫星传输变为全球共享。网络空间正在演变为政府管制的更为强大的工具。经济国家主义之路注定很快成为过去时代的副产品。新经济秩序的现实迫使政府和跨国企业改变其运行模式。

这个地区和这个半球的国家对这一转变并不是不受影响的。为了与时俱进，它们采取了一些措施将西半球经济融入一个单一的自由贸易区——美洲自由贸易区（FTAA）。全球化概念对于加勒比国家如巴哈马来说已经成为现实。

自1992年以来，自由民族运动政府开始了一项进程，即似乎严重倾向于使用全球化方法来促进贸易、投资和创造就业机会。

全球化方法建立在自由化的基础上，但是也必须考虑到发展的不同层次，特别是人力资源和部门发展，从而使巴哈马的利益最大化。

目前，巴哈马在困境中苦苦挣扎。在新普罗维登斯岛的一些经济部门，特别是建筑业、金融服务业和酒店业，有一种经济繁荣的感觉。然而，还有一些部门因为人力资本开发水平的不足，正在经历着"繁荣不足"。

"繁荣不足"的原因是经济一体化、培训、某些地区的基础设施建设和财政资源等方面存在不足，这里仅举几例。这些问题对全球化概念至关重要，因为它们是可持续发展的总体目标中的不可或缺的组成部分。

当把经济变量和犯罪、住房条件差、家庭不稳定等社会层面的问题置于一起考量时，巴哈马的经济和社会重建变得举步维艰。为了使全球化在这种情况下发挥作用，在制定公共政策时，就必须考虑到这些因素。

在政治层面，对于国家选择哪条道路来改善每个巴哈马人的社会经济命运，我们必须有清晰的认识。这一信息常常是混乱的、引起误解的。

在商业层面，许多商业实体还在评判巴哈马人，因为在商业周期的关键时刻常有陋习——交通运输便是其中之一,尤其在集装箱业务中。

由于竞争激烈,食品和商品零售商似乎在给巴哈马消费者更多的优惠。

在一般公众层面,全球化创造了一个新的世界,带来了新的挑战,需要做出与经济国家主义主导时所不同的行为反应。技术和业务方式的变化会导致技术过时,工作岗位不再有保障,这就需要持续的再培训计划。

基本原则已经改变,那些无法适应的人将被抛在后面。

家庭岛的移居机制

第二次世界大战后,巴哈马实际上是一个城市社会,因为成千上万的巴哈马人为了工作、教育和从事服务业从家庭岛或外岛迁到拿骚。弗里波特和大巴哈马岛的发展进一步加剧了城市化综合症。

然而近来,马什港、阿巴科岛、西班牙韦尔斯、北伊鲁萨拉岛和长岛的克拉伦斯镇/戴德曼斯凯正以充满魅力的非城市社区的形象兴起,像 20 世纪四五十年代的拿骚那样简单和友好。

拿骚的转变正式始于波特斯凯发展为国内航运枢纽以及天堂岛大桥的建设。与此同时,约瑟夫·加芬克尔先生把他的加芬克尔垒球场改建为帕姆代尔购物中心,将帕姆代尔发展成一流的可选择的商业中心。这对于将帕姆代尔从一个高级住宅区转变为今天的商业区来说,起到了催化剂的作用。

随着帕姆代尔的扩张,为了使来往车辆能够方便地进入该区域,推倒柯林斯墙成为必然。而且,已故的罗兰·西莫内特爵士开发了布莱尔庄园,作为大量正在迁出帕姆代尔的人的替代住宅区。这就导致了城市的扩张,因为其他区域如东拿骚、海风、西维拉斯、西海湾街的格鲁夫声名鹊起。由于旅游业的蓬勃发展,拱门以南的格鲁夫和金门吸引了成千上万想出人头地的人。

大规模的公共资金建房从黄色老年人项目开始。伊丽莎白庄园、火烈鸟花园及新普罗维登斯岛的其他社区在政府的资助下继续扩建。

在大巴哈马岛,城市化延伸到了八里岬。就像乔·加芬克尔在拿骚建的那座购物中心一样,在八里岬,一座耗资数百万美金的现代化购物中心即将竣工并将奠定基调。城市化带来了许多挫折,改变了人们的生活方式和社会的功能。“老拿骚”狭窄的街道不能很好地调节来往车辆。房地产的压力引发了住宅用地和商业用地价格的飙升。

单一住宅所有权正岌岌可危,许多城市住宅现在都是公寓和共管公寓。

在新普罗维登斯岛,每平方英里人口为 2 152.5 人,在巴哈马,大概是 47.4

人。这意味着在拿骚人们住得更为密集。再加上平均住户人数约为 4 人，平均寿命延长（男性 68 岁，女性 75 岁）和大部分人口处于育龄阶段，人口激增可能会进一步加剧城市化综合症。

目前是否有解决方案？有，我们正开始体验它。最大的变化发生在工作岗位上，因为企业不一定要位于市中心或商业区。信息时代使通过传真机、移动电话和互联网做生意成为可能，并且几乎不损失工作效率。

为了享受一定品质的生活，人们不必住在离本国首都很近的地方就可以体验某些便利的设施。录像机、卫星和有线电视将来自世界各地的体育、新闻和娱乐传播到最偏远的地方。兰德瑞尔角、阿克林斯岛、狐狸镇、阿巴科岛上的家庭就像拿骚、迈阿密或伦敦的人们一样习惯于收看美国有线电视新闻网（CNN）和娱乐体育节目电视网（ESPN）。

有了高效的远程通信系统，家庭岛的居民可以电视购物，参与到电子商务的新世界中去。

唐·金通过他与美国有线电视 HBO 频道的关系将拳击提升至一个新的水平。这个频道也使美国职业篮球联赛（NBA）付给迈克尔·乔丹百万美元成为可能，使职业棒球大联盟与山米·索沙等人签订长期合同成为可能。

巴哈马的规划者们没有充分利用这些可能性。要高度重视那些有意识的启动计划，使更多类似家庭岛的岛屿吸引人们前来居住。安德罗斯岛太大，有丰富的物质资源供人们开采。

在海绵开采时代，曼格罗夫岛是巴哈马第二大人口中心，但今天它几乎荒无人烟。长岛的情形也如此，在巴拿马运河建造之前，大量巴哈马居民住在崎岖岛——阿克林斯岛地区，临近世界重要的大洋航线之一。

信息时代使诸如曼格罗夫岛、猫岛、玛雅古纳岛、阿克林斯岛和崎岖岛等地的人口再生成为可能。在巴哈马，由科技带来的可能性基本上还处于认识和接受的萌芽阶段。然而，利用这一机制来促使人们迁回家庭岛似乎被忽视了。

城市化

世界正在经历一种叫作城市化的现象。1950—1980 年，世界城市或都市人口从 3 亿增加到 18 亿，巴哈马也不例外。

1953 年，巴哈马的城市人口约为 4.6 万人，到 1980 年，已增加到近 12 万人。这一数字在 27 年里增长了近 300%。1990 年的人口普查还没有发布，但是数据应当会持续攀升。

鉴于巴哈马的情况,这意味着新普罗维登斯岛和弗里波特是人口稠密的城市中心,而家庭岛上的居民则属于人口数量下降的少数派。在过去 30 年间,巴哈马的大多数人口集中在其两个城市。

1901—1943 年,巴哈马 66% 的人口居住在家庭岛上。1953 年以来,发生了戏剧性的变化。

随着城市人口的增加,新普罗维登斯岛和大巴哈马岛的人口更加集中。因此,这些岛屿的人口密度也大幅度增加。1980 年,新普罗维登斯岛的人口密度为 1 693 人 / 平方英里,大巴哈马岛为 62.5 人 / 平方英里。

大量城市人口和人口高密度这两个因素改变了巴哈马人的生活品质,特别是在拿骚和弗里波特这两个城市。

巴哈马城市发展的非凡热潮源自 20 世纪 40 年代后期开始的经济增长与发展的过程。拿骚在物质基础设施(电力、公路、供水)和社会基础设施(学校、卫生设施、娱乐)两方面都进行了集中建设。

基础设施的集中建设连同经济增长和发展(建筑业和旅游业)导致大批人离开家庭岛到拿骚寻求经济机会。找工作是城市化的关键推动力。

城市化也有不利的一面,特别是拿骚,面临着诸多消极的副作用,尤其在人口稠密地区,交通拥堵、间歇式供电供水、环境污染、废物处置不当以及犯罪率上升。

巴哈马在某种程度上是幸运的,那里没有棚户区或贫民窟,但是有些地区仍然使用户外厕所,居民需要用抽水机抽水,垃圾无人清理。

巴哈马人对城市化进程已有其应对措施。许多巴哈马人返回各家庭岛,只因拿骚的生活已经处于不堪忍受的境地。

那些达到退休年龄的人、那些获得工作机会的人或那些希望建立新的商业基础的人,均属于离开都市生活去家庭岛过慢节奏悠闲生活的人。

反城市化的趋势是一项艰巨的任务,因为绝大部分人困于城市化的生活方式,他们是在这一社会化进程中被培养起来的。

巴哈马依然处于一个特殊位置,其城市问题还没有达到像我们这个地区的几个国家那样无法解决的地步。

城市化中的问题必须得到解决,需要规划和管理。国际规划师预测,到 2000 年,第三世界国家 51 亿人口中近 45% 的人将生活在城市地区。巴哈马已经超过了这个比例。

巴哈马城市人口迅速增长的原因被归结为家庭岛的大规模迁出。1901—

1943 年，主要的人口中心在新普罗维登斯岛、安德罗斯岛、猫岛和伊鲁萨拉岛以外。曼格罗夫岛上的居民人数曾一度仅次于拿骚，位居第二。

在过去 30 年里，猫岛的居民数量急剧减少；安德罗斯岛和伊鲁萨拉岛的人口增长不明显，比较平稳。

是的，城市化是无法更改的事实，而且这一现象很可能会加速。然而，解决方法是通过更加均衡、高效地发展家庭岛来创造充足的就业机会。若不如此，人们还将继续向拿骚和弗里波特迁移。

第 3 章 ››

旅游业：食品生产的新维度

> "加勒比经济是宗主国经济发展的延伸，是帝国体系不可分割的部分。它们的贡献基本上是提供原材料。"
>
> ——安东尼·希尔，牙买加人，圭亚那大学讲师，英国伦敦高级专员公署

在加勒比殖民地长大和生活的人被诱导着相信几乎所有东西都来自母国。这一误解源于这样的事实：像巴哈马和加勒比其他地区的殖民地都是宗主国的市场。

糖是甘蔗的副产品，但我们认为糖来自英国。咖啡是一种昂贵的混合商品，牙买加的蓝山咖啡也来自英国。另一方面，像猪油这样的制造或加工商品，是烹饪和烘烤的主要原料，是非常不健康的食品。咸猪肉和咸牛肉是英国畜牧业中类似的不健康的副产品。这些和其他一些食品都是导致心血管疾病的重要因素，正在今天的加勒比人口中显现出来。

在今天的牙买加，鳕鱼仍然是千里之外的人们的重要食物。他们同样依赖像沙丁鱼、金枪鱼和鲑鱼这样的罐头产品。健康爱好者们视这些商品为不健康食品。

在世界贸易组织的规章制度之下，加勒比共同体国家失去了在欧盟的优惠市场地位。当这些国家还是殖民地时，英国是甘蔗和咖啡豆等原材料的市场，这些原材料经过加工之后又重新出口到殖民地。这些商品享受特惠关税待遇，意味着来自英国的商品被征收的关税比来自邻近国家（如古巴、海地、多米尼加共和国甚至美国）的商品所要收取的关税要低。

1968 年，巴哈马还是英国殖民地，其采取了一些措施来确保英国的糖配额。当时美国木材公司巨头——欧文斯-伊利诺伊公司在阿巴科岛上种植了约 2 万英亩的甘蔗。欧文斯-伊利诺伊公司能够确保美国配额，巴哈马政府则尝试获得英国配额。

商品会议在国际糖业组织的总部伦敦召开。这是巴哈马首次参与此类谈判，而通常被称作"糖岛"的其他英属加勒比殖民地，与国际糖业组织打交道的历史已久。英国一度通过在加勒比、非洲、亚洲和太平洋地区的各个产糖殖民地来控制全球食糖市场。英国可以通过英联邦优惠关税制度来操纵甘蔗的买价和卖价。因此，这些殖民地不仅是糖的安全市场，而且是一系列其他商品的安全市场。其中，许多商品导致了不健康的食品配制，一些原料如猪油、咸牛肉和咸猪肉会引发严重的健康问题。

殖民体验的一个重要方面是食品控制。随着旅游业的发展，食品也通过改变消费模式或膳食模式成为一种控制商品。

旅游业和地区食品生产

每年到加勒比的游客有 4 000 万—5 000 万。这些游客大多是从美国乘坐邮轮来的，乘坐飞机在中途停留的游客也占了很高的比例。中途停留的美国游客如果能在加勒比感受到一丝"美国感"会觉得非常舒适。然而，这并不会减少对加勒比事物的尝试所带来的加勒比体验，如异国水果和蔬菜、烹饪、工艺品、手工制品。

加勒比体验受到房产类型和区域的限制。许多房产都有试图留住游客的项目，如像地中海俱乐部那样包含一切的度假机构，或者像亚特兰蒂斯那样有 38 家饭店和加勒比最大赌场的超级酒店。

"美国感"的结果是引入了美国快餐特许经营店。在整个加勒比，可能除古巴之外，都存在快餐经营的扩张——加勒比人所有的美国特许经营店以及一些加勒比快餐连锁店。

美国快餐特许经营店既影响了食品进口又影响了食品种类。快餐给加勒比人的健康状况带来了消极影响。

例如，在巴哈马，几乎有所有种类的快餐专营店。从专门经营比萨（达美乐、必胜客）和汉堡（麦当劳、汉堡王、温迪快餐）的美国连锁店，到赛百味、奎兹诺斯或像卢西亚诺那样的美食机构，以及让·乔治、鲍比·弗雷、卡迈恩和诺布那样的高端餐厅，还有高端咖啡厅星巴克。

加勒比本地的鸡肉快餐店不得不和肯德基竞争；帕蒂外卖不得不和美国汉堡特许经营店竞争；（加勒比）烙饼店不得不和比萨店竞争。

酒店和美食餐厅吸引着欧美顾客。这些餐厅需要一些优质的水果、蔬菜、肉类、鱼类、奶酪和香肠。其中某些食物，尤其是新鲜水果、蔬菜以及某些肉类和鱼类可由当地来供给，但要可靠地持续供应一整年高品质产品，也是种挑战。

表 3.1　2003 年加勒比到访游客

目的地	到访邮轮游客	中途停留游客	合　计
安圭拉岛		46 915	46 915
安提瓜和巴布达	385 686	224 030	609 716
阿鲁巴岛	542 327	641 906	1 184 233
巴哈马群岛	2 970 174	1 428 973	4 399 147
巴巴多斯	559 122	531 211	1 090 333
伯利兹	575 196	220 574	795 770
百慕大群岛	226 097	256 563	482 660
博内尔岛	44 601	62 179	106 780
英属维尔京群岛	304 338	278 114	582 452
开曼群岛	1 818 979	293 515	2 112 494
古巴		1907320	1907320
库拉索岛	279 378	221 390	500 768
多米尼克	177 044	72 948	249 992
多米尼加共和国	398 263	3 268 182	3 666 445
格林纳达	146925	142 333	289 258
圭亚那		100 911	100 911
牙买加	1 132 596	1 350 284	2 482 880
马提尼克岛	268 542	453 160	721 702
蒙特塞拉特岛		8 375	8 375
波多黎各	1 234 992	1 321 846	2 556 838
萨巴岛		10 260	10 260
圣尤斯泰希厄斯岛		10 788	10 788
圣卢西亚	393 240	276 948	670 188
圣马丁岛	1 171 734	427 587	1 599 321
圣文森特和格林纳丁斯	64 965	78 535	143 500
特立尼达和多巴哥	55 532	409 007	464 539
特克斯和凯科斯群岛		163 584	163 584
美属维尔京群岛	1 773 948	618 703	2 392 651
合计：38 352 342			

来源：加勒比旅游组织（CTO）

　　此外，还有特色食品。这些特色食品是为了美食大厨的方便而制作或加工的，或者是为了保持特许经营者的水准。加勒比农业综合企业有时不具备生产某些特色食品的能力。

一个典型例子是食用蛋农业综合企业。根据加勒比家禽协会所说，食用蛋是加勒比共同体国家能够自给自足或接近自给自足的商品。然而，较大的加勒比共同体国家（牙买加、巴巴多斯、特立尼达和多巴哥、巴哈马）并没有开展鸡蛋加工业务来专门处理鸡蛋产品，如蛋黄、打蛋器、蛋粉、巴氏杀菌蛋、冷冻蛋或液体蛋。在酒店，尤其是超级酒店中，糕点师和美食大厨却需要这些特色产品。这对食用蛋经销商有着消极影响。

这导致了双重市场——一个新鲜食用蛋市场和一个为旅游业提供特色产品的市场。

旅游业不再是加勒比国家经济单独的附属物。旅游食品文化正在并且已经与国家食品消费融合在一起。这意味着越来越多的原住民正在获得旅游者的口味和饮食习惯，在这一地区的每个岛国和附属国，游客的身影随处可见。

加勒比人前往北美和欧洲进行商务旅行、疯狂购物、度假或者参加各种学科培训也加快了这一融合。

与旅游者饮食的这种密切联系加重了本已严重的健康状况。加勒比食品营养研究所（CFNI）报告称：

> "非传染性疾病已经逐渐取代传染性疾病成为加勒比地区人们死亡的主要原因。在一些区域，和营养有关的慢性病，如肥胖症、糖尿病和高血压，是导致残疾、疾病和死亡的主要因素。在加勒比人口中，高血压和糖尿病被列为两大主要慢性病，也是导致其他疾病如心血管疾病（中风）和冠心病的主要危险因素。"

并非只有加勒比处于这一困境中。联合国粮食及农业组织和世界卫生组织（WHO）发起了一个推动"水果和蔬菜的生产、供应和消费"的项目。

联合国粮食及农业组织指出：

> "研究表明，每天摄取足够的水果和蔬菜是均衡饮食的一个部分，水果和蔬菜有助于预防重大疾病，包括心脏病、中风、糖尿病、癌症以及缺乏重要微量营养元素和维生素。在全球人类死亡的20个危险因素中，世界卫生组织将水果和蔬菜摄入不足排在第六位。"

情形更加恶化，因为女性在加勒比国家的劳动力中占40%—50%。

在巴哈马，女性在旅游业中占主导地位。2005年，女性工作者比男性工作

者多 6 000 人。（见表 2.1）

随着女性成为劳动力的重要组成部分，超市取代市场成为购买食材的首选，快餐店取代家常菜，"方便"食品将变得重要起来。

许多方便食品源自北美，正在取代本土或传统食品，因为后者并不容易准备，不适合职场母亲或职业女性——她们很可能是单亲母亲、妻子或母亲。

随着工资的增长，特别是在像旅游业等服务部门是主要经济部门的加勒比国家，小岛国家如巴哈马、巴巴多斯、安提瓜和巴布达，将指望进口来满足它们的食品需求。

2006 年 5 月，特立尼达和多巴哥的农业、土地和海洋资源部部长霍恩·贾勒特·那莱恩阁下在第一届加勒比农业食品交易会上讲了下面一段话：

> "今天在座的许多人都痛苦地意识到，加勒比作为一个地区，其每年进口将近 15 亿美元的农产品。作为一个有能力生产比目前更多农产品的地区，这一事态让人无法接受。据估计，在一些加勒比国家，每 1 美元的旅游支出中便有 0.6—0.8 美元用在了这个地区的进口食品上。"

在巴哈马，这一数字约为 0.85 美元。这种局面使大多数加勒比国家位于粮食净进口国之列。

联合国粮食及农业组织在一份名为《基本食品商业进口的正常融资水平》的文件中，根据硬通货花在进口食品上的比例确认了一些国家。根据 1995—1998 年的数据，以下加勒比国家较为显著。（表 3.2）

表 3.2　加勒比地区食品进口一览表

占硬通货的百分比	国　家
现有硬通货的 10% 以上 （货物出口和服务业的税收减去所偿还的债务）	巴巴多斯 多米尼加共和国 牙买加 特立尼达和多巴哥
10%—20%	圣卢西亚
20% 以上	海地
无数据	古巴 多米尼克 圣基茨和尼维斯 圣文森特和格林纳丁斯

这种情形可能变得更为严峻。据加勒比旅游组织关于到访游客的最新数据，这个地区任何一天的游客数量都在 11 万至 13.7 万之间。这是一个高消费市

场，因此，将会增加对进口食品的需求。

联合国粮食及农业组织将 2004 年这一地区的食品进口评估为 22 亿美元。（见表 3.3）

挑战：本地供给

几个世纪以来，加勒比农业一直为工业化欧洲提供农业原料。直至独立时期，才开始重视满足国内需求。随着优惠市场的衰落、旅游业的兴起以及由于服务部门出现而不断上涨的工资，满足食品需求的生产能力得到了加强。

加勒比的存在立足于农业贸易。在整个殖民时期，农业出口是殖民地的生存基础，就像许多殖民地一样，是唯一的外汇来源。随着经济变得更加复杂，外汇收入来自类似旅游这样的产业。

加勒比国家开始面对全球化的问题，农业贸易在独立时期呈现了与以往不同并且更为复杂的维度。对于这个地区的大多数国家来说，全球化体现在四个贸易体制上。受到小岛国家在贸易规模和经济类型方面的限制，情况更趋恶化。

这个地区的大多数国家不得不应对四个贸易体制。1995 年以来，除了巴哈马，所有独立国家都成了世界贸易组织的成员国。就这一点而言，世界贸易组织的《农业协定》主宰着全球农业贸易。在这个半球层面上，将拟建一个美洲自由贸易区，它其实是世界贸易组织的附加物。

对于这些欧盟国家的前殖民地来说，有非洲、加勒比和太平洋（ACP）协议。非加太集团的加勒比成员国由加勒比共同体国家和举办加勒比论坛的多米尼加共和国组成。

欧盟给予非加太国家的特惠协定始于《洛美协定》，后发展为《科托努协定》以及后来的《欧盟合作伙伴协议》。

在地区层面上，有加勒比单一市场和经济，它是整合加勒比共同体国家经济体系的机制。

除巴哈马之外，所有加勒比共同体国家都必须对接这四个贸易体制。从一个技术专家的视角看，没有一个加勒比共同体国家拥有足够的人力来有效参与和监控这些体制中的各种协商和活动。在此方面，加勒比共同体建立了加勒比地区谈判机制，作为加勒比共同体国家制定贸易政策和策略的机构。

加勒比地区谈判机制的工作人员来自加勒比共同体的各成员国，其方针决策反映着来自各加勒比共同体国家的各类贸易部门的投入。

加勒比地区谈判机制作为一个区域团体，证明其协商效力的最佳例子是它

表 3.3　加勒比食品进口值（以 1 000 美元为单位）

食品进口值（以 1 000 美元为单位）	1990	1991	1992	1993	1994	1995	1996	1997	1998	1999	2000	2001	2002	2003	2004
安提瓜和巴布达	28 158	26 336	26 446	24 434	23 939	24 718	24 350	28 362	26 373	23 098	24 316	19 404	21 644	23 466	21 772
巴哈马	179 109	195 970	170 534	161 772	178 882	205 563	220 156	215 182	213 914	226 570	320 220	282 429	204 469	168 353	197 765
巴巴多斯	90 806	95 433	86 280	87 868	97 044	104 629	113 355	132 100	73 859	127 729	95 180	130 571	131 183	139 425	103 619
伯利兹	42 616	25 745	49 085	42 556	39 740	41 959	45 633	48 286	46 373	39 360	78 189	53 726	48 385	57 530	60 640
多米尼克	18 984	19 054	18 340	16 099	17 108	21 566	24 832	24 717	23 393	19 867	23 256	21 310	20 503	21 320	22 468
多米尼加共和国	219 370	243 457	248 461	305 394	326 710	394 092	438 566	491 681	478 736	410 961	429 581	415 181	515 919	466 250	490 610
格林纳达	25 956	26 063	23 231	29 708	28 969	33 579	40 061	32 171	37 398	33 923	32 433	26 917	35 347	29 836	23 619
圭亚那	33 280	31 929	374 440	42 240	37 825	51 930	52 888	77 426	79 669	107 213	72 067	74 959	74 087	65 956	68 085
海地	167 035	160 999	186 618	158 659	156 367	293 267	295 911	335 659	330 400	307 195	269 481	258 435	323 580	318 111	372 917
牙买加	197 588	196 982	202 924	225 744	201 084	305 122	312 581	367 038	351 866	362 345	323 402	423 277	421 954	365 256	380 784
圣基茨和尼维斯	15 764	15 313	14 061	15 050	15 827	19 382	22 629	20 472	20 149	18 954	28 039	25 464	24 872	26 568	18 832
圣卢西亚	44 773	53 326	55 903	56 855	60 639	64 875	63 626	69 381	68 829	65 414	68 988	61 839	58 457	69 625	41 366
圣文森特 / 格林纳丁斯	25 235	25 795	26 540	28 348	27 499	29 247	31 279	36 723	37 623	29 819	22 740	25 029	37 324	36 005	30 472
苏里南	40 162	41 651	48 938	37 376	38 502	45 374	116 348	131 389	128 857	81 439	72 728	74 301	49 866	61 837	69 510

续表

食品进口值 （以 1 000 美 元为单位）	1990	1991	1992	1993	1994	1995	1996	1997	1998	1999	2000	2001	2002	2003	2004
特立尼达和多巴哥	196 804	205 029	204 512	172 008	165 761	221 764	229 637	243 580	263 649	255 116	257 594	290 132	276 688	293 634	316 019
加勒比论坛	1 325 640	1 363 088	1 399 313	1 404 111	1 415 896	1 857 067	2 031 852	2 254 167	2 181 452	2 109 003	2 118 214	2 182 974	2 244 278	2 143 172	2 218 478

来源：联合国粮食及农业组织统计数据库，2006 年

与各个国家合作，共同保护几乎影响每个加勒比共同体国家食品生产的一种商品。在此提到的商品是肉食鸡或鸡肉。

1990/1991 年，加勒比生产肉食鸡的家禽类农业综合企业受到了进口廉价鸡肉产品的威胁，如鸡翅、鸡脖和鸡背，它们都是美国家禽业的副产品。这些不同部位的鸡肉产品的销售价格低于生产成本。

加勒比食品进口商利用这些低成本的副产品将其"推向"加勒比市场。其后果是破坏了加勒比共同体国家的当地产量的稳定。

禽肉生产是牙买加、巴巴多斯、特立尼达和多巴哥、圭亚那和伯利兹等大型加勒比共同体国家的农业综合企业。这种一体化通过合同已将小农和饲料生产商或禽肉加工商结合起来。

加勒比家禽协会在其执行董事罗伯特·贝斯特先生的领导下，已经能够将农业经营企业统一起来，从而使该协会成为这个地区最有效率的商业集团。

禽肉生产已经转变为小农活动，整个地区大约有 10 万个饲养者。肉食鸡肉现在是这个地区蛋白质的主要来源。

禽肉作为农业综合企业，除了具有经济价值，还具有交叉性的影响。在此方面，加勒比共同体的各国政府已经开始认识到禽肉生产在各国农业部门中所扮演的包罗万象的角色。

由于加勒比家禽协会通过加勒比共同体秘书处和加勒比地区谈判机制在国家层面和区域层面开展活动，禽肉作为一种敏感商品已经在贸易谈判中，特别是在美洲自由贸易区被突显出来。

图 3.1　加勒比国民担任美洲农业合作研究所总干事 [1]

① 图中人物为多米尼加共和国的卡洛斯·E. 阿基诺博士（1992—2000 年）和巴巴多斯的切尔斯通·布拉思韦特博士（2001—2010 年）。

贸易和人类发展问题使加勒比各国政府对全球规划变得敏感，从而促使他们在全球、半球和地区授权上签字。这些授权在食品生产框架内已经启动了旨在解决饥饿、贫困和食品不安全问题的政策和规划。

主要的全球授权如下：

① 2015 年目标——全球繁荣和农业；

② 2015 年目标——千年发展目标（联合国）；

③ 2015 年目标——世界粮食首脑会议（联合国粮食及农业组织／全球）；

④ 2015 年目标——农业计划（联合国粮食及农业组织／半球）。

鉴于这些全球授权，国家级和地区级的部门贡献必须协调一致，以实现这些倡议的目标和指标。

这些全球和半球倡议正在塑造加勒比地区和国家的农业战略。实施这些倡议的是一些机构，如联合国粮食及农业组织在巴巴多斯有一个分区办事处，在牙买加、特立尼达和多巴哥没有代表，又如美洲农业合作研究所在除古巴以外的所有独立国家均有代表。

联合国粮食及农业组织和美洲农业合作研究所签署了一份协议，共同向各国政府提供协调的技术支持，特别是在将政府与全球授权联系在一起的地区。

加勒比共同体以贾格迪奥倡议作为回应。该倡议正在执行社区农业政策，其主要目的是使加勒比农业转型成为以市场为导向的，具有国际竞争力的和对环境无害的粮食生产者。与此同时，还有东加勒比国家组织的农业政策和战略计划。这个计划建立的前提是次区域国家最好采用集体方式解决问题。

在整个地区和个别国家面临挑战的现实之下，加勒比地区的专家们表示他们主要关心的是对待加勒比农业的方式。

美洲农业合作研究所的加勒比总监——圭亚那籍的 H. 阿灵顿·D. 切斯尼博士指出："这个地区处于粮食匮乏状态，无论在数量还是所需品种上，自然灾害发生后通常情况会更加恶化。"如果这种情况真的发生，正如目前显示，农业实质上不能减少这种短缺，使粮食不安全对我们的主权、社会平等、稳定和治理构成威胁。我们必须做出努力来加强自己的粮食安全，集中精力发展"新型"农业。

除了发展"新型"农业，联合国粮食及农业组织的前雇员、格林纳达籍的温斯顿·菲利普斯博士把加勒比大陆（圭亚那、苏里南和伯利兹）和小岛国家对立起来看待。他的评论如下：

"① 今天很难从一个区域整体的角度谈论加勒比农业，就像20 或 30 年前所做的那样。现实是，多年以来每一个国家都经历了巨大的政治、经济、社会等变化，这些变化以不同的方式塑造着每个国家的农业部门。

② 几乎在每一个加勒比国家，宏观政策对农业部门的影响都要比部门政策本身的影响更大和更为普遍。这一想法几乎公然违抗另一种意见，即需要通过增加财政资金分配来给予强有力的保证。

③ 每个国家农业部门的潜力并不相同。尽管如此，区域层面的讨论往往给人一种印象，即每个国家的潜力都是一样的。鉴于这一事实，部门发展的区域性解决方法需要采取不同的战略。在此方面，许多国家都会有一些附带后果。"

我认为正是由于上述原因，我们必须把"加勒比农业作为一个区域整体"来谈论。巴德鲁姆认为需要采取不同战略，我完全同意他的观点，其中之一就是以跨国私营部门投资为导向。几年前，在我说我们需要以这种方式看待地区农业时，一位加勒比同事嘲笑了我。我同意，农业部门已经受到这些国家发展方式的影响。除了特立尼达岛，在那里石油一直占主导地位，其他国家的农业已经不同程度地受到旅游业和其他服务业增长的影响。然而，正如巴德鲁姆正确指出的那样，我们的专业人员仍然认为该行业"在每个国家都相同"。正因如此，我们更为关注的是局限性而非可能性（农业规模太小、信誉不佳、无生产成果等）。

现实是，小国家的农业除了失去传统市场之外，已被服务行业所取代。有较大国土面积的国家——圭亚那、苏里南、伯利兹，依然是农业占主导地位。从近年来鼓吹的数字看，圭亚那生产了最便宜的鸡肉、菠萝、蔗糖和大米；我也大胆猜测，该地区生产了最便宜的牛肉和牛奶。

就农业而言，小岛从地形上就几乎注定了要栽培乔木作物。表面上看，果树栽培、香料和精油的生产是值得认真考虑和检验的。农业部门的方针和潜力因不同国家而异，这为这场辩论增加了重要的一点。坦率地说，我对贾格迪奥倡议的发起者完全忽略了地区农业政策方向感到惊讶。该方向强调了由那些国土面积较大的国家来为加勒比地区提供粮食的潜力；以及由圭亚那、苏里南或伯利兹邀请私营部门投资，而由政府为基础设施建设提供资金来发展贸易的潜力。

就像嘲笑我的那位同事所想的那样，如果这听起来很像地区粮食计划，我们应当意识到这些想法来源于政府投资的项目（我甚至不确定是否该称其为投资）。有迹象表明，地区私营部门越来越有兴趣进行区域内农业投资。无论其实质是什么，政府正在为这个地区的跨境投资铺平道路，这是值得鼓励的。我本以为就此事而言，即使是出于具体的国家利益，考虑到其他国家农业部门所发生的情况，圭亚那作为一个粮食生产/加工国，也会看到在圭亚那积极推广地区私营部门投资的好处，伯利兹和苏里南也是如此。

无论我们是否喜欢，当今世界私营部门投资的趋势是向资源可用、价格更便宜以及鼓励投资的地方转移。我并不认为加勒比的投资者有任何特殊之处，或者能够承受不同的方向。这是 21 世纪初制造业从巴巴多斯转移到特立尼达所突显出来的。巴巴多斯人并不愉快，但这就是今天发生的事情。有人回想起当初特立尼达的电话系统落后到极点，特立尼达商人飞到巴巴多斯打电话和发传真的事吗？（一个人即使去巴巴多斯打电话，据说是在批评巴巴多斯，因为与特立尼达不同，巴巴多斯"一切都正常"。）

小国可以把自己的农业定位于生产高附加值的产品，如特选香料加工和其他专为中美生物医药协会生产的产品。或许在丹尼斯·诺尔的"美德能"产品里有一个极大的教训，而我们所有的专家和政府都没能看到。观察加勒比单一市场和经济如何帮助促进这些发展会非常有趣。我们中一些人将会回想起，当我们还在想方设法改善地方政府对于农产品的运输服务时，马库斯·德弗雷塔斯已能把农产品从圣文森特运到迈阿密。

加勒比粮食生产市场被认为具有局限性。圣卢西亚的常务秘书马丁·萨特尼先生评论说：

> "我很有兴趣地追踪了这场辩论/讨论，同意目前为止所做的许多评论。我认为除非我们解决根本起因，否则我们将永远不能使地区农业部门和农村经济完全转型。基本问题本质上是结构性的，涉及生产系统（从农场到市场，包括附加值）中创造/产生的价值的管理和所有权。如前所述，岛屿经济完全由生产驱动，受市场终端控制，几十年来直至最近都被外部商业实体掌握和支配——我们很难发展出一种商业和企业文化，无论我们做了什么，都被保守地局限于商品价值链的低端。我们在为现成的定制市场生产原料商品方面几乎成了专家，但在塑造方面所起的作用非常有限。当市场发生巨大改变并持续改变时，我们完全误读了这个故事。为什么我们在那条路上走了那么久，是我们对种植度修改相对'满意'的另一场

辩论。

因为我们对市场和市场营销总体所知有限（从实际业务 / 价值管理的角度），如今由可替代商品 / 非传统商品提供的现有机遇即使在国内也很难抓住，除非实现重大结构改革或传统的'香蕉'模式重新出现（鉴于贸易环境显然不可逆转，我们都知道这是一种幻想）。

现实是，从促进贸易和出口的角度看，我们仍需完成本该几十年前做的那些事情，比如通过香蕉或任何其他商品发展出一种企业文化并推动创新（一个整体策略），既关注部门之间的后向联系也关注前向联系，把食品安全问题和自然资源的可持续利用和管理问题纳入考虑。这一战略性方法不应局限在国家层面，从长远来看应扩展到区域层面。"

美洲农业合作研究所的圭亚那雇员多莱特·巴德哈姆博士就加勒比农业的方案进行了以下总结。

"① 加勒比农业长期以来一直在衰退（和其他大多数国家一样）。这不是一个新情况。真正的问题在于所有国家的历任政府长期以来采用不同政策和战略，并不能促进农业部门的发展。蔗糖和香蕉业的缓慢消亡（通过欧盟和美国市场的持续保护）实际上延缓了这个部门衰落的速度。在几个国家独立 45 年之后，人们听到了关于香蕉和蔗糖的相同论点，这不足为奇。

② 今天人们很难像 20 或 30 年前那样把加勒比农业作为一个整体来谈论。现实是，这些年来每个国家都经历了巨大的政治、经济、社会等方面的变化，这些变化以不同的方式塑造着每个国家的农业部门。这些国家唯一的共同之处是确保少数商品（可能还有其他一些商品）进入受保护的市场。

③ 在几乎每个加勒比国家，宏观政策对农业部门的影响都要比部门政策本身的影响更大和更为普遍。再加上多年来所执行的这种农业政策，农业部门滞后和衰落的结果就不足为奇了。

④ 每个国家的农业部门的潜力不尽相同。尽管如此，在区域层面上的讨论经常给人以印象——每个国家的潜力是一样的。鉴于这一事实，部门发展的区域性解决方法需要采取不同的战略。在此方面，许多国家都会有一些附带后果。

⑤ 即使有了健全的政策和策略，除非通过财政资金拨款给予强有力

的保证,农业(或者任何其他部门,就此事而言)还是无法得到发展。农业部门的一系列地区计划,从 20 世纪 70 年代的地区粮食计划到目前的贾格迪奥倡议,(仍然处于初期)在部门内收效甚微,这正是由于缺乏政府的资金保证。美国和欧盟农业的发展在很大程度上归功于那些政府持续多年的巨额资金保证。

问题是,该地区的发展重点在哪里,以及为达成目标政府准备在多大程度上分配必备资源。政府仍在努力,以资助贾格迪奥倡议所提出的地区农业发展基金。"

插曲:《埃尼亚斯文集》 巴哈马人吃得健康吗?

在我的书《巴哈马农业历史沿革:1492—2012)》中,我指出:当克里斯托弗·哥伦布和他的随从们离开欧洲登陆这个群岛时,他们发现了一个富饶的环境。

> "欧洲人遇到了亚热带气候……,丰富的植被包括可食用的水果:牙买加酸橙、海葡萄、椰李、菠萝、松果和李子;根茎类作物:木薯、甘薯、花生以及带有药性的植物,如愈疮树。"

在前哥伦比亚时期,这种环境养育了早期住民,如泰诺人、阿拉瓦克人和可能来自佛罗里达的塞米诺尔人。因几乎没有食品贸易,所有的住民们消耗了这些岛屿的物产。最初,粮食作物来自天然植物,最后发展成为栽培作物,如甘薯和木薯。

在气候温和的欧洲,人们不得不培育可储藏作物以便在漫长的冬季月份里维持生活;而在这个亚热带环境里,住民们极大地依赖季节性水果和蔬菜,它们通常由于新鲜而营养价值较高,并且由于耕作方式和收获方法的缘故口感极好。

到 19 世纪中期,巴哈马不仅为本国种植丰富的粮食作物,而且还用于出口。从哥伦布及其随从在这些岛屿上发现的有限几种粮食看,粮食生产能力已经极大地提升了。

多样化和扩展是食品供应的支柱,维持着临近佛罗里达海岸的这个英国小殖民地上住民的生活。

大多数巴哈马人的饮食以畜牧业系统为中心。该系统生产了农作物、家禽以及大量海产品来提供健康而均衡的饮食,它们新鲜、美味并且大多数都是有机产品。这一点由水果的营养成分可见一斑。这些水果曾经非常重要但如今却濒临绝种。如罗望子果，其果肉具有很高的营养价值，富含钙、磷、铁和维生素B 族。

富含钙、磷、铁、钠、钾、胡萝卜素以及维生素 B1、B2 和维生素 C 的人参果，如今许多巴哈马人已经很少吃了。

黄酸枣、红李、牙买加酸橙和红枣也是如此，但这些水果已经从我们的日常饮食里消失了。

和 50 年前相比，今天巴哈马的饮食已经被快餐所主导，如袋装鸡肉、鸡块和鸡翅以及淋上番茄酱的油炸薯条，或者罐装的进口食品——新鲜时也是机械催熟，食之无味。它们大多数都是用商业肥料种植的。此外，越来越多的这种进口食品是转基因的。这些转基因农作物在欧洲食品商店是被禁止出售的，因其对人类健康的影响尚不明确。

20 世纪后半叶，男性和女性的平均寿命都有了很大的变化。1990 年，男性的平均寿命是 68.32 岁，女性的是 76.528 岁。和 1980 年相比，那时男性的平均寿命是 64.26 岁，女性的是 72.06 岁。

对于这一变化，有专家将其归结为医疗技术的进步、卫生服务的可用性以及大范围的工作人群更广泛地利用健康保险计划，而非普通公民正在消费的食品种类和质量。

上周，《时代》杂志刊登了一种名为"低碳（碳水化合物）"的新型饮食方式。有多少巴哈马人会尝试这一新时尚？你猜的跟我一样乐观。我知道一定会有人尝试。问题是这些时尚节食是否是健康饮食。答案是像我们的祖先那样吃饭吗？不排除这一可能性。

为了国民的健康，我们应该认真考虑采取措施来确保食品供应运转良好。

转基因生物

巴哈马人需要熟悉转基因生物（GMOs）这个术语。对于普通消费者来说，这是个新词，但对于科学家来说，它是未来的方向。

下一个千年，这个词将对人类发展方式产生严重的影响。在科学上，这是生物遗传学的新时代，影响着所有形式的有机体。遗传学家未来将能够复制人类，推动农业发展，开创其他基因产业。

即将于下个月在华盛顿州西雅图召开的世界贸易组织洽谈会上，转基因生物将成为最有争议的话题之一。这一争议源自这样的事实——转基因生物因与食品安全和人类健康息息相关，引起了人们的深切关注。

目前,一场三方辩论正在进行中。那些推广转基因生物的国家(美国、阿根廷、加拿大和墨西哥)认为,转基因作物对人类健康的威胁并不比非转基因作物更大,它们反对区分转基因和非转基因作物。若无标识,消费者将完全不知道他们吃的是转基因的还是非转基因的食品。

拉丁美洲、亚太地区的发展中国家,如马来西亚,希望从另一个角度采取一种更为谨慎的方法,要求在商业化前对转基因生物进行大量的测试以确定其对人类健康和环境构成的风险。

另一方面,欧盟坚持走中间路线,因为欧洲的消费者群体反对使用转基因生物,但是欧洲政策制定者及科学界并未禁止在其食品生产系统中使用转基因生物。

在过去的 18 个月中,欧洲已经暂停了对转基因生物的批准;然而上周,总部设在英国的阿斯特拉·塞内卡公司获准销售转基因番茄。

一份关于这一批准的新闻报道指出:

> "业界群体对这一决定持谨慎的欢迎态度,他们目睹了欧洲公众和政界对转基因产品不断飙升的反对意见,与美国对此事的漠不关心形成了鲜明的对比。"

英国消费者非常积极地阻止将转基因生物引入其食品系统中,他们经历了疯牛病危机,因此较为谨慎。英国消费者的抗议如此强烈,以致转基因的番茄酱立刻就从超市下架了。公众的反对基于这样一个事实,即产品缺乏适当检测,因而不能确定它对人体的影响。

另一方面,巴哈马消费者则处于不利地位。首先,巴哈马是一个食品净进口国,食品进口商在很大程度上决定着巴哈马人所吃的食物种类。其次,我们的食物中有 85%—90% 是从美国进口的,美国是从事转基因生产的主要国家之一,并且不支持给产品贴上标签以区分它们属于转基因还是非转基因。在这种情形下,巴哈马人将不知不觉地成为转基因产品最大的消费者之一。

所有这些关于转基因的问题还没有得到解答。这是一个相对较新的领域,由科学家和消费者组成的评审团仍在讨论这个问题。长久以来,发展中国家行动迟缓,依赖发达国家来确定行动方案。在巴哈马,我们应当对转基因采取折中的态度,因为根据科学进行区分并不意味着我们可以简单地忽视那些和科学无关的担忧。

关于此事,加勒比共同体国家在一份最近的报告中声称:

"基因工程产品在许多国家的接受度通常很低，但对动物产品的接受
度远远低于农作物。在此方面，使用基因改造作物喂养动物可能导致肉食
市场的过度细分。"

近年来，许多巴哈马人对有机种植的作物、施以商品肥料的作物、可能含有
生长激素的肉类产品，以及在树上或藤上自然成熟，而非用气体催熟的水果和
蔬菜都非常了解。现在，转基因生物成了新成员。

多年来，由生活方式和消费习惯引发的疾病的发病率有所增加。如果没有
一个通过标签标明的适当的监管体系，我们就会不加选择地消费转基因产品，
可能会产生一系列全新的、不同以往的健康问题。

有一种说法是人如其食。

第 4 章 ››

自我新意识

> "为了相对地脱颖而出,每一代人都必须找到自己的使命,完成它或者
> 辜负它。"

> ——马提尼克岛弗朗茨·法农的《地球上受苦的人》

加勒比很难发展自我意识,除非黑人真正得到承认。正因为非裔移民的存在,加勒比才能开发出具有全球重要性的资源和商品。

亨利·霍布豪斯在他的著作《变革的种子》中将非洲人在加勒比的角色作为重点。霍布豪斯是这样说的:

> "一个不必要的'傻瓜'是如何对加勒比的非洲化负责的。它(加勒比)只涉及世界上很小的一部分地区,但到 1800 年,却担负着超过 80% 的蔗糖和奴隶贸易。一个直接结果是,这个小地区同时担负着西欧国家所有航海工作的近一半,包括海军的和民用的。"

新世界的奴隶制度给体力劳动这一整体概念遗留了不尊重的问题吗?这种联系给新世界的黑人打上了烙印,无论其成就如何,这一遗留问题可能是导致整个地区食品生产失败的根本原因。

加勒比是高附加值商品蔗糖的主要产地和把非洲人作为财产进行交易这一赚钱行业的市场,拥有一片加勒比土地对欧洲人来说是有利可图的。因此,这个地区受到了西班牙、荷兰、英国和法国的影响。加勒比成为欧洲国家的蔗糖殖民地。后来,美西战争见证了美国对波多黎各和维尔京群岛地区的入侵。

由于殖民历史,加勒比从来不是一个同质区域。在大安的列斯群岛的北部,有三种语言:西班牙语(古巴、多米尼加共和国和波多黎各)、法语(海地)和英语(牙买加)。在小安的列斯群岛,有荷兰语(库拉索岛、阿鲁巴岛、博内尔岛)、法

语(马提尼克岛和瓜德罗普岛)和英语(加勒比共同体国家和美属维尔京群岛)。

在小安的列斯群岛上,英语语系的影响占主导地位。1958 年,前英国殖民地和牙买加组成了命运多舛的西印度群岛联邦。

除了联邦的这一尝试之外,我们还意识到了某种区域性团体的需求,于是加勒比自由贸易区(CARIFTA)建成了。然而,1972 年,加勒比各国领导人在第七届政府首脑会议上决定通过建立加勒比共同体(共同市场将是其一个重要组成部分),使加勒比自由贸易区转变为一个共同市场。

加勒比共同体自有其挑战并将继续接受挑战,但它已经成为这个地区的核心机构,或许比其他任何机构都更能促使这个地区明确其"自我意识"。

近年来,这种"自我意识"的定义历经了加勒比共同体的几项举措——关于人口的自由流动、加勒比单一市场和经济以及加勒比法院(CCJ)。

加勒比共同体已在这个地区扩大其影响范围,首先通过接受说法语的海地而打破了以英语为母语的垄断,继而促进了准会员的加入。通过加勒比论坛,多米尼加共和国加入其中。

总共约有 20 个区域性机构在加勒比共同体秘书处的管理范围内。

加勒比共同体已经在国际社会脱颖而出,因为它是一个所有成员国都遵守民主原则和法治至上的集团。该地区的希望是这一民主遗产将由其新成员海地采纳并实行。

从表面看,基督教给加勒比留下了不可磨灭的印象。在前英国殖民地,基督教是英国的国教。随着独立,一个由"西印度群岛人"领导的本土教会出现了。

西印度群岛教会的大主教、都主教和首席主教已经成为全球圣公会的领导者。德雷克塞尔·戈麦斯大主教阁下已经成为关于圣公会所面临问题的第三世界发言人。

西印度群岛教省包括所有前殖民地的主教教区,这些殖民地现为独立国家。教省统一了这个地区的精神力量。这在英国圣公会和教省神学院的礼拜仪式上得到了体现,巴巴多斯的科德林顿学院则维持了那些在该地区担任圣公会社区神职人员的学术水准。

本土的加勒比圣公会向教省的教会提供了一种加勒比视角来看待全球圣公会所面临的重大问题。

古巴、海地、多米尼加共和国和美属维尔京群岛有圣公会或新教圣公会。在古巴,有古巴新教圣公会(圣公会),由古巴大主教委员会管辖。该委员会由西印度群岛的大主教、美国圣公会第九教省的高级主教以及加拿大圣公会的首席主教组成,后者担任委员会的会长。

图 4.1 西印度群岛教会的大主教、都主教和首席主教,巴哈马以及特克斯和凯科斯群岛的主教,德雷克塞尔·戈麦斯阁下

古巴新教圣公会的主教负责加勒比联盟的圣公会教省。该教省包括海地、多米尼加共和国和波多黎各。美属维尔京群岛的新教圣公会教徒属于美国圣公会。这个地区建立了完善的圣公会制度。

罗马天主教统治着讲西班牙语和法语的国家以及圣卢西亚、特立尼达和多巴哥。安的列斯群岛主教团是天主教团体,由这一地区的大主教和主教组成。例如,在海地,前天主教神父让·贝特朗·阿里斯蒂德采纳了拉丁美洲的解放神学,他最终成为海地的第一位民选总统。

基督教遍及这一地区。主要的教派是天主教、圣公会和浸信会。基督教是加勒比认同感的一个特征。

体育在加勒比认同感中扮演着一个重要的角色。在加勒比共同体,板球将除海地之外的所有加勒比共同体国家联结在一起。在大安的列斯群岛(古巴、多米尼加共和国和波多黎各)和库拉索岛、美属维尔京群岛上,棒球占主导地位。

西印度群岛板球队是板球界最佳球队之一。加勒比的板球受到的评价如此高以至于 2007 年的板球世界杯在这个地区举行。这推动了旅游业。

加勒比棒球是职业棒球大联盟的一支主要力量。加勒比球员代表着 20%—25% 的大联盟球员。

然而,田径运动联结着所有加勒比国家。在 1968 年的奥运会上,加勒比的古巴选手(胡安·陶林,400 米和 800 米)、牙买加选手(唐·夸里,400 米)以及特立尼达和多巴哥选手(哈尔西·克劳福德,100 米)赢得了 100—800 米的金牌,在这些项目中占绝对优势。在随后的奥运会中,奥运奖牌得主来自古巴、巴哈马、牙买加和多米尼加共和国。最近,体育节目广播员在多数情形下能认出该地区的运动员,从而突出了该地区在体育界的地位。

雷克斯·内特尔福德教授创造了"加勒比文化符号"这种说法,把加勒比定义为带有"非洲节奏"的欧洲旋律。正如内特尔福德教授所指,贯穿整个加勒比文化的主线是欧洲和非洲之间的纽带。尽管加勒比经历了欧洲的殖民统治,并且故意断开与非洲的联系,加勒比文化仍根植于欧洲和非洲文明中。

这种二元根系结构缔造了一个独特的民族。由于这个民族的独特性,已逐步形成一种不同于欧洲或非洲的生活方式。这反映在音乐、烹饪、礼拜活动、生活方式、对大多数事物的基本态度、建筑以及加勒比人民的沟通方式上。

这个地区正着手发展一个新的经济部门——旅游业,也正采取措施创建一个地区性高等院校——西印度群岛大学。这是 1948 年。

1948 年以来,西印度群岛大学在加勒比英语区发挥着关键作用,培养了数以千计的人才。然而,在整个地区,每个加勒比国家都存在高等院校的扩建。老牌独立国家(古巴、海地和多米尼加共和国)几十年前就建有大学和学院。在新独立的国家,由于政府和私营部门的举措,高等教育也得到了发展。

西印度群岛大学一直是加勒比共同体最好的高等院校,然而,加勒比知识学习网(CKLN)最近的数据表明,加勒比大约有 150 所高等院校。

西印度群岛大学通过校外项目扩大了它的影响。在这个信息和通信技术的时代,加勒比知识学习网将"连接这个地区的学院和大学,促进区域性电子学习课程的合作和开发"。这也将有助于实现加勒比共同体的目标——确保至 2010 年 30% 的人口接受过高等教育。

一些国家,如牙买加,也制定了国家目标——到 2015 年实现加勒比共同体 30% 的目标。

毫无疑问,西印度群岛大学在它存在的近 60 年中被国际社会赞誉为一所突显了加勒比学术形象的大学。在此期间,西印度群岛大学已成为一所能力和声誉兼具的真正大学,能够与全球老牌大学相媲美。

在 150 所高等院校中,有一些海外学术机构,其中包括 24 所医疗(和 1 所兽医)学校。这些机构不同于普通的医学院,因为它们更便宜,而且在加勒比建立一所海外医学院也更容易,那里的认证条件不包括研究课程、全方位服务的大学或医院。

这种偏离规范的做法已将海外加勒比医学院与传统的医学院区分开来;由于 1910 年发表的《弗莱克斯纳报告》,美国和加拿大的医学院经历了改革。

这份报告的基础是"有太多的学校,其中许多学校不达标,需要明确学医的先决条件和医学教育的内容"。作为评估的结果,这份报告建议,医学院教育的最低要求应为四年(两年基础科学和最后两年的临床工作)。

弗莱克斯纳对美国和加拿大的 155 所医学院进行过调查,他视约翰·霍普金斯医学院为典范。那时只有"16 所医学院要求两年或两年以上的大学学习作为入门条件。"

海外加勒比医疗机构已将加勒比建立为医疗培训的中心。该地区总共有 37 所在世界卫生组织注册的医学院。特立尼达和多巴哥(1 所)、牙买加(1 所)和多米尼加共和国(9 所)均设有医学院;其中,圭亚那的 1 所学校为国内或地区学生提供服务,还有几所在东加勒比国家(格林纳达、圣卢西亚)。

《世界银行报告》指出:

> "1984—2004 年进入美国的国际医学毕业生中的 70% 都来自海外加勒比医学院。据估计,目前有 11 000 名海外学生就读于这些学校。"

加勒比是第三世界国家的一个地区,正在为向美国和加拿大等发达国家输出医师提供环境。

加勒比地区谈判机制是一个重要的区域机构。越来越多的加勒比国家将服务业视为其外汇收入的主要来源。尽管旅游业是一个变幻无常的行业,但与其他服务或商品相比,它为加勒比国家的经济提供了更多的外汇。

2006 年 11 月,圣基茨和尼维斯政府成立了糖业多元化基金会(SIDF),这是"自我新意识"的最佳例证。这一决定源于这样的事实——政府决定放弃几百家小农从事的甘蔗种植,转而开启一项将圣基茨和尼维斯的经济转变为以服务为基础的规划。

糖业多元化基金会的成立反映了总理登齐尔·道格拉斯博士这一届政府有信心使这个双岛之国走上一条新的经济发展道路。这届政府认为,糖业多元化基金会是"实现圣基茨和尼维斯人民各种抱负"的最佳途径。

除了古巴,美属波多黎各和维尔京群岛,法属岛屿马提尼克岛和瓜德罗普岛以及荷属库拉索岛、阿鲁巴岛、博内尔岛和萨巴岛,加勒比地区谈判机制能够为该地区的大部分国家制定出一个共同的贸易政策。通过一个共同的贸易政策,加勒比在一系列贸易体制(世界贸易组织、美洲自由贸易区以及《欧盟的合作伙伴协议》)中统一了口径。

这个地区有很多面。在作为旅游目的地方面,加勒比旅游组织在把加勒比推广和发展成为世界独一无二的目的地方面发挥着战略性作用。

加勒比旅游组织是一个相对较新的组织,成立于 1989 年 1 月。它由加勒比旅游组织(成立于 1951 年)和加勒比旅游研究和发展中心(成立于 1974 年)合并而成。加勒比旅游组织把自己归类为国际性发展机构。

加勒比旅游组织的效能取决于其推销和壮大加勒比市场的能力。因此,其成员由各旅游目的地国家组成,每个国家都各具特色;然而,在我看来,共同之处使这个地区仍然被视为一个目的地。

诸如加勒比共同体、西印度群岛大学、加勒比地区谈判机制、教会、体育和文化等加勒比机构,正在帮助这个地区发展一种"自我意识",目的是使潜在的游客关注这个地区。

例如,在加勒比文化中,音乐尤为突出。无论是牙买加的雷鬼乐、非洲—古巴爵士乐、特立尼达岛的钢鼓乐队,还是巴哈马的卡里普索或贾卡努,这些声音的共同点是"非洲节奏"。在加勒比音乐中,正是"非洲节奏"使这个地区的音乐闻名遐迩,独一无二。

在基督教的敬拜和礼拜仪式中也发现了这种节奏。随着天主教和圣公会神职人员的本土化,敬拜的节奏被改变了。

正是通过制度的同步,加勒比地区开始发展出一种"自我意识"。

朗姆酒之于加勒比,如同红酒之于欧洲。在加勒比种植甘蔗的地方,有一种特殊种类或牌子的朗姆酒就是在那里加工出来的。这导致整个加勒比地区生产出了一系列的朗姆酒。其中某些朗姆酒国际闻名,一些在本地区有名,还有一些是岛屿独有的。

人们总能找到一家朗姆酒馆,出入的通常是男人,讨论着各种话题,吃着当地食物,这里也有娱乐活动。

朗姆酒有很多用途。它获得了麻醉剂的美誉,但其药用价值没有被开发,也没有被作为烹饪或烘焙的佐料。尽管如此,朗姆酒依然是加勒比社会经济结构中一个重要的方面。它是加勒比地区的一个显著特色。

在过去的 500 年里,甘蔗生产经过了诸多技术变迁,特别是在植物遗传学和育种方面,这反映在甘蔗的成熟率、含糖量、对土壤类型反应等的改进上。这些因素影响了在各个岛屿上生产的朗姆酒的类型。在这个全球化的时代,各种规章制度管理着知识产权,朗姆酒是一种独特的饮品,基于原产地命名保护制度,特殊的朗姆酒应当作为一种加勒比产品被保护起来。

20 世纪 90 年代，澳大利亚葡萄酒和白兰地公司同欧盟签署了一份协议；2003 年，加拿大和欧盟达成了协议。加勒比地区谈判机制亦应当为加勒比共同体的朗姆酒达成此种协议。

加勒比经历了奴隶制和殖民主义两个时期，现正处于第三个时期——独立时期。奴隶制和殖民主义的经历在该地区人们的头脑中留下了精神烙印，这一烙印正被新的意识所替代。正是这一"自我意识"驱使该地区的人们达到新的高度。加勒比国家正左右着自己的命运。

插曲：《埃尼亚斯文集》《巴哈马日报》 加勒比单一市场和经济：巴哈马是去还是留？

特立尼达的西班牙港——35 年前，到特立尼达还是一件烦琐之事。今天，从迈阿密到西班牙港轻而易举，只需 3.5 小时。

双岛之国（特立尼达和多巴哥）经历了很多变化。这里经济繁荣，而且它可能是加勒比地区讲英语的国家中工业化程度最高的。

特立尼达和多巴哥的经济表现出了很大的弹性。在石油市场触底后，其经济受到了猛烈的冲击，因为其外汇主要来源被严重破坏——储备下降，国家基础设施开始分崩离析，失业率开始飙升，毒品交易泛滥。

现在经济更加健康，因为外国投资已经注入几个地区，以建设高度多样化的经济。

本周，加勒比地区的焦点再次聚集于特立尼达，因为加勒比地区的政府首脑在该区域第 20 届加勒比共同体峰会上举行会晤。

这个峰会对于该地区未来的发展至关重要。峰会的首要议程是建立单一的市场经济。以此为方向，加勒比共同体国家需要极大地变更现行做法，特别是在发展加勒比共同体货币、国家之间的资本流动、人力资源利用以及贸易方面。这对巴哈马的影响是巨大的，无疑将涉及相当大的争论。

加勒比一体化和巴哈马的问题很棘手。尽管我们与其他加勒比英语区有着许多共同的问题，巴哈马人依然存在总体政治和经济融入的心理障碍。

为了更好地理解和体会，在这个问题上需要更多的公共教育。在政治、职业和公共服务层面上，我们对于巴哈马参与加勒比一体化有着深入的理解和体会；然而在公民和商业层面上存在着极端不适。

加勒比共同体领导人认识到了这一事实，即因为失败的西印度联邦的记忆导致了对一体化进程的猜疑。为了解决实施单一市场和经济的不确定性,政府首脑决定实施一项区域范围的方案,向人们宣传一体化运动及其好处。

加勒比共同体领导人有个共识,即这个一体化概念并不容易推销,也不应该在一个国家培养此种理念。在此背景下,人们普遍认同,一些国家会比其他国家进展得慢。

在举办政府首脑峰会的同时,加勒比农业部也出现在特立尼达和多巴哥,因为那里正在举办加勒比农业周以及其他一些和农业综合企业有关的活动。

主办这些峰会的加勒比领导人总喜欢"炫耀"自己国家最好的一面。特立尼达的经济正在好转,这一点大家可以看到并感觉到。

这里通常会有美国快餐特许经营店,如肯德基、必胜客、汉堡王和麦当劳。卫星和有线电视传输使人们可以跟上习惯收看的节目。男女时尚在拿骚、迈阿密或纽约都是相同的。手机以及最新的信息技术小配件随处可见。

30 多年前我是这个岛国的一名学生,那时这里似乎是个遥远的地方。随着科技、通讯和交通的进步,西班牙港似乎并不那么遥远了。加勒比和巴哈马的关系日益紧密;今天,它们的同远大于异。

巴哈马应当畏惧加勒比一体化吗?

1992 年,国际发展专家认为加勒比未来的经济前景岌岌可危。他们认为,该地区支离破碎、负债累累,而且越来越被高犯罪率和影响社会稳定的毒品贩运所困扰。

加勒比联邦的未来如此让人胆战心惊,以至于政府首脑们成立了西印度群岛委员会以推荐加强区域合作和一体化的方法。委员会由施里达斯·兰法尔爵士担任主席。顺便一提,他正带领加勒比共同体谈判团队进入美洲自由贸易区。

在我看来,巴哈马商会的成员反对加勒比共同体在这次谈判过程中为巴哈马履行代理职能。感觉巴哈马应当独立谈判。

几个星期前,巴哈马驻加勒比大使 A·伦纳德·阿切尔先生曾说,巴哈马是时候认真考虑加勒比一体化了。他的论据是加勒比国家的经济看起来越来越相像——旅游业、金融服务业以及其他服务业,特别是那些和信息技术紧密相关的行业。

在国际发展机构、联合国机构当然还有欧盟看来,加勒比被视为一个有其自身权益的地区。美国在里根政府期间采取了这种做法,并启动了加勒比盆地计划(CBI)。此种方式已经流行起来。

巴哈马人难以认同其余的加勒比人。在地理上,这个群岛的岛屿分为两部分,每部分都连接着大陆。大安的列斯群岛,如古巴、海地、多米尼加共和国、牙买加、波多黎各以及维尔京群岛,代表着加勒比盆地的北部秘境。小安的列斯群岛形成了盆地的东部秘境。这些岛屿包括从安圭拉岛到格林纳达的岛屿。地理学家认为,特立尼达可能还有巴巴多斯在地理上与委内瑞拉相近。

巴哈马位于大安的列斯群岛的北部,在严格意义上超出了加勒比海盆地的范围。在更广泛的背景下,加勒比海界定了加勒比地区的范围。然而,在此更广泛的背景下,巴哈马被视为加勒比的一部分。由于其英国殖民背景,其与加勒比海盆地讲英语的国家有着天然的政治亲和关系。因此,巴哈马与加勒比共同体结盟。

1997年之前,金融专家和分析人士经常以东南亚国家和地区——亚洲四小龙为加勒比海盆地国家效仿的榜样。然而,东南亚的经济和金融方面出现过一些引人注目的逆转,其中几个国家的经济模式被作为可供采纳的典范。

自1992年以来,加勒比共同体的经济一直朝着积极的方向发展。1997年,旅游业在该地区经济表现中仍然是主导部门,对境外金融部门的增长做出了越来越大的贡献。这支持了阿切尔大使的观点——加勒比共同体国家的经济看起来越来越相像。

加勒比开发银行最近的统计数据证实了经济的积极表现:

> "安圭拉岛的经济增长了大约6.5%,开曼群岛为6%,英属维尔京群岛为4.5%,特克斯和凯科斯群岛为4%。安提瓜和巴布达的增长估计为4.8%。对于巴哈马来说,据报道,其经济已连续五年增长,实际国内生产总值增长了3.5%,比1996年的1%有了大幅度增长。

> 巴巴多斯也经历了连续五年的经济增长,但其4.3%的增长无法和上一年的5.2%相提并论。伯利兹增长了3%,相比1996年的1.5%翻了一番;格林纳达增长了4.3%,高于上一年的3.4%。在圭亚那,增长率估计为6.1%,远低于1996年的7.9%。

> 牙买加的经济继续停滞不前,其增长率或许在1%左右。在圣基茨和尼维斯,与1996年的4.8%相比,有迹象表明其产量提高了8%;在圣文森特和格林纳丁斯,增长极小。特立尼达和多巴哥的经济复苏仍在继续,预计增长率为3.2%。多米尼克和圣卢西亚的经济似乎在衰退,因其经济极为依赖香蕉出口。"

从所有迹象来看,加勒比共同体国家做出了合理的调整,正朝着正确的方向前进。拥有如此强大的经济,加强与加勒比共同体的关系符合巴哈马的利益,特别是在《洛美协定》和美洲自由贸易区的谈判过程中。

伦纳德·阿切尔一语中的。我们需要更加仔细地研究加勒比一体化的含义。

加勒比一体化:我们的立场是什么?

加勒比英语区把自己界定为加勒比一体化的主要发起者。一体化进程虽然经过了起起伏伏,但在过去的 40 年中,特别是独立时期以来,取得了稳步进展。然而纵观这一时期,巴哈马只是参与了这一进程的一部分。

最常用来解释巴哈马部分参与的原因是赞同一体化进程不符合其利益。

西印度群岛大学成立时,白人寡头政府认为大学教育远远超出了大多数黑人的目标。因此,巴哈马选择不参与资助这所大学。直到进步自由党接管政权,巴哈马才成为西印度群岛大学的经费资助方。

巴哈马从未将自己视为西印度群岛的一部分。其板球队签字加入西印度一体化才表明它在国际上认同了这种身份。

20 世纪 50 年代,西印度田径队的教练们急于想要把汤米·罗宾逊归入自己队中,特别是短跑接力队,但未能如愿,因为巴哈马不是加勒比团体的成员。

20 世纪 70 年代,如果不是财政部部长卡尔顿·弗朗西斯先生如此坚持和有远见,巴哈马将不会成为加勒比开发银行的董事会成员。就像今天一样,当时的想法是我们在某些方面不能从加勒比开发银行获益,把我们的钱放进加勒比银行不符合我们的利益。

加勒比自由贸易区运动会花了近五六年的时间,才为这一地区的年轻人承办了最重要的运动赛事。B. J. 诺塔奇博士在担任巴哈马业余体育协会主席期间参观了巴巴多斯的运动会,决定巴哈马应当参加加勒比自贸区运动会。自从参加加勒比自贸区运动会后,看看巴哈马在体育上收获了什么?这是金牌女将大获成功的基础。

一些国际组织,如欧盟、泛美卫生组织以及联合国粮食及农业组织将巴哈马置于加勒比地区的背景之下。

提到欧盟,巴哈马可以获得很多项目的资助,然而这些资助的地区总部或在牙买加,或在巴巴多斯,或在特立尼达。因为出于行政目的,巴哈马隶属于这些被列为地区办事处的国家之一。在很多时候,由于我们在地区“圈子”之外,巴哈马并未获得它有资格得到或符合条件的好处。

作为一个地区，加勒比所面临的最重要的挑战之一是全球化问题，以及像大多数加勒比共同体国家那样的小经济国家将如何应对这一问题。由于参加美洲自由贸易区所面临问题的复杂性，加勒比建立了地区谈判机制，汇集了贸易方面的技术专长，以呈现一个统一的立场。

这种做法已经得到了回报。就在最近，加勒比在世界贸易组织的《农业协定》中表明了自己的立场。其陈词深受好评，因为该文献的关键部分得到了发达国家的认可，尤其是美国和欧盟那样的大国。

在当今世界上，对于巴哈马这样的小国来说，单打独斗是鲁莽的。政府在处理我们的金融服务黑名单时所采取的策略和加勒比共同体把问题交给世界贸易组织的方式将被评判和比较。巴哈马民众，在某一时刻，将会判定每种方式的结果。

一体化进程现已触及我们文明的一个非常基础的方面——通过加勒比法庭解释我们的法律。巴哈马已表态，它希望英国枢密院继续发挥这一作用。加勒比共同体称，其已发展到可在本地区内实现此方面治理的水平了。

许多人将保留枢密院看作是我们殖民地遗产最后的遗留之一。另一方面，英国也已摊牌，它在无数个场合表示其未来是和欧洲其他国家在一起的，并以欧盟的形式将其自然生活的基本成分融入单一体中。

在不久的将来，我们巴哈马人将醒来，发现英国人表示他们不再对裁定我们的法律事务感兴趣了。他们在独立过程中身体力行，英联邦已成为"空谈俱乐部"，例子不胜枚举。

在这发展的关键时刻，值此 21 世纪之际，巴哈马依然不明白加勒比一体化的重要性。矛盾的是，在加勒比所有国家中，巴哈马或许是最具世界性的。居住在中部的是每个加勒比岛屿的原住民——牙买加人、海地人、巴巴多斯人、特立尼达人、圣卢西亚人、多米尼加人、圣文森特人、圭亚那人、伯利兹人、古巴人等。

第 5 章 »

"9·11" 事件

"没有文明应对外部世界如此毫无准备;没有国家如此容易被袭击和掠夺,并且从灾难中几乎什么也没学到。"

——特立尼达人 V. S. 奈保尔的《印度:受伤的文明》

2001 年的"9·11"事件,表明了旅游作为一种商品之变幻莫测,以及严重依赖旅游收入的经济之脆弱。由于没有航班可以进入或离开美国,加勒比地区受到了空中禁运的打击。

空中禁运使加勒比旅游业损失了数百万美元的收入,并使数千人暂时失业。"9·11"是一个破坏经济、社会和政治稳定的事件。尘埃落定后,其影响甚至更为深远。一场以反恐战争为形式的新战争已经成为现实。这场战争将使加勒比各国的政府投资数百万美元用于机场和邮轮码头安检,以及一批新的工作人员的专业安检培训。

对于巴哈马来说,"9·11"的代价昂贵。9 月 11 日,美国联邦航空管理局停止了美国机场所有的航班运营,直到 9 月 13 日才恢复航班。

2001 年,巴哈马平均每天有 4 211 名游客,每人每天至少花费 250 美元。一天的平均支出为 1 052 750 美元。航班取消,巴哈马每天损失超过 100 万美元。

没有哪个加勒比国家拥有巴哈马那么多的机场;2005 年有 64 个,其中 30 个铺设了跑道。在一些岛屿上,如伊鲁萨拉岛,有 3 个机场(北伊鲁萨拉岛、总督港和罗克桑德),并且每个都可接待国际航班。

在机场系统安装安检设备需要基本建设费用。此外,因为整个群岛都需要治安保卫人员,所以招募人力的费用也增加了。

在 2002 年 3 月发表的预算中,巴哈马总理和财政部部长声明如下:

"在 2001 年的最后一个季度,现有统计数据显示,总到访游客数量缩减了 11%，逆转了 2000 年同期增长 15.3% 的趋势。航空游客受到的冲击最大，减少了 22.8%；邮轮游客受到的冲击略小，减少了 5.1%。据估计，这段时期总的游客开销减少了约 28.5%。

据报道，'9·11' 后，相对于正常时的 57%，酒店的平均入住率低至44%；房地产通过大幅折扣和削减成本的措施做出回应，其中包括部分关闭、临时裁减员工和缩短工作时间。

同样地，很多极其依赖旅游业的零售商店采取了节约劳动力的措施，金融机构为可能受到财政困难影响的工人们做好了准备，为个人和家庭债务提供机会以便实行更易管理的服务措施。

由于第四季度的损失，2001 年总到访游客缩减了 0.4%，为 419 万人；航空游客减少了 2.9%，为 144 万人；邮轮游客的增速放缓了 1%，为 275 万人。由于那些往往待的时间最长、花费最多的中途停留的旅客呈现疲势，再连同价格折扣，估计 2001 年的行业收益会减少 3.5%，为 17.5 亿美元。

相应的酒店业趋势表明，尽管平均房价上涨了 2.9%，至每晚 153.03 美元，但是入住率减少了 4.4%，造成预计的客房收入减少了 1.7%。"

归根结底，巴哈马政府不得不借款 1.25 亿美元来完善 2001 年 2 月的财政状况的融资。这从根本上导致了 "9·11" 事件的余波，私营部门的损失估计达数亿美元，尤其是和酒店及旅游相关的行业。

酒店一周工作时间的缩短对女性产生了不利影响，她们很多都是单身母亲和养家糊口之人。

这概括了 "9·11" 事件对巴哈马造成的直接影响。

美国政府的国土安全部实施了西半球旅游倡议。这项倡议要求：

"美国人以及加拿大人、墨西哥人和百慕大人从西半球的任何地方通过航空或海运方式抵达美国时，必须出示护照。"

在此倡议之前，来到巴哈马的美国人只需某种身份证明，即驾照或社会保障卡就足够了；"9·11" 改变了这一约定。

几名 "9·11" 恐怖分子持有美国大学的学生签证。鉴于这些学生签证被用于进入美国，美国出台了颁发学生签证的新政策。这个过程严格而且选择性很强，导致许多加勒比学生无法获得学生签证。

这给指望在这个地区接受高等教育的加勒比学生带来了极大的困难，因此，这也强调了地区性高等院校的重要性，如西印度群岛大学、国家级大学和社区学院以及许多外商独资和经营的人文类和兽医类专科大学/学院。这个地区的高等教育培训已深化到拥有 150 所高等院校的程度。

美国和加勒比各港口以及邮轮码头也开展了反恐努力。其主要关注的是水下爆炸装置或任何可能危及邮轮安全的机械装置。

2006 年 8 月 10 日星期四,加勒比各国政府再次受到惊吓。当时,机场接到了来自美国运输安全管理局的高度安全警报。起因是发现了一起恐怖分子企图阴谋炸毁从英国伦敦飞往美国的飞机。这一警报包括往返美国的飞机以及往返英国的飞机。

英国航空公司——英国航空和维珍航空,以及牙买加航空都有从英国直飞加勒比的航班。随着新安全规则的出台,这个警报暂时中断了旅行,避免了一次可能发生的"9·11"事件。

在 2001 年 9 月 11 日之前的任何一天,加勒比地区都会有大约 10 万名游客,他们人均花费为 100—250 美元。在 2001 年的最后四个月中,这种游客涌入的状态被打断了,每天的收入损失为 1 000 万—2 500 万美元。回顾巴哈马的情况,该行业在 4—6 个月内都无法恢复到常态。该地区的收入损失接近 10 亿美元。

"9·11"事件使该地区的这些小岛国家遭受了重大的经济衰退。

插曲:《埃尼亚斯文集》《巴哈马日报》 深远影响

在世界贸易中心和五角大楼遭到袭击后,旅游业遭受重创,加勒比国家正准备渡过一个经济难关,这个过程可能持续到 2002 年中期或后期。

本周,加勒比政府和旅游业的领导人在巴哈马回顾了形势,希望这场灾难的共性能导向一种视角,以缓冲落势或在某种程度上减轻正经受的损失和下滑的金融指标。

在纽约市、奥兰多和拉斯维加斯等地,人们正在利用各种各样的噱头和措施来吸引游客回到赌桌、沙滩、主题公园、博物馆和表演场所。酒店和航空公司在这些努力中发挥着重要作用。它们的成功程度还有待确定。这场把戏美其名曰"价格共享",这只是在经济上存活下去的必要条件。

这是旅游业面对的普遍情况。在袭击发生后的几周内,询价越来越多。就拿骚的一处房产而言,自恐怖袭击前以来,该房产价格已逐渐上涨 70%;感恩节和圣诞节期间的预订态势良好,旅行作家的到访人数再次出现上升趋势。这些全是积极的迹象。

整个局势取决于安全程度。到目前为止,每个人都应意识到世界处于战争状态。

这并非遥不可及。本周早些时候，联合国秘书长科菲·安南先生非常关注一份来自美国安全理事会的备忘录——除了阿富汗，可能还有其他东方国家被指派进行轰炸。这是火上浇油。

这就是今天的危机。经济预测显示事态日益恶化——这一状态可能会持续两年之久。若此情况属实，这对许多国家来说可能意味着经济崩溃。

据全球贷款机构评估，恐怖袭击将对未来两年全球经济增长的预测产生负面影响——是的，未来两年。此外，第三世界或发展中国家的经济增长和发展将会严重滞后。

预计大约 1 000 万人可能陷入贫困，每天只靠不到 1 美元过活。

在袭击发生前，经济学家就观察到，在一些工业化国家，如欧洲、美国和日本，经济增长放缓。袭击事件导致预期的经济复苏推迟了。

与旅游相关的行业遭受的打击尤为严重。这一观点使加勒比和巴哈马这样的国家陷入目前的困境——约 65% 的度假预订被取消了。

20 世纪 90 年代，由于外国投资的大量涌入，巴哈马处于极为沮丧的经济状况。这种情形并不长久，因为资本流向发展中国家的速度肯定会放缓，可能会变为涓涓细流。记住：依赖旅游业的经济已不再盛行。

巴哈马经济发展政策基于旅游业和金融服务两大支柱，必须对这一政策进行调整，引入宏观经济政策来反映更好的投资环境，既强调外国投资也鼓励本地投资。

毫无疑问，加勒比共同体政府首脑会议的紧急会议将重点关注袭击事件引发的经济后果，特别是旅游业、航空业和金融服务部门。

对于巴哈马来说，其影响是严重的。我们已经感受到了其对旅游业和金融服务的影响。就航空业而言，这意味着分散在我们群岛四面八方的 20 个机场将扮演新的角色。

更严格的安全规则将授权优先使用我们的家庭岛机场。许多机场将不再作为入境港，在一些原本有多个机场的岛屿上，只有一个可被指定用来接待国际航班——私人航班和商业航班。

世界处于战争模式的时间越久，袭击的影响就会越大。

我们的世界安全吗？

自 2003 年 3 月以来，美国、英国以及其他多个国家开始入侵伊拉克。入侵的最初原因是为世界清除大规模杀伤性武器,萨达姆·侯赛因政权被认为拥有这些武器。

推翻萨达姆政权相对较快,没有多少人员伤亡。一旦被击败,解放者就成为占领者。这一占领在该国引发了许多内乱,每天的新闻广播中都充斥着人们被汽车炸弹炸死或被武装人员袭击的报道。当年 6 月,该国的统治权移交给当地人。

上周,美国参议院的一份报告得出结论说,中央情报局对伊拉克构成的威胁提供了虚假的、没有根据的评估,布什政府据此说服英国和其余国家入侵伊拉克。

这份报告被驳斥,因为得到的结论是如果美国的立法者知道真相,美国国会可能不会批准伊拉克战争。这份报告影响了美国人、美国总统以及国务卿科林·鲍威尔的信誉,鲍威尔必须通过联合国安理会向世界推销这一入侵想法。

此次入侵的一个方面是根除恐怖主义和那些支持或庇护恐怖主义者的国家。基地组织也是全球共同的恐怖主义仇敌。

所有这一切的结果是,世界已被颠倒,每个国家的每个角落都受到了冲击。世界考虑的主要因素是安全方面——我们的海港、机场、人员的安全,以及对在这些国家旅行的个人的审查级别,特别是在北美和欧盟。

让我们首先看看一个国家的情况,然后再看看我们的地区。

曾几何时,旅行是令人愉快的,那时人们未经历小老太太们用金属探测器对身体进行严格检查,人们不禁想她们是否知道自己在找什么。

整个安检业务使拿骚国际机场成为一场灾难。以前乘飞机离开需要一个小时办理登机手续。由于美国国土安全部要求所有的安检程序,旅行已变得以安全为主了。

首先,你要办理登机手续。然后,带着或拖着行李走到值机区。根据你的起飞时间,如果是在下午 4 点之后,那么只有一扇门通向美国预检区。这可能意味着和 100、150 或 200 人一起排队,这取决于你前面的航班。

当你到达安检机器后,希望你的行李不要太重。如果你前面有一位携带大包的女士,那么她或女安检员中的一位不得不费力地把包拎到安检传送带上。所有的安检人员都是女性,周围没有男性提供帮助。

想想这个刚在天堂里度过了五天四夜的游客——他或她度过了一个愉快而放松的假期,即将回家。在机场接受安检是其和巴哈马当局的最后一次接触。

当你通过美国移民局审查进入美国海关之后,你可能不得不接受由巴哈马安检人员进行的另一次搜查，然后把你的包放在行李带上。之后，你上楼，随身行李由另一组安检人员检查。根据航班、时间段和目的地，缉毒人员可能会带着狗嗅嗅你已被检查过的手提行李。如果你经美国转机，那么整个安检过程必须重复。安全似乎是个无止境的任务。

基地组织对加勒比共同体来说是个威胁吗？美国或英国在加勒比共同体国家的利益可能会受到威胁，但对加勒比共同体国家的政府却没有构成真正的威胁。那么为什么从拿骚到蒙特哥湾或从蒙特哥湾到拿骚的航班也有相同类型的安检规定呢？更荒谬的是，在金斯敦和布里奇敦或西班牙港之间也有严格的安检措施。整个地区被要求花费巨额资金在机场和海港建立安检设备，只是为了满足美国国土安全部的要求。

美国已将这场反恐战争变为全球性的战争。由于国际贸易和旅行的安全需要，像巴哈马这样的小国每天都面临这种情况。此外，安检已经影响了我们的生活成本，因为运输成本的很大一部分源于安全需求。

这些安检措施对普通旅行造成了极大的破坏。比如，尝试获得欧盟的签证。由于历史关系，巴哈马人可以去英国旅行。到欧洲大陆不是一件容易的事，可能需要两个星期才能获得签证。为什么？因为安全。

尽管有着所有这些安全倡议，我们的世界更安全了吗？

佛罗里达港口在和平时期和战争时期的重要性

几乎 50% 的游客乘坐邮轮而来。邮轮业已经成为加勒比地区推动大众旅游的主要交通工具。对于巴哈马来说，50% 这一数字代表着大约 200 万名游客，其中大多是美国人。

迈阿密和劳德代尔堡也已成为通往巴哈马和加勒比的邮轮枢纽门户。这是笔巨大的生意，为南佛罗里达的这两个城市创造了可观的收入和就业机会。

在这两个港口，安全是个大问题。美国处于战争时，迈阿密和劳德代尔堡被视为敏感的安全点，这使得新的国土部门加强了对这一地区的安全介入，因其被认为可能易于遭受恐怖袭击。

这些措施包括打算全部或部分关停这些港口。进入这些地点的邮轮在到达之前要靠岸搜查。在某些情况下，美国国土安全部官员会前往外国港口，检查经由迈阿密或劳德代尔堡前往美国的船只。

在迈阿密和劳德代尔堡，官员们现在都在使用高科技安检设备来检查行李，以确保诸如生化产品或脏弹等物品没有被安放在旅客的包里。

对于商船来说,须提前 24 小时提交航运声明,以便安全人员对装在集装箱里的物品有所了解或查明集装箱里的货物。

迈阿密、劳德代尔堡、西棕榈滩、皮尔斯堡、杰克逊威尔 / 圣奥古斯丁是大西洋上佛罗里达的主要东海岸港口。大部分运往巴哈马的货物都是在这些港口装船的。佛罗里达西海岸的萨拉索塔、坦帕 / 圣彼得斯堡和彭萨科拉港口濒临墨西哥湾,然而与佛罗里达东海岸港口相比,从这些港口出发运往巴哈马的货物相对较少。

这两岸的港口处于警戒状态;战时,其状态将变为高度戒备,执行严格的安全措施。这必将影响邮轮旅客和货运的进出。就巴哈马来说,80%—85% 的货物是巴哈马人所消费的食品。我们的其他经济部门,如建筑业,尤其是建筑材料,将受到影响。

这些安全措施将影响游客到访,因为邮轮港口,如迈阿密和劳德代尔堡,将被关停或以 50% 的载客量运营。这将极大地影响巴哈马的收入,因为从到访游客那里所得的收入将减少。对巴哈马南部旅游目的地的影响将更加严重。

三大集装箱公司——热带、先锋和海岸是我们货运的主要承运商。因为安全措施会产生费用,运输成本很可能会增加,而我们的衣食父母不得不缴付费用,从而影响总运费。

像贝蒂船运公司那样的船舶,更倾向于用货盘装运货物并且在迈阿密河以外运营,也要接受严格的安全检查。

从海运的视角看,这就是巴哈马面临的局面。"9·11"事件导致了我们对航空港的高度关注,因为穆罕默德·阿塔及其同伙利用飞机制造破坏。安全网络现已被扩大到涵盖美国的海港,这反映在迈阿密和劳德代尔堡已经加强了安全意识。无论哪个周末,这些海港加起来可能有 20 艘邮轮在港内,等待着将成千上万的美国人运往巴哈马和加勒比。

这个地区的旅游业已经发展到乘坐邮轮来的游客多于乘坐飞机的地步。邮轮市场在旅游方程式里是一个极其重要的因子。如果它减速或暂时退出,这个地区的旅游业将被摧毁。

货运业务的影响在经济上之深远,就如同这个地区所有国家的食品都依赖美国农业综合企业,多米尼加共和国除外。他们的情况更趋恶化,因为他们的农业出口商品不得不运往美国。对于那些遥远的加勒比群岛,特别是东加勒比的背风群岛和向风群岛链,返程空载是维持合理的低运费的一个重要因素。

佛罗里达西海岸港口在巴哈马和加勒比的经济生存中发挥着关键作用。在未来几天和几个星期里，美国和伊拉克的战争将使我们认清这个事实。

反恐战争与巴哈马

在巴哈马的我们对恐怖主义行为免疫吗？答案是否定的。恐怖主义是全球关注的重大问题，对每个国家的国家安全来说都是一个威胁。2001 年 9 月 11 日之后，美国通过建立新的国土安全部，赋予其内阁地位，加强了对这一新的战争策略的关注。

随着对恐怖主义的担忧，美国国会正被敦促通过联邦恐怖主义保险法案，这实质上是一个针对工人的补偿型安全保障。无论是何种原因导致工作中的伤亡，它都将支付医疗费、误工费、死亡抚恤金。"9·11"事件导致保险公司向那些受伤或丧生者的配偶和子女支付了 30 多亿美元的赔偿金。这种恐怖主义保险应该是为了保护工人免受另一次可能发生的类似"9·11"事件的恐怖袭击。

这类保险的一个原因来自这样一个事实——美国的保险公司不愿为像世界贸易中心那样工人高度集中的工作场所或像五角大楼那种知名场所提供保险。

我们北面强大的邻居已经配置了巨大的资源——重构了金融、立法和政府资源，以使美国、其人民和经济免受这场反恐战争的影响。

对于第三世界或发展中国家来说，它们面临的威胁与美国、加拿大和西欧等发达工业化国家的威胁一样真实吗？或许是联合国通过反恐怖主义委员会竭尽全力来保护世界以及像巴哈马这样的小国。

这个委员会的作用是通过规则评估和技术援助的协调项目来加强这一领域的全球能力。联合国计划的一个重要部分是通过加强禁止使用或扩散大规模杀伤性武器的全球规范，并向那些寻求遏制武器、资金和技术流向恐怖分子的国家给予技术支持，从而实现裁军。正是从这个角度出发，美国—英国倡议获得了联合国批准，搜查并销毁伊拉克的大规模杀伤性武器。

反恐专家越来越一致认为，恐怖组织尤其是基地组织，正在瞄准西方游客。在巴厘岛发生的针对外国游客的袭击，只是在亚洲发生的针对西方人的最近的、最致命的一次袭击。令人担心的是，这种恐怖主义可能会出现在美洲，可能是诸如巴哈马和加勒比这样的近海旅游区。

我们每天的新闻广播中充斥着关于恐怖组织及其行动的声明，大多发生在中东和亚洲其他地区。

巴哈马畏惧的是国际恐怖主义，因为国内恐怖主义在这里不是问题，至少此时此刻不是问题。作为一个国家,我们可能成为国际恐怖主义的受害者,因为在巴哈马,任何一天都能发现大量的美国人出现在海湾街、我们的国际机场、亚特兰蒂斯那样的酒店以及邮轮停泊处的赌场和码头。我们的游客是被袭击的目标,这些地方是恐怖分子确认的犯罪场所,这对我们来说是个威胁。

像巴哈马这样的小国既没有财政资金来开展反恐活动,也负担不起一个煞费苦心的情报部门为我们提供预防模式。这一情况的解决方案是与专门研究反恐措施的国际机构结盟,联合国就是这样的机构。

美国反恐政策的关键之一是增强那些与美国合作并且需要帮助的国家的反恐能力。对于巴哈马来说,这或许是应对国际恐怖主义的最佳方式。

自 2001 年 9 月 11 日以来,目前有 69 个国家支持全球反恐战争。就我所知,我们的政府从未告知巴哈马人我们是否是这 69 个国家中的一个。另外,20 个国家已经向美国中央司令部的责任区部署了 16 000 多名士兵。我们的国防军中是否有人被部署或派往此部队?对我们的军队来说,接触这些情况并且在这种国际环境中得到训练符合我们的利益。

巴厘岛事件在全世界引发了轩然大波,因其表明了国际恐怖主义的无情。数百个家庭遭受了严重的痛苦。该事件对印度尼西亚的经济和福祉造成的伤害或许无法估量。身在巴哈马的我们不得不在这场反恐战争中保持警惕。

"9·11" 后的世界

2001 年 9 月 11 日,我们的世界发生了翻天覆地的变化。这一天的缩略词——"9·11",其自身已经成为一种表述,无论在哪里都被认为极其重要。

在一个国家的生活、一个社会的生活以及我们的生活中,有些场景令人难忘。"9·11"便是其中之一。很多上了年纪的巴哈马人可以告诉你 1967 年 1 月 10 日他或她在哪里;同样可以说出约翰·F. 肯尼迪总统在得克萨斯州的达拉斯被暗杀的那天。"9·11"就是那些事件之一。

根据主要大国领导人的说法,"9·11"标志着世界处于战争状态。这次是反恐战争。这是一场与人类已经习惯的传统战争完全不同的战争。

第一次世界大战以壕沟战和刺刀冲锋为特征,敌人就在那里,进行面对面对抗和徒手搏斗。在第二次世界大战中,原子弹是用来杀死成千上万的日本人以及摧毁长崎市的工具。这场反恐战争则不同,因为它在许多方面影响着全球社会。

"9·11"事件影响了我们的旅行方式。对于我们这种生活在像巴哈马这样的流动社会中的人来说，这是最突出的。每次去机场，无论是在国内航站楼还是国际航站楼，我们都要面对安检措施。我们中的许多人还记得安检措施不必要的那个时候。"9·11"之后，安检措施开始实施。

安检是"9·11"之后世界的标志之一。

与安检一起的，还有个人审查。每个人都需要护照。一些政府要求其公民如果想去旅行就得获取护照。美国尤为明显。美国人曾一度不需要护照就可到巴哈马旅行，"9·11"导致这个规定被修改了。

想到美国高等院校上学的学生必须能够证明他或她有经济能力来资助自己的教育。这已成为一种非常死板的做法。这些指导原则亦适用于英国大学。这是因为几名"9·11"恐怖分子持学生签证进入了美国。这是美国对此的回应方式。

西方国家的政府，特别是那些欧洲国家的政府，正警惕地修改他们的移民政策。在社会层面，大家普遍关注某些民族团体的宗教宽容以及"多元文化对一体化"的概念。

在此方面带头的是澳大利亚。澳大利亚政府表明，澳大利亚是一个建立在基督教原则上的国家，希望自己的公民能在这一背景下履行职责。如果他们做不到，那么应当离开这个国家。这是一个非常大胆而且审慎的立场。当数百名澳大利亚公民在巴厘岛被一枚恐怖主义炸弹炸死炸伤时，澳大利亚感受到了反恐战争的后果。巴厘岛，位于印度尼西亚。

电视使我们每天都能看到这场战争。我们知道人体炸弹，因为我们常常在电视上看到。最近，以色列和真主党在黎巴嫩的战斗表明了战争所造成的苦难。

"9·11"创造了一个新的世界。这种态势可能会伴随我们很久。一些人说情况可能恶化，只有时间能给出答案。

第 6 章 »

残留社会

"最后,整个西印度的传统是反知识的。人民的生活局限于狭隘的唯物主义考虑,或对产品价格,或对生活成本,或对工人的懈怠,或对犯罪和违法的增长,或对赌博,或对追求女人(视情况也可能是男人),或对简单的暴饮暴食。"

——特立尼达和多巴哥前总理、特立尼达人埃里克•威廉姆斯博士的

《内心的饥饿》

无论是在法国、西班牙、英国的管辖之下,还是在荷兰的管辖之下,每个加勒比国家都经历过奴隶制和殖民主义。作为殖民地,其政治和经济之存在一开始都围绕着奴隶制,然后是殖民主义,于是一种独特的、不同类型的社会——残留社会产生了。

加勒比社会不得不内化所经历的奴隶制和殖民主义的后果,这导致了几个世纪以来的一种行为模式——以欧洲为中心并且脱离了其非裔侨民的根。

1804 年,非洲奴隶的后裔在海地通过革命摆脱了法国的束缚。在加勒比英语区,已有 172 年(1834 年)的历史,束缚最早在 1962 年,即 44 年前牙买加从英国获得独立时被割断。对这些前英殖民地来说,拥有主权的经历相对较短。大安的列斯群岛的古巴和伊斯帕尼奥拉岛(海地和多米尼加共和国)独立的时间更长。(见表 6.1)

表 6.1　加勒比地区附属国和国家

英国殖民地	独立日期	附属国(地)	废除奴隶制日期	奴隶贸易
安提瓜和巴布达	1981 年	安圭拉岛	1807 年	贩卖人口终止

续表

英国殖民地	独立日期	附属国（地）	废除奴隶制日期	奴隶贸易
巴巴多斯	1966 年	英属维尔京群岛，开曼群岛	1834 年	解放（4 年学徒期）
巴哈马	1973 年	特克斯和凯科斯群岛		
伯利兹	1981 年	蒙特塞拉特岛		
多米尼克	1978 年			
格林纳达	1974 年			
圭亚那	1966 年（1970 年成为共和国）			
牙买加	1962 年			
圣基茨和尼维斯	1983 年			
圣卢西亚	1979 年			
圣文森特和格林纳丁斯	1962 年（1976 年成为共和国）			

法国殖民地	独立日期	附属国（地）	废除奴隶制日期	奴隶贸易
海地	1804 年（第一个黑人共和国以及西半球第二古老的共和国）	法国海外部：圣马丁岛，瓜德罗普岛，马提尼克岛，卡宴岛（法属圭亚那）	1848 年	殖民地解放
			1830 年	奴隶贸易终止

荷兰殖民地	独立日期	附属国（地）	废除奴隶制日期	奴隶贸易
尼德兰		特别海外身份：圣马丁岛，库拉索岛，阿鲁巴岛，博内尔岛，萨巴岛，圣尤斯泰希厄斯岛	1863 年	奴隶制废除 / 解放
苏里南	1975 年			

美国殖民地	独立日期	附属国（地）	废除奴隶制日期	奴隶贸易
波多黎各		国内自治	1865 年	美国宪法第十三条修正案正式废除"非自愿奴役"

续表

美国殖民地	独立日期	附属国（地）	废除奴隶制日期	奴隶贸易
美属维尔京群岛		美国领土：圣托马斯岛，圣克罗伊岛，圣约翰岛	1865 年	美国宪法第十三条修正案正式废除"非自愿奴役"
西班牙殖民地	**独立日期**	**附属国（地）**	**废除奴隶制日期**	**奴隶贸易**
古巴	1902 年		1820 年	奴隶贸易废除
多米尼加共和国	1844 年		1870 年	殖民地解放

　　尽管 1834—1838 年是被解放的奴隶学习手艺的学徒期,奴隶制在个别岛屿殖民地被解除,但成千上万人的基本培训仍然是耕种土地。这一分组成了小农,他们遍及整个地区。小农是奴隶制的遗留。

　　奴隶制发展出一种阶层社会——主人／奴隶关系。另一方面,殖民主义的特征是政治统治和经济剥削,前奴隶子女的机会非常有限。独立带来了社会、政治以及经济的转型。

　　通过这一转型过程,旅游业出现并发展为该地区价值数十亿美元的产业。

　　第二次世界大战后,加勒比的经济以农业为基础;蔗糖是主要的出口作物。农业生产是主业,这些岛屿殖民地以农村人口为主,其中小农是主要类别。由于独立后若干年的经济转型,到 20 世纪末,小农将成为濒危物种。尽管牙买加和圭亚那有铝土矿,特立尼达和多巴哥有石油,小农对这两个国家的农业部门来说依然很重要。

　　经济转型在加勒比各国进行的速度有所不同。20 世纪 50 年代,作为巴哈马发展委员会主席,斯塔福德·桑德斯爵士开始将巴哈马从以农业为基础的经济转变为以旅游业为主导的经济。外国在酒店建设方面进行了大量投资,政府在改善基础设施方面亦进行了大量投资。

　　1968 年,巴哈马的到访游客达百万大关。到 1969 年,巴哈马吸引了 100 万名游客,超过了其最近的加勒比共同体旅游目的地竞争者——牙买加。对于其他加勒比共同体国家来说,在 1960—1970 年的十年中,旅游业将成为加勒比共同体国家经济的一个主要部门。

表 6.2　1969—1971 年加勒比共同体到访游客

国家(地区)	数　字		
	1969 年	**1970 年**	**1971 年**
巴哈马	1 332.4	1 298.3	1 463.6
牙买加	279.9	309.1	359.3
百慕大群岛	281	302.7	319.3
巴巴多斯	134.3	156.4	189
特立尼达和多巴哥	117	117	136
安提瓜	61.2	65.3	67.6
多米尼克、格林纳达、蒙特塞拉特岛、圣基茨—尼维斯—安圭拉、圣卢西亚、圣文森特	97.7	115.5	123
英属维尔京群岛	29.5	33.1	46.1
开曼群岛	19.4	23	24.3
英属洪都拉斯	28	31.5	45.6

来源:《加勒比的稳定》(巴哈马以百万美元为单位;其他国家以千元美元为单位)

　　加勒比提供了阳光、沙滩和大海以培育新兴的旅游业。发展这一产业的投资来源主要来自美国,美国也是加勒比旅游的主要市场。

　　从地缘政治上说,加勒比被视为美国的后院,位于美国的势力范围之内。

　　多年以来,随着该地区成为劳动力、农业原材料、铝土矿、石油和天然气的来源地,加勒比同美国发展出一种共生关系。作为回报,美国提供了市场和外国直接投资,作为旅游和其他项目的汇款和资金。

　　美国 2000 年的人口普查报告显示,2 800 万移民中大约有 10% 或者说 300 万人来自加勒比,主要是古巴、牙买加、多米尼加共和国和海地。移民向该地区的汇款数额很可观,在 20 世纪 90 年代是 4 亿美元。到 2002 年,该数额已上升到 40 亿美元。

　　关于贸易,2003 年美国从加勒比进口的商品中有 45% 享有优惠待遇。加勒比盆地计划是在里根执政期间提出的。2002 年,《加勒比盆地贸易伙伴法案》开始实施。

　　加勒比和北美经济之间的相对开放性推动了加勒比旅游业的发展,旅游业又刺激了该地区服务的扩张。

加勒比旅游业的面貌

加勒比旅游业具有很多含义。对加勒比人民来说，旅游业意味着就业。这是一次从事他或她的岛上最重要的行业——服务业的机会。对游客来说，这是一次展现了阳光、沙滩或大海的体验。对外国企业家来说，这是一次投资并获利的机会。

这三个因素以各种形式呈现，每个岛屿均不同。对旅游业并无一个统一的观点，每种方式都有利弊。

在过去 50 年里，加勒比的旅游文化一直在发展，已经影响了加勒比人民的社交，他们不得不与游客交流。这些游客可能是邮轮乘客、住在酒店或家庭旅馆的过境旅客、把这儿当成第二故乡的冬季住客、寄宿生或者度春假的人。所有这些类型的游客都给岛民留下了印象，影响着他或她的眼界。

• 综合旅游

在巴哈马旅游的早期，酒店、高档餐厅、高尔夫球场和上流赌场禁止黑人入内。巴哈马黑人主要是酒店工人——侍者、酒保、女花匠或表演者。管理层是外国人，前台接待要么是白人，要么是浅肤色的人。

拿骚大肆宣扬其殖民地建筑、英国传统以及高档免税店，使其成为一个独特的海上殖民地。游客的夜生活在黑人社区——"下坡路"。巴哈马的夜生活集中在这个地方。本土乐师演奏着卡里普索①和谷贝音乐，由本土舞蹈者表演歌舞，盛极一时。

20 世纪 60 年代中期，隔离墙已被推倒；到 60 年代末，随着赌博业和超级酒店设施的引入，天堂岛作为新普罗维登斯岛第二个旅游目的地开放了。

巴哈马的旅游文化开始转变。巴哈马人开始频繁出入旅游场所，"下坡路"社区的夜生活开始衰落，因为酒店开始成为本地人和外国人娱乐的中心。

20 世纪 70 年代早期到中期，旅游文化融入了巴哈马人的生活方式。政治会议、婚礼、舞会、派对、宗教仪式、大型会议和商业会议全都在酒店举行。唯一不允许巴哈马人参与的旅游活动是进赌场，巴哈马人参与赌博是非法的。

旅游业也有助于巴哈马人饮食习惯的改变。这里有大量的美国快餐特许经营店。进口的食品经过加工，含有大量的糖和饱和脂肪。

通过卫星传输、无线电广播再加上邻近佛罗里达大陆，巴哈马充斥着美国广告。这影响了包括食品在内的一系列购物。或许只有波多黎各和美属维尔京

---

①　译者注：起源于西印度群岛，关于现代主题的歌曲。

群岛更加融入美国经济并受其广告影响。

• 飞地旅游

飞地旅游已经成为加勒比旅游体验的一个方面。基本上有两种类型：全包式度假机构（地中海俱乐部、桑多兹酒店、微风酒店）和封闭式社区，后者通常是冬季住客或非长住客人的住处以及分时公寓／共管公寓综合体。所有这些都具有排他意味。

例如，在牙买加，一些地方犯罪盛行，为了应对，北海岸发展了许多全包式度假机构。对于地中海俱乐部、桑多兹酒店和微风酒店来说，全包是一个产品，也是体验本身。

在大多数情况下，即使是在像巴哈马的亚特兰蒂斯这样的巨型加勒比超级酒店，总体思路也是让客人多在酒店内花钱。在某些情形下，有一些微妙的设计，阻止客人游览海岛社区。

• "两个世界"

因为旅游部门的发展以及由开发商引入的产品类型或体验，各国政府必须小心，以免造成"两个世界"。

当存在"两个世界"时，这种局面导致的社会压力会有消极影响，因为生活方式上的差异日益明显。在奴隶制的背景之下，旅游业可以是过去时代的一个提示，黑人基本上为白人提供服务，而财产所有权归外国人所有。

• 旅游基础设施

发展旅游部门的一个重要部分是基础设施。"9·11"以来，机场和邮轮码头的安全特性带来了旅游新维度。加勒比的新机场必须是"9·11"兼容的。

机场、邮轮码头、良好的道路和可靠的公用设施，如通讯、电力和供水，并不能完全胜任，生产力和竞争力将是决定因素。这两个因素取决于加勒比国家为其人力发展和产业扩张提供尖端技术的能力。

加勒比国家面对的挑战是是否有能力通过技术进步把这个地区定位为世界级的旅游目的地。

世界银行报告说，加勒比必须就不断变化的全球环境做出更积极的回应。加勒比旅游业自 1995 年以来经历的市场下滑已经表明对此缺乏及时的响应。竞争力的下降源于"不断上涨的高工资，缺乏技能形成和技术吸收"。

为了在全球背景下生存下去，如果想保持国际竞争力的话，加勒比旅游业必须使其劳动力更富有成效。

结　论

加勒比人民有过奴隶制和殖民主义的经历,把他们对旅游的认识植入发展方程式中是非常重要的。为了使旅游业在该地区全面发展和扩大,各个国家和附属国的人民必须认同呈现给全球市场的产品,必须部分拥有所有权——桑多兹酒店和微风酒店就是加勒比国民创建的世界级酒店的绝佳例子。

加勒比旅游必须反映加勒比社会的精神。这个多元而独特的社会诞生于探险、灭绝和剥削,自有其特色。正是这种特色形成了加勒比旅游产品的核心,并推销给全球社会。

插曲:《埃尼亚斯文集》《巴哈马日报》 缔造美国/加勒比共同体学说

上周二,美国国务卿康多莉扎·赖斯博士来到巴哈马会见加勒比共同体的外交部部长。这一会晤每年举行一次。七年前,美国前国务卿科林·鲍威尔将军也会见了加勒比共同体外交部部长。

比尔·克林顿在其执政期间曾多次会见加勒比共同体首相;有一次他去巴巴多斯进行洽谈。

加勒比属于美国的势力范围,被视为美国的第三条边界。大多数加勒比国家的第一贸易伙伴是美国。

就巴哈马来说,这一数字是 90%。相反,美国是加勒比产品的大市场。除了圭亚那、特立尼达和多巴哥外,大多数加勒比国家都指望美国游客。几乎在每个国家,旅游业都取代了农业成为主要经济部门。

国务卿与加勒比共同体的议程包括贸易、竞争力以及其他问题,如移民、贩毒和洗钱。

从正确的角度看待赖斯博士的访问,她是来商谈加勒比共同体所面临的问题的。作为加勒比共同体国家的巴哈马是东道主。据可靠的消息来源,巴哈马被视为这个地区最安全的地方之一,故选此为会议地点。是的,赖斯博士礼节性地拜访了总理及其内阁,这是加勒比共同体的一件大事。

巴哈马人对于加深与加勒比共同体的关系一直持有矛盾心理。去年,巴哈马打算在《查瓜拉马斯条约》上签字并加入加勒比单一市场和经济,这引发了一场全民骚动。有人强烈拒绝加入加勒比单一市场和经济。

然而,巴哈马人并不领会或理解一个事实——这是一个地缘政治集团的时代。加勒比共同体是世界最古老的组织之一。巴哈马人在未来的某一时刻将不得不决定我们是否加入加勒比共同体。当我们做出最有利于自己的选择时,他们的"半成员资格"对我们来说并不总是一个好的选择。加勒比共同体领导人容忍我们的这种态度,但当这个地区的生活水平和收入水平提高时,这条路可能会被封闭。

上个周,枢密院裁定巴哈马的强制死刑是违宪的。另一方面,加勒比共同体建立了加勒比法院作为上诉的终审法院;大多数国家选择不把案件移交到枢密院。随着英国加深对欧盟的依附,枢密院自身也改变了。唯一一扇向巴哈马敞开的大门是加勒比上诉法院。进一步说,在巴哈马法律界某些地方,人们不愿使用加勒比的法庭。既然枢密院有这样的裁决,那些赞成死刑的人将对加勒比法院的看法稍有不同。

加勒比共同体国家获得了良好声誉,一个特点是其民主的复杂性。在加勒比共同体国家中,巴巴多斯和巴哈马拥有本半球两个最古老的议会传统。巴哈马从1729年开始实行代议制。布什政府一直在拉丁美洲、中东和其他地区吹捧民主原则,因此,加勒比共同体是采取民主行动的一个楷模。这是国务卿赖斯博士的议程之一,她赞扬了加勒比国家坚持民主原则的历史。

独立时期以来,加勒比共同体发生过一次未遂的政变,是在20世纪70年代的特立尼达。总而言之,除了海地,其次是苏里南,加勒比共同体国家政府换届的机制是投票,这使得加勒比共同体不同于拉美国家。

加勒比共同体大约有2 000万居民。也有成千上万加勒比共同体的后裔居住在美国,其中很多人这些年来帮助建设了美国。许多美国黑人领袖,其中一些是民权运动领袖,继承了加勒比传统。

加勒比共同体构成了美国边境的一个战略部分,保持一种健康的关系符合加勒比共同体和美国的最大利益。希望赖斯博士为加勒比共同体缔造一种学说以反映这些国家在这个全球化时代所面对的现实,并且加强加勒比共同体国家的可持续经济增长和发展。这一点十分重要,因为加勒比共同体国家的发展方式具有特殊性,全都出自奴隶制的残留。大多数国家不是具有发展潜力的多民族复杂社会,然而,美国有能力帮助加勒比共同体国家创建框架来达到或实现新的高度。

海地加入加勒比共同体:错误决策还是明智之举?

最近在特立尼达和多巴哥的西班牙港召开的政府首脑峰会上,海地被准许加入加勒比共同体。这个地区对这一决定的批评在增多,很多人认为这个决定是仓促的。

自从脱离法国独立以来，海地一直在财政上遇到困难。西方或欧洲的殖民主义势力使海地向法国付出了巨大的代价。当时，海地是加勒比的明珠，也是法国重要的海外领土。海地的财富来自其制糖生产带来的经济回报。

今天，海地是西半球最贫穷的国家，政府无法运转，文盲率和失业率高。这个国家已经被美国人以及来自这个地区其他国家的联合国维和士兵占领，包括巴哈马。然而，海地共和国仍然缺乏政治、社会和经济上的稳定。

这一背景使很多加勒比人感到不安。理由是，一些加勒比共同体国家有类似问题，但不像海地那样根深蒂固。许多加勒比共同体国家没有对加勒比机构，如西印度群岛大学和加勒比共同体秘书处，履行其财政承诺。海地自己都处于金融困境中，如何能履行其财政承诺？很多人怀疑，海地不能履行承诺，将耗尽加勒比共同体有限的财政资源。问题是，海地能支付自己的费用吗？

有些人认为，加勒比共同体应当遵循欧盟用来接受新成员的模式。欧盟的前身——欧洲经济共同体，制定了入会标准。其中一些标准是具体的人均收入、识字水平、运作正常的民主制度以及公正的司法体系。一旦一个国家能够达到这些标准，就给予其成员资格。

所有迹象表明，加勒比共同体没有走这条路线。正因如此，这个地区的很多人对这个决定极其怀疑。随着海地的加入，加勒比共同体包含了这个半球最贫穷的两个国家——圭亚那和海地。

海地的事态关乎这个地区的每一个国家。继海地的岛屿邻居——多米尼加共和国之后，其对巴哈马的社会经济稳定构成了极大的威胁，因为许多海地人似乎认为他们拥有某种到巴哈马避难的权利，要么藐视要么忽视这片土地的法律。

很多巴哈马人认为新普罗维登斯岛的"下坡路"地区被新来的海地人或第一代在巴哈马出生的海地人所占据。从社会方面来说，这些社区恶化到了在房屋、卫生设施、获得更多医疗保障和培训以及公共机构方面极度需要重建的程度，以使这些社区再度成为社会认可的人类居住地。

加勒比共同体正迈向一个单一的市场和经济。由于有这么多国家处于经济阶梯的底端，这个目标似乎遥遥无期。而且，人口在这个地区内自由流动的构想在当前环境下绝不可能被巴哈马人接受。

随着海地成为加勒比共同体成员，巴哈马的一体化方程式现在变得更为复杂了。海地的生活节奏不仅与巴哈马不同步，与整个地区也不同步。因此，于此时接纳海地是个草率的决定。当海地展示出其有能力更好地管理其政治、社会和经济事务时，才应做此决定。

加勒比共同体和古巴：加勒比倡议

在冷战时期，加勒比国家允许以美国的外交政策来决定这些国家如何反应并与其他国家共存，特别是那些在这个半球和地区的国家。

这个政策阻碍了这个地区的国家和古巴打交道，巴哈马也不例外。

在推翻巴普蒂斯塔政权之后，菲德尔·卡斯特罗掌管了古巴，引入了马克思社会主义。这对美国来说是政治侮辱，因为它公然对抗门罗主义，这是美国在这个半球外交政策的基石。

牙买加在诺曼·曼利执政时期对古巴实行门户开放政策，开始了劳动力和文化的交流，并且建立了贸易关系。由于牙买加向古巴示好，里根政府大幅削减了美国的对外援助。

当莫里斯主教的新宝石运动从埃里克·加里手里接管了格林纳达的政府时，格林纳达与古巴建立了外交关系，这最终导致了美国入侵格林纳达。

也正是在此期间，"弗莱明戈号"事件在 20 世纪 70 年代后期造成了巴哈马和古巴之间的紧张关系。"弗莱明戈号"上的三名国防军船员由于遭到一名古巴人的攻击而身亡。古巴向被杀船员的家属和巴哈马政府做出了赔偿。

"弗莱明戈号"事件发生后不久，联合国粮食及农业组织在哈瓦那召开了一次半球会议。

巴哈马由当时的农业和渔业部部长乔治·A. 史密斯阁下、常务秘书伊德瑞斯·里德先生和时任农业署署长的我为代表。

当时，格林纳达的大使邀请我们到他家吃晚餐。晚餐期间，大使解释了古巴之所以给予格林纳达援助，是因其刚刚摆脱了殖民身份。古巴的援助是真诚的，因为这个援助不带附加条件；这对于来自巴哈马的我们来说是一次具有启发性的交流。

在联合国粮食及农业组织会议代表的官方招待会上，卡斯特罗主席要求私下会晤史密斯先生。正是在这次会晤中，卡斯特罗先生表达了对于"弗莱明戈号"事件的遗憾，表明了其政府想要加深古巴与巴哈马之间关系的愿望。

在和古巴官员的会谈中，提到了古巴和巴哈马从前的联系，特别是来自茵那瓜岛和拉吉德岛，甚至安德罗斯岛的某些地方的人的自由流动。

在巴哈马商业中曾有一段时间，巴哈马人在古巴求职，做蔗糖业工人。当我还是个孩子时，我记得拉吉德岛的船只载着各式各样的古巴产品——朗姆酒、糖、番石榴和奶酪等运达兰热市场。

在 20 世纪 70 年代和 80 年代期间，约翰・麦卡特尼博士和莱昂内尔・凯里以及其他人频繁造访古巴学习马克思社会主义。他们的行为在政界被视为近乎煽动性的，不被认同。古巴被视为一个向外输出革命的威胁。

这个地区的各个国家，以前不得不在这种情形下发挥作用。现在环境发生了变化。

上个周，加勒比共同体和古巴官员在牙买加的金斯敦商谈古巴加入加勒比共同体的事宜。应当铭记，这发生于美国对古巴的禁运仍然有效时，但这种情况正在发生。加勒比共同体国家已不再准备与美国所支持的邻国建立关系。这与过去的时代截然不同。

去年，加勒比共同体接受海地成为其一员。随着该地区国家的经济、社会和政治关系日益紧密，旧的禁忌正在逐渐消失。

加勒比共同体正处在发展一个单一市场和经济的过程之中。随着地区经济一体化倡议的实施，加勒比市场因古巴的加入而急剧扩大，几乎增加了 2 000 万人。海地和多米尼加共和国已经为加勒比共同体的产品打开了新的市场，反之亦然。

考虑到这个地区的发展，巴哈马是时候增加对古巴的影响力了。它是我们最近的邻居之一，通过加勒比共同体，两国的关系将得到加深。加勒比地区的地理政治气候将在新世纪提供一系列新的挑战。

克里斯蒂的加勒比共同体初体验

就职两个月后，总理克里斯蒂将参加在圭亚那乔治敦召开的加勒比共同体政府首脑会议第二十三次会议。这次会议将在 7 月 2 日至 3 日召开。

过去十年间，前总理休伯特・A. 英格拉哈姆阁下是加勒比共同体一股强大的力量。他与巴巴多斯的总理欧文・亚瑟、牙买加的 P. J. 帕特森、特立尼达和多巴哥的巴斯迪奥・潘迪之类的加勒比共同体重量级人物一起发起了几项行动并坚持自己的立场。在这点上，人们非常期待克里斯蒂先生能继续发挥已故的林登・O. 平德林爵士在其总理任期内开创的并由英格拉哈姆先生继续持有的这种领导作用。

这也将是克里斯蒂先生作为总理第一次邂逅国际关系。首次邂逅非常适时，是在地区舞台上，而且他处于跟巴哈马同样面对全球化和贸易自由化问题的同行之中。

在巴哈马的背景下，人们期待外交和公共服务部部长弗雷德·米切尔阁下展示不同的观点，在处理与加勒比共同体的关系时提出新的巴哈马视角。上一届政府期间，英格拉哈姆先生的观点似乎在巴哈马占主导地位。当时的外交部部长是珍妮特·博斯特威克夫人，更多的是附和英格拉哈姆先生对加勒比的看法。种种迹象表明，米切尔先生在制定巴哈马与加勒比共同体（如加共体单一市场和经济）新的政策立场时发挥了强有力的作用。

加勒比共同体首脑会议在其议程中采用了新维度。在"共同前进"的主题下，将有一个民间团体和首脑的对话。

加勒比共同体秘书处一直敦促其成员国在民间团体的问题上开展国家对话。在共同前进会议上，各成员国将向政府首脑汇报公民对于涉及民间团体的各个主题的看法。

安提瓜和巴布达以及圣卢西亚将做关于加勒比单一市场和经济的报告。显然，这两国的公民把其作为重点关注事项。对我们巴哈马人来说，这是一个低优先级的事项，因为巴哈马无意于最近加入单一市场和经济。

另一方面，海地的主题是"民间团体的角色"。在一个面对政治动荡、经济不稳定再加上拥有很长的军事独裁统治传统的国家，了解民间团体的角色或许是这个国家走向更民主社会的一个中心议题。

大多数成员国（准确地说是 2/3）已经表明了他们的主题。根据最近加勒比共同体的报告，巴哈马还没有提交主题，尽管上周外交部和巴哈马民间团体的代表举行了一次会议。所有迹象表明，会议的反馈是与会人员没有充足的时间为会议做准备，会议的目的也不明确。

在这次会议上，加勒比共同体将庆祝其作为一个团体成立 30 周年。加勒比共同体是世界上最古老的区域性政治组织之一。它做了大量工作把这个地区团结起来。很难想象这个地区没有加勒比共同体会怎样，即它对这个地区的影响度。近年来，一个与之匹敌的实体形成了——加勒比国家联盟。其成员范围更为广泛，包括所有分享加勒比海海岸线的国家，也包括中美洲国家。

克里斯蒂先生和他的代表团不得不面对很多议项，包括单一市场和经济、安全和犯罪以及海地。有国内事务，也有地区事务。对巴哈马来说，后两项对我们的社会极为重要。看我们的代表团如何在地区面前提出这些问题将会很有趣，尤其是海地已经成为加勒比共同体的一员。

关于这一议程的国际方面，加勒比共同体正努力解决自由贸易问题，特别是即将到来的美洲自由贸易区，预计于 2005 年实施。这对于巴哈马来说是一种双重负担，与其他成员国不同，它不是世界贸易组织的成员，因此，必须应对这两个组织。加勒比共同体主要关注的问题是美洲自由贸易区，因为它有可能对加勒比的农业、纺织业和制造业造成严重的社会经济破坏，从而引发巨大的社会混乱和经济衰退。

这个地区希望巴哈马在地区事务中发挥越来越大的作用。人们希望米切尔先生能够发现一个机制，把巴哈马经济各部门面临的问题编入外交政策要点中去，并找到办法把巴哈马的专业人士推到加勒比共同体的领导位置上去。

加勒比一体化仍是巴哈马人尚未解决的一个问题，应在我们的外交政策中予以优先考虑。

旅游业与世界贸易组织：我们准备好了吗？

旅游业无法逃避世界贸易组织的规则。无论我们愿意与否，旅游必须像我们经济的每个部门一样面对贸易自由化。我们越早意识到这一点并尽可能地应对加入世界贸易组织的影响，就会越好。

旅游业是世界上最大的产业。就全球总影响力而言，其价值相当于国内生产总值的 3.5 万亿美元。这代表着全球国内生产总值的 11%、2 亿份工作和全世界总就业的 8%。就业预测显示，到 2010 年为止，全球旅游业有能力每年创造 550 万份新工作。

旅游业不仅对巴哈马和加勒比很重要，对全世界也很重要。然而，主导这个产业的大玩家是发达国家的旅行社、连锁酒店、航空公司以及现在的计算机预定或全球分销系统的运营商。这些没有一个是由第三世界控制的。

面对全球的发展，在过去 30 年里，世界旅游业的增长速度是国内生产总值的 2 倍，其中发展中国家所占份额增长到总数的 1/3 左右。

全球旅游业被欧洲、美国、加拿大、中国（唯一的亚洲国家）和墨西哥（唯一的拉美国家）的旅游目的地所主宰。

法国每年吸引 7 000 多万的游客，而美国为 5 000 万。尽管有 2 000 多万的差别，美国每年赚 700 亿美元，而法国赚 300 亿美元。

当前十名的数字和巴哈马的数字相比时，巴哈马在世界舞台上只是一个小角色；当与欧洲、亚洲和拉丁美洲等其他地区相比时，加勒比地区则是一个大玩家。

在过去的 50 年里，旅游业使巴哈马从一个渔村转变为一个生机勃勃的小群岛国家。巴哈马今天的成就来之不易。巴哈马花了 20 年才达到第一批百万游客。

第二个百万是在 13 年内实现的,第三个百万只用了四年。实现第四个百万是虚幻的,因为 20 世纪 90 年代的十年间,我们一直徘徊于 360 万的水平。

巴哈马的游客开销在 20 世纪 80 年代达到了 10 亿美元的水平。15 年之后(1998 年),其最高总成绩是 14 亿美元。

从到访游客和开销的数字来看,种种迹象表明巴哈马的旅游业较为平稳。这个产业需要新的推动力——动力。

今年早些时候,巴哈马在世界贸易组织中选择了观察员身份而非直接正式会员身份。也有许多人认为,世界贸易组织只关心贸易。服务业是一个重要的领域,因此,作为服务业的旅游业也很重要。

巴哈马在国际舞台上表现出诸事落后的综合征。相对于经济合作与发展组织(OECD)的表现,我们都知道金融服务业发生了什么。那些从事国际贸易的人都知道大玩家玩的那些把戏。前十名中的许多国家都是经济合作与发展组织的成员。经济合作与发展组织已经尝试在旅游投资上设置参数,这势必将损害像巴哈马这样依赖外国投资来扩建和改善旅游设施的发展中国家。其口号是限制性商业惯例。

未来图景可见于美国和中国的双边协定。

> "对酒店和饭店来说,到 2003 年底,商业存在[①] 的股权限制将被取消。至于旅行社和旅游经营服务,2003 年 1 月 1 日之后将允许外商控股,2005 年底之后将允许外商独资的子公司。"

如果这发展成一个标准合约,对我们来说将有严重的后果,唯一的差别就在于这些方面于哪一年开始生效。这取决于像巴哈马这样的国家通过谈判成为正式成员国的条款。巴哈马人民需要一个解释。

加勒比共同体旅游业的今天

20 世纪 60 年代,当我身为特立尼达西印度群岛大学圣奥古斯丁校区的一名学生时,大多数加勒比国家的经济主要靠出口农产品来赚取外汇。糖是这些前英国殖民地的主要支柱。

35 年以后,大部分经济体实际上已发生转变。如巴哈马,其现在外汇的主要来源是旅游业。本周我才完全领会这个事实,尤其在听到围绕加勒比共同体

---

① 译者注:商业存在是指某一成员的服务提供者在另一成员领土内设立商业机构或专业机构,从而为后者领土内的消费者提供服务。

政府首脑会议的所有吹嘘之后。

看起来似乎大多数加勒比国家都仿照巴哈马的发展模式，不仅跳上了旅游这列列车，而且看到了金融服务部门的好处。

早在 20 世纪 60 年代，巴哈马和南加勒比的交通很差。从拿骚到特立尼达的西班牙港，几乎要花 24 个小时。在那些岁月里，英国西印度航空有限公司是唯一的运输公司，几乎每个岛屿它都停留——波多黎各、牙买加、安提瓜、圣卢西亚、巴巴多斯和特立尼达。似乎要花很长时间才能到达。

岛屿之间的通讯很差。我祖母去世时，我母亲和叔叔花了两周时间才和我取得联系。我的宿舍米尔纳公寓甚至没有电话。英尼斯太太，一位经营餐厅的女士，允许我使用她的办公电话来接听电话。

通过收音机和电视收听新闻绝无可能。为了收听棒球、足球和篮球比赛，我不得不调到美国武装部队的无线电网络。

无论在哪里，都要花费很长的时间才能收到邮件，通常为 2—4 周。我母亲会给我寄《论坛报》和《卫报》，看起来好像巴哈马处于另一个大陆而非同一地理区域。那些年，距离对人们有不同影响——人们感觉距离遥远。今天，互联网使人们可以每天与同事和朋友们通信。

在今天的加勒比，旅游业产生了一定的影响。生活和时代已经完全改变，所有事都变了。人们可以在几小时内到达任何一个加勒比岛屿。从前到特立尼达西班牙港的 24 小时的旅途，现在从迈阿密到特立尼达的皮亚科机场只要 3.5 小时的航程，且中途不停。

卫星传输使人们在那里或在这里观看同一电视节目成为可能。

联邦快递和敦豪快递可在 24 至 36 小时内送来信件和包裹，即使是到圭亚那和苏里南。

促成这大部分变化的原因，源于想在这个获利丰厚的旅游市场中具有竞争力，这使得加勒比成为全球最热门的旅游目的地之一。

在克林顿执政期间，美国人有许多可支配收入，这些钱花在了旅游上。拜访稀奇古怪的热带隐秘之所很时髦。旅游开发者利用这一点，花了数十亿美元打造豪华、高雅的场所。

三四十年前，旅游的概念对南加勒比来说相对较新。当我试图向西印度群岛大学的同学们描述巴哈马的旅游时，他们嗤之以鼻，并说巴哈马正在餐桌旁等着富有的美国人和欧洲人。多么损人！

巴哈马认识到旅游业远比那个复杂。通过认识到该行业的复杂性，我们能够把它从一个季节性的经济活动变为一个全年兴旺的产业。大多数加勒比人还不能复制这一转变的技术性细节。这就是为什么巴哈马旅游需要专业人士，且主要的加勒比旅游目的地为他们提供高职位的原因。牙买加聘请了巴兹尔·史密斯，吉姆·赫普尔已经离去，克利夫·汉密尔顿掌管特立尼达和多巴哥的旅游业多年，桑迪·桑兹在圭亚那，这样的例子不胜枚举。

上周，我的一个朋友去了马提尼克岛。那里的旅游业依赖每天从巴黎飞来的一次法航航班。安提瓜的旅游业处于困境，因为主要来自欧洲的航班减少了。因为不良市场和经济状况，圣卢西亚恢复为冬季型产业；因为西金斯敦骚乱的失稳效应，牙买加的旅游业陷入了极大的困境。

整个加勒比地区的报纸标题没能展现这里是一个安宁的地区以及让游客感到有安全保障的旅游目的地。

星期二的头条新闻写道："在牙买加暴动中9人被杀""持枪歹徒杀害巴哈马医院的护士""圣文森特有了旅游警务室""安提瓜酒店暂时关闭""圣卢西亚经济迫使酒店关门""特立尼达和多巴哥在美国联邦航空局降级"以及"加勒比的艾滋病处于紧急状态"。

不足为奇的是，英格拉哈姆先生在加勒比共同体会议期间呼吁明年10月召开旅游高峰会议。种种迹象表明，加勒比旅游产品可能存在严重问题。总理是对的；这需要地区关注，因为今天加勒比太多地区依赖它了。

巴哈马人和旅游经济

第三世界国家的旅游业有别于发达国家的旅游业。差异的主要方面在于第三世界的本地居民通常不会关照自己国家的旅游经济。本地居民通常要么是社会精英或拥有可支配收入的人，而人口的另一部分是旅游业某个领域的雇员。

几年前，我和家人去肯尼亚进行了一次观兽之旅，那真是最纯粹的生态旅游。这次观兽旅行的一个重要特点是从一个野生动物保护区到另一个野生动物保护区，并且在各式各样的地方住宿。在整个旅途中，我们接触的肯尼亚人都是工人——女仆、侍者、导游或好奇的人。

加勒比的很多地方，尤其是牙买加和古巴，为游客建立了单独的旅游飞地，几乎与社会的其他地方隔绝。这两个国家都强调了当地居民和外国人之间的分隔。

在古巴，巴拉德罗和可可岛禁止古巴人入内。在这些地方唯一能见到的古巴人是在这里工作的人。古巴政府不鼓励古巴人和游客深交。参与仅限于工作。

最近在牙买加召开的一个旅游会议上，该国的旅游部部长宣布，政府打算利用度假地的士兵来减少针对游客的犯罪以及制止当地人对游客的骚扰。

这一意外举措并非由政府发起，而是牙买加酒店和旅游协会要求的。在牙买加的观光胜地部署军队被视为向打击犯罪迈出了一大步。其他人则认为，这是将旅游经济和大多数当地人分隔的另一控诉。

当分析肯尼亚、古巴和牙买加的情形并跟巴哈马比较时，可以确定的是，巴哈马的情形完全不同，不同于其他相关的第三世界国家的规范。

在巴哈马，巴哈马人是旅游经济不可或缺的部分。巴哈马人不仅在这个行业工作，而且支持它并经常光顾。

所有当地酒店都有涉及岛上的营销和销售的项目。许多项目依靠本土市场来产生足够的销售额，特别是在发展缓慢时期，从而提高盈利。

关于国民经济中的旅游总收入，很多旅游业的统计数字未能反映出巴哈马人对旅游收入的贡献。

如果你想要证据，那么问自己这些问题：大多数婚宴在新普罗维登斯岛的什么地方举行？"海葡萄"周日早午餐的主要顾客是谁？社交和慈善的盛大活动在哪里举行？政治会议呢？

在旅游附属业务中，巴哈马人租下"黄鸟"进行社交活动，夏天带家人去蓝色珊瑚岛度假野餐。旅游业的每一部分都得益于巴哈人的惠顾。

巴哈马的旅游业已被塑造成具有同时吸引游客和居民的特色。二者能够共存并享受一个产品，这刺激了巴哈马的经济，把巴哈马推向一个层次——本地居民将其生活融入旅游经济的结构之中。

旅游业是金蛋，但是鹅可能被伤害到其生存能力严重受限的地步。保持多年发展而来的和谐很重要。这一和谐的秘诀是保持一种氛围，使每个巴哈马人都能享受旅游经济的好处。人民的权利不应被践踏或忽视。这种融合生成了独特的产品。它应该被不断加强而非受到短视的政策和项目的阻碍。

第 7 章 ››

海地人：一个坚韧的民族

> "杜桑之败在于方法，而非原则。"
>
> ——C. L. R. 詹姆斯，特立尼达历史学家、记者、社会主义者，
>
> 《黑人雅各宾派》

　　海地是脆弱的，其脆弱性集中体现在国内的普遍贫困、社会不平等、经济衰退、高失业率、治理不善和暴力犯罪上。一直以来，世人都认为海地是一个风雨飘摇的弱国。由于社会、经济、政治上的动荡，海地成了西半球 34 个国家中最贫穷的一个。在这一地区，海地比其他岛国都更早独立，是第一个独立的黑人共和国（1804 年）。

　　海地有 830 万人口，平均寿命 52 岁，人均收入 361 美元，长期深陷贫困。

　　距其最近的邻国（巴哈马和多米尼加共和国）一直阻止海地的非法移民涌入。这是由人口状况造成的，海地的年均人口增长率为 2.2%。加上现有的 830 万，海地的人口将在未来 25 年内超过 1 200 万。2003 年，40% 的海地人居住在首都太子港，海地日益发展成一个城市社会（城市中心包括戈纳伊夫、太子港、海地角），城市人口数量庞大，接近 400 万。尽管在西半球，海地的艾滋病发病率最高，每年约有 38 000 人死于这一疾病，但海地的人口增长仍然未受影响。

　　对海地人来说，移民是解决缺少工作机会和收入来源的方法，因为"30% 的家庭和 44% 的城市家庭会接收海地移民的汇款"。年均汇款量为 8 亿—9 亿美元，占海地家庭收入的 30% 左右。仅次于巴巴多斯，海地是美洲人口第二稠密的国家。

　　就业岗位主要来源于非正规经济和农业部门，而后者又由小自耕农构成，占海地劳动力人口的 50%。

　　另外，海地的基础设施存在严重问题。一半的城市人口没有饮用水，约 1/3

的人口卫生条件不足，只有 10% 的人能用上电，也只有 20% 的道路能通行。

委婉地说，海地的经济一直存在问题。过去的 40 年里（1960—2000 年），有 30 年经济呈负增长。虽然有十几年（20 世纪 70 年代和 20 世纪 90 年代后半段）经济确实增长了，但增长缺乏可持续性，很快便停滞不前。

人们可能认为，经济发展停滞的根源在于政局不稳。但事实并非如此。世界银行指出：

> "海地政府不断采取限制私营部门发展和对出口不利的财政及贸易政策，建立垄断性的公营企业，而且公共资金并未用于提高国家的生产和吸收能力。"

从本质上说，糟糕的政府政策是经济发展迟滞的原因。

海地的坚韧

海地宣告国家独立的过程堪比难产。独立革命使殖民地的重要商品——蔗糖遭到破坏性威胁。殖民列强不希望类似革命在加勒比其他殖民地再次发生。

对英国殖民者来说，1804 年海地独立比废除奴隶贸易，停止从西非贩卖人口早了三年，比美国的奴隶解放运动早了 30 年。

由于海地的民族反抗，殖民列强对其施加惩罚，这让海地争取独立的过程与在战场上战胜拿破仑的军队一样无比艰难。

（1）海地的治理

1804 年海地宣告独立后，欧洲列强不仅拖延国际社会承认海地为主权国家，发起类似美国对古巴的经济禁运，对海地实施经济封锁，拒绝与其贸易，而且还针对海地实行国际外交抵制。这导致海地无法建立大使级外交关系。为了让海地付出代价，法国政府向这个新生的共和国施以国际压力，强迫其赔偿法国因海地革命而遭受的损失。

穆拉托（黑白混血人）精英阶层和新近解放的非洲黑奴之间的争斗造成了多年的政治和社会动荡。尽管海地的非洲黑奴在形式上获得了解放，但是在海地独立后的 30 年里，奴隶制仍是该地区的常态。

近一个世纪以来，海地持续政局不稳，经济动荡，这导致美国从 1915 年开始军事占领海地直至 1934 年。虽然这一时期美国的占领在一定程度上使这个国家处于稳定状态，然而，美国撤军后，海地又陷入了政治混乱之中。

1957 年，绰号"老大夫"的乡村医生弗朗索瓦·杜瓦利埃成为海地总统。他去世后，他的儿子"小大夫"让－克洛德·杜瓦利埃继任海地总统。杜瓦利埃政权统治海地将近 30 年(1957—1986 年)。

杜瓦利埃政权被认为是海地历史上最专制的政权。其统治被推翻后,海地经历了政治转型,成为一个民主国家。1905①—1987 年,海地先后颁布了 21 部宪法。

在民主化进程中,海地从 1986 年到 2005 年经历了 15 届不同的政府。(见表 7.1)有几位曾多次出任总统(亨利·南菲(2 次)、让-贝特朗·阿里斯蒂德(3 次)和勒内·普雷瓦尔(2 次))。

表 7.1   1986—2005 年海地政府

政　府	姓名及职位	任　　期	时　长
1	亨利·南菲总统(军政府)	1986 年 2 月至 1988 年 2 月	2 年
2	莱斯利·马尼加总统	1988 年 2 月至 1988 年 6 月	4 个月
3	亨利·南菲总统(军政府)	1988 年 6 月至 1988 年 9 月	3 个月
4	普罗佩·阿夫里尔总统(军政府)	1988 年 9 月至 1990 年 4 月	20 个月
5	埃拉尔·亚伯拉罕总统(军政府)	1990 年 4 月	3 天
6	埃尔塔·帕斯卡尔-特鲁约总统	1990 年 4 月至 1991 年 2 月	10 个月
7	让-贝特朗·阿里斯蒂德总统	1991 年 2 月至 1991 年 9 月	7 个月
8	约瑟夫·C. 内雷特总统	1991 年 10 月至 1992 年 5 月	7 个月
9	无政府状态		
10	埃米尔·若纳桑总统	1994 年 6 月至 1994 年 9 月	3 个月
11	让-贝特朗·阿里斯蒂德总统	1994 年 10 月至 1996 年 2 月	16 个月
12	勒内·普雷瓦尔总统	1996 年 2 月至 2001 年 2 月	5 年
13	让-贝特朗·阿里斯蒂德总统	2001 年 2 月至 2004 年 2 月	3 年
14	博尼费斯·亚历山大总统	2004 年 2 月至 2006 年 5 月	2 年
15	勒内·普雷瓦尔总统	2006 年 5 月至今	

来源:世界银行(1998 年)及媒体的统计

虽然 20 世纪 60 年代加勒比逐渐兴起成为主要的旅游目的地,但"老大夫"杜瓦利埃的专制统治阻碍了海地的经济发展。1960—2000 年,海地的人均国内生产总值呈负增长。仅在 1971—1980 年的十年期间实现正增长。(见表 7.2)。

---

① 译者注:原文如此。

表 7.2　1961—2000 年人均国内生产总值年均实际增长率（单位：%）

	1961—2000	1961—1970	1971—1980	1981—1990	1991—2000
海地	−1.0	−1.4	2.6	−2.3	−2.3
拉美地区	1.7	2.6	3.1	−0.8	1.7
撒哈拉以南非洲地区	0.2	1.9	0.8	−1.3	−0.4
全球	2.5	3.2	2.5	2.3	2.0

来源：世界银行

农业仍是海地经济的重要部门，服务业则为主导行业，旅游业因受政局动荡的影响一直被边缘化。

（2）海地的应对机制

海地人制定了各种机制来应对政局不稳和经济衰退，二者已成为制约海地经济可持续发展，提高人民生活质量的主要障碍。在摆脱法国统治宣告独立后，海地随即陷入政治动荡和经济落后的双重危机之中。

此外，艰难独立的海地还遭到了经济封锁和外交孤立。多年来，海地人民已经学会如何在国家所处的大环境中生存下来。

• 海地的移民

据世界银行估计，巴哈马有 7.5 万名海地人，多米尼加共和国有 50 万名，美国和加拿大约有 200 万名。第二次世界大战后，这些境外海地人成为海地应对机制的一部分，他们给国内亲属的汇款现已接近 10 亿美元，占海地国内生产总值的 25%。

自 1950 年起，海地人陆续离开海地，其中以技术人员、熟练技工和商人居多。他们中大多数人离开是出于政治原因。20 世纪 60 年代，杜瓦利埃政权统治时期人才外流的现象加剧；到 20 世纪 80 年代，非熟练工和农民也开始加入海地的移民大军。

移民不仅为数百万境外海地人提供了避难之地，也为那些仍留在海地境内的人提供了一个社会安全网。后者用从境外收到的汇款购买生活必需品，如食物、教育、医疗、住房。（见表 7.3 和表 7.4）

表 7.3　收款居民支出一览表

汇款支出项目	百分比（%）
食物	81

续表

汇款支出项目	百分比(%)
教育	74
衣物	64
储蓄	34
医疗	28
住房	27
生意	14
其他	11
偿债	9
还债	7

来源:世界银行

表 7.4 汇款金额

金额区间	百分比(%)
≤ 100 美元	41
101—300 美元	42
301—500 美元	9
>500 美元	8
其 他	1
合 计	100.0

来源:世界银行

· 非正规(部门)经济

海地曾一度吸引外商直接投资其制造业和服务业(旅游业),然而糟糕的财政政策阻碍了制造业的发展,政治动荡又使海地成为一个没有吸引力的旅游目的地。因此,政府主导的公营企业成了最主要的雇主。因为海地政局长期不稳,私营部门发展受困,所以规模相对较小。

在这种环境下,海地的非正规部门用人规模庞大,根据世界银行的统计,海地约有 100 万的个体经营者践行着"便士资本主义"。

这些"便士资本家"从事各种小生意,比如在农村开修理店、在街边摆摊卖日用品、在建筑工地当临时工、在乡下种地。

· 文化生活

海地的文化生活充满活力,体现在艺术和音乐方面。尽管国家贫困,但作为登上国际舞台的第一个黑人共和国,海地有着强大的国家意志。这是海地人一直引以为豪的原因，对海地侨民来说尤是如此。

投资下一代

以加利福尼亚卡梅尔山谷的圣邓斯坦教区的名义，美国圣公会国内外传教协会的教徒在海地安什建立并资助圣安德烈基督学校，以帮助当地孩子的发展。（见图7.1）

安什的环境如下：

> "5月以来，安什市政府便无法保障市民用电（照片摄于2006年9月）。城市晚上漆黑一片。由于道路状况恶化，油槽车无法将燃油运往城市电力系统或当地零售加油站。油槽车在崎岖不平的道路上行驶，要么故障频发，要么陷进泥里。这时就会有人来偷车上的燃油。
>
> 安什的市政供水中断。当地人不得不在浑浊的泥水中洗澡、洗衣。河水就是他们的饮用水。"

圣安德烈基督学校既是学校也是教堂，可以说是安什的一处绿洲。这里全天供电，保证学校、教堂、设备运作。

学校现在有750名学生。早上6:30开始，小至3岁，大至高三的600多名学生陆续到校，早上7:00正式上课，周六不休。上课期间，学校每天为所有学生和当地遗孀提供一顿热饭。

启动这一项目时，圣邓斯坦教堂还只是一个有着混凝土地板和屋顶的单坡屋顶建筑；1993年，该教堂接纳了33名学生。

图 7.1　海地安什圣公会资助学校的孩子们

抵达美国

对海地人来说，前往美国必经巴哈马。非法移民的交通工具通常是摇晃破旧的小船,并不适合长途航行,然而,海地人为了更好的生活愿意铤而走险。

　　成千上万的海地人乘船途经巴哈马,他们或将巴哈马作为中转站短暂停留,或在巴哈马永久定居。但不管最终决定如何,他们都是非法移民。

　　由于大量海地人偷渡,巴哈马如今面临着严峻的非法移民问题。这种情况给巴哈马的社会和经济造成了深刻影响。偷渡来的海地人不会说巴哈马本地语言,又目不识丁(47%的海地人不识字)。非法移民最担心的是住不起房,因此,成千上万的海地非法移民不得不到贫民区找房子暂住。这些海地人不仅给巴哈马的医疗基础设施造成了严重压力,同时,危及当地的公共教育系统;因为在一些学区,数以百计的不会说英语的海地儿童占用了巴哈马当地孩子的教育资源。

　　这导致大量海地非法移民的孩子在巴哈马出生。他们将巴哈马视作祖国,可获得巴哈马国籍却成了一场官僚主义的噩梦。

　　海地的非法移民已经演变为巴哈马的一个情绪化议题。很多巴哈马人认为,海地非法移民已威胁到巴哈马的种族构成。但也有巴哈马人将海地人视作熟练和非熟练劳动力的来源。

　　巴哈马和非法移民所面临的一大问题是,海地人是否有能力融入一个基督教根深蒂固、政治体制民主、基于英国普通法系、成熟且国际化、以旅游业和金融服务业为主的服务型经济社会。

　　由于海地现在是加勒比共同体的成员国,海地问题成了巴哈马加入加勒比单一市场和经济的绊脚石。加勒比单一市场和经济的核心纲领是促进区域内人口的自由流动。

图 7.2　海地非法移民的单桅船被巴哈马皇家国防军舰船拖走

插曲：《埃尼亚斯文集》《巴哈马日报》 海地与 18 世纪 90 年代

（编者按：时值美洲首个独立的黑人国家——海地庆祝独立 200 周年之际，戈弗雷·埃尼亚斯从不同角度阐述了海地革命及海地迈向独立的征程。）

18 世纪最后十年的历史主要围绕法属圣多明戈的战事展开。法属圣多明戈位于伊斯帕尼奥拉岛西部，占该岛面积的 1/3。伊斯帕尼奥拉岛的意义十分重大。1492 年哥伦布在圣萨尔瓦多岛登陆，之后他向东南方继续航行，发现了更大的岛屿，为致敬西班牙，哥伦布将这座岛屿命名为西班牙岛或伊斯帕尼奥拉岛。

法属圣多明戈的重要性主要体现在两个方面：第一，它提供了法国 2/3 的海外贸易；第二，它是欧洲奴隶贸易最大的独立市场。非洲奴隶已成为新大陆大部分地区如美国、巴西、中南美洲的其他国家以及加勒比地区经济发展的基础。18 世纪 90 年代发生在法属圣多明戈的战事对整个加勒比地区今后的政治、社会和经济都至关重要。

17 世纪中叶以来，欧洲各国将加勒比视作新大陆制糖业的基地，因此，加勒比诸岛逐渐成为殖民者的赚钱宝地。

由于创造了大量的赚钱机会，加勒比地区的制糖业成为欧洲人金钱和物质财富的重要来源。这让欧洲各国如西班牙、葡萄牙、荷兰、英国以及法国的企业家们在航运、贸易、商品销售、金融等方面发展壮大，并为其国内提供了大量的衍生经济机会。

加勒比成为欧洲经济剥削的重点区域。古巴和多米尼加共和国是西班牙的殖民地；英国人拥有牙买加、巴巴多斯、特立尼达、大部分背风和向风群岛；荷兰人控制了库拉索岛和圣马丁岛；马提尼克岛、瓜德罗普岛、圣卢西亚和圣多明戈则是法国的属地。

圣多明戈很快便成为法属加勒比的主要获利来源。到 18 世纪中叶，圣多明戈发达的制糖和咖啡业对牙买加在加勒比地区的地位构成了严重威胁，因为牙买加曾自称为加勒比地区首屈一指的奴隶殖民地。这就是 18 世纪最后十年法属圣多明戈所处的经济结构。它将成为海地建国的重要因素之一。海地或阿依提，意为"多山的地方"。

法属圣多明戈还有另一个重要因素——非洲黑奴。1763—1789 年，圣多明戈的奴隶人口从 206 000 人暴增至 465 429 人。在这么短的时间内，大量非洲奴隶进入美洲殖民地，特别是加勒比的殖民地，这是前所未有的。

当然还有第三个因素。1789 年，法国大革命爆发，其自由、平等、博爱的革命思潮成了推动圣多明戈奴隶起义的助燃剂。

当时圣多明戈的种族构成复杂，包括将近 50 万的非洲黑奴、有色人或黑白混血人组成的中产阶级、法国白人财阀及法国官员执掌的殖民政府。法国的政治动荡致使了法国大革命的爆发，由此引发了法属圣多明戈的政治动荡。有色人及黑白混血人对白人，中产阶级对上层中产阶级，法国人对殖民者之间的混战接踵而至。就在这些动乱爆发之际，非洲黑奴抓住机遇，发起了武装起义。

起义的正义性对评判这场革命至关重要——种族平等、奴隶解放推动了起义的发展。杜桑·卢维杜尔军事才华出众，他率领的奴隶军不仅打败了拿破仑的法国军队，也战胜了西班牙和英国军队。

1804 年 1 月 1 日，卢维杜尔的接班人让-雅克·德萨林将军在戈纳伊夫宣布海地独立。如今，这位胜利将军的纪念碑矗立在广场上的显著位置，海地总统让-贝特朗·阿里斯蒂德将在此主持纪念海地独立 200 周年的官方庆典。

海地宣布独立是意义深远的，因为它是非洲之外的首个黑人共和国，也是近代的第二个后殖民国家（继美国之后）。这表明，在军事领导下，一支由曾经的奴隶组成的军队，联合其游击队或抗击小分队能够战胜欧洲最精良的军队（如法国、英国或西班牙的军队）。

海地革命威胁到了 19 世纪初主宰加勒比地区的经济状况和种族基础。欧洲奴隶主们被他们的非洲黑奴打败，这让各地奴隶主们意识到海地发生的一系列战事不仅影响了加勒比其他地区，也波及包括美国在内的美洲各地种植园。他们对此深感恐惧。

海地共和国的新领导人制定了一部宪法，规定任何黑人，无论男女老幼，不管从新大陆的任何地方来到海地，都将在这个新共和国被授予公民身份。

经过 13 年的革命，海地终于在 1804 年 1 月 1 日正式独立。然而，随之而来的却是全世界的孤立。直到 21 年后（1825 年），法国才承认海地独立。这是海地支付给法国 9 000 万金法郎赔款之后换来的主权认可。1862 年，英国承认海地为主权国家，但这距离法国认可海地独立又过了 37 年。由此可见，海地的国家地位是欧洲列强勉强施舍的。

海地的"无敌舰队"

提到"无敌舰队"一词，几乎总是让人想起那支 1588 年远征英格兰失利的西班牙著名海上舰队。这支舰队之所以建立是因为克里斯托弗·哥伦布在西班牙的资助下发现了美洲这块新大陆，于是西班牙宣称，新大陆上已经开发和正在开发的大笔财富都归西班牙所有，致使西班牙与英格兰交恶。

西班牙决定亮出自己的军事实力，创建一支强大的海军攻击英格兰。这支强大的舰队被称为"西班牙无敌舰队"。

美国海岸警卫队最近的情报显示，在伊斯帕尼奥拉岛西部，巴哈马以南，另一支"无敌舰队"正在集结。据近期的一次统计显示，约有 600 艘小船已经造好，另有更多在建，目的是将大量人口从海地经巴哈马运送至美国。

这支"无敌舰队"的创建源于候任总统比尔·克林顿最近发布的一项政策声明，即美国不会拒绝寻求庇护的海地人入境。1993 年 1 月 20 日，克林顿政府就职；与此同时，"无敌舰队"也准备好向美国进发。

这项政策将给巴哈马造成巨大且深远的后果，并对巴哈马的社会经济结构产生重大影响。

克林顿的政策与老布什的正好相反。老布什政府主张在公海上拦截海地的小船，要么把船上的难民遣返回海地，要么将他们送到古巴关塔那摩湾的收容所接受询问和处置。

因此，老布什政府饱受批评，舆论认为这是一项种族歧视的政策，因为海地人是黑种人。另一方面，批评人士称，美国之所以欢迎大批古巴人的到来，据说是因为古巴人大多为白人，且古巴裔美国人在美国有强大的游说集团。

海地人说，他们之所以寻求新的家园是由于军政府的政治压迫。老布什政府则认为海地人是因为经济原因离开海地，因此，才制定了在公海上拦截他们的政策。

在海地，军事统治已司空见惯，这种情况屡见不鲜。军事压迫的同时，杜瓦利埃时期海地的经济状况并未好转，于是大量海地人外逃。由于西半球国家的经济抵制，海地目前的经济形势严峻，极其困难。

克林顿宣誓就任美国总统之时，数千艘海地小船可能已经造好，为海上长途跋涉做好准备，从海地经巴哈马最终到达美国的佛罗里达。

众所周知，过去这些海地小船能容纳 200—300 人。海地"无敌舰队"的第一次远航大概会运送 200—300 000 人。一、二月份是一年中最冷的时候，海水冰冷刺骨，海面风大浪急。数百艘海地船只可能会在巴哈马海域遭遇严重困境，因此，数以千计的海地人不得不在巴哈马群岛下船。

其后果就是成千上万的海地人在巴哈马群岛各处寻求庇护。对巴哈马政府来说，这事关重大。或许这是继美国南北卡罗来纳州的保皇派及其奴隶来到这片群岛定居之后最大规模的一次人口涌入，男女老幼皆有。

鉴于这些可能性，预估巴哈马国防军会命令所有舰队保持待命，阻止这些海地人突袭巴哈马海岸。

此外，还可预见的是在美洲国家组织（OAS）及联合国的会议上，西半球国家乃至全世界都会注意到明年初巴哈马可能遭遇的问题。毫不夸张地说，灾难可能就在巴哈马的东海岸。

《出埃及记》仍在上演

最近几周，巴哈马的海地非法移民泛滥成灾。据信，这种大规模的人口偷渡是组织严密的团伙所为；许多人认为，这些团伙由在巴哈马的本地人或海地人组成。

从一开始，克里斯蒂政府就试图严打海地人非法偷渡到巴哈马。此外，巴哈马外交部部长也在国际场合（如出席美洲国家组织和加勒比共同体论坛时）积极讨论海地当前面临的问题，以及海地尚未解决的非法移民情况对加勒比地区和海地的近邻（如巴哈马、多米尼加共和国）的负面影响。

5月22日至23日，巴哈马政府与海地恢复谈判，希望能够达成一项新条约。据巴哈马外交部部长米切尔所述，新条约中的一个重要方面是"所有情报收集工作都是为了找到这一问题的根源"。

过去一周，巴哈马的报纸头条刊登了大量海地人涌入巴哈马的报道。日常脱口秀节目也遭到巴哈马民众的电话轰炸，表达他们的不满情绪，抱怨海地非法移民占用其卫生、教育、社会服务等资源，导致巴哈马本国人民税负过重。甚至卡迈克尔路拘留中心也因过去几周大量非法移民涌入而几近满员。

巴哈马缺乏资源来解决当前这些非法入境者的冲击所带来的挑战。造成这种情况的根源正是海地从法国殖民地转变为世界上第一个黑人独立国家。

作为法国殖民地，海地曾是法国殖民帝国中的明珠，也曾是加勒比最富庶的殖民地。海地土地肥沃，其生产的甘蔗以及糖浆、朗姆酒等蔗糖副产品带来了大量财富。在海地击败拿破仑军队获得独立，脱离法国统治时，法国便失去了一块重要的殖民地。

海地为其独立付出了高昂代价，时至今日，海地仍未恢复元气。西方列强迫使一代又一代的海地人民为自己的自由付出代价。2004年1月，海地人民迎来了海地独立200周年。

宣布独立后不久，海地很快就陷入了经济困境。从19世纪后期起，海地开始遭受日益严重的经济不稳定和政局动荡，其中部分源于对法国的赔款。美国占领期间（1915 年至 20 世纪 30 年代），海地一直被赔款问题困扰。一直以来，海地从未能在经济和政治上取得平衡，从而充分解决这个贫困国家所面临的巨大问题。

　　海地已成为西半球的问题所在。西半球有能力影响海地局势的国家似乎都对此置若罔闻。冷战时期，海地受到美国的大量援助，因为美国视海地为共产主义渗透的潜在滩头阵地；因此，美国选择支持像杜瓦利埃这样的独裁者。

　　如今世界正处在全球化的新时代，然而在海地落后于西半球其他国家，深陷经济与政治困境时，国际社会却鲜有伸出援手。海地曾一度是加勒比最富有的殖民地，现在却落得西半球最贫穷国家的恶名。

　　米切尔的外交政策妥善地解决了海地给巴哈马带来的挑战，理应受到褒扬。米切尔还应考虑直接援助海地，不管是提供医疗、教育设施方面的专业知识，还是提供种子、种植材料、农具、肥料等农业投入。巴哈马必须更加积极主动，而不是采取一贯的处理方式。

　　20 世纪 50 年代，加纳国父、非洲独立运动领袖克瓦米·恩克鲁玛向全非洲人民敞开了加纳的教育之门，启迪他们寻求独立。特立尼达和多巴哥前总理埃里克·威廉姆斯博士曾用这个双岛之国的巨额石油收入援助西印度群岛以及非洲人民。20 世纪 60 年代，我曾在特立尼达求学，当时一些非洲学生能在此学习得益于威廉姆斯政府颁发的奖学金。今天，菲德尔·卡斯特罗也效仿这一做法。因其颇具前瞻性且大有好处。

　　巴哈马可将这种前瞻性计划作为解决途径，缓解海地人大量涌入的问题。

非法移民：海地劳动力过剩的出路

　　尽管处理海地问题并非易事，但巴哈马新一届政府仍将其作为首要任务。上周三，外交部部长弗雷德·米切尔阁下与劳工和移民部部长文森特·皮特阁下对海地进行了正式访问。访问的核心议题即从海地这个贫困国家持续涌入巴哈马的非法移民。

　　由于巴哈马是毒品走私至美国的中转站，巴哈马国防军的主要任务之一便是打击毒贩。然而数月来，源源不断的非法移民涌入巴哈马，这给巴哈马国防军增加了额外压力。巴哈马的整个南部边境极易遭到非法人口贩子和毒品走私者的袭击。无论是人口贩运还是毒品走私，最终目的地一般都是美国，而巴哈马仅是临时停靠站。

两位部长此行的目的就是为了使海地政府意识到，巴哈马民众对待海地非法移民问题的耐心已几乎耗尽，容忍程度达历史新低。

出于各种原因，巴哈马人民很排外，对侵犯其国家资产的外来者极为防范。在巴哈马人民眼中，巴哈马是他们的家园，这片国土上产生的利益应归巴哈马人民享有。凡是侵犯巴哈马国家利益的行为，都会给巴哈马人民造成极度不安。正是这种不安促使巴哈马政府派出两位部长赴海地解决问题。

众所周知，海地是西半球最贫穷的国家。加勒比共同体在接纳海地为其成员国时就充分认识到海地与其他成员国不同，其政治结构脆弱，没有民主传统。而另一方面，美国已经暂停了对海地的财政援助，直至海地恢复其国内的政治秩序。这阻碍了海地的经济增长与发展，巴哈马代表团承诺会游说美国政府发放这些援助金。

巴哈马人民对上述因素均有了解。尽管存在语言差异，巴哈马基督教会对身处巴哈马的海地人和海地本国人民都表现出了强烈的基督教兄弟情谊。几乎每个在巴哈马的基督教教派都有针对海地国民的所谓拓展计划；有些教派甚至在海地建立了基督教宣教团。

同教会一样，巴哈马政府通过米切尔和皮特两位谈判代表向海地提供人力、设备等形式的技术援助。就援助而言，巴哈马正帮助海地采取各种措施，进一步解决巴海两国的人口偷渡问题。

与此同时，巴哈马以积极的姿态收集情报，并更严厉地打击偷渡行为。

各种迹象表明，巴哈马外交部似乎正与加勒比共同体协调巴哈马的这一倡议。近日，圣卢西亚外交部部长朱利安·亨特阁下与美洲国家组织副秘书长就共同目标刚结束对海地的访问返回。若西半球各组织机构和各国政府齐心协力，海地面临的问题可能会得到更快的解决，最终为改进海地政治制度和建立新的政治秩序奠定基础。

仅30万人口的巴哈马向人口约800万的海地提供援助，两国间的这种双边关系为巴哈马处理区域问题提供了的新角度。佩里·G. 克里斯蒂阁下领导的新政府应受到赞赏，外交部采取的这一新政策也应得到肯定。显然，米切尔为巴哈马的外交政策翻开了新的一页。

巴哈马人民必须认识到，海地的经济以劳动力过剩为主要特征。另一方面，由于"无就业增长"这种新现象抬头，许多欧洲国家纷纷预测将面临劳动力短缺的局面。这源于全球经济环境发生了根本性变化，原来以自然资源和原材料为基础的产业发展已转型为知识型的产业发展。这意味着发展中国家生产的初级产品逐渐变得边缘化。在这一新经济形势下帮助海地脱贫绝非易事，特别是如果海地不理解围绕其发展的变化。

海地必须建立公信力

巴哈马和海地一直在定期磋商，尝试解决大规模海地非法移民涌入巴哈马的问题。从各方面来看，外交部部长兼议员弗雷德·米切尔阁下之所以赢得高度赞誉，很显然是因为他竭尽所能为巴哈马当局解决了这一日益严峻的问题。

米切尔让加勒比共同体的外交部部长们注意到了海地的非法移民偷渡问题，并将此问题上升到整个西半球的高度，这是他此番努力的主要特点。他已成功引起美洲国家组织的关注。我认为，下一步米切尔会在联合国论坛上提出该问题，并将问题上升到全球高度，因为他需要在联合国获得更多支持。

同样显而易见的是，各方正积极劝说世界银行、国际货币基金组织（IMF）等全球性大型组织以及泛美开发银行（IDB）等西半球多边机构提供资金，帮助海地进行其急需的基础设施升级。

上周，在《巴哈马日报》头版文章中，米切尔表示：

> "泛美开发银行会继续为海地提供其所需的开发贷款，以发展海地各领域经济，这在以前是不可能的，因为海地尚未还清欠款和利息。"

海地经济陷入这种困境实在见怪不怪。这并非始于阿里斯蒂德总统执政期间；这种进退维谷已成为海地经济、财政所面临的各种问题的一部分。因此，我对给予海地贷款发展经济的举措表示怀疑，同时，我怀疑泛美开发银行是否会像米切尔所说的那样大方。几十年来，就发展而言，海地最大的敌人是其自身。几个月前，美国国务卿科林·鲍威尔将军访问加勒比时重申，没有任何明确迹象表明海地政府正着手进行政府体制改革，从而有效利用数百万美元的机构拨款、外国援助或贷款。鲍威尔是对的。在向海地政府拨款方面，所有组织机构都银根紧缩。

海地属于这样一类国家——"全球数百万人因第三世界债务及其后果而陷入贫困"。每次国际会议上，像海地一样处境艰难的国家都会大声疾呼要求减免债务。

世界银行和国际货币基金组织设有一个名为"重债穷国倡议"的项目，其目的是为那些有良好政策的贫穷国家提供债务减免。正是从这个角度来看，海地被一些机构和国家拒之门外，因为几乎没有证据表明海地正在实施"良好政策"来减轻其面临的贫困负担。

海地正深陷危机，而美国等援助国或国际货币基金组织、世界银行等组织似乎不愿意伸出援手。但事实并非如此。这些机构已经为海地花费了大量资金。国际货币基金组织向成员国提供备用贷款是为了应对紧急情况，避免危机再次发生。然而这一情况已演变成"危机—救助—危机—救助"的无限循环。海地已经接受过 22 次紧急救助，比利比里亚（13 次）、厄瓜多尔（16 次）和阿根廷（15 次）的次数都多。

海地非法移民的大规模偷渡正在影响巴哈马人民的生活质量。最近一期《人类发展指数报告》显示，虽然巴哈马仍名列世界前 50 位；然而，2003 年，我们的排名已从第 43 位降至第 49 位。排名下滑的原因就是穷困潦倒的海地非法移民大量涌入。

国际社会采取措施为海地提供资金改善局势，给海地人民创造就业机会，尤其是那些农村地区的海地人，因为正是这些人寻求偷渡到我国。这符合我们的利益。据报道，就在上周，有 22 艘船驶入拿骚港。对大部分巴哈马人来说，这实在让人气愤。

如果海地想要获得国际机构的信任，必须首先自行整顿。

海地：把握机遇，开启新篇章

上周日，巴哈马、加勒比共同体以及全世界其他地区的人们一觉醒来发现海地的反政府武装叛乱致使其局势极度恶化，总统让-贝特朗·阿里斯蒂德被迫逃离海地。有人称阿里斯蒂德已经辞职，也有人认为他是被逼离开的。阿里斯蒂德表示，他离开海地是为了避免这个饱受战乱折磨的国家发生更多流血事件，让 800 万海地贫民受苦。

作为西半球第一个黑人共和国，海地为此骄傲自豪，然而颇具讽刺意味的是，时值庆祝从法国独立 200 周年之际，海地国内却法治缺失、政治混乱。

鉴于其目前的局势，海地是否已将主权交予国际社会？显然，在这个特殊时期，海地没有自治的能力；并且现在它还威胁到了北加勒比的社会和经济稳定。巴哈马的海地人几乎占巴哈马总人口的 20%，因为在阿巴科岛、大巴哈马岛、新普罗维登斯岛和伊柳塞拉岛都有大型的海地人聚居地。

过去 40 年来，巴哈马人深受海地政局不稳的影响。谁能轻易忘记"老大夫"杜瓦利埃的独裁统治和他直接领导的国家安全志愿军——令人闻风丧胆的通顿马库特，还有"老大夫"的继任者——"小大夫"杜瓦利埃，他奢靡腐败，最终被赶下台。杜瓦利埃家族以所谓终身总统的方式统治了海地近 30 年，导致大批海地人出逃至巴哈马。"小大夫"之后，海地由军方接管，同时出现了一位神父，他宣扬解放哲学并让海地人民心向往之。这位神父就是让-贝特朗·阿里斯蒂德。1988 年阿里斯蒂德被鲍思高慈幼会开除，后来他成为海地 200 年来首位民选总统。

在海地，军方一直扮演着权力掮客的角色。阿里斯蒂德暂时被迫离开海地期间，军事巨头拉乌尔·塞德拉斯执掌海地。不久，塞德拉斯下台，流亡巴拿马，阿里斯蒂德重回海地再任总统。

然而，有史以来，卫星转播第一次将海地危机直接展现在我们客厅的电视上，我们看到屠杀、战乱就发生在邻国，发生在加勒比共同体的姊妹国家。转播画面呈现的是一个想把政治分歧推向极端的民族形象。这种场景让人恐惧，它显示了一个国家体制基础的失败。

国际社会对于像海地这样的国家已逐渐丧失耐心。在我的一生中，这种情况一再发生。许多人认为，是时候让海地人民拿出点尊严，摆脱这种不断依赖的状态了。加勒比和拉丁美洲地区是全球较为进步的区域之一，但海地却几乎长期处于不发达状态。

海地问题的政治解决办法可能是其作为被保护国由联合国再管理一段时间，因为海地人民似乎没有自治的政治意愿。海地必须从全球社会经济瘫痪国家的名单中脱身。

从其目前的态势来看，海地对北加勒比地区构成了威胁。未受教育的劳动力涌入他国。医疗基础设施年久失修，不得不依靠古巴医护人员的支援，国民健康得不到保障。国内经济乱作一团，主要收入来源是国外汇款。

无论我们承认与否，海地在自治方面非常令人失望。我们要通过加勒比共同体和美洲国家组织坚持在海地实行严格措施，改善并升级其体制结构，加强民主，将海地建成为一个现代国家，这符合巴哈马的利益。

海地是一个"倒退"的国家，其治国理念是旧时代的体现。全球化环境下的现代国家治理模式与之截然不同；海地已然落后，留给加勒比共同体、美洲国家组织和联合国的挑战是提升海地的治理能力。

阿里斯蒂德在其身处海地政治权力中心的 14 年里，从未在海地奠定参与式民主制的基础。尽管他拥有强大的宗教和神学背景，但阿里斯蒂德的执政理念十分专制。正鉴于此，阿里斯蒂德的一些亲密支持者和盟友（如美、法两国）均对其产生了怀疑,怀疑在其执政下海地的前途。

阿里斯蒂德成功地解散了军队,然而除此之外并没有其他可说的了,因为他可能是第二次世界大战后离开海地的领导人中最落魄的一个。

发展专家预测,海地需要几十年的时间才能恢复一些表面秩序,建立起现代国家所需的体制结构。这必须在联合国、美洲国家组织以及一定程度上加勒比共同体等国际机构的范围内进行。这是一项长期工作,不能速战速决。

然而,巴哈马必须负起责任参与进来,因为这符合我们的国家利益。在独立 200 年后,作为世界上历史最悠久的黑人共和国,海地必须抓住机遇,为其国民生计开启新的篇章。

海地——加勒比共同体的最新成员

上周,加勒比共同体政府首脑会议在牙买加蒙特哥贝举行,会上加勒比共同体接受了海地的加入申请。

这是件值得关注的大事,原因如下。第一,其为深化区域一体化迈出了切实的一步,因为海地是第二个加入加勒比共同体的非英语国家,而且过去并不是英国殖民地。前荷兰殖民地苏里南是第一个加入加勒比共同体的非英语国家。第二个重要原因要从新大陆的黑奴贸易说起。作为世界上第一个黑人共和国,海地为新大陆的黑人点亮了自由之光。这个新生的共和国从法国独立后,立即针对从事奴隶贸易的所有国际势力、殖民大国,如英国、荷兰、葡萄牙、西班牙、法国和美国,实施了一项革命性的移民和公民政策。

海地共和国向世界宣布,任何来到海地的黑人都是自由人,如果他愿意,他将成为这个刚刚独立的共和国的公民。

那是 1804 年,当时加勒比的奴隶贸易兴旺发达。海地的所有邻国都有大量的奴隶人口,特别是古巴、波多黎各、牙买加和巴哈马。

就巴哈马而言,海地的移民和公民政策在巴哈马废除奴隶制之前已经实施了 30 年。可以想象,因为这一政策赋予的自由和公民身份,巴哈马的奴隶逃往了海地。

海地对利润丰厚的奴隶贸易构成了威胁,于是欧洲列强决定让其为反抗法国的"罪行"付出经济上的代价。

对法国而言,海地比其在加拿大的殖民地还要重要。海地土地肥沃,盛产糖、咖啡、香料、柑橘,矿产资源也十分丰富。因此,当富饶的海地脱离法国独立后,殖民列强最初拒不承认海地主权,以示惩罚。为了获得主权承认,海地不得不向法国支付高昂的赔偿金。财政负担让这个新生的共和国元气大伤，直至今天，经济复苏仍是海地的一项艰巨任务。

在独立近两个世纪后，海地现已成为加勒比共同体组织的一员，不仅受到加勒比共同体的认可，同时，能在没有怀疑和猜忌的真诚氛围中发挥作用。

加入加勒比共同体的过程并不简单。加勒比共同体秘书处的工作组与海地官员进行协商、调查，达成具体条款和条件，海地只有完全满足其要求，才能正式获得加入加勒比共同体的资格。

牙买加总理 P. J. 帕特森先生提到海地的加入时说道："通过加强与加勒比姊妹国家间的联系，将极大地促进海地国内民主结构建立的进程。"

对巴哈马人民而言，海地加入加勒比共同体不仅能推动其改善自身的"民主结构"，而且加勒比共同体会对其给予体制上的支持，促进海地的经济发展，从而提升海地人民的生活质量。从长远来看，加入加勒比共同体会促使海地采取一系列举措，以改善教育机构、医疗制度，使文化和体育活动相互促进，为加勒比地区创造一个大市场，同时，遏制海地经济难民涌入巴哈马。

普雷瓦尔总统政府在推动海地加入加勒比共同体方面所做出的努力值得赞赏。这对海地人民来说是一个新的开始。地区参与或许是推动海地政治朝着积极方向发展的途径。长期以来，海地一直被贴着"西半球最贫穷国家"的标签，加勒比共同体有望让海地摆脱这种耻辱的国际形象。

近两个世纪前，海地曾帮助那些因奴隶贸易迁徙而来的黑人受害者，如今，那些迁徙而来的黑人，随着社会经济条件和政治地位的提高也向海地施以援手。

非正规经济

经济学家为特定的经济因素、经济形势甚至经济理论命名的方式真是奇妙。就本文而言，经济学家将非正规经济或非正规部门定义为小规模进行的、形式多样的生产活动，内容包括商品，尤其是服务。这种生产活动完全或部分逃避了制度、财政或保险义务。

可以说，巴哈马是一个高度成熟的经济体，统计局和中央银行从巴哈马的银行业、制造业、旅游业、建筑业和农业等部门获得经济、金融以及其他重要的统计数据。

所有这些信息都定期发布，提供有价值的经济数据，用于确定经济增长率——正增长或负增长、通货膨胀水平、国际收支平衡等。

尽管巴哈马经济成熟,但其非正规部门正发展迅速。一位经济学家将此称为"人民对国家无力满足贫困群众基本需求的自发性和创造性回应"。其他经济学家们表示,"目前非正规部门的发展似乎反映了纯粹的生存逻辑"。

国际劳工组织(ILO)等国际组织正密切关注经济的非正规化。据该组织估计,巴哈马等发展中国家创造的新就业岗位中,至少有70%目前处于非正规部门。

这是由于私营部门、政府私有化项目规模缩减,公共部门就业机会减少,经济不振。人们为了生存才进入非正式部门就业。

塞奇•拉图什在其著作《弃儿之星》中提出了一种源于弃儿发展的自发力量的发展模式。这一观点源于这样一个事实,即非正规部门的存在和日益发展只是排外的经济表现。

毫无例外,巴哈马的非正规部门也呈增长态势,体现为以下各种形式。

① 几乎未受过正规培训、没有固定工作场所的个体经营者从事的小型贸易,如路边修车工、增长迅速的客/货运"黑车"(常出没于玛格丽特公主医院门诊部、各种城市市场、超值食品店、拿骚各地的贝类摊和水果蔬菜摊)、物业和景观维护公司的经营者、在建筑工地上从汽车后备厢卖食品的小商人、向酿酒厂出售啤酒瓶的拾荒者,以及卖花生和报纸的小贩。

② 技能水平低,雇佣劳动力少,特别是食品外卖行业;99美分的早餐市场在拿骚随处可见。这些类型的经济实体需要一定数量的启动资金才能开展业务。

在新普罗维登斯岛的很多低收入地区,相当多的人按月做着小生意,卖汽水、馅饼和"酷爱"牌自制冰棍等。

③ 也有个人从事更高调的经济活动,但其逃避手续制度,没有经营许可证,不为员工缴纳国民保险,无视保护雇员和消费者的其他监管准则,在家中经营或使用有关政府机构没有批准的场所。

这些人可能在正规部门受过良好的专业培训,具备专门知识,但已决定在非正规部门从业,为的是抵制"现行经济体制"。

上周,财政部部长表示,自1992年8月以来,在自由民族运动的执政下,正规部门创造了大约14 500个就业岗位。我想知道是否有人能告诉我们,因裁员等措施以及老百姓赚钱求生的意愿而产生的非正规部门的就业岗位又有多少。随着劳动力市场的变化,雇主需要适应性更强的员工,因为新技术开始发展,员工需具备更多知识和技术。非正规部门将在巴哈马经济中发挥非常重要的作用，正如国际劳工组织估计的那样，非正规部门会创造更多的就业机会，远超统计局和中央银行发布的数据。

像巴哈马这样的发展中国家所面临的挑战是制定适当的机制，让非正规经济中正在发生的经济活动合法化。

非正规经济或许是挖掘第三世界国家人民真正创造性潜力的途径，特别是那些以前被抛弃、现在被排除在正规经济之外的人。目前巴哈马社会中非正规经济的从业者很可能是 20 世纪 90 年代真正的企业家。

非正规经济：人力资本投资

上周，本专栏界定了什么是非正规经济，并举例说明了非正规经济在巴哈马，尤其是在城市飞地的情况。经济学家认为，限制非正规经济增长的要素是加大对人力资本的投资。简言之，人力资本是劳动力的同义词。

为实现有效的人力资本投资，必须首先建立一个全面的经济政策框架。该框架包括以下内容：

① 善政廉政，确保稳定；

② 经济管理，最大限度地调动资源，促进可持续发展；

③ 人力资源管理，支持创造就业和创收，减少贫困；

④ 企业发展，突出私营部门在过度发展中的关键作用；

⑤ 科学技术提高人口效率，促进基础设施建设。

与此同时，还必须有恰当的投资激励机制，和正常运行的资本、金融及劳动力市场。

第①条巴哈马政府做得相对成功。至于第②条，巴哈马政府高度重视旅游业和金融服务业，因此，建立了各种机构如巴哈马酒店培训学院，并在巴哈马大学内设置相关系部，支持这些领域的人力资源开发，符合上述第③条的内容。第④和第⑤条做得不好。这表明巴哈马政府在很大程度上依赖公共部门创造就业机会，因此，无法满足不断增长的人口就业需求。巴哈马技术职业学院努力满足经济发展中贸易、技术就业，特别是建筑业、轻工业和制造业等行业的人力培训需求。

从这五个方面来看，人力资本不足愈发明显。因此，人力资源投资的需求变得更加重要。这是未来一个世纪中政府会面临的挑战，而解决这些问题的能力将决定能否凭借正规经济结构真正减少贫困，增加就业机会。这一机制能够带来可持续增长，从而改善广大民众的总体生活质量。

非正规经济的存在表明，人力资源中的一部分人只有通过这一途径才能生存下去。而这些人并不具备在非正规经济中竞争的技能，另外，非正规经济的发展尚不足以满足巴哈马的就业需求。

正规部门和非正规部门的规模将表明国家对人力资本的投资是否朝着正确的方向发展。

第8章 ››

加勒比巴哈马：找寻粮食生产的解决之道

> "单靠政治法令想要成功孕育一个土生土长的新社会是不可能的，即便法治能推动并维持这一进程。但是人，无论其文化、种族或阶级出身如何，必须投资于两种本质上仅为人类所有的文明设施。对此，我指的是智力和想象力。"
>
> ——牙买加和加勒比文化偶像，雷克斯·内特尔福德教授

加勒比各国之间差异很大。然而，当人们将该地区视为一个整体时，由于岛屿国家与大陆国家在农业产量、出口能力、自然资源上各不相同，会呈现出高度的多元化。

加勒比经济体的多元构成体现在这些国家为赚取外汇而出口的产品上。

1995—1999 年，加勒比共同体中有 5 个蔗糖出口国（巴巴多斯、伯利兹、圭亚那、牙买加以及圣基茨和尼维斯）。现在，只剩伯利兹、圭亚那和牙买加。巴巴多斯、圣基茨和尼维斯已转为发展服务业（旅游和金融服务）。

由于欧盟终止了对加勒比地区的香蕉优惠政策，加勒比东部国家的香蕉产业遭到冲击。在东加勒比的次区域，多米尼克、圣卢西亚、圣文森特和格林纳丁斯的经济受到了不利影响，因为有大量小农从事香蕉生产。

从工业角度看，加勒比出口一系列产品：电子元件、服装等制造业产品，化学品、钢材、机械、运输工具等工业产品，以及石油和燃料、霰石、盐、铝土矿和氧化铝等矿物产品。（见表 8.1）

欧盟对加勒比和 / 或加勒比论坛存在贸易顺差。（见表 8.2）15 个国家中仅有 4 个国家（牙买加、圭亚那、伯利兹和多米尼克）因农产品出口而对欧盟有贸易顺差，有 10 个国家（巴哈马、多米尼加共和国、特立尼达和多巴哥、圣文森特和格林纳丁斯、安提瓜和巴布达、巴巴多斯、圣卢西亚、海地、格林纳达以及圣基茨和

表 8.1 加勒比地区出口额占世界出口总额的百分比(1995—1999年,5年平均值)

加勒比共同体	朗姆酒、糖、糖蜜	香蕉	柑橘	黄金	石油和燃料	化学品	铝土矿和氧化铝	肥皂	电子元件	机械和运输工具	服装	海鲜	香料	可可	木材	大米	面粉	钢材	霰石	盐	娱乐
安提瓜和巴布达①																					
巴哈马②	x		x									x							x	x	x
巴巴多斯	16.2					10.1			10.3												
伯利兹		13.8	18																		
多米尼克	26	32.3						30.1			9.6	9.9			1.1						
格林纳达		5.4									4.8	13.7	22.0	11.9							
圭亚那	24.6			22.1			15.6								2.2	14.5					
牙买加	7.4						42.6				14.9										x
圣基茨和尼维斯	35.0									50.9											
圣卢西亚		41.3									9.9										
圣文森特和格林纳丁斯		35.3														11.6	15.0				
苏里南					3.6		76.9					7.8				7.1					
特立尼达和多巴哥					46.2	24.3												7.8			

来源:国际货币基金组织工作人员评估测定

① 2003年:数据不足。
② 巴哈马向美国市场出口一系列柑橘类水果(酸橙、橙子、葡萄柚),价值1 460万美元;向欧盟出口龙虾,价值1.08亿美元;霰石价值50万美元。
2004年:盐价值1 240万美元,朗姆酒价值3 130万美元,电影业(大巴哈马电影制片厂)。
1985—1993年:牙买加的娱乐业不断扩大,涉足电影拍摄(价值5 000万美元)和音乐制作(有50个录音棚)。

尼维斯)与欧盟存在贸易逆差,还有 1 个国家(苏里南)与之持平。

表 8.2　2005 年欧盟—加勒比贸易概况

加勒比论坛	欧盟 25 国出口额 (百万欧元)	欧盟 25 国进口额 (百万欧元)	欧盟贸易差额 (百万欧元)
巴哈马	1 591	1 027	+564
多米尼加共和国	793	474	+319
牙买加	406	751	−345
特立尼达和多巴哥	536	507	+29
圣文森特	286	263	+23
安提瓜和巴布达	219	121	+98
巴巴多斯	157	88	+69
苏里南	192	192	0
圭亚那	60	170	−110
圣卢西亚	159	60	+99
伯利兹	99	114	−15
海地	109	16	+93
格林纳达	37	11	+26
多米尼克	18	21	−3
圣基茨和尼维斯	22	8	+14
			+861

来源:农业贸易

　　对于加勒比的大多数国家而言,糖和香蕉一直是传统出口商品。然而由于这两种商品的全球环境不断变化,加勒比的大部分国家已转向发展服务业或增加农业生产的多样性,实现粮食安全目标,和 / 或为旅游市场提供特定服务。

　　部分岛国已开始实施经济多元化战略,以减少对出口农业的依赖,同时满足国内需求,从而解决粮食安全问题,满足旅游市场,如推广有机农业以满足新鲜蔬菜的市场需求。

　　为发展新兴行业,有的多元化战略是横向的。这体现在加勒比盆地计划的推行实施上。该计划在牙买加、海地、多米尼加共和国以及像巴巴多斯这样的其他加勒比共同体国家中建立自由贸易区。

　　有些行业已经出现了纵向多元化现象,比如旅游业内部就出现了多元化发展。在农业方面,牙买加和伯利兹正效仿巴西,用甘蔗生产乙醇。

旅游业的这种纵向多元化表现在健康水疗（牙买加、英属维尔京群岛），医学教育（格林纳达、多米尼克、多米尼加共和国），生态旅游和体育旅游方面。亚特兰蒂斯等超级酒店给加勒比旅游业带来了新的发展空间。

单靠阳光、沙滩和大海不足以吸引游客。自 1995 年以来，加勒比旅游业所占的市场份额就在一直下滑。加勒比共同体的情况尤其如此，1960 年其游客量占全球游客总量的 0.91%，而 2002 年已降至 0.69%。据世界银行称，这是受古巴新兴产品的影响。

世界银行的报告指出，下滑体现了竞争力不足的问题，即劳动力薪水高，技能不足且技术适应性差。

以特立尼达和多巴哥在石油行业的纵向多元化为例。20 世纪七八十年代，其出口产品几乎全是原油。20 世纪 80 年代以来，该国的石油行业开始向多元化发展，涵盖油气精炼、液化天然气生产和石油化工产品。

行业纵向多元化的优点是不易受到外部市场冲击的影响。

加勒比各国政府仍然认为有必要多元化发展经济，从严重依赖农业出口转向其他经济活动，因为人口数量不断增加，与之相适应的工作岗位亟待解决。例如海地，移民问题正是由于新增人口缺乏就业机会造成的。

像海地一样，牙买加也一直在努力应对创造就业的挑战。1990 年美国人口普查显示，有 159 913 名牙买加人移民美国，占牙买加总人口的 15%。

这意味着牙买加的人才外流。在这些移民中，23% 受过中等教育，67% 受过中等以上教育。

移民已成为失业问题的表现。据国际货币基金组织统计，加勒比已有 10%—40% 的劳动力移民至经济合作与发展组织成员国。对一些加勒比国家而言，形势相当严峻，因为在受过 12 年完整学校教育的人中有多达 70% 的人选择移民。如此高的移民率使加勒比成为全世界接收汇款最多的地区，甚至占国内生产总值一定的百分比。据国际货币基金组织统计，2002 年，加勒比地区的汇款占区域内国家生产总值的 13%。

加勒比单一市场和经济关于人员自由流动的规定对解决移民问题将有很大的帮助。尽管巴哈马不是加勒比单一市场和经济的成员国，但非官方报告显示，巴哈马的加勒比共同体公民比其他任何加勒比共同体国家的都多。在巴巴多斯，对熟练建筑工人的需求给其带来了大量的圭亚那商人。

过去几十年（20 世纪 60 年代至 90 年代），加勒比各国的三个主要行业（农业、工业和服务业）均发生了转变。全球化的现实对加勒比经济的结构调整产生了巨大影响。农业的跌幅最大，其国内生产总值的增长率不超过 1.4%，对国内生产总值的贡献微乎其微。另一方面，服务业，尤其是旅游业的国内生产总值增长十分显著。

为了扭转加勒比农业衰退的局面，加勒比共同体发起了贾格迪奥倡议。这是最近的一项举措，此前还有其他的应对措施。1975 年推出的地区粮食计划旨在增加国内生产，但以失败告终。失败的原因之一是加勒比共同体各国政府未能兑现承诺。

1983 年制定的地区粮食和营养战略遇到了与地区粮食计划类似的问题。六年后（1989 年），加勒比共同体农业发展计划开始实施，取代了地区粮食和营养战略。

同年，东加勒比国家组织制订了自己的农业多元化计划。

加勒比共同体农业发展计划于 1995 年接受评估，评估发现该计划存在几处缺陷，即公共部门和私营部门认识不足。1996 年，区域农业转型计划得以制订，目的是纠正其他区域计划的一些局限性。

自 2002 年起，农业区域转型计划的框架便以六种商品为基础，即椰子和油脂、小型反刍动物——绵羊和山羊、家禽、甘薯、辣椒和木瓜。该计划得到了加勒比共同体秘书处的支持，另有成员国代表的协助，目的是在国家层面落实该计划。

反思上述这些计划，可以得出加勒比农业衰退的几个原因。由于各国政府害怕将行业控制权交给区域官员，因此，从未有过成功的区域性计划。

投资农业，实现区域粮食安全

温斯顿·菲利普斯博士建议如下：

"大约 25 年前，有人建议加勒比共同体各国政府从进口粮食总量中拨出一部分，专门从加勒比共同体国家进口。尽管这一想法旨在鼓励各国为实现加勒比共同体的目标付诸行动，但在当时，该想法被认为是给各国政府强加数量限制，因而被毫不客气地抛弃了；即使现实情况是，在不作为（即没有'数量限制'）的情况下，区域内贸易相对于粮食进口总量几乎不存在。至此，农产品销售协议以失败告终。我认为，现在是加勒比共同体各国政府和我们的专业人员面对现实，甚至是面对加勒比共同体的部分政治错误的时候了。首先通过争取区域内私营部门的投资，其次鼓励私营部门参与投资，来设法发掘某些国家在农业生产方面的相对优势。例如，主亚那和伯利兹需要加强农业基础设施建设,并开展审慎的计划来吸引加勒比地区的投资者投资其农业部门,其他国家则需要鼓励本国投资者积极参与投资。石油储量丰富的特立尼达不仅有可能投资农业生产,还可能投资农产品加工。在加勒比地区,我们长期以来一直在争取旅游业,甚至银行业和互联网服务的投资;为什么不采取同样的方法吸引农业投资呢?除非各国政府和人民采取审慎措施,利用好加勒比地区的相对优势,否则,加勒比共同体建立的所有促进框架,如加勒比单一市场和经济框架,都将毫无意义。据我所知,有些观点认为,在这个以知识为基础的世界,相对优势的概念早已改变,但请告诉我,加勒比共同体中哪些国家称得上拥有成本相对较低的(农业)生产?"

找寻解决之道

加勒比地区各国政府、农业专业人员以及农学家无力发展可持续农业,本地区的人民对此颇感失望。这反映在过去 40 年来,农业部门的国内生产总值不断下降,农业对加勒比地区经济的贡献微不足道。(见表 8.3)

表 8.3　各行业国内生产总值增长率及其对国内生产总值增长的贡献

	农　业	工　业	服务业
行业增长率			
20 世纪 60 年代	1.4	4.9	5.3
20 世纪 70 年代	0.5	7.0	5.8
20 世纪 80 年代	0.3	4.6	4.9
20 世纪 90 年代	1.2	3.9	3.3
对国内生产总值增长的贡献			
20 世纪 60 年代	0.2	2.0	3.9
20 世纪 70 年代	0.0	2.0	3.3
20 世纪 80 年代	0.1	1.1	2.8
20 世纪 90 年代	0.1	0.8	2.4

来源:世界银行(世界发展指标)

加勒比农业一直以小农为基础,但政治当局为了赢得选票,支持非竞争性的"福利农业"制度,尤其是在内部自治阶段和独立时期,几乎没为小农群体带来什么创新技术。

农业是保持农村人口"就业"的机制,以防城市人口膨胀。尽管如此,农村青年还是想到城市中心寻求就业机会。

农业的纵向多元化可以避免农村人口向城市迁移。农业产业化会在农村地区提供与农业相关的就业机会，从而为农村青年和女性创造新的就业机会。

找寻加勒比农业发展的解决之道必须从三个关键要素或方面考虑，分别为小农、可持续农业、贸易。

从这三个关键方面看区域内农业部门的表现，可清楚地发现：过去 40 年（1960—2000 年）中，加勒比地区的农业发展欠佳，这对本地区各国的经济增长和发展产生了负面影响。

1. 小农

20 世纪五六十年代，西印度群岛大学的农业经济学家大卫·爱德华兹教授在其著作《牙买加小农经济研究》中强调了小农的状况以及牙买加小农经济的状况。阿瑟·刘易斯爵士也指出，有必要发展工业或服务业，以便吸收农业部门的剩余劳动力。圣卢西亚经济学家阿瑟·刘易斯爵士曾担任西印度群岛大学副校长、加勒比开发银行总裁，1979 年因提出"二元经济模型"和"贸易条件模型"理论获得诺贝尔经济学奖。在二元经济模型中，刘易斯研究了劳动力从传统部门（农业）向现代部门（服务业，如旅游业）的转移。在贸易条件模型中，他概述了发达国家和发展中国家之间贸易往来的运作方式。在巴哈马，旅游业的增长和发展能吸收家庭岛（农村地区）未充分利用的劳动力进入酒店业工作，尤其是女性。在特立尼达和多巴哥，石油行业一直是主要的就业部门。

几十年来，上述情况并未发生。巴巴多斯、安提瓜、圣基茨和尼维斯以及特立尼达和多巴哥等国在一定程度上减少了对甘蔗生产的依赖。

家禽子产业是农业纵向多元化的一个典型例子。在牙买加、巴巴多斯、特立尼达和多巴哥，家禽综合企业以小农为基础。小农与企业签订合同，企业参与饲料生产、家禽加工，或二者兼营，这促进了家禽综合企业的发展。

通过加勒比家禽协会的努力，该行业已成为区域农业中最具竞争力的子产业之一。这是因为小型家禽合同农户已然成为农业综合企业经营者，对世界贸易组织规定的食品安全、技术、等级、标准以及国际贸易规则十分敏感。

在整个加勒比地区，特别是在加勒比共同体国家，有超过十万名小农从事禽肉农业综合企业生产。加勒比家禽协会通过其项目表明，小农可以成为农业综合企业经营者，并颇具竞争力；然而，必须对家禽子产业进行结构调整，以增强大型农业综合企业的实力，从而弥补小农自身的缺陷，如规模经济。

在贸易自由化的时代,小型家禽合同农户必须在市场力量驱动的环境中求生存。在这种环境中,一方面从给予农户国内资助和出口补贴的国家进口家禽副产品,另一方面市场准入规则十分严格。通过其自身的竞争力,这些小型家禽合同农户得以生存。而禽肉是加勒比地区蛋白质的主要来源。

据估计,2006年加勒比有4 000万—4 500万人。有些国家,如海地、伯利兹、圭亚那,还有牙买加,仍存在大量小农。小农人口的数量多达本地区农业总人口的10%—15%。这体现在以农业为经济基础的国家,农业对国内生产总值的贡献率高,而国民的人均收入较低。

20世纪六七十年代,农业占加勒比地区就业的30%。(见表8.4)到了20世纪80年代,情况出现重大变化,这主要是受到全球化的影响,加勒比地区不再享有欧洲市场的特惠待遇。

表 8.4　农业就业率(20 世纪六七十年代)

农业就业人口占总劳动力人口的比率		
国家	20 世纪 60 年代	20 世纪 70 年代
巴巴多斯	26	16
圭亚那	37	29
牙买加	39	29
特立尼达和多巴哥	21	16
东加勒比国家组织	46	32

来源:世界银行

随着加勒比共同体经济从20世纪70年代开始向旅游业方向发展,就业开始从农业转向服务业。

为实现这一转变,劳动力必须迁至工业或服务业,而且相关行业也必须达到更高程度的纵向多元化。

20世纪下半叶,农业在加勒比地区已不占优势,不再是主导这些岛国经济的支柱产业。新世界秩序的确立,促使旅游业兴起。财富增加了,交通方式也在改变,殖民主义瓦解,曾经被征服的人民如今大步向前,掌握了政府统治权,为其国家开辟出一条全新的、不同的发展道路。

服务业,特别是旅游业,是加勒比共同体国家独立时期的产物,也是古巴和多米尼加共和国战后兴起的产业。尽管太子港的旅游业有一定程度的发展,但旅游业对海地的影响并不像对整个加勒比地区那样深远。

尽管加勒比的旅游业在总体上取得了成功,但从区域角度来看,它正在全球市场上失去一席之地。为使加勒比地区发展为旅游目的地，加勒比旅游组织应发挥更大作用，包括调查研究，通过建立标准和认证机制实现区域质量控制，成立评估机构，从而确保该地区作为旅游目的地的竞争力。加勒比旅游机构认识到，必须采取积极行动，将加勒比作为一种旅游产品进行推广。2006 年 11 月在古巴哈瓦那举行的第一次大加勒比旅游部部长会议上，与会部长签署了《最后声明》。

《最后声明》是一项战略计划，其重点在于吸引游客赴加勒比旅游，据联合国世界旅游组织预测，未来四年旅游业将会增加。

尽管《最后声明》是一项战略计划，但其没有反映食品生产和安全情况。应对加勒比地区的食品供给进行有效预测，以满足区域内旅游市场不断扩大的供应量，同时确保食品链安全。

这应是加勒比旅游组织和相关食品监管部门向所有成员国规定的区域目标。

（1）小农：背景分析

爱德华兹在《牙买加小农经济研究》中提到了一些有意思的观点，有助于了解牙买加小农经济的起源，并进而得窥加勒比小农的开端。

其研究表述如下：

> "一个多世纪以前，奴隶尚未被解放，牙买加的农业以种植园的组织形式为主。从那时起，奴隶的后代建立起数以千计的小农场……在总共 150 万人口中，约有 90 万人以务农为生。在近 61.5 万有偿就业人口中，约有 30 万人从事农业工作。因此，在牙买加农业为 1/5 的全国人口或者近 1/3 的 14 岁以上人口提供了就业机会。农业占其国内生产总值的 19%。"

这是 20 世纪 50 年代牙买加小农经济的情况。当时，牙买加的"人均收入为 78 英镑"，在今天还不到 200 美元。

爱德华兹教授声称：

> "小农经济的出现虽然主要与牙买加有关，但也适用于西印度群岛及其他许多不发达国家的小农式农业，尽管环境不同，但基本特征是相似的。"

这项研究由殖民地经济研究委员会发起，该委员会成员由英国各大学的经济学家组成，目的是就"殖民地"的经济研究向殖民地大臣提出建议。

当时牙买加政府正在考虑启动一项重大农业发展计划，于是这项研究随即展开。小农在农业部门中发挥着重要作用,因此,有必要对其进行研究。研究工作由三方共同开展,主要参与者包括殖民地经济研究委员会成员爱德华兹、牙买加政府和西印度群岛大学的社会与经济研究院。

殖民地部也非常关注移民问题。1953—1955 年,有 27 000 名牙买加人移民到英国,这不包括来自西印度群岛的英语殖民地的移民。这项研究旨在帮助"了解牙买加一些更为重要的小农经济制度的经济和其他相关方面,以便评估改进小农经济制度的可能性"。

牙买加努力应对小农社会的挑战之时,巴哈马正在将其经济结构从以农业为基础调整为以服务业为基础,即旅游业;旅游业正从季节性活动转变为全年生意,最终发展成巴哈马经济的主要部门。

随着这种调整,人力从农田大规模流向酒店业。这种转变的受益者之一是现在在酒店业占主导地位的女性。

在《经济增长理论》一书中,阿瑟·刘易斯爵士就小农问题指出了以下几点。

> "实际上,在大多数经济落后的(发展中)国家,为家庭消费提供食品的农业部门是众多产业中发展最缓慢的,因此,制约了整体经济增长。这是因为当农业掌握在小农手中时,新技术的引进更多地取决于政府而非私营企业主的主动性。[①]
>
> 但是,要增加农民的农业产量,需要采取一系列基本上属于政府范畴的措施;首先是在农业研究和推广上投入大量资金,其次在公路建设、农村供水、农业信贷设施等方面加大经费支出。"

农业部门投入低的状况一直持续到 21 世纪。在以下所选的加勒比共同体国家中,政府的农业支出相对较低。各国的农业支出占其国内生产总值的百分比,从 6.8%(2001 年)低至 0.6%(2002 年)不等。(见表 8.5)

表 8.5 政府用于农业和研究的支出占所选国家国内生产总值的百分比

所选国家	年 份	
	2001	2002
安提瓜和巴布达	1.9	无
巴哈马	0.8	0.6

---

① 正是这一事实促使人们更关注农业综合企业的发展。农业综合企业在加勒比地区禽肉生产中取得了成功。

续表

所选国家	年　份	
	2001	**2002**
巴巴多斯	2.7	2.6
格林纳达	6.3	5.7
圭亚那	5.0	3.9
牙买加	0.7	0.7
圣卢西亚	6.8	6.0
特立尼达和多巴哥	2.6	2.2

来源：2005 年 6 月美洲农业合作研究所区域总监在巴哈马的讲话

农业投资下滑的现象一直持续到新世纪。

刘易斯进一步解释道：

> "日本的经验表明，政府在农业领域的适当投入会对农民增产有显著效果。这样农业非但不会落后于其他部门，阻碍经济发展，反而会起到带头作用，对其他产业有所需求，并向其提供资金。但在这种情况下，大多数国家的政府忽视了小农农业，导致其发展受阻，拉低了其他产业的增长率。"

事实上，这一点在加勒比得到了反映，即该地区粮食短缺，无法为区域内各国人民和数百万游客提供足够的粮食。造成这种情况的原因是以小农为主的农业部门的效率低下。

在加勒比，农业部门的创新仅限于农业综合企业这一子部门，在小农中并不普遍。然而，旅游业却是创新基础广泛。刘易斯指出："除非其他部门也适当发展，否则单个经济部门的创新会受到制约。"尽管旅游业有所增长，但整个加勒比地区的农业产量没有跟上。刘易斯认为，"经济的平稳发展需要工业（和／或服务业）和农业共同增长。"然而这并未实现，因为农业发展一直滞后。

爱德华兹的《牙买加小农经济研究》表明，在 20 世纪 50 年代，约有 90 万人（也可能是 100 万人）从事小农经济，占牙买加人口的 60%。刘易斯比较后发现：法国在 20 世纪 50 年代需要全国 25% 的人口务农才能保证国内供给，而在美国和加拿大等工业化国家，这个数字仅接近 10%。

加勒比的小农农业若不想被淘汰，必须变得更精简、更高效，并通过技术和加大研究投入来提高生产力。为了实现这一目标，加勒比地区各国政府必须增加对农业的支出，因为正如爱德华兹的《牙买加小农经济研究》中所述，半个世纪前小农群体面临的诸多问题，今天仍然存在。具体表现在：无论在国家层面还是地区层面，农业对国内生产总值的贡献都不理想。

（2）小农：一种资源

小农在加勒比农业中并没有明确的界定。在有些国家，小农被认为是向旧时代的倒退，是一种社会负担，对国库没有贡献抑或浪费国家财政。这一群体已被丑化，成为加勒比农业失败的替罪羊。

在某些方面，小农经济往往意味着失败和过时。对许多决策者来说，小农经济存在的问题很多，但解决方案十分有限。从一个时代到另一个时代，人们对小农经济的关注逐渐减弱。从国家层面看，小农经济在各国农业部门中所起的作用有时取决于政治气候、捐助者的态度或者国际机构的议程，而不是帮助这一群体克服市场力量等经济挑战，或者提高利益攸关方的竞争力。

在国家和地区层面分别确定小农的战略作用之前，小农经济将继续下滑，并最终从加勒比各国的农业部门中消失。

20 世纪 50 年代中期，90 万牙买加人被束缚在这片土地上。小农经济被指责是死路一条。当时，这些小农都寄希望于牙买加政府，指望政府能在英联邦的特惠市场上为他们的甘蔗、香蕉、柑橘或咖啡谈一个好价格和配额。然而如今，世界贸易组织的《农业协定》取消了这一优惠政策，导致加勒比地区的数百万小农面临经济不确定、社会不稳定的局面，造成数千人流离失所。随着工业化国家逐步停止接收移民，移民不再是条可靠的出路。正是在这种背景下，加勒比各国政府必须为小农制订可持续发展的经济计划。

这些计划必须包含两个方面。第一，削减赤字，由于无法满足本国的粮食需求，所有国家均面临赤字问题；第二，减少进口，目前加勒比地区的进口主要是为了满足数百万乘飞机或船来此旅游的游客的粮食需求。

小农是奴隶制的传统。加勒比的奴隶获得解放，赢得自由后，为了维持生计，他们沿用从奴隶主那学来的技术进行耕作。对他们来说，耕作没有科学指导，而是反复试错后得出的经验传统。这种传统逐渐演变成一种技艺，年复一年，地复一地，世代相传。

一般很少有人意识到要将耕作的技艺与科学结合起来，或者用技术专家的话说，将本地的农耕经验与科学知识结合起来。

20 世纪 60 年代，我在特立尼达的西印度群岛大学攻读研究生，我的毕业论文研究的是特立尼达洛皮诺／拉帕斯托拉地区采用的农耕方式。洛皮诺／拉帕斯托拉位于北部的一个农村公社，距东主道约 8 英里。可可和咖啡是那儿的主要作物。种植园归一名法国人所有，但由奴隶负责种植可可和咖啡，经营庄园。对于洛皮诺 / 拉帕斯托拉地区的农耕经济来说，更好的农耕指南是《麦克唐纳的农民历》。

当时，我作为农业部的技术推广官员在巴哈马的东南部群岛上工作。这些岛上的小农是奴隶的后代，从 20 世纪 60 年代至今，他们仍然在"坑洞"或矮林地上采用刀耕火种的原始技术。其耕作依赖于较低的外部投入。

1776 年前后，一群保皇派农场主来到巴哈马谋生，他们在巴哈马的东南部种植棉花，由此形成了一些农村公社，当时美国正在争取脱离英国独立。

这些保皇派农场主主要来自美国南部，他们带着各自的奴隶到巴哈马东南部的群岛上定居。出于各种农艺原因，他们试种的棉花未能成功，这让他们和奴隶们在养殖小型反刍动物（绵羊和山羊）的同时，不得不从事劳动密集型的作物耕作。

在洛皮诺 / 拉帕斯托拉地区和巴哈马东南部，小农只能依靠本地的农耕经验，而政府机构几乎毫不关心他们所使用的耕作技术或技艺的科学价值。

尽管资源匮乏，小农还是生存了下来。他们的生存本能应该具体化为可以提升的技术，从而增强他们在小农经济中的竞争力。但决策者们往往忽略小农的潜力，在制定政策和计划时将其排除在外。另一方面，私营部门的立场则全然不同。

家禽类农业综合企业的合同养殖户之所以成功，是因为私营部门的经营者与利益攸关的小农通力合作，成果显著，这才使家禽类农业综合企业在加勒比地区得以幸存。自上而下式的殖民传统依旧影响着政府部门和机构的管理理念。而这可能正是加勒比地区农业失败的主要原因之一。

小农在农业多功能性中发挥着举足轻重的作用。是小农与环境直接接触，是小农维系着农村地方社区，是小农的价值体系和职业道德为国家建设和良好公民的塑造树立了楷模。

经过多年甚至几代人的努力，小农已经设计出了与环境相适应的耕作制度，使其能生产和养殖一系列作物和牲畜。而他们面临的挑战是如何使这些耕作制度适应市场力量。为此小农必须发挥自身实力，与那些得到研究扶持、国家资助、出口补贴和规模经济下的商品进行竞争。

加勒比是一个粮食短缺的地区，许多国家都面临粮食不安全问题。服务业，尤其是旅游业的增长，加剧了粮食短缺问题。服务业的收益用于进口粮食，其中一部分可由小农供应。

一些国家近期出现了粮食短缺问题。究其原因，是过去这些国家的小农社会能满足国内若干食品的消费需求，能在一定程度上实现自给自足。然而，随着经济的变化，人们对方便食品的需求越来越大。城市化发展，女性逐渐成为劳动力的关键组成部分，这导致本土食品在国民消费中丧失了原本的重要地位。

许多国家的决策者忽视了小农在维持自给自足方面的作用。例如，就圣基茨和尼维斯而言，政府已决定将其经济转向服务业，并引导小农经济团体到其他领域就业。

确定小农的数量并对小农经济做出界定绝非易事。一般来说，可以查看农业普查的结果；但农业普查每十年才进行一次。在一些国家，农业部出于各种原因仍然将务农人员登记在册。例如，在飓风、干旱、火灾、洪水等自然灾害过后用来核对登记农户受灾情况是否属实，是否有资格获得补贴、免税优惠或者援助。另外，也可以通过协会、合作社或者商业团体得知小农数量。牙买加、巴巴多斯、特立尼达和多巴哥政府认可农业协会为小农的代表。

表 8.6 显示了整个加勒比地区小农的分布。小农是个特殊群体，需要具体计划来提升其竞争力，但有的国家没有将小农与资源丰富的大农区分开来。

表 8.6　各国小农情况

国　家	年　份	类　　别	农民数量	小农数量	来　　源
安提瓜和巴布达	2005	牲畜	2 000	?	联合国粮食及农业组织登记资料：管控圈养和散养牲畜技术合作计划①；该数据已在网上发布
			5 000	?	国家中期投资计划（NMTIP）文件：50% 全职，50% 兼职
巴巴多斯				?	无数据；农业部承诺给予数据，但并未细分为小农和大农；国家中期投资计划文件中没有相关数据
		已登记	3 000	2 000	巴巴多斯农业协会正在建立农民登记数据库，并估算小农数量
巴哈马	2004	已登记	2 000	1 242	联合国粮食及农业组织登记资料：2004 年 9 月 10 日致 H. 克拉伦登的附信；农业部审批登记的农民；详情参见章节注释
伯利兹	2004	农作物和牲畜，以小农为主	12 000	12 000	登记资料：2004 年，农业部门战略项目文件草案；国家中期投资计划文件：小农遍地，但无具体数据

① 译者注：TCP 为 Technical Cooperation Programme 缩写形式，意为技术合作计划。

续表

国　家	年　份	类　别	农民数量	小农数量	来　源
多米尼克			?	?	国家中期投资计划文件：无数据
多米尼加共和国			?	?	国家中期投资计划文件：无数据
格林纳达	2004	根据登记信息，至少有 14 000 个小农		14 000	登记资料：2004 年 8 月至 9 月，飓风后恢复农业部门的投资建议；国家中期投资计划文件：无数据；详情参见章节注释，土地利用调查
	2006	肉豆蔻		10 000	国家中期投资计划文件
	2006	可可		3 500	国家中期投资计划文件：大约 14 000 人是正确数据
圭亚那				5 000	联合国粮食及农业组织登记资料：2005 年 3 月，紧急援助受洪水影响的农民项目文件草案；国家中期投资计划文件：无数据
海地	2004				联合国粮食及农业组织登记资料：2004 年 8 月至 9 月，飓风后恢复农业部门的投资建议；海地暂无数据
牙买加	2004		200 000	100 000	联合国粮食及农业组织登记资料：2004 年 8 月至 9 月，飓风后恢复农业部门的投资建议；国家中期投资计划文件：无数据；详情参见章节注释中的 H. B. 伯纳德备忘录
圣基茨和尼维斯			3 084	?	圣基茨和尼维斯：国家中期投资计划和 2000 年银行担保投资项目概况；农业和渔业普查；国家中期投资计划文件：农作物、小型反刍动物、牲畜、商业；无数据
圣卢西亚	2006		841	?	国家中期投资计划文件："农民"；无资质认证或数据
圣文森特	2006		1 000	?	国家中期投资计划文件：1 000 名农民准备接受培训
苏里南					
特立尼达和多巴哥			?	?	国家中期投资计划文件：农民数量下降 37.5%；无农民资质认证，未提及具体数量

来源：联合国粮食及农业组织登记资料，2006 年国家中期投资计划文件，互联网；联合国粮食及农业组织统计数据库中没有数据

在拉丁美洲，小农和勉强糊口／没有土地的农民分属两类，这种区分更为

明显。在一些加勒比国家，勉强糊口／没有土地的农民可能是拓荒者，也可能是佃农以租佃分成或者其他形式维持生计。无论属哪种情况，小农都是一种未充分利用的资源。

在牙买加等国家，棘手之处在于如何处理那些没有土地或者持有土地面积超过 1 公顷但不足 5 公顷的农民问题。解决办法是在国有土地上实施土地安置计划，或者通过分割大型种植园将有经济效益的地块分配给没有土地和土地稀少的农民。

由于缺少这类土地规划师，这群农民中很大一部分要么涌入城市，要么移民到国外，目的地通常是给其汇款的国外亲属的所在国。亚拉斯谷土地管理局就是牙买加政府专门设立的用来解决没有土地或土地边缘化问题的机构。

作为加勒比共同体最大的国家，牙买加有 15 000 名佃农，另有 115 000 多名小农仅靠不到 1 公顷的土地维持生计。这两个群体合计包括 130 000 个小农。

再看看加勒比共同体中的小国格林纳达的农业部门的构成，其 71% 的农场面积不到 5 英亩。还有相当多的农户（27%）仅拥有 1—2 英亩土地。

若都像牙买加和格林纳达的情况一样，即小农所持土地面积如此之少，那么想通过务农改善生活几乎是不可能的。

（3）小农经济：逆转命运

加勒比地区的一些国家和农产品集团正逐渐认识到，必须采取措施改善小农的命运，并将这一群体作为其农业发展计划的重要组成部分。

多年来，小农一直被丑化成一种负担；如今，在一些国家，他们的命运正在被逆转。

• 古巴

古巴是加勒比地区最大的国家，其人口接近 1 200 万。过去 40 年里，古巴一直受到西半球乃至全球首富——美国的经济封锁。

古巴在政治和经济意识形态上是社会主义国家，与苏联和东欧集团同属一个阵营。随着冷战结束和苏联解体，古巴需要在其粮食生产计划上开辟一条新的道路。

古巴农业的工业化体现在对拖拉机的使用和对人造化肥，特别是氮肥（192 千克／公顷）[1] 的高投入方面。由于失去了苏联和东欧集团的特惠市场，古巴的糖价是世界市场价格的 3 倍。这一变故使古巴不得不参与世界市场竞争。实际

---

[1] 赖特，朱莉娅 . 古巴实施生态学习的经验 [J]. 可持续农业，2006，22.

上，古巴当时的处境与因世界贸易组织的考验而失去欧盟特惠市场的加勒比共同体国家的处境如出一辙。

古巴目前正面临粮食危机，因为无法进口供工业化粮食生产所需的农机和化肥，导致粮食生产受挫，粮食严重短缺。

为了扭转这一局面，古巴政府决定将粮食生产系统的重点放在以下几个方面上。

> "以当地知识、技能和资源为基础的技术上，而不是依赖进口生产资料……通过改善农村环境、增加农村就业机会、精简农场数量，让农民回到农村务农"。

这一战略的关键要素是扩大研究范围，更加重视推广服务以及让农民有地可种。

事实证明这一战略是成功的，因为粮食产量有所增加——"主食生产及产量翻了一番并持续增长，最重要的是，粮食供应基本恢复到可接受的水平"。而这一切主要归功于小农的农业产量。

• 圭亚那和苏里南

据圭亚那和苏里南的报道称，美洲农业合作研究所正在推广良好农业规范（GAP）[1]的概念，且这一举措正在小农中产生积极影响。这对于那些从事出口农业的小农尤为明显。

农作物的质量和数量都提高了；水污染和虫害也减少了。这得益于综合管理和农药的使用。

良好农业规范概念是小农经济生产转型的重要手段。详情参见章节注释。

• 加勒比共同体的家禽业

在加勒比共同体国家，禽肉是蛋白质的主要来源。就食用蛋而言，加勒比地区的自给率相当高（90%—95%）。而生产食用蛋的农业综合企业的支柱是小农。加勒比家禽协会对本地区农业综合企业的估值为 4.6 亿美元，这些企业在加勒比地区 14 个国家雇用了 30 000 人。

当加勒比地区受到可能暴发禽流感的威胁时，数以千计的人的生计会受到波及。在牙买加，家禽类的农业综合企业以小农为主，估计约有 10 000 人，其中大概 2 000 人是鸡蛋供应商，平均每人只有 25 只母鸡。

肉鸡的加工也多为小农经营。在加勒比共同体中，农产品加工商大致分三

---

[1] 章节注释里概述了良好农业规范的具体内容。

种(大型、小型和农舍加工)。小农和 / 或加工数不足 5 000 只禽类的加工商被归为农舍类别,具体情况如下。①

表 8.7　农舍家禽加工商与小农的概况

农舍家禽加工商在各国的市场份额		各国小农数量
巴巴多斯	30%	75
伯利兹	无数据	380
多米尼加共和国	80%	无数据
圭亚那	50%	100
牙买加	30%	10 000
东加勒比国家组织	无数据	380
苏里南	>96%	25
特立尼达和多巴哥	55%—60%	50

加勒比地区有 3 000—4 000 个农舍家禽加工商和大约 11 000 名小农。

为促进整个家禽业的发展,加勒比家禽协会开展了系列活动,无论是否是协会成员,无论经营规模的大小,均可参加。这对小农而言是巨大的财富,许多小农与饲料厂或加工厂签约,成了合同种植 / 养殖户。

小农和农舍家禽加工商为国家乃至整个加勒比地区的家禽生产做出了重大贡献。其家禽产量所占的市场份额已然印证了这一点。

小农和农舍家禽加工商的作用不言而喻;不过,要想使其更深入地融入整个农业综合企业,必须采取深思熟虑的举措。其中一项举措是三方合作,由加勒比家禽协会、国家政府机构(如农业部)和地方农民协会共同制定战略,推动小农和农舍家禽加工商加入农业综合企业,提高这一群体在全球化领域的竞争力,并鼓励和促进其采用新技术提高效率和产量。

加勒比家禽协会的计划旨在提高农业综合企业中所有参与者的竞争力,包括小农和农舍家禽加工商。具体举措如下所述。

① 地区学校和培训研讨会(2003—2005 年)。加勒比家禽协会就家禽农业综合企业的多个方面(技术升级、疾病预防和管理、编写农场和食品安全手册以及制定行业战略等)创办了六所地区学校并举行了十次国家培训研讨会。

② 调查。对家禽农业综合企业的多个子部门开展各项调查,旨在量化加勒比地区家禽业的产业构成及其对国内生产总值的价值和贡献。这包括国家登记

---

① 加勒比家禽协会,加勒比共同体农舍家禽加工商,操作守则。

计划。

③ 宣传。加勒比家禽协会作为行业代表分别在政府首脑和国家级会议上发声，反映业内关切的问题。还与农业协会、农民团体和合作社等非政府组织开展国家级合作。

④ 贸易谈判。加勒比家禽协会携手加勒比地区谈判机制，积极参与同世界贸易组织、美洲自由贸易区和加勒比单一市场和经济的谈判，设法将家禽申报为敏感性大宗商品。

加勒比家禽协会一直是帮助从事家禽业的小农在全球化时代谋生的力量。

本节中的三个例子是小农的未来如何由失败或边缘化转变成具有某种形式的经济可行性的示范。上述这些举措能真正把小农经济变为国家资源，并有助于加勒比地区农业的持续发展。

2. 可持续农业

加勒比地区生产的糖、香蕉、咖啡和柑橘在全球市场的同类商品中具有相对优势。加勒比的旅游业因阳光、沙滩和大海闻名于世。在农业和旅游业部门，环境是关键因素。

本地区所有独立国家都是联合国及其专门机构，如联合国粮食及农业组织的成员，这些国家也是国际公约（ICs）的签署国，尤其是与环境和贸易有关的公约。

（1）这意味着什么？

关于环境的国际公约有四项，即《联合国气候变化框架公约》（*UNFCC*）、《联合国防治荒漠化公约》（*UNCCD*）、《联合国生物多样性公约》（*UNCBD*）以及联合国森林论坛，其中联合国森林论坛基本上算是一项进程，而非公约。

国际社会通过这些公约引发关注，呼吁各方采取行动解决与人类命运息息相关的全球环境和发展问题。其中许多问题与环境有关，因为它们波及农业、渔业和林业。

在加勒比地区的一些国家，处理这些问题的责任由政府的几个部委分别承担。例如，在巴哈马，这些问题就由三个不同的部／司来分管：农业（农业和海洋资源部）、林业（土地和服务部）和环境部。国家政府面临的问题是能否在负责国际公约具体方面的各个部／司之间形成协同效应。

农业、渔业和林业都与环境关系密切。如果放松对土地和土壤的管制，农业生产就难以为继（《联合国防治荒漠化公约》）。如果为了获取柴薪或兴建度假区而随意地乱砍滥伐，生物多样性将不复存在（《联合国生物多样性公约》），随之而来的就是影响气候和降雨量(《联合国气候变化框架公约》)。

加勒比各国政府必须保证环境或生态系统服务(水、海洋生物、森林)不受破坏，从而确保农业和旅游业可持续发展，因为环境是二者赖以生存的保障。

就农业而言，尽管在食品消费和 / 或使用生物燃料(甘蔗、玉米、油棕)满足能源需求方面体现了农业的多样化发展，但其竞争将日益激烈。因为城市化进程和度假区开发，耕地正逐步减少。有句澳大利亚的土著谚语说得好，"你爱护土地，土地也会爱护你"。

在加勒比地区，高质量的耕地是有限的，因此，必须采取措施保护本地区的粮食生产能力。

（2）为何需要国际公约？

对加勒比国家来说，国际公约是新的国际承诺，为加勒比各国明确自身发展目标，推动其走上可持续发展道路提供了新的机遇，农业和旅游业尤为如此。

认可国际公约的国家承诺，允许进行各种比较研究。另一方面，国际公约反映了当今知识、技术、制度、国际关系、外国调查发现和投资机会的发展情况。把履行各种国际公约的责任分摊至各部 / 司，却导致加勒比各国无法好好利用这些公约带来的机会。正是国际公约间的协同效应使加勒比各国受益，因此，需要通过主管部委在国家一级进行更有效的协调。

3. 贸易

贸易一直是加勒比经济生活中的重要因素。作为曾经的殖民地，如今已独立的加勒比国家仍向欧洲的殖民市场出口农产品。它们与前欧洲殖民者建立起联盟。作为受欧盟资助的非洲、加勒比和太平洋地区国家集团的成员，这些加勒比独立国家在对欧洲市场的贸易中享有特惠待遇。这便是刘易斯贸易条件模型的背景。

特惠待遇终止后，加勒比地区的对外贸易必须遵守世界贸易组织的规则和条例。在西半球，自由贸易协定(FTAs)逐步推行。为应对这些全球化布局，加勒比共同体建立了加勒比单一市场和经济。

就这点来说，贸易具有全球性，因为农业贸易受《农业协定》管辖；而《农业协定》又是在世贸组织的框架内制定规则和条例的。2001 年的《多哈部长级协定》涵盖货物贸易和服务贸易。自由贸易协定也涉及环境和农业方面。

在这种贸易环境下，加勒比地区的农产品必须具有竞争力。因为特惠市场已不复存在，它们不仅要在全球市场上更胜一筹，还必须在地区市场(岛间贸易和岛内贸易)上占有一席之地。

世界市场对加勒比地区的产品是有需求的,为满足当地人民和游客的需求,国内的食品市场日益扩大。加勒比各国政府必须出台相应的监管机制,确保区域内有竞争力的产品比欧盟或美国的产品更具市场优势。因为在欧盟和美国,农民享有大量补贴。

值得注意的是,如《多哈部长级协定》所述,环境和 / 或生态系统服务对旅游部门十分重要。

关键因素

对国民经济中的农业部门进行评价的依据是,小农是否已转变成为农业综合企业的经营者,他们的农业综合经营和农作系统是否在环境上可持续并能在一定的贸易框架内成功经营。

这些关键因素为加勒比地区的农业提供了前进的道路。

几乎所有加勒比国家都把旅游业作为其经济的一个部门。然而,只有少数几个国家(巴哈马、巴巴多斯、特立尼达和多巴哥)完成了从农业经济向服务业(旅游业)或工业经济的转型。

另一方面,那些仍以农业为基础的国家已然缺乏竞争力,因为他们必须依赖特惠贸易政策才能进入出口市场。缺乏竞争力是过去 40 年来(1960—2000 年)农业部门发展失败和拖加勒比地区国内生产总值增长后腿的主要原因。

旅游业在创造就业和吸引外国直接投资方面给加勒比地区带来了革命性的变化,不过也导致了粮食进口的增加。但总体而言,旅游业改变了加勒比地区。

在独立时期,加勒比各国政府必须在全球化、贸易自由化和市场力量的背景下施政。这就要求政府采取新办法来发展经济,而对于以农业为基础的经济体来说,这并不好解决,突出问题在于小农经济缺乏竞争力。

在这种环境下实现经济转型成为加勒比各国正在努力应对的挑战——有的国家成功了,有的仍在挣扎。

2006 年 10 月版的《孢子》杂志——国际农业和农村合作技术中心官方期刊,在其"农业政策文章"版块的"观点"一节中刊登了彼得·黑兹的文章《小而美》。他提出用以下方式来改变农业的发展面貌。

　　"农业的作用会随国家的发展而变化。当人们越来越富裕时,农业在国民收入和就业中的比重便逐步下降,小农场更难以与规模更大、机械化程度更高的农场竞争,消费者对饮食的需求呈现多样化,高价值、深度加工和熟食产品备受青睐。

城市化发展加剧了这些趋势。总之,随着国家越来越富裕,农场也越来越大,农场经营变得更加商业化,更专注于生产高价值产品。许多小农场消失了,剩下的要么投资有竞争余地、高价值的小众市场,要么成为兼职农户。这些变化是一个国家经济转型过程中的正常现象。"

《巴哈马日报》农业综合企业版

农业综合企业:加勒比地区农业的希望

加勒比地区农业部门的利益攸关方之间正展开一场激烈的辩论。辩论的目的是为了让私营部门的经营者能与公共部门和非政府组织竞争,获取地区农业部门的自然资源,从而生产在全球市场上具有竞争力的粮食产品。

地区农业部门组织

以下组织被视作实现这些目标的关键。一是有政府资助的加勒比农业研究与发展研究所。该研究所是加勒比共同体的主要研究机构。但多年来,其对加勒比共同体农业所起的作用一直倍受质疑,行政重组时常发生。相关人士纷纷呼吁加勒比农业研究与发展研究所重整旗鼓,发挥应有作用。

另一个组织是加勒比农业综合企业协会。该协会是在美洲农业合作研究所的倡议下成立的。美洲农业合作研究所认为,推进加勒比农业发展的办法是将农业商业化,而不是由非熟练工兼职。因此,加勒比共同体国家建立了各种类型的农业综合企业协会。从美洲农业合作研究所在加勒比各国均设有办事处来看,其价值已获认可。

还有一个组织是联合国粮食及农业组织驻巴巴多斯的分区办事处。设立该办事处是为了让像联合国粮食及农业组织这样的全球性组织能及时应对国家层面的农业问题或挑战。

农业贸易

贸易自由化和全球化促使加勒比各国政府和农业经营者用一种全新的视角看待农业。1995年,除巴哈马外,所有加勒比共同体国家都加入了世界贸易组织,再次强化了这一视角。

世界贸易组织的规章制度迫使各国政府和经营者改变农业的经营方式。为此,加勒比共同体建立了加勒比单一市场和经济,目的是在加勒比地区采取措施,提高加勒比共同体国家的竞争力并鼓励加勒比共同体国家之间扩大区域内贸易。

农业贸易的角色转变随即开始。由加拿大、墨西哥和美国三国签署的北美自由贸易协定开创了自由贸易的新纪元。这最终引发了关于建立西半球自由贸易区即美洲自贸区的讨论。正是在这种大环境和世界贸易组织的共同作用下,加勒比各国政府和私营部门的经营者认识到,如果不采取必要措施将加勒比农业提升至一个新水平,农业商业化就是不可能完成的任务。

在此形势下,公共部门和私营部门开始重新审视加勒比共同体国家与农业综合企业增长和发展有关的机构。

农业综合企业的驱动力

重建加勒比农业研究与发展研究所势在必行。为了让新研究所发挥应有的作用,加勒比家禽协会执行主任罗伯特·贝斯特建议研究所必须"在私营部门与我们密切合作。这是个绝佳的机会。调整计划并以加勒比地区协会为中心"。

近年来,在贝斯特先生的领导下,加勒比家禽协会一直是左右各国及区域家禽产业政策的重要力量。该协会能有效地让各国政府和加勒比地区谈判机制认识到进口家禽对国内生产者造成的冲击。市场准入问题及其对本地生产者的持续影响一直十分惊人。

格莱斯顿农场是加勒比家禽协会的创始成员之一。其首席执行官布鲁斯·汉森首先提出了设立加勒比家禽协会的想法。当时汉森先生在佐治亚州亚特兰大市参加年度家禽大会,他把加勒比共同体的家禽生产商召集起来共同商议,而这次会议促成了加勒比家禽协会的诞生。如今,格莱斯顿农场已不复存在,这是由于目光短浅的食品进口商支持进口美国禽肉,因其享有补贴,十分廉价,导致巴哈马农业部门最大的生产商被迫退出市场,关门倒闭。

而加勒比家禽协会让本地区各农业综合企业的经营者意识到,要想在以市场力量驱动的世界中生存下来,团结一致是基础。

农业综合企业组织的作用

如今,加勒比地区有以下几类组织代表农业经营者的发声。

在牙买加、巴巴多斯、特立尼达和多巴哥,小农倾向于加入农业协会。例如,在巴巴多斯,巴巴多斯农业协会为其成员提供推广服务。这实际上替代了巴巴多斯农业部的相关责任。在特立尼达和多巴哥,农业协会一直在竭力保护家禽合同养殖户的权利。该协会认为,大型家禽公司通过为这些合同养殖户提供饲料、雏鸡和市场分销渠道的方式剥削其劳动成果。

作为牙买加政府的游说机构，牙买加农业协会主要代表小农的利益，具有极大的影响力。在牙买加，政客们会听取牙买加农业协会的意见。

其他组织还有各行业协会。大多数加勒比地区的经济体以农业为基础，在出口市场上竞争，并向其前殖民统治者争取出口配额。一些商品起步较早，为当地经济和就业，尤其是农村地区就业，赚取了大量外汇。糖和咖啡等商品为欧洲的大都市经济创造了巨大财富。

糖、大米、柑橘、香蕉和咖啡等商品的协会都是以出口为导向的。随着粮食安全问题日益严峻，旨在满足国内粮食需求的商品变得越来越重要，由此，适应本地市场的商品协会应运而生，如家禽、猪肉、蔬菜和奶制品协会。

去年，在美洲农业合作研究所的支持下，巴巴多斯举办了一次研讨会，目的是鼓励扩大加勒比地区的羊肉生产。巴哈马农工公司的副总经理阿诺德·多塞特先生和伊柳塞拉岛的农民艾德林·西莫内特代表巴哈马出席了会议。会议中值得注意的几个重要因素有：

① 艾德林·西莫内特是加勒比地区最大的羊肉生产商。

② 巴哈马是加勒比地区主要的羊肉生产国，为牙买加和巴巴多斯的优良种畜提供了巨大的市场。

③ 巴哈马有潜力将其生产基地多样化，分别生产羊肉和牛奶。

这次研讨会的结果是多塞特先生被选为地区羊肉生产委员会成员。

其他行业协会正在加勒比各地兴起，如园林绿化协会、观赏园艺协会、水产养殖（鱼类养殖）协会。

农业综合企业经营者的影响

贝斯特先生为农业综合企业的经营者做了出色的辩解，他是这样说的：

"① 是谁在推动游说工作，在地区和国际上推动和维护我们主要行业的区域观？是谁为那些代表地区利益参加国际会议的公共部门买单？

② 是谁正在积极地为农业部门寻找新的商机，并研究提高包括农业卫生在内的效率的途径？又是谁拥有并推动业内大量的技术研究站？

③ 是谁不断地与公共部门角力，敦促其根据我们签署的贸易协定修改过时的法律和监管制度？

④ 是谁在农业卫生和食品安全系统出问题时，承担缺乏应对措施的代价？"

所有这些问题的答案都是农业综合企业的经营者。

加勒比是一个相对较小的区域，其生产能力有限。因此，区域内各行业集中起来，提出所有经营者共同关心的问题至关重要，尤其是国际和西半球层面的问题。因为没有哪个加勒比共同体国家能独自完成，巴哈马也不例外。

巴哈马的农业综合企业可在加勒比地区发挥一定作用。事实上，巴哈马的农业综合企业与加勒比共同体较大国家的相比不相上下，然而长期以来我们都退居次位。巴哈马的柑橘种植面积在加勒比共同体各国中位居第三，仅次于伯利兹和牙买加。巴哈马在一个松树岛上种植的蔬菜种类比其他任何一个加勒比共同体国家都要多。而巴哈马已然是区域内羊肉生产的领跑者。随着更多研究、人力培训和资金的投入，这一领先优势可以扩展到农用工业。

农业综合企业是加勒比地区和国家农业发展的希望。为了提高农业综合企业的竞争力，公共部门和私营部门必须齐心协力争取最大利益。国家和区域集团（如协会、合作社）则要增强农业作为经济活动的生存能力。

插曲：《埃尼亚斯文集》《巴哈马日报》　巴哈马与加勒比共同体

距巴哈马上一次主办加勒比政府首脑会议已经快八年了。在这之前，巴哈马还举办过两次政府首脑会议——分别在 1984 年 7 月和 1993 年 7 月。

20 世纪 90 年代，由于不可控因素，巴哈马参与了加勒比共同体的事务中。

巴哈马是加勒比国家，这是不争的事实，然而，巴哈马不顾大环境的影响，不仅拒绝承认，而且拒绝接受这一事实。巴哈马是个资源极其有限的小国，我们无法面对这一现实的根本原因是什么呢？

分析过去 20 年的全球性事件，全球化、世界贸易组织、美洲自由贸易区、经济合作与发展组织打击有害税收行为的倡议、非法移民、艾滋病肆虐、贩毒和洗黑钱等，都不是单个国家能够独自应对的，需要区域内各方携手合作，共同处理这些问题。孤军作战是非常鲁莽的行为。

在深度参与加勒比共同体事务之前，巴哈马对南加勒比群岛或人称西印度群岛采取的是边缘化的态度。

学术上，在普及免费中等教育之前，很多巴哈马人在牙买加著名的私立寄宿中学接受中等教育。

随着西印度群岛大学进一步发展并拓宽其学术基础，巴哈马政府认识到其作为一所区域性高等院校所存在的价值，决定给予其财政资助，从而确保巴哈马人在各种学术和专业领域的地位。

巴哈马的英国圣公会与加勒比地区的学术生活保持着长期关系,在巴巴多斯的科德林顿学院,巴哈马的黑人曾在此接受英国圣公会神职人员的神学培训。如今,巴哈马与科德林顿学院的关系更为紧密,近半数的神学院学生是巴哈马人。

20世纪60年代后期,当时进步自由党政府领导的巴哈马决定参与创建加勒比开发银行。20世纪70年代,通过参加加勒比自由贸易区运动会,巴哈马进一步扩大了在加勒比地区的参与度。巴哈马曾多次主办该运动会。除田径外,巴哈马和加勒比的兄弟国家共同参与了各种体育赛事。

21世纪初,巴哈马与加勒比共同体的关系正处于十字路口。加勒比共同体各国政府已决定深入推进一体化进程。一些国家呼吁各国允许国民在没有护照或任何证件的情况下在加勒比共同体国家间自由流动。巴哈马不支持这一提议。

然而,在本次第22届加勒比共同体政府首脑会议上,有两项倡议得以大力推进——建立加勒比单一市场和经济以及加勒比法院。

巴哈马律师协会成员公开反对巴哈马加入加勒比法院。他们认为巴哈马应当坚持拥护枢密院。

大多数巴哈马人并不清楚什么是加勒比单一市场和经济。然而,在加勒比地区,这并不是什么新鲜事,自加勒比共同体作为一个贸易和政治集团成立以来,加勒比共同体国家就一直朝着这个方向发展。

各国的岛际贸易,加上便利的共同关税制度,逐渐将加勒比共同体推向单一市场和经济的发展方向;这与欧洲共同体的进程非常相似。

加入这个单一市场和经济会对巴哈马造成重大影响,因为巴哈马经济开放,依赖服务业,且货币与美元等值。在加勒比地区,各国的币值并不相同,存在巨大差异。

贸易是加勒比地区的一个重要问题,因为大多数加勒比共同体国家依赖出口作为其国家收入的主要来源。除巴哈马外,加勒比的所有岛国均是世界贸易组织的成员。随着美洲自由贸易区逐步成型,并计划于2005年投入运行,加勒比共同体各国政府已经同意,如果巴哈马主动参与进来,那么各国将通过加勒比地区谈判机制就其加入美洲自贸区一事进行统一谈判。

无论我们巴哈马人是否意识到这一点,每一个倡议的实施都将使我们与加勒比共同体的联系变得愈发紧密。加勒比共同体第22届政府首脑会议的开幕式上,巴哈马总理在致辞中强调,加勒比应不分你我,共同推进本地区各国旅游产业一体化。他还提议 2002 年 10 月在巴哈马举办一次区域旅游峰会。届时，加勒比旅游业将成为关注的焦点。

作为巴哈马人，我认为巴哈马普通民众并不清楚政府有意参与加勒比的一体化进程。但不管我们大多数人是否承认，巴哈马的各个机构正逐步融入加勒比共同体。

这是事实。

我们的加勒比：进步还是停滞？

上周，加勒比开发银行举行了行长年会。有意思的是，30 年前时任进步自由党政府的财政部部长，如今已故的卡尔顿·E. 弗朗西斯，因推动加勒比开发银行资本化而遭到强烈批评。当时，巴哈马是该行在加勒比地区三大融资国之一。

怀疑论者认为巴哈马永远不会从这项投资中获益，资金会被我们"西印度群岛"的表兄弟挥霍和滥用。地区主义是一个饱受质疑的概念。

然而，本周初，我们了解到巴哈马开发银行（BDB）借了 1 000 万美元来资助新企业家的发展。于是财政部部长迅速补充道，巴哈马开发银行已经进行了改革，现在的目标是提供急需的创业投资，促进我们日益扩大的商业阶层的形成和发展。

多年来，巴哈马人并未完全理解和意识到加勒比开发银行、加勒比共同体和西印度群岛大学等区域机构发挥的作用。经常有人抱怨，这些机构总是纸上谈兵，没有实际行动。因此，与其他地区的类似机构相比，它们的增长和发展速度一直很慢。

这种批评并非完全正确。例如，加勒比共同体一贯实行兼容并蓄的"大帐篷政策"，即允许区域内所有国家加入，而不论其发展水平如何。这是加勒比共同体一直以来发展缓慢的主要绊脚石。

最近海地加入加勒比共同体就是一个典型示例。不像欧盟，申请加入其的国家必须达到一定经济发展的标准，海地的人均收入是加勒比地区最低的，而加勒比共同体仍旧接纳其为成员国。

巴哈马总理休伯特·A. 英格拉哈姆阁下在加勒比开发银行会议上致开幕词时说道，巴哈马正为"看似无限涌入的经济移民所困扰"。

过去几周里，大量海地人涌入巴哈马，试图逃离本国的经济和政治危局。

海地的政治环境变得动荡不安，这导致了暴力事件的激增，威胁了拖延已久并原定于本月下旬举行的立法和地方政府选举。

美国对海地政府施压，要求其重新确定选举日期，并警告说："如不能在6月12日前组建议会，海地将可能受到民主国家共同体的孤立，并危及今后的合作。"

像海地一样，还有很多国家的大量民众身陷贫困。为此，英格拉哈姆总理再次呼吁加勒比开发银行：

> "采取更多举措减少贫困，遏制经济移民的流动。在这方面，我们必须更加重视减贫和帮助区域内最贫穷国家的目标。"

得益于大量的外国投资，巴哈马的经济一直欣欣向荣，而且前景十分被看好，因为今年的经济增长率预计将达到4%。这种良好的经济状态对那些身处贫困地区的人们来说非常具有吸引力。

但巴哈马并不是加勒比地区唯一拥有健康经济的国家。多米尼加共和国鼓励投资者到该国投资。该经济在1999年增长了8.3%，预计今年将继续以7%—7.5%的速度增长。

然而，加勒比地区仍然严重依赖农业部门提供就业，现在的农业受市场驱动，不像过去几十年那样由生产驱动。人们的饮食习惯发生了巨大变化，特别是随着加勒比地区越来越倾向发展旅游业，对一些岛国来说，旅游业已取代农业成为其主要的外汇收入来源。

总体而言，加勒比地区仍在努力寻找其经济出路。在社会层面，存在很多问题，尤其是在医疗、教育和住房方面。在政治层面，本地区依然处于各自为政的分裂状态，这在很大程度上源于其殖民地的历史。

新世纪，加勒比的未来将主要取决于我们所选择的领导层、经济发展的道路以及我们在营造区域环境中呈现出的社会化程度。

40年后的牙买加（第一位女总理）

金斯敦是牙买加的首都，有约75万居民。它是加勒比英语区最大的城市。第一次与这座城市产生交集是在我八岁的时候，那是半个多世纪以前的事了。

作为前英国殖民主义在加勒比地区的中心，牙买加独立的时间比任何加勒比共同体国家都要长，已有约40年的历史了。40年来，这个国家为应对不断变化的全球环境经历了巨大的社会经济变革。

世界银行等国际机构将牙买加视作发展中国家。第一世界国家或所谓的发达国家称，牙买加在过去40年中的发展每况愈下。

发展评论人士指出，牙买加的货币贬值，失业率估计高居加勒比地区榜首，财政赤字过大且国家无力偿还外债。

还有另一种不同的观点。这种观点认为原因在于，像牙买加和巴哈马这样的发展中国家，其发展进程主要掌握在发达国家手中，后者用自己的标准对发展中国家该如何发展指手画脚。

如今，牙买加是一个有约 200 万人口的国家，在评价其发展形势时，有几点是必须考虑的。独立之初，牙买加的人口不足 100 万。殖民主义造成了收入上的巨大差距，但并没有导致什么分化。许多牙买加人在独立后一穷二白。曼利总理时期，人们渴望国家的社会经济制度更加公平，然而社会主义的尝试以失败告终。

这一尝试致使牙买加人大量外流，这些人中有许多专业人士、中产阶级和商业阶层，后者离开时也将财富转移到了国外。这对牙买加来说无疑是沉重的打击，牙买加至今尚未完全恢复。

尽管遭遇了这种挫折，牙买加人还是有着强烈的进取精神。随着国家的经济基础从农业转向旅游业，牙买加经历了深刻的经济转型。铝土矿是牙买加在世界市场上主要的出口矿物之一，但随着铝的价格下跌，铝土矿的价格也相应降低。由于糖、香蕉等传统农产品失去了特惠市场，农业生产随之改变，加之铝土矿价格下降，牙买加的经济成了主要问题。

如今，牙买加有着极其庞大的非正规经济。一些专家甚至认为，非正规经济的规模要大于正规经济。那么什么是非正规经济呢？从理论上讲，非正规经济是不计入国民经济统计的那部分经济。

在牙买加，经济学家所谓的"便士资本主义"的例子比比皆是。人们在路边、街角、人行道、马背、车里等地方贩卖各种各样的东西。成千上万的牙买加人每天都以此谋生，但世界银行和其他机构的统计数据将他们归为穷人和失业者。这是国际经济分类体系中的谬误。

毒品贸易是非正规经济的重要组成部分。

据说，牙买加境外的国民比境内的多。其国民收入的很大一部分是境外牙买加人的汇款。

与大多数国家一样，为促进国家发展，牙买加面临建设教育、医疗、服务和基础设施的挑战。而要建成这些必要设施，牙买加不得不大量借款。当一个国家的大部分人口都处于低收入阶层时，就会影响税收收入。这也是为什么在整个加勒比地区，可能除了特立尼达和多巴哥这种能从石油和天然气领域获取巨额税收的国家之外，其他大部分国家的政府都相对贫困。

相较而言，巴哈马是一个还算富裕的国家，人均收入较高。可即便政府有盈利能力，由于税收收入不理想，巴哈马政府也是入不敷出。所有加勒比共同体国家都面临同样问题。

1976 年以来，牙买加的汇率一直在下跌；然而，从某种程度上说，这使他们的旅游产品更具吸引力。此外，牙买加的旅游业与其他经济部门建立了强有力的联系，将大量本国特产纳入旅游产品中，最大限度地增加了旅游收入。

正如牙买加音乐、美食和人民所展示的那样，牙买加是一个生机勃勃、充满活力的国度。

区域可持续性

发展中国家总是受到西方媒体的大量批评。但如果考虑到很多国家原先的经济发展水平，那么一些第三世界国家领导人对其国家发展做出的贡献的确不可思议。

当其中许多国家实现独立时，人力资源十分落后；其基础设施均围绕国家自然资源获取和开发而建设。然而，纵览加勒比地区的发展情况，尤其是加勒比共同体各国，牙买加是最早实现独立的国家，已有 43 年之久。

尽管加勒比共同体国家都曾经历经济不稳定和困难，但都努力生存了下来。加勒比地区经济发展的兴衰是由政府掌控的，政府运作是其经济发展的动力。随着全球化的到来，一切都必须改变，因为全球化进程的标语是竞争力。

政府促进竞争力，私营部门则推动竞争力。这种重新定位不仅逐渐转变了政府的应对举措，也改变了社会——私营部门、工会、非政府组织、国际机构、融资机构等的思维方式。

这一新观念的影响已在加勒比地区表现出来，在加勒比共同体各国中都能看到并感受到这一变化。

应当记住的是，加勒比共同体实际上是由三类国家组成的。以牙买加、巴巴多斯、特立尼达和多巴哥及巴哈马为代表的小岛经济体是一种发展方向。其次还有像东加勒比国家组织这样的次区域集团，正在形成自己的社会经济发展模式。第三类是加勒比共同体的大陆国家圭亚那、苏里南和伯利兹。这些国家地广人稀，农业综合企业潜力很大，目前他们正在转变食品生产系统，提高其在全球市场上的竞争力。

海地虽然是加勒比共同体的成员国，但由于其历史和发展模式，在我看来，它仍是一个特例。所有加勒比共同体国家的前身都是殖民地，其发展进程均会受到之前殖民统治的影响。

在加勒比共同体的内部，目前有上述三种不同的发展模式。但对这些国家来说至关重要的是，必须推动其经济以实现可持续增长和发展。

在加勒比共同体的所有国家中，民主原则都深入人心，且各国政府也十分稳定。最大的问题在于这些国家政府的执政水平，尤其是决策过程。人们非常关注政府如何处理社会问题，如两性平等、社会经济边缘化、人力资源开发、住房、艾滋病、扶贫。大部分加勒比共同体国家政府都没能找到可持续解决这些问题的办法。其结果就是城市生活水平日益下降，导致犯罪率上升且往往是暴力犯罪。

几乎每个加勒比共同体国家都存在这些问题。在牙买加，谋杀率急剧上升。最近在西班牙港发生了一系列恐怖分子爆炸袭击。在巴哈马，毒品贸易一直在助长暴力犯罪。

在20世纪下半叶的大部分时间里，加勒比一直努力把自己打造成世界顶级的旅游目的地，并迈出了勇敢的步伐。各国政府因无力解决上述社会问题，使加勒比的阳光、沙滩、海洋等优势得不到发挥，从而阻碍了本地区各国政府实现经济的持续增长和发展。为了让加勒比共同体的岛屿国家和大陆国家实现真正的独立，各国政府、民间团体和私营部门必须共同努力，一起成就在社会、经济、政治及文化生活上均可持续发展的加勒比海地区。

加勒比单一市场和经济：对全球化的回应

全球化的特点之一是遵守国际标准和法规。人们期望各国在一系列经济、社会、政治活动中能依规行事。要想成为一个稳定且对国际社会有贡献的国家，该国的立法和法律必须与全球化世界的步调保持一致。这就是我们生活和竞争的环境。

专家们给全球化下了如下定义：

> "通过跨国投资完成世界文化、经济、基础设施的一体化和民主化，凭借通信技术实现信息的迅速传播以及自由市场力量对地方、区域和国家经济的影响。"

这是对全球化意义的阐释。关键在于身处加勒比群岛的我们必须掌握世界看待自己的方式。

全球化的种子早在工业革命时期就已种下。它是一个不断演变的过程。除非我们了解全球化的起源，否则我们许多人将难以理解其对现今巴哈马的影响。

工业革命是很多相互关联的根本性变革的结果，这些变革将农业经济转变成为工业经济。其中最直接的莫过于生产性质的变化，即生产什么、在哪儿生产以及如何生产。生产力和技术效率显著提高，部分原因是在生产过程中系统地应用了科学知识和实践经验。另外，一大批公司企业迁至划定区域办公，也使其效率得到提高。工业革命使人们从农村搬到城市生活、工作，促进了城市的发展。

这些变化彻底改变了人们的生活和工作方式。工业革命是人类成长和发展的决定性时期，其从未停下前进的脚步；全球化只是工业革命的强化和延伸。

工业革命促使经济变革和社会转型。经济变革加速深化了社会转型，如人们从农村地区向城市中心迁移。今天，这种迁移变成了国家间的人口流动。人们从农村搬到城市的主要原因是城市地区物资丰富、供应充足、设施便利且触手可及。如今，86% 的巴哈马人生活在大巴哈马岛和新普罗维登斯岛之间，这是我们群岛的城市中心。

工业革命期间，科学和技术受到越来越多的关注，并改变了房屋的建造方式。今天，信息技术也是如此，互联网创造了一个无国界的世界。

工业革命始于 18 世纪下半叶；三个世纪后，我们进入了全球化时代，这实际上是 20 世纪 /21 世纪版本的工业革命。

欧洲和美国是工业革命最初的受益者，其经济因此而高度工业化。到了 20 世纪，随着日本、韩国、中国成为工业大国，在世界范围内，工业化延伸到了亚洲和太平洋的部分地区。然而，在全球的大部分地区，尤其是那些提供原材料和人力促进工业革命发展并最终造福欧美经济的国家，至今仍无法实现机械化生产和更大的经济增长。

为了自身的利益，欧洲在共享其前殖民地的市场时建立了一个由加勒比、非洲和太平洋地区新独立国家组成的非加太国家集团。另一方面，美国利用地缘政治的优势将拉丁美洲和加勒比国家变为其客户市场。尽管工业革命的影响在此已存在近三个世纪，但构成客户市场的国家依然在与不发达的经济现实做斗争。

为了加快全球化进程，工业革命的受益国——主要是欧盟、美国和日本，将全球化的概念强加于这些不发达国家，其中很多国家是小规模经济体，其人力、物力和自然资源都十分有限。

全球化的主要推动者是世界贸易组织，全球经济一体化机制一直是贸易自由化的工具。应对这一新世界经济秩序的办法是建立经济集团，利用规模经济的优势。一些小国家，特别是那些作为客户市场的国家，已将经济一体化作为应对机制，以达到某种程度的经济规模。

正是在这种情况下，世界贸易组织才在全球层面制定了贸易规则和条例。为了通过经济一体化发挥规模经济的优势，欧洲建立了欧洲联盟，而美国建立了北美自由贸易区，并打算到 2005 年建成美洲自由贸易区，即在北美自贸区国家（美国、加拿大和墨西哥）的基础上，加入拉丁美洲和加勒比的客户市场国家。

认识到自身经济和政治的局限性后，作为欧洲和美国客户市场的加勒比各国成立了加勒比共同体。起初，加勒比共同体是摆脱了殖民主义的国家针对国际环境做出的政治应对。但经济现实是，只有一体化才能确保其主权国家的地位。因此，必须建立加勒比单一市场和经济，这是利用贸易自由化应对全球化的机制。

在未来十年的某个时刻，巴哈马将势必改变和决定应对全球化的机制。

后记：新加勒比

加勒比地区的每个国家和属地都经历了奴隶制、殖民主义和内部自治／独立的三个时期，进而在社会、经济、政治孕育与发展方面达到成熟水平。

这是由自然资源、人力资源基础、地缘政治环境、贸易路线以及姊妹国家和／或属地的相对优势等多种因素造就的。这些因素在海岛民族一体化、文化与美食的交融中也发挥了重要作用。由此形成的融合在区域范围内和外观呈现上都显得趋同而非趋异。正是这一点，在多样性中催生出了加勒比地区的独特性。这种多样性对该地区的每个国家来说，无论大陆、岛屿还是属地国家都是与生俱来的。

20 世纪 50 年代，好莱坞电影《日光岛》取材于加勒比，由加勒比演员哈里·贝拉方特主演。影片中令人难忘的一幕是贝拉方特和一群小农一边唱着《香蕉船之歌》一边把香蕉装到货轮上。独立时期诞生了一个新的加勒比，《日光岛》中的贝拉方特形象已退出大众视野。

回顾历史，西印度群岛联邦的解体或许是塞翁失马焉知非福。加勒比共同体便是在吸取其经验后创立的，并发展成为一个区域性组织。加勒比共同体主要在加强体制化建设等若干方面发挥了引领作用，建立了强有力的参与式民主和牢固的民主原则基础，提高了加勒比地区的国际声誉。

为了响应世界贸易组织，加勒比共同体建立了加勒比地区谈判机制。加勒比法院将取代枢密院，成为加勒比地区的终审法院。

加勒比共同体不断扩大，接纳了海地为其新成员。通过加勒比论坛，多米尼加共和国也加入了该阵营。如今，加勒比共同体需要通过扩大加勒比论坛的格局来吸引古巴的加入。古巴是加勒比地区最大的岛国，若其参与到本地区最主要政治集团的事务中，必将加强加勒比地区在西半球和全球的影响力。

作为旅游胜地，古巴越来越受欢迎。2006 年古巴的游客接待量达到 200 万。

安全的旅游环境、丰富的历史文化价值以及古巴人民的热情是其受游客青睐的主要原因。

加勒比是全球重要的旅游目的地，每年吸引 4 000 万—5 000 万游客乘坐轮船或飞机前来游览。大量的游客和支持旅游业发展的基础设施建设极大地改变了几乎每个岛屿的风貌。

加勒比已成为医学教育中心。西印度群岛大学医学院因其热带医学奖学金而闻名。东加勒比沿海和多米尼加共和国的众多医学院里，大批主要来自北美的学生在接受培训。

尽管加勒比发展势头良好，加勒比人仍继续向美国和加拿大移民。随着加勒比地区日渐成熟，建立起自我认同感并培养出自我意识，公共部门和私营部门的领导阶层将会各自找到多元化发展小岛经济的新途径。当人们看到在加勒比地区有更多成功的机会，移民的冲动就会减小。而单一经济和市场以及区域内人口的自由流动，会大大降低移民的必要性。已有证据表明，数以千计的加勒比共同体人民在巴哈马获得了就业机会。同样地，数百名圭亚那人正在巴巴多斯的建筑行业工作。

美国移民局和人口普查局的统计数据显示，自 2000 年以来，有 800 万外国出生的美国居民前往美国就业或求学。

在这 800 万人中，约有 6% 即 48 万人来自加勒比地区。他们平均年龄为 27.6 岁，其中约 24 万人将其收入的 30% 或更多用于住房花销。男性收入为 22 656 美元，女性为 20 485 美元。约有 12 万人生活在美国贫困线以下。

他们就业的主要领域是建筑业，其次是住宿业、餐饮服务业以及制造业。

将这些数据，特别是人均收入和就业机会与加勒比国家进行比较，可以得出结论，即一些加勒比国家提供的人均收入和就业机会与之不相上下，从而减少了（前往别国）移民的必要性。

随着经济转型，移民的需求将减少。公共部门和私营部门双管齐下，可在很大程度上帮助大多数加勒比国家调整或精简农业（小农）和服务业（旅游业及金融服务业），以及帮助特立尼达和多巴哥重整石油业。

作为 2007 板球世界杯这一国际盛会的主办地，加勒比已成为全球瞩目的焦点。尽管赛事只在加勒比英语区举行，但整个加勒比地区势必会得到广泛宣传。预计此次赛事将吸引大量来自英国、澳大利亚、新西兰、印度、巴基斯坦、斯里兰卡以及东非和南非等板球国家的游客。本次大赛将带来不同地区的游客，不再仅限于北美或欧洲。

　　加勒比共同体的各国政府和私营部门花费数百万美元用于赛事准备，前者进行接待培训，后者负责基础设施升级和翻新，尤其针对即将成为比赛场地的九个岛国。

　　此次板球世界杯的宣传将聚焦整个加勒比地区，而非个别赛事地点。同样，呈现给世界的是整个加勒比地区，而非个别赛事的承办国家。

　　第二次世界大战之后，加勒比地区的经济从以农业为基础转型为以服务业和／或工业为基础。对于大多数加勒比国家来说，这一转型始于20世纪60年代，而今天，加勒比地区已成为著名的旅游目的地。

　　新加勒比崛起的经济助力包括临近北美的地理位置、相对稳定的政治环境以及承袭欧洲殖民统治的社会、宗教和教育机构。这些因素加上气候条件（太阳、沙滩和海洋）、热情的民众、文化的多样性、民主原则和资本主义环境，使加勒比地区成为投资旅游业发展和建立离岸金融机构的理想场所。于是，加勒比各国政府纷纷建设必要的基础设施，以推动新产业的发展。

　　这一举措改善了人们的生活水平和生活质量，提高了本地区大多数经济体的人均收入，实现了国内生产总值的快速上涨。

　　独立时期的加勒比与殖民时期的加勒比有很大不同。外地人来此置业定居，并在大多数岛国形成了聚居地，这使加勒比的区域形势复杂化。在这里，金融服务业是经济的重要组成部分，离岸银行家、会计师、律师和其他金融专业人才为高端住宅、学校和社会设施创造了市场。在金融服务业成熟的国家，本地专业人士已然融入这种生活方式。

　　无论是人类医学还是兽医学，加勒比地区已成为全球医学专业教育的中心之一。医学院所几乎遍布加勒比各岛，由此产生了如下市场需求：一方面是解决教师、学生和行政人员的住宿问题，另一方面是建设为教学、管理和其他设施服务的基础设施。

　　这一切造就了新的加勒比。

章节注释

第 1 章

美中央情报局《世界各国纪实年鉴》

加勒比共同体网站

历史渊源

加勒比的稳定

加勒比的地缘政治

第 2 章

《巴哈马手册》

巴哈马统计局

巴哈马的农业

巴哈马的历史

第 3 章

《农业观察》第 2 期第 11 卷, 第 1 期第 12 卷

美洲农业合作研究所背景: 目标 2015——贾格迪奥倡议

联合国粮食及农业组织杂志《聚焦》: 多吃水果和蔬菜

加勒比食品与营养学会

《加勒比地区肥胖, 糖尿病和高血压营养管理协议》

联合国粮食及农业组织加勒比地区清单, 巴巴多斯

第 4 章

世界银行报告:《抉择时刻: 21 世纪加勒比的发展》

免费百科全书维基百科——弗莱克斯纳报告

第 5 章

2002 年财政预算案

第 6 章

安东尼·希尔——《旅游业的发展》(第 46—48 页)，小国的经济稳定，加勒比的稳定

表 6.2　1969—1971 年加勒比共同体到访游客

第 7 章

世界银行——海地	包容性增长的选择与机遇
	海地经济增长的趋势、决定因素及制约因素
世界银行——海地	社会适应能力与国家脆弱性
	世界银行报告第 36069 号——海地
	2006 年 4 月 27 日——加勒比海国家管理部门

第 8 章

卡斯滕斯，阿古斯丁 (2016 年 5 月 1 日)	《全球化世界的区域一体化：加勒比的头等大事》
	双年度商业、银行业、金融业国际会议主旨演讲，西班牙港，特立尼达和多巴哥
	http://www.imf.org/external
世界银行报告	《加勒比国家必须提高生产力和竞争力，以加快经济增长》
安斯蒂，卡罗琳	《抉择时刻：21 世纪加勒比的发展》
	http://web.worldbank.org
威廉·阿瑟·刘易斯	《经济增长理论》

迈克尔·格里芬先生：

　　针对上述情况，敬请留意，就我们在农业和土地部的调查而言，我们结合过往经验将"小农"定义为经营少于 5 英亩(2 公顷)土地的农民。根据 1996 年的农业普查，牙买加有小农 158 795 人。其构成如下：

无地小农	14 980 人
土地面积小于 1 公顷的小农	115 267 人
土地面积 1—2 公顷的小农	28 548 人
合计	158 795 人

下一个区间(即土地面积 2—5 公顷的小农)有重叠部分。这部分包括 22 332 名农民。但如您所见,这些农民中有的属于我们定义的"小农",有的则超出定义范围。我认为之所以出现重叠,是因为就我们的情况而言,5 英亩对于小农来说是一个合理可控的农地面积,也是针对小农的调查中我们碰到的最普遍的农地面积。然而,当我们采用米制衡量时,界限就会有些模糊不清。2 月份还会进行一次农业普查,我们希望能尽快更新上述信息。

1996 年的农业普查将农地 / 农场定义为"全部或部分用于农业生产的土地……"

为了把真正的农业用地与家庭菜园和后院农舍区分开来,特做出以下区分。

农地或农场指至少满足以下一项条件的农业经营:

① 种在温室 / 遮阳棚或室外的 1 面积尺(0.41 公顷)栽培作物,包括花。若农民只有 1 间温室 / 遮阳棚,其面积不得少于 4 400 平方英尺;

② 有 12 棵经济果树,如柑橘、芒果、面包果树;

③ 有 1 头牛;

④ 有 2 头猪、2 只山羊或 2 只绵羊;

⑤ 有 12 只家禽,包括鸭子、火鸡等;

⑥ 有 6 个蜂箱;

⑦ 有 1 个任意大小的鱼塘。

仅从事下列经济活动的经济单位不被视为农业用地:

——狩猎、诱捕、猎物繁殖;

——林业、伐木;

——海洋捕捞。

仅从事植物育苗的单位也不被视为农业用地。

如前所述,这些信息有些过时。但 1996 年的农业普查确实指出,当时的农业用地面积在下降,并且最近的发展表明其下降的趋势更为严峻。这些信息应该能提供一些我们此前的情况以供参考。我们正将普查系统落实到位,以确保信息及时更新。

致敬,

H.D. 伯纳德

以下信息源自格林纳达重建和发展局（ARD）的土地利用调查。格林纳达的农民正在经历老龄化，但 60% 的农民表示，他们退休后，家里会有人继续经营家庭农场。

这是 2005 年 11 月土地利用调查中反映的若干情况之一，该调查由格林纳达重建和发展局与农业部、土地部、林业部和渔业部联合发起。

调查显示农民的平均年龄为 53.7 岁，比 1995 年农业普查时偏高了约 2 岁。

然而，尽管农民的平均年龄有所增加，但 62% 的受访者说他们可以找到一个亲戚作为接班人。

此次调查是按照地理位置分层划分的，在 100 个普查区中开展。其中包括对 1 016 名随机挑选的农民进行面对面访谈。调查问卷包含 104 个问题，分属于下列主题：

① 土地状况；

② 劳工资料；

③ 土地利用；

④ 肉豆蔻和可可；

⑤ 其他作物；

⑥ 未来打算；

⑦ 土地侵吞；

⑧ 财政和技术援助；

⑨ 农业协会和市场营销；

⑩ 劳动力储备和土地银行的吸引力；

⑪ 务农对收入的贡献。

以下是此次调查中收集到的关于格林纳达农地状况和农业人口构成的重点：

① 73% 的受访者是男性；

② 62% 的受访者的年龄为 41—70 岁；

③ 77% 的受访者的最高学历是小学；

④ 68% 的受访者表示务农为其主要职业；

⑤ 71% 的农地不到 5 英亩；

⑥ 27% 的农地为 1—2 英亩；

⑦ 24% 的农地为 2—5 英亩；

⑧ 89% 的农民拥有自己的农地并持有地契；

⑨ 77% 的农民无法使用灌溉用水；

⑩ 69% 的农民使用化肥；

⑪ 40% 的农民使用粪肥。

此次土地调查的结果于 1 月 19 日在重建和发展局董事会会议室向各利益攸关方正式发布，农业、土地、林业和渔业部部长格雷戈里·鲍文表示，格林纳达政府，特别是农业、土地、林业和渔业部将根据该调查结果行事。

鲍文部长说：

"鉴于资源有限，我们将尽一切可能与重建和发展局、商品委员会、农村公社以及所有其他涉农的利益攸关方合作，进一步推动及实现农业部门的现代化。"

2006 年 1 月 23 日

重建和发展局

格林纳达圣乔治植物园

电话：473-439-5606/07/08

传真：473-439-5609

电子邮件：mail@ardgrenada.org

《孢子》杂志——"观点"

截至 2005 年 5 月 18 日在巴哈马群岛已登记的农民数量汇总表

岛　屿	已登记农民人数
阿巴科岛	64
阿克林斯岛	4
安德罗斯岛	182
安德鲁斯岛——南部	7
猫　岛	245
崎岖岛	2
伊鲁萨拉岛——中部	90
伊鲁萨拉岛——北部	60
伊鲁萨拉岛——南部	121
伊克祖马斯岛	71
大巴哈马岛	20
茵那瓜岛	1

岛　屿	已登记农民人数
长　岛	182
玛雅古纳岛	7
新普罗维登斯岛	184
圣萨尔瓦多岛	2
合　计	1 242

来源：良好农业规范

简　介

21 世纪，全球农业主要面临三大挑战：① 改善粮食安全、农村生计和收入；② 满足人们对安全食品和其他产品日益增长的多样化需求；③ 节约和保护自然资源。国际社会在世界粮食首脑会议行动计划和联合国千年发展目标中阐述了这些挑战，并提出了 2015 年之前需要实现的具体目标。

无论现在还是将来，人们都期望农业能在一系列的环境中保证粮食安全，并不断要求农业产生积极的环境、社会和经济效益。虽然农业是可持续发展和应对这些挑战的关键因素，但在迅速变化的食品经济和全球化背景下，农业初级生产者的生产模式正在发生巨大变化。

良好农业规范是一种具体促进农产品生产的环境、经济和社会可持续性的手段。部分挑战可通过良好农业规范来应对，从而确保安全健康的食品和非食品农产品。良好农业规范既能满足以需求为先的消费者和零售商，还能满足以供应为先的生产商和劳动力以及连接供需双方的机构和服务。虽然良好农业规范可以应对日益全球化和一体化的农业部门不断增长的需求，但它仍能对地方和国家市场产生重要影响。

在农业生产和农产品的准则、标准以及方案不断增加的背景下，联合国粮食及农业组织制定了良好农业规范方法。因此，"良好农业规范"一词有许多不同的含义。例如，它可指为了满足农民和消费者的需要以及食品生产链的具体要求，由私营部门、民间社会组织和政府制定且形式多样的个人、自愿及非监管性的方法。良好农业规范也正式被国际监管框架和相关操作规程认可，用来尽量减少或防止食品污染。

鉴于不同参与者在制定和采用准则和标准时的趋势以及对世界农业挑战和承诺的认识，联合国粮食及农业组织启动了一项磋商进程，旨在各方就良好农业规范的应用原则、指标和手段达成理解和共识。经过两次初步的电子会议，并在可持续农业与农村发展的背景下细化了良好农业规范的概念后，2003 年 4 月，农业委员会（COAG）第十七届会议建议联合国粮食及农业组织继续开展良好农业规范方法的前期工作。

这可能包括提高认识、信息交流、经济分析、试点项目、技术援助和能力建设，要特别注重发展中国家的需求。

在农业委员会讨论之后，2003 年 11 月 10 日至 12 日召开了关于良好农业规范方法的专家磋商会。其目的是审查和确认总体概念，提出解决问题的指导意见，确定实施战略，为联合国粮食及农业组织制定和实施良好农业规范方法推荐行动方案。来自各学科以及社会各界，如阿根廷、加拿大、克罗地亚、埃塞俄比亚、法国、德国、印度、纳米比亚、新西兰、马来西亚、菲律宾、乌干达、英国和美国的私营部门、公共部门和民间团体的专家，与联合国粮食及农业组织指定的专家一道参加了磋商会。

此次专家磋商会由主持报告、促进对话、工作组讨论和一般性评论几部分组成。会议向与会者提供了三份背景文件[①]：一份是有关制定良好农业规范方法的总体概念文件；另两份是其辅助文件，重点体现为以下两点。

① 对与农业生产相关的现行准则、标准和指南的类型进行总结分析。

② 鼓励农民和农业部门的其他参与者采用良好农业规范。

这些文件旨在为讨论提供出发点。

磋商会提供了很多意见和建议，其中最重要的是，应将良好农业规范方法视作达到目的的手段（即实现农产品生产的环境、经济和社会可持续性，从而确保安全健康的食品和非食品农产品），而非目的本身。给予联合国粮食及农业组织的初步建议包括以下几个方面。

① 描述和定义良好农业规范的概念，包括以下方面：

可持续发展的三大支柱：良好农业规范应具有经济可行性、环境可持续性和社会可接受性；包括食品安全和质量方面；

重点关注初级生产；

考虑现行的自愿及强制性农业操作准则和指南；

有既定的鼓励措施和体制环境。

② 找到并比较现有的良好农业规范相关计划（为确保一致性）以及驱动因

---

① 这三份文件是制定良好农业规范的方法；良好农业规范相关准则、指南和标准的总结分析；采用良好农业规范的鼓励措施。

素及动机，发现不同国家以不同形式实施良好农业规范的经验。

③ 在既定环境下（以可能的应用场景和期望的成果为依据），为制定和调整良好农业规范，拟定全球原则和指导方针。

④ 组织各利益攸关方开展国家和地区级研讨会，以构建联网和促进机制，从而在当地达成一致的良好农业规范。

⑤ 通过以下方式提升能力：

提高市场链中的参与者（包括消费者）的认识和教育水平；

提高决策者的认识；

通过数据库、门户网站、网络（生态系统、商品等）共享信息；

开展国家和地区性试点项目——培养培训师和农民带头人。

⑥ 为制定和应用良好农业规范方法调动资源。

Acknowledgements

I wish to express my thanks to Ms. Shantel Stuart who was responsible for typing manuscript and preparing the electronic edition. Her assistance was an invaluable component in this project.

Too often the help of family members are taken for granted. However, this book[①] would never have been completed without the encouragement of my wife, Sandra; my sons, Geoff and Tim; and their wives, Vanessa and Suzy. Their editing was extremely important and their critique of the document provided invaluable insights for me.

The Bahama Journal and its publisher, Wendall Jones enabled me to explore the Caribbean for years via *The Eneas Files* which has provided a special forum in the book itself.

Several people were involved with the preparation of the manuscript in its various stages. These individuals, Rachela Tirelli and Latricia Musgrove, had to decipher my handwriting in order to use their computer skills in several critical areas of the manuscript.

An important element in the preparation of this book has been the utilization of information and communication technology in conjunction with the assistance of international agencies like the Food and Agriculture Organization (FAO) and the Inter-American Institute for Cooperation on Agriculture (IICA). The FAO offices (Sub-Regional in Barbados and Representative in Jamaica, Liaison office in The Bahamas) have been extremely effective in the compilation of data. I single out Dr. Barbara Graham and Mr. Hesdie Grauwde in Barbados, Mr. Greg Bethel in The Bahamas and Dr. Dunstan Campbell in Jamaica.

---

① 本书英文部分于 2009 年由 Authorhouse 出版。

IICA's local representative, Dr. Marikis Alvarez has always displayed a great deal of cooperative spirit in the exchange of views on agriculture in the region and in the provision of data.

Both FAO and IICA, through their decentralization policy, have been useful as a conduit for the dissemination of the information around the region. In every instance the professionals went the extra mile to obtain the requested information and data.

The Executive Director of the Caribbean Poultry Association, Mr. Robert Best has been helpful in the provision of data on poultry in the region. Networking with other professionals in the region was invaluable, particularly through the FAO Caribbean List on the Internet.

The information on the work of the Episcopal Church in Haiti was provided by Mr. George Lockwood who was also instrumental in locating the textbooks, *The Theory of Economic Growth* and *An Economic Study of Small Farming in Jamaica*. These books were used in my studies at the University of the West Indies, St. Augustine, Trinidad and were misplaced by me.

Special thanks are extended to Bahamian artist, Ms. Abby Smith, for book cover. Her artwork depicts "the small farmer in the Caribbean." The small farmer is a legacy of slavery. During the colonial years he or she was exploited and now in the Independence Era, he or she remains marginalized economically and socially.

This work would not have been completed without the support of those mentioned as well as several others.

Introduction

My fascination with the Caribbean region began when my maternal aunt moved from The Bahamas to Jamaica after marrying a Cuban born to Jamaican parents. It was in the late 1940s when my aunt Vernie and her husband Roy Johnson, went to Jamaica to take up residence.

Uncle Roy was a communications officer with the West Indies Regiment and was stationed in The Bahamas. Now that World War II had ended, he was demobilized, hence his return to the homeland of his parents, Jamaica.

My aunt's marriage and eventual move to Jamaica were the factors which were responsible for the family visits to Jamaica as well as facilitated my exposure to Jamaican culture and two languages of the Caribbean, the Spanish of Cuba and the creolized English of Jamaica. On occasions, uncle Roy would lapse into a Cuban dialect or Jamaican Creole depending on the situation and the tenor of the conversation.

This exposure to Jamaican culture combined with the Cuban-rooted antics of uncle Roy was instrumental in stimulating my interest in the region as a whole, resulting from what I had seen in Jamaica and imagined for the other Caribbean islands which I had yearned to visit. By the time my aunt and uncle Roy returned to The Bahamas, I had received a glimpse into the culture of one island, Jamaica. It was at this point that the fascination began.

Cuba held significance. As a boy I accompanied my maternal grandfather, John Henry Saunders, who operated a native restaurant just off Bay Street in the 1940s and part of the 1950s, when he made his daily purchases for fresh fruit, vegetables, fish and native meats on the Market Range, now Woodes Rodgers Drive in downtown Nassau.

One of his stops was to the Ragged Island boats which were known to ply between

Ragged Island and Cuba to buy products to sell on the Nassau market. This was my introduction to a variety of Cuban items, one of which has remained a favorite today— guava cheese, which was packed in rectangular wooden boxes about 3×12 inches. Of course, there were the rums, liqueurs, sugar and one or two other products. If my memory serves me right, I do not remember cigars. The Ragged Island connection was the chief mechanism through which trade was conducted with Cuba on a sustained basis.

The thirst for a greater understanding of the region had been piqued by a number of other events and scenarios. There was the periodic influx of West Indians into The Bahamas and this led me to ponder the peripatetic nature of Caribbean peoples.

West Indians from the Anglophone colonies had, over several decades, been migrating to The Bahamas to find work as skilled tradesmen, policemen, household workers, educators, clergy men or to take up appointments in various professional positions as civil servants or in the private sector. Immigrants came from Jamaica, Barbados, Trinidad, Tobago, and some islands of the eastern Caribbean and even the South American mainland, specifically Guyana and Belize (formerly British Honduras), to join the workforce of The Bahamas. Most were assimilated into the Bahamian society through marriage, just like my aunt and her husband.

The assimilation process was rooted in the commonalities of language (English), British educational system, Anglicanism, the legal system and the legacies of colonialism and slavery. Another important ingredient in the assimilation process was the University of the West Indies (UWI).

As a university student at the UWI campus in St. Augustine, Trinidad during the 1960s, I was once again exposed to natives from every Anglophone Caribbean island. Bahamians were perceived as being different from other West Indians because of a noticeable twang in our speech. This resulted from our proximity to the United States (US) and also from the fact that our economy was tourist driven, hence service-based whilst their economies were export driven based on agricultural commodities grown on estates or by small farmers.

While at the UWI, one acquired the facility to discern speech patterns in order to identify the accents or dialects of the peoples of each island. In my role as a public official, I have traveled to most of the island nations and attended many conferences, workshops and seminars. This constant exposure to different island countries served to deepen my fascination with the Caribbean as a region.

In 1980, as a member of the Bahamian delegation to the Food and Agriculture Organization Caribbean and Latin American Regional Conference in Havana, Cuba, I had the opportunity to have an audience with the President of Cuba, Fidel Castro. On another fact—finding mission to Guyana in 1973, I had several meetings with the late President of Guyana, Forbes Burnham. In 2000, as a member of a Caribbean Poultry Association (CPA)'s group, we had a meeting to discuss poultry production in the region with the Prime Minister of Barbados, Owen Arthur.

A notable CARICOM leader was Sir Lynden Oscar Pindling, who has been revered as the Father of the Independent Bahamas. Sir Lynden led The Bahamas for 25 successive years from 1967 to 1992 as Premier (1967 to 1973) and Prime Minister from (1973 to 1992). He held the distinction of being the longest serving Head of Government in CARICOM. I had the honor of being a candidate with him and on his Party's ticket in the 1997 General Election for the Honorable House of Assembly of The Bahamas, the second oldest parliament in the hemisphere.

Because of our geographical position between the US and Hispaniola, there would be contact with Haiti and the Dominican Republic. My contact with the Dominican Republic has been superficial with separate visits to Romania to view farming in that area and Punta Cana, one of the all-inclusive hotel properties in that country.

On the other hand, Haiti has evolved into a special case with the government of The Bahamas and Bahamians in general. Prior to the second half of the 20th century, the connection with Haiti was principally through trade. One of the biggest traders with Haiti was Mr. Wilfred Toothe, the brother of my godfather, the late Hon. T. A. Toothe, a prominent lawyer and Member of Parliament.

Mr. Toothe's warehouse was adjacent to my grandfather's restaurant and near the Market Range. His living was trading with Haitians, just like the Ragged Islanders whose business was trading with Cubans.

During the repressive presidencies of Haiti's Francois "Papa Doc" Duvalier and his son, Jean Claude "Baby Doc" Duvalier, the migration of Haitians en masse to The Bahamas commenced.

Prior to the Duvaliers, the Haitians who sought refuge in The Bahamas were skilled tradesmen or artisans. Under the Duvalier Regime, this changed as the exodus brought thousands from rural Haiti. These people had little education and were poor. Their rural background enabled them to become farm labourers in many farming communities in The Bahamas.

This category was in sharp contrast to the Haitians who were my schoolmates at St. Augustine's College in Nassau. St. Augustine's was a Benedictine Monastic School which was operated by Benedictine monks from Minnesota. The Haitian boys boarded and came from wealthy and influential families. They had come to The Bahamas to study for the Cambridge Overseas Examination from the United Kingdom (UK).

In 2003 I was appointed The Bahamas Ambassador to United Nations' FAO. In this regard, the Director-General of FAO, Dr. Jacques Dior, was to address the Caribbean Community Heads of Government Conference in Jamaica. In my capacity as Ambassador, the Prime Minister of The Bahamas, the Rt. Hon. Perry G. Christie, included me as member of The Bahamas' delegation to the conference. It was this occasion which heightened my appreciation for the political development of region as one could see in action Caribbean leaders working together to address the challenges facing the region at this juncture of the 21st century.

I have had a wide spectrum of interaction with Caribbean peoples through visits around the region and by coming in contact with large numbers of them who reside in The Bahamas. It is this background plus the fact that as a Caribbean agriculturist with expertise in agricultural development, I, like others, are cognizant of the fact that Caribbean agriculture is in a state of decline while Caribbean tourism has emerged as the dominant sector in most of the economies of these small island states. As a result of this, the region is being transformed in a number of areas. This book will, hopefully, shed some light on the transition which has taken place and is still taking place during the second half of the 20th century and at the dawn of this new century.

Chapter 1

A New Era

"The existence of slavery and its aftermath is the most fundamental factor in the history and development of Caribbean societies. Without taking account of the significance of slavery, it is impossible to understand the nature of the contemporary Caribbean."

—Fernando Henriques, Jamaican, UWI Professor

With the ending of World War II, the geopolitical scene would be altered. Europe was ravaged by the war and it would require the USA's Marshall Plan to rebuild the nations of Western Europe. The Soviet Union would emerge as the power in the east thus changing the global paradigm as the Cold War sets in. This would have implications for the colonial possessions of European states. In less than a decade after World War II, the commencement of the dismantling of the various colonial outposts would begin.

In the British Empire, this meant the attainment of independence by India in 1950. Seven years later, in 1957, the West African colony of the Gold Coast became Ghana and the first Anglophone colony in Africa to gain its independence. The independence movement would also reach the Caribbean when Jamaica, in 1962, would achieve the distinction of becoming the first colony in the British West Indies to achieve its independence. By 1983, virtually all of the former colonies had gained their independence from Britain. Only the smaller territories (Turks and Caicos Islands, Montserrat, Anguilla, British Virgin Islands, Cayman Islands and Bermuda) have remained dependencies. Three South American countries (Belize, Guyana and Suriname) have aligned themselves as members of the CARICOM. Independence brought to a close some 300 years of British control of the region.

The Caribbean was a region born out of exploration, extinction and exploitation. Growing up as British subject in a British colony like The Bahamas, we were taught that Europeans discovered the New World of which the first landing was the Caribbean archipelago of The Bahamas. Christopher Columbus' encounter with the Arawaks whom he met on the island of Guanahani, which he renamed San Salvador, ended in the depopulation of The Bahamas. The inhabitants whom he met were, in a short time, taken against their will to Cuba and Hispaniola, today's Haiti and Dominican Republic, to perform work which eventually led to their extinction. In order to exploit the resources of the region, the Europeans turned to Africa for manpower thus commencing the African Diaspora in the New World and placing Caribbean region at the very centre of the phenomenon which would evolve into the inhumane institution of slavery.

Slavery would form the backdrop to the march for independence. Despite being abolished in the British Empire in 1834, the psychological impact of slavery has manifested itself on the descendants of the African slaves in the Caribbean in various ways—politically, socially, economically and spiritually. With the abolition of slavery in the New World, the era of the indentured labourer ushered in the influx of Asians, mostly East Indians, Indonesians and Chinese, thereby diversifying the ethnicity of the region. It is this potpourri of people which comprises the independent states of the Caribbean region.

The interaction between geography and politics has played a significant role in shaping the Caribbean as a region during the Colonial Era and now during the years as sovereign states. At the height of the Colonial Era, the Caribbean was a critical component in the Triangular Trade which facilitated the shipment of rum and sugar from the region to Britain which, in turn, sent firearms, cloth, salt and other items to West Africa from where black men and women were bartered for those items and sold in the Caribbean as slaves to the owners of the plantations where sugar cane was grown.

Today, the Caribbean's geography and politics have placed the region in a different role. The complexities of nation building of which economic transformation is vital have presented a new set of challenges. With independence came, all of the reigns of governance thereby differentiating it from the colonial period. This would become a transforming experience.

The Anglophone Caribbean, as a result of the number of states which became independent in the second half of the 20th century, has been driving the geopolitical affairs of the region. These mid-20th century independent states have been able to undertake this through CARICOM, which has evolved into a body which embraces multicultures and different languages. CARICOM states of former British colonies have stepped into independence with strong democratic traditions—the Bahamian and Barbadian parliaments are two of the oldest parliaments in the hemisphere. There is also a strong institutional base, notably the UWI, which is truly a regional tertiary institution, the Caribbean Development Bank (CDB), the Caribbean Agricultural Research and Development Institute (CARDI), Caribbean Regional Negotiation Machinery (CRNM) and Caribbean Single Market and Economy (CSME). These independent states via CARICOM have had a catalytic effect in moving the region and keeping it on a progressive path. The task was and continues to be challenging.

Figure 1.1   Caribbean Leaders: Christie (left), Castro (centre) and Bird (far right)[1]

Table 1.1   CARICOM—15 Member States and 5 Associate Members

Member State	Population (2006 est.)	Per Capita Income (2005 est.)
The Bahamas	320,665	$17,800
Barbados	279,912	$17,000
Belize	287,730	$6,800

(to be continued)

[1] Fidel Castro, President of the Republic of Cuba (longest serving Head of State in the region), the Rt. Hon. Perry G. Christie, M. P. Prime Minister of the Commonwealth of The Bahamas. (The Third Prime Minister of The Bahamas) and the Hon. Lester Bird, former Prime Minister of Antigua and Barbuda at a CARICOM meeting with Cuba in Havana during 2005. Photo courtesy of: Peter Ramsey.

Member State	Population (2006 est.)	Per Capita Income (2005 est.)
Guyana	767,245	$4,600
Haiti	8,308,504	$361
Jamaica	2,758,124	$4,400
Suriname	439,117	$4,100
Trinidad & Tobago	1,065,842	$16,700
	Subtotal 14,227,139	

CARICOM comprised the members' states of which all of the Organization of Eastern Carribbean States (OECS) are included with the exception of Anguilla and the British Virgin Islands which are associate members.

The population and per capita data obtained from Central Intelligence Agency (CIA)—World Factbook, World Bank (Haiti).

Sub-Region

Table 1.2   OECS

State	Population (2004 est.)	Per Capita Income (2002 est.)
Anguilla	13,008	$8,600
Antigua & Barbuda	68,320	$11,000
British Virgin Islands	22,187	$16,000
Dominica	69,278	$5,400
Grenada	89,357	$5,000
Montserrat	9,245	$3,400
St. Lucia	164,213	$5,400
St. Kitts & Nevis	38,836	$8,800
St. Vincent & the Grenadines	117,193	$2,900
Subtotal	591,637	

Table 1.3   CARICOM Associate Members

State	Population (2004 est.)	Per Capita Income (2002 est.)
Bermuda	65,773	$69,900 (2004)
Cayman Islands	45,436	$32,300 (2004)
Turks & Caicos Islands	21,152	$11,500 (2002)
Subtotal	132,361	
CARICOM Total	14,951,137 (2006)	
		$3,500 (2005)
Cuba	11,382,820 (2006)	$7,000 (2005)
Puerto Rico	3,927,188 (2006)	$14,500
Dominican Republic	9,183,984 (2006)	$16,000
US Virgin Islands	108,605	
Netherlands Antilles	221,736	
Caribbean Region Subtotal	39,775,470	

(to be continued)

State	Population (2004 est.)	Per Capita Income (2002 est.)
		$14,400 (2003)
Martinique	436,131	$7,900 (2003)
Guadeloupe	452,776	
St. Martin		
Caribbean Region Total	40,664,377	

Intermezzo: *The Eneas Files, The Bahama Journal*   The Caribbean's Geopolitical Mix

Whether we want to accept it or not, The Bahamas is hitched to the CARICOM wagon. Last week at the 20th Heads of Government Summit, CARICOM states admitted Haiti to its fold.

The Bahamas is the closest CARICOM country to Haiti and Haiti has created possibly more concerns for The Bahamas than any of the other CARICOM states which are further south and deeper in the Caribbean Basin.

In addition to CARICOM, there is another Caribbean grouping called the Caribbean Forum (CARIFORUM), which, prior to last week, comprised CARICOM states plus Haiti, and the Dominican Republic. In the foreseeable future, probably early in the next century, Cuba will join one of these groupings.

Within CARICOM, there is the seven member grouping—OECS. These states comprise Grenada, St. Vincent and the Grenadines, St. Lucia, Dominica, Antigua and Barbuda and St. Kitts and Nevis.

With Suriname being a part of CARICOM, now Haiti and in the near future Cuba, trilingualism (Dutch from Suriname, French from Haiti and Spanish from the Dominican Republic and Cuba) will become the spoken languages in various fora of the Caribbean.

Also, at the recent summit, Venezuela made serious overtures to CARICOM. Its president came personally to address the Heads and made some proposals which CARICOM may not be able to ignore.

Venezuela is an oil rich state where democracy is in its embryonic stages; its financial clout from its oil resources cannot be ignored.

This is the geographical scenario which is developing in the Caribbean. The Caribbean is no longer confined to the islands in the Caribbean Sea. It is now inclusive of those states whose shores feel the warmth of the Caribbean Seas like Venezuela.

Excluding Cuba and Venezuela, the population of CARIFORMUM in 1996 was approximately 22 million people—38% located in the Dominican Republic, 34% in Haiti and then the percentages drop off substantially as the next highest is 12% in Jamaica.

With Cuba's 11 million people, CARIFORUM's population increases by 50%. If an arrangement evolves with Venezuela's 20 million plus, then CARIFORUM's population doubles.

Globalization has exacerbated the move towards trading blocs. It has been demonstrated that countries are able to expand their exports through the vehicle of trading blocs. This has been very obvious in CARICOM and as liberalization gains more and more prominence, trade will continue to increase.

All of these countries have huge labour pools with unemployment running high throughout the region with Barbados and The Bahamas being the exceptions. By putting the labour force of these countries to work, exports from these countries can be extremely competitive intra-regionally and globally.

During the last 50 years of this century, there have been serious changes in the politics of the Caribbean. The rise of Castroism in Cuba isolated Cuba from its Caribbean neighbours for almost three decades; however, this is changing. The decolonization of the region by the British and Dutch has established a number of independent states like those which comprise CARICOM.

With independence, these states have attempted to a fashion regional identity which cuts across language difference and culture peculiarities in order to build, in the case of the Anglophone Caribbean, on the strengths of commonalities embedded in democratic principles and British jurisprudence.

For three centuries, no overseas region was contested more vigorously by the imperial powers of Britain, France, Spain and the Netherlands. Today, the Caribbean is one of the most politically stable regions of the world. Its chief challenge now is orientating its economies to function effectively in the global economy.

Chapter 2

Economic Transformation

Creating an Urban Society

"In the middle of the yard, there was kindled a massive fire, which provided illumination as well as a spirit of warmth and jollity, to the event. It also served to tune the goatskin drums, which they used to provide rhythm for the dance... moved by the rhythm and music anyone could jump into the ring, and dance to his or her soul's delight."

—Dr. Cleveland W. Eneas, Bahamian, *Bain Town*

A Case Study: The Bahamas

The Bahamas has a geographical position which has enabled this archipelago to enjoy the advantages of proximity to the US. The island of Bimini in the northern Bahamas is only forty-eight miles away from the Florida coastline. It is said that on a clear night one can see the glare of Miami lights from Bailey Town.

It is this proximity which has been in a major factor in the post war economic boom which The Bahamas experienced with the ending of World War II and the recent post 9/11 boom.

The post war boom was the catalyst for the transformation of the economy of The Bahamas from an agriculture-based economy and seasonal tourism to an industry which became a 12-month commercial business. It also led to the creation of an urban society centered around the capital city of Nassau in the island of New Providence and the newly established city of Freeport on the island of Grand Bahama.

The post 9/11 boom would bring an unprecedented level of investment in the Family Islands resulting from the Christie Administration's economic development strategy of encouraging the development of an anchor touristic project on each Family Island. This strategy would assist in the reversal of migration from the Family Islands to the urban centers, alleviate poverty by creating jobs and bring sustainable economic activity on the islands of the southeastern Bahamas and facilitate the trickling down of the tourism dollar to a broader segment of the population.

Post War Boom

Prior to the ending of World War II, most Bahamians lived on Out Islands, which today are referred to as the Family Islands. In 1943, the population of The Bahamas was just under 70,000 of which about 30,000 lived on New Providence, near and around the capital city of Nassau. The remaining 40,000 were scattered throughout twenty (20) islands with a significant number of inhabitants.

During the 1940s, 57% of the population lived on the Family Islands or in rural Bahamas. In those days, most islands of The Bahamas had a lifestyle which depicted that of a quaint fishing village. This was reflected in the societal mores, diet and attachment to the land as small farmers in many instances as subsistence farmers, and to the sea as fisher folk.

In his book, *A History of The Bahamas*, Michael Craton, an Englishman and former secondary school history master at the prestigious Government High School in The Bahamas, captures the mood of The Bahamas at the end of the war. Graton stated the following:

> "The end of the war, so joyfully celebrated, was not followed by the traditional slump. Indeed, the two and half decades after 1945 were a period of unparalleled, almost uninterrupted expansion and success. Soaring tourist and investment figures and a corresponding rise in government revenue were accompanied by huge improvements in living standards, education and political sophistication. At the same time, encouraged by a declining will or ability to rule on the part of the British government, steady progress was made towards full self-determination."

Political power in the 1940s was in the hands of the white minority which comprised a group of merchants who controlled commerce in The Bahamas enabling them to dictate the rate of economic development in this archipelago. Their businesses on the main street, Bay Street, of the capital city Nassau labeled them the Bay Street Boys. This oligarchy wielded political and economic control of The Bahamas.

As a colony with a Royal Governor who headed an executive council and parliamentary bodies, the Bay Street Boys dominated the chambers of government and guided the reigns of governance in the colony.

There was no ministerial government until 1964. The board system prevailed. One of the important boards was The Bahamas Development Board.

In 1949, Stafford Loftus Sands became Chairman of the powerful Bahamas Development Board. He would retain his position for 15 years. In 1964, it would evolve into the Ministry of Tourism. For almost 18 years, Mr. Sands, who eventually was knighted and later known as Sir Stafford, was visionary for tourism growth and development; he was also responsible for identifying offshore banking a viable economic activity which would eventually become an important sector in the economy of The Bahamas during this period.

As Chairman of the Development Board (1949–1964) and Minister of Tourism and Finance (1964–1967), Sir Stafford was the most powerful political figure in The Bahamas. He was able to achieve this status because of his legal training, business acumen and political clout.

Ministerial government came when internal self-government was granted under 1964 constitution. Prior to this, there were electoral abuses which enabled the Bay Street Boys, who eventually formed the United Bahamian Party (UBP) whose political base was the white minority. One of the elements in the political arsenal of the UBP was the company vote.

Figure 2.1   Sir Stafford Lofthouse Sands[1]

---

[1] Chairman, Bahamas Development Board (1949–1964); Minister of Tourism (1964–1967).

Companies were eligible to vote in elections. Sir Stafford, who represented the city constituency, had some 300 companies registered in his chambers; it is said that he would sit in the voter's booth and vote for himself 300 times.

Sir Stafford was a product of a Bay Street business family. He was an articled clerk in the Chambers of Sir Kenneth Solomon. His secondary education was obtained at the Government High School and not the segregated Queen's College.

Sir Stafford was educated, trained as a lawyer, and developed his business acumen and political skills in The Bahamas. He was a product of The Bahamas.

The Majority Rule came on January 10th, 1967. Lynden O. Pindling led Progressive Liberal Party (PLP) defeated UBP, Sir Stafford went into voluntary exile in Spain. On January 25th, 1972 at the age of 59 years, he succumbed to cancer in a London hospital; he never returned to The Bahamas. However, his legacy of having transformed the economy of The Bahamas from one dependent on agriculture to one dominated by success i.e. tourism and financial services has established him as a Bahamian visionary. The Sands model for a small island developing state is being duplicated throughout the region.

The Bahamas was early on the Caribbean tourism radar. Sir Stafford recognized this and The Bahamas Development Board sought to improve airlift in order to take advantage of The Bahamas' proximity to the US, particularly the highly populated urban centers along the US eastern seaboard. Combining the charm of Old Nassau with the sun, sand and sea, visitor arrivals grew.

Developments in the Transformation Process (1943–2000)

The second half of the 20th century for The Bahamas would be a period of prolific growth and development in all spheres of life. The economy of The Bahamas was dramatically altered by the developments which would take place in the burgeoning tourism industry and an embryonic offshore banking centre.

The Bahamas Development Board under its first chairman, Harold G. Christie embarked on a program to promote The Bahamas. Mr. Christie's objective was "to turn this insignificant community into the new Mecca of the world's rich." In 1949 when Sir Stafford Sands became Chairman, The Bahamas attracted some 32,018 visitors.

By the end of the 1950s, visitor arrivals would reach 264,758. Sun, sand and sea were the centerpieces of the tourism promotional programme. This was further enhanced by the introduction of *The Hotel Encouragement Act* in 1949.

The Hotel Encouragement Act was a piece of incentive legislation which provided hotel developers with duty-free concessions on a range of items in the construction of hotels as well as equipment and materials. In conjunction with this legislation came the construction of the Cable Beach Golf Course by the Canadian millionaire, Harry Oakes, who was said to be one of the richest men in the British Empire at that time. With this new thrust to attract visitors, provisions had to be made for an expanded airport.

In 1957 the National International Airport became operational and Oakes Field Airport which was located just outside of Nassau was closed.

Development activities were not confined to New Providence. With the signing of *The Hawksbill Creek Agreement* in 1955, the island of Grand Bahama would undergo transformation creating the second city of Freeport.

Politically, there was much agitation. In 1953, PLP was formed with Lynden O. Pindling, a young British trained attorney as its leader. From its inception, the PLP became a thorn in the side of the white power structure, the Bay Street oligarchy which would eventually form themselves into UBP.

Political tensions were inflamed when the Taxi Cab Union initiated a blockade of Nassau International Airport in order to protest the utilization of buses by tour companies and hotels to transport guests. This situation ballooned into a national strike in 1958 when hotel workers aligned themselves with the cab drivers. The matter was resolved with cab drivers having the exclusive right to transport arriving tourists.

It was during this decade that migration to New Providence reached the point where more Bahamians resided there than all the other islands of The Bahamas combined. The Bahamas had become an urban society.

The 1960s would be a landmark period in Bahamas tourism. 1968 would become the year when The Bahamas would receive its 1 million visitors.

A number of factors would contribute to this upsurge. The most important would be the introduction of casino gaming in both Nassau and Freeport.

Freeport would come into its own as a touristic destination with the construction of a 18-hole golf course and two miniature 9-hole courses plus the construction of the Lucayan Beach Hotel. On the island of Abaco, the Treasure Cay development would come on stream.

Hog Island, which is located less than a mile from New Providence, would undergo a name change and become Paradise Island. By the end of 1960s, a bridge would connect Paradise Island to New Providence thereby providing New Providence with two destinations, Cable Beach and Paradise Island.

Politically constitutional change would usher in ministerial government in 1964 giving The Bahamas internal self-government.

The general election of 1967 would see the political demise of the Bay Street oligarchy, UBP and the emergence of PLP under Pindling.

For the black majority, the general election of 1967 would become the most significant political event since Emancipation in 1834.

The 1950s and 1960s were decades of dramatic changes in the sociology of The Bahamas. This change stemmed from the introduction of women not only in the workforce, but also in the political affairs of the archipelago.

Women became an important part of the hotel labour force as thousands of women left their homes in New Providence and the Family Islands to seek employment in the hotels, principally as maids. A significant number of women became income earners. For those who were single mothers, they became head of households with an income. Women also dominated the market as vendors of souvenir items, particularly the native straw items which became a key aspect of Bahamian tourism. In 1960 women gained the right to vote and sit in the legislator of The Bahamas.

The Bahamas had acquired the reputation of being a stable developing country in contrast to events which were taking place in countries coming out of the colonial experience. This stability attracted foreign investment in the tourism sector.

By mid 1970, visitor arrivals had climbed to 1.5 million. The golf course became an element of attraction for visitors as new courses were constructed in Freeport, Grand Bahama, Treasure Cay, Abaco and in New Providence (South Ocean and Coral Harbour). Recognizing the growth and development of the tourism sector, the Hotel Training College and the Hotel Corporation were established. In order to deepen the visitor experience at the community level, the Ministry of Tourism implemented the People-to-People Programme.

The People-to-People Programme was committed to bringing the visitor into the home of the average Bahamian.

With the US being the main market for Bahamian visitors, The Bahamas government was able to negotiate an agreement with the US government to operate a pre-clearance facility in Nassau (1974) and Freeport (1976). This was a tremendous tool in accommodating the large number of Americans returning to the US from The Bahamas.

After almost a decade of internal self-government and five years of PLP governance, The Bahamas attained its independence in 1973, ending almost 300 years of colonial rule and bringing a close to the colonial experience.

The Bahamas would now embark on a new chapter in its national life. The 1980s would highlight phenomenal growth and development in tourism.

Sir Clement held a portfolio with tourism on three different occasions.

① Ministry of Tourism and Telecommunications (14th October, 1969–30th November, 1971).

② Ministry of Foreign Affairs and Tourism (9th October, 1984–19th August, 1992).

③ Ministry of Tourism and Public Personnel (9th October, 1987–30th September, 1990).

Figure 2.2 Sir Clement Maynard[1]

Overall, Sir Clement served as the minister responsible for tourism in The Bahamas for 13 years. Under Sir Clement's leadership, The Bahamas became the tourism mecca of the Caribbean.

---

[1] Former Deputy Prime Minister of The Bahamas (29th October, 1985–18th August, 1992).

Table 2.1   Tourism Workers by Gender (Hotels and Restaurants) 1991–2005

Year	Total	Male	Female
1991	21,180	8,800	12,380
1992	21,175	8,950	12,225
1993	18,895	8,385	10,510
1994	18,385	8,850	10,030
1995	19,405	7,625	11,780
1996	20,360	8,655	11,705
1997	21,440	9,240	12,200
1998			
1999	23,300	9,630	13,670
2000			
2001	25,515	10,800	14,715
2002	25,690	10,890	14,800
2003	27,920	11,985	15,935
2004	23,765	9,180	14,585
2005	29,095	11,380	17,715

Source: Dept. of Statistics

In early 1980, 2 million tourists had visited The Bahamas. By 1983, the figure had climbed to 2.6 million; in three yeas (1986), it topped off at 3 million. It is during this decade that cruise ship passengers would exceed stopover visitors by air. The cruise ship business would become the dominant source of visitors to The Bahamas.

After 25 years as the governing party, PLP would experience its first defeat in 1992. The reigns of government would fall into the hands of the Free National Movement (FNM) under the leadership of Mr. Hubert A. Ingraham.

The Ingraham Administration would seal a deal with the South African Hotelier, Sol Kerzner, who would bring a new dimension to tourism in The Bahamas with his purchase of the Resorts International Holdings on Paradise Island. The Kerzner purchase rejuvenated tourism in The Bahamas and by the end of the 1990s, the number of annual visitors had increased to 4 million.

At the dawn of the 21st century, The Bahamas had undergone a transformation of its economy, its demographics and its way of life as a result of the growth and development of tourism into the most important sector of the economy. In 55 years, The Bahamas had evolved from an agricultural dependent archipelago to a thriving touristic urban centered sovereign state with a per capita income approaching $20,000.

Tourism in conjunction with financial services had created a service-based economy.

Post 9/11 Boom

9/11, for Americans, was a second Pearl Harbour. For the rest of the world, it would mark a new era of terrorism; it would change the manner in which people travel and bring a higher level of intensity to security.

In The Bahamas and the Caribbean, 9/11 was a wake-up call for many of these small island states as the vulnerabilities of their economies were exposed because everything stopped—the tourists stopped coming, the airplanes stopped flying because the airspace over North America was shut down, the cruise ships stopped sailing and the container ships were moored to the docks in Miami, Ft. Lauderdale, Rivera Beach, Jacksonville and elsewhere with food, supplies and animal feeds destined for an import dependent region.

The two vital links of air travel and cruise ships to Bahamian and Caribbean tourism were suspended. Americans themselves began to view foreign travel from a different perspective and seemed more interested in traveling to nearby destinations. The Bahamas was ideal for leisure trips and the establishment of second homes. Being only 48 miles from the Florida coast and about 1,000 miles from New York, The Bahamas was about to receive a windfall of foreign direct investment.

Figure 2.3   Atlantis on Paradise Island—Flagship property of Kerzner International

The centerpiece of the government's economic development strategy was the establishment of anchor projects on the various Family Islands, particularly those in the southeastern Bahamas which are less developed than Pine Islands (Abaco, Andros and Grand Bahama) in the northern Bahamas. This strategy has attracted some $11.5 billion in foreign direct investment by mid 2006.

The architect of this strategy was the Christie Administration which succeeded the Ingraham Administration in May, 2002. Hon. Perry G. Christie, the Prime Minister of The Bahamas has put much emphasis on making this strategy a reality, hence its implementation among the Family Islands.

Projects have been approved and are at the constructional/operational stage on Abaco, Andros, the Berry Islands, Crooked Island, Eleuthera, Exuma, Grand Bahama, Mayaguana, New Providence, Rum Cay and San Salvador, as shown in Table 2.2.

The government of The Bahamas has signed a contract with a Canadian firm to manage the Lynden Pindling International Airport which is undergoing a massive expansion and upgrading programme. This programme will modernize the airport facilities and make it the premier airport after 9/11 in the region.

In conjunction with this, the government has initiated a redevelopment plan for the city of Nassau and the Nassau Harbour. The transformation of the city of Nassau and its harbour from the "Old Nassau" which was the centre of The Bahamas Development Board's tourism promotion will take place under a public-private sector arrangement. The entity which will implement the transformation is the Nassau Economic Development Commission and the Nassau Tourism and Development Board.

The mechanism to sustain this process is through a committee called the Business Improvement District, a Canadian pioneered body with units in 1,500 cities around the world.

In 2005, The Bahamas hit the 5 million visitor arrivals' mark. The post 9/11 boom will possibly result in the number of visitor arrivals doubling the 2005 figure of 5 million within the next 2 to 3 years.

The Bahamas in 2006 had a population which was estimated to be about 324,000 of which 85% live between New Providence and Grand Bahama, the urban centers of this archipelago. These anchor projects will create new employment opportunities on islands with communities which depend solely on farming and fishing for their livelihood. In a

Table 2.2   Developments in the Transformation Process (1943–2005)

| Decade | Year | Visitor Arrivals | Tourism Product Components | Major National Developments/Tourism | Demographics (Population Growth and Change) | | | Labour Force Engaged/Employed by Sector | | | Labour Force All Bahamas | Employed | |
					Nassau	Freeport, G.B.	Family Island	Agriculture (Small Farmers)	Tourism	Financial Services		Women	Men
	1943				29,391	2,333	37,122						
1940s	1949	32,018	Sun	*The Hotel Encouragement Act*									
	1950	45,371											
	1951	68,502											
	1952	84,718		Cable Beach Golf Course									
	1953	90,485	Sand		46,125	4,095	34,614						
	1954	109,605											
	1955	132,434		*The Hawksbill Creek Agreement* (Freeport, G.B.)									
1950s	1956	155,003	Sea (cruise ships, yachting)										
	1957	209,713		Opening of Nassau International Airport									
	1958	196,658		General Strike									
	1959	264,758		Castro overthrows Batista									

(to be continued)

Decade	Year	Visitor Arrivals	Tourism Product Components	Major National Developments/Tourism	Demographics (Population Growth and Change)			Labour Force Engaged/ Employed by Sector			Labour Force All Bahamas	Employed	
					Nassau	Freeport, G.B.	Family Island	Agriculture (Small Farmers)	Tourism	Financial Services		Women	Men
1960s	1960	341,977		a 18-hole golf course and 2 miniature 9-hole courses (Freeport, G.B.)									
	1961	368,211											
	1962	444,870		Hog Island renamed Paradise Island									
	1963	546,404	Gambling, golf course	Lucayan Beach Hotel opens casino, Treasure Cay, Abaco	80,907	8,230	41,083						
	1964			Paradise Island development, internal self-government, cabinet govt., first Minister of Tourism									
1960s	1965												
	1966												
	1967			Pindling Administration									
	1968	1,072,213		Bridge construction, Paradise Island									
	1969												
1970s	1970			Introduction of Cruise Statistics Hotel Act	101,503	25,859	41,450	3,099					

(to be continued)

Chapter 2 Economic Transformation | 179

Decade	Year	Visitor Arrivals	Tourism Product Components	Major National Developments/Tourism	Nassau	Freeport, G.B.	Family Island	Agriculture (Small Farmers)	Tourism	Financial Services	Labour Force All Bahamas	Women	Men
1970s	1971		Golf course	5 18-hole golf courses and 2 miniature courses (Freeport), Treasure Cay, Abaco									
	1972												
	1973	1,500,010		Independence/establishment of The Bahamas Hotel Training College				3,320					
	1974		Nassau & US opened pre-clearance facility	Hotel Corp. (promote tourism); South Ocean/Coral Harbour; golf course									
	1975			People-to-People Program				3,797					
	1976		Freeport	US opened pre-clearance facility									
	1977												
	1978			Centre for Hotel and Tourism Mgt., UWI Bahama Host Programme				4,214					
	1979												
1980s	1980	1,904,560			135,437	33,102	40,966						
	1981		Paradise Island	Club Med									

(to be continued)

Decade	Year	Visitor Arrivals	Tourism Product Components	Major National Developments/Tourism	Demographics (Population Growth and Change)			Labour Force Engaged/ Employed by Sector			Labour Force All Bahamas	Employed	
					Nassau	Freeport, G.B.	Family Island	Agriculture (Small Farmers)	Tourism	Financial Services		Women	Men
1980s	1981		Family Island	Eleuthera and San Salvador									
	1981		Freeport	Re-opening Lucayan Beach Hotel and casino									
	1982												
	1983	2,631,970		Cable Beach Hotel									
	1984												
	1985		Cruise ships	Exceed 1 m passengers									
	1986	3,007,300		Casino, Cable Beach									
	1987												
	1988	3,158,091		Cruises exceed air									
	1989				172,196	40,898	41,955						
1990s	1990		Cruise ships	Accounts for 2 m visitors, expansion of Prince George Dock									
	1991		Cruise ships						21,180	7,955	114,400	55,000	59,400
	1992		Cruise ships Family Island	Ingraham Administration/ Princess Cay, Bannerman Town, Eleuthera					21,178	7,940	114,700	54,300	60,400

(to be continued)

Decade	Year	Visitor Arrivals	Tourism Product Components	Major National Developments/Tourism	Demographics (Population Growth and Change)			Labour Force Engaged/Employed by Sector			Labour Force All Bahamas	Employed	
					Nassau	Freeport, G.B.	Family Island	Agriculture (Small Farmers)	Tourism	Financial Services		Women	Men
1990s	1993		Nassau Intl. Airport	New Terminal (pre-clearance facility and US departures)					18,895	11,465	121,800	57,400	64,400
			Nassau	Bahamas Tourism Training Centre									
	1994		Paradise Island Theme Resort	Sun International Atlantis ($140 m) Phase III				1,727	18,880	12,190	124,600	59,100	65,500
			Cable Beach	Super Club Breezes buys Ambassador Beach Hotel									
	1995			Sandals takes over Le Meridian, formerly Balmoral Beach Hotel					19,405	10,580	127,440	60,925	66,515
	1996								20,360	11,125	129,765	59,385	70,380
	1997								21,440	12,420	135,255	63,940	71,315
	1998			Phase II ($ 650 m), Atlantis; British colonial re-opened downtown, Nassau; School of Hospitality & Tourism; COB					22,120	13,970			
	1999								23,300	13,350	145,350	68,105	77,745

(to be continued)

Decade	Year	Visitor Arrivals	Tourism Product Components	Major National Developments/Tourism	Demographics (Population Growth and Change)			Labour Force Engaged/Employed by Sector			Labour Force All Bahamas	Employed	
					Nassau	Freeport, G.B.	Family Island	Agriculture (Small Farmers)	Tourism	Financial Services		Women	Men
2000s	2000	4,203,831	Freeport	Our Lucaya/Lucaya Harbour	212,432								
	2001		9/11	Isle of Capri/Harbour Island		46,954			25,515	16,330	153,310	74,230	79,080
	2002		FAA Certified International Airport, San Salvador	Christie Administration New Gov. Cruise Facility Welcome Centre, Prince George Dock ($ 2.8 m)			45,451		25,690	16,475	152,090	74,280	78,410
	2003	4,594,042	Exuma, Family Island	Emerald Bay Four Seasons					27,920	15,595	154,965	75,825	79,140
	2004	5,000,000	Freeport	Grand Bahama International Airport (9/11…); Hurricanes (Francis and Jeanne)					23,765	17,575	158,340	76,560	81,780
	2005		Paradise Island	Kerzner Group (Phase III) ($1 billion)				1,242	29,095	16,180	160,530	77,740	82,790

Source: Bahamas Department of Statistics

Agriculture comprises farming, fishing and forestry. This column relates to the number of small farmers actively engaged in farming.

Fishing employment increased from 9,300 in 1995 to 12,304 in 2004. These figures are compiled from the Department of Agriculture and Marine Resources.

Forestry is limited to Agro-Forestry i.e. Cascarilla bark in the south-eastern Bahamas.

socio-economic environment where the youth of these islands are not attracted to farming, these anchor projects will arrest the movement of women and youth to the urban centers.

In addition, this anchor project strategy is consistent with the UN Millennium Development Goals.

① Goal 1: Eradicate extreme poverty and hunger, particularly in rural communities.

② Goal 2: Promote gender equality and empower women. Tourism in The Bahamas has been effective in this regard in New Providence and Grand Bahama, and no doubt will be just as effective in Family Islands.

③ Goal 3: Ensure environmental sustainability. Environmental impact studies are required for all of these projects in the Family Islands.

With reference to healthcare, there are 12 community health districts with polyclinics, main clinics and satellite clinics relative to the population of the island in question. On New Providence and Grand Bahama, there are major hospitals; mini-hospitals have been planned for Abaco, Eleuthera and Exuma.

Regarding education, there are 13 educational districts under the aegis of the Ministry of Education offering primary through secondary schooling. In conjunction with the ministry network, there are 41 independent schools; these are operated chiefly by the various Christian denominations.

The healthcare and educational services fall within the 21 administrative districts which provide local government services to the inhabitants throughout the Bahamian archipelago. The 64 airports, of which 30 are paved, along with public docks and private marinas comprise the numerous ports of entry on the various Family Islands.

Through the anchor projects, the transformation process is being deepened to include all of The Bahamas.

Tourism Impact

The tourism journey in The Bahamas since the ending of World War II has been nothing short of spectacular. There has not been a decade when tourism has brought tangible rewards to The Bahamas and its people.

The benefits which have accrued to this archipelago have come not only from the geographical position of these islands to one of the richest nations on earth but also from the ingenuity of the people who inhabit these islands called The Bahamas. Those benefits have also brought challenges, such as economic marginalization to sections of the populace, disparity in development, a dichotomous Bahamas with the haves and have-nots and the influences of foreign dietary habits, culture and lifestyle.

In a recent statistical analysis by The Bahamas Department of Statistics revealed the following:

① Tourism's total economic contribution tallied $2.8 billion in 2003, comprising 51% of the Gross Domestic Product (GDP) of The Bahamas.

② This economic activity generated $1.6 billion in local wages or 61% of all wages.

③ In terms of employment, tourism is the catalyst for 97,383 jobs, or 63% of the employment base.

Tourism in The Bahamas has directly influenced virtually nine areas of the economy of The Bahamas namely hotels, restaurants, recreation, transportation, real estate, government, manufacturing, agribusiness and fisheries. In more recent times, the educational system from primary to tertiary levels respectively, have been oriented to meeting the human resource needs of a burgeoning tourism industry.

In small island developing states, tourism can be, in some respects, a savior and, in some other respects, it could bedevil the economy as was seen during the 9/11 episode.

Overall, The Bahamas has benefited, is benefiting and will continue to benefit from tourism. The impact of the post 9/11 boom has been projected to sustain the economy for decades.

Table 2.3　Post 9/11 Projects—Major Foreign Direct Investments

Island	Approved Projects Not Commenced	Approved Projects Constructional/Operational Stage
Abaco	Neandross & Zimmerman	The Abaco Club on Winding Bay
		New Plymouth Development Co.
		Abaco VI, Inc.
		Ocean Frontier
		Passerine at Abaco
Andros		Coconut Farms Ltd.
Bimini		Bimini Bay Resort
		Bimini Sands
Berry Islands		International Marinas—Chub Cay

(to be continued)

Island	Approved Projects Not Commenced	Approved Projects Constructional/Operational Stage
Cat Island	Crystal Mount Ltd.	
Crooked Island		Pittstown Point Landings Ltd.
Eleuthera	Powell Pointe at Cape Eleuthera	Windermere Development Co.
		Governor's Harbour Resort
		Eleuthera Properties Ltd.
		Two Seasons Resort
		Pineapple Fields
		Runaway Hill Club
		Romora Bay
		Coral Sands Hotel
		Valentine's Resort and Marina
Exuma	80/50 Private Residential Resort	Holmes Crab Cay
	Exuma Resort Developers Limited	Emerald Bay Resort and Marina
	Little Bay (Marvin Parker)	Roker's Point at Emerald Bay
	Three Sisters Hotel	Grand Isle Villas
	Kravitz Multimedia	L'lle D'Agnes
		Lignum Vitae Ltd.
		The Village at Hopper's Bay
Grand Bahama	Marriott Vacation Club International	Gold Rock Creek Enterprises
	Seaward of Grand Bahama	Island Seas Investments Ltd.
	William and Ruth Hamisch	Pharmachem Technologies Ltd.
Inagua	Flamingo Nest Resort	
Mayaguana		I-Group
New Providence		Atlantis Resort—Phase III
		Charlotteville Development
		BH RIU Hotels Ltd.
		Paradise Island Condominium Join Venture Ltd.
		Whispering Winds
		The Marley Freedom Resort
		Azura Development

(to be continued)

Island	Approved Projects Not Commenced	Approved Projects Constructional/Operational Stage
		Baha Mar Developers Ltd.
Rum Cay		Montana Holdings Ltd.
San Salvador		Club Med—Columbus Village

Source: Ministry of Financial Services and Investments (Newspaper Supplement)

Agriculture in Decline

Agriculture in The Bahamas is in a state of decline. This is reflected in two areas—a shrinking group of small farmers and a sectoral output which has been stagnant over the past quarter of a century (1980–2005).

Small Farmers

There have been two censuses of agriculture, one in 1978 and the other in 1994. In 1978, there were 4,214 small farmers; by 2005, that figure had decreased to 1,242. This reflected a loss of 2,972 from the sector. Over the 25-year period, the sector has been losing almost 120 small farmers per year, or ten farmers per month.

The small farmer is an endangered species as this grouping is aging and there are few replacements by the youth who, over the years, have migrated from the Family Islands to the urban centers of Nassau and Freeport in search of employment opportunities and tertiary education.

In 1994 census, 1,176 farmers representing 65% of the total number of small farmers (1727) were between the ages of 55 to 75 years. With a life expectancy for males at 68–69 years, by 2008 virtually all of these farmers are likely to be dead, though some may live longer. About 30% of this number are females who have a slightly longer life expectancy (75.3 years).

Farm Output

Farm output from agribusinesses and small farmers has peaked around $60 million in 2002. The agricultural sector of The Bahamas comprises three components:

① the small farmer;

② agribusinesses;

③ export agribusiness (US agribusiness companies operate offshore export farming operations in winter vegetable and citrus production respectively).

In all of these components, there have been substantial decline and this has adversely affected investment in the sector, employment, technology transfer, manpower development and the general growth of the sector.

Growth in the agribusiness subsector was led by the poultry industry both in broiler meat and table eggs production. In 1998, poultry was a $21 million industry with broiler production accounting for $21 million. In November 2002, however, the largest broiler unit, Gladstone Farms, went into receivership and closed its doors leaving a production vacuum $8–10 million and more than 300 unemployed farmer workers about 60% of whom were single mothers.

The main reason for the Gladstone closure was the reduction of duty on broiler meat from 70% plus stamp tax to 35% plus stamp tax. The government of The Bahamas' decision was influenced by pressure from food importers who supplied the hotels, gourmet restaurants and fast food businesses.

With the closure of Gladstone Farms, the broiler meat market is now dominated by imports as Bahamas Poultry in Grand Bahama, now the largest producer, fights for survival in an environment which is dominated by poultry product of leg quarters and wings which are being "dumped" not only in the Bahamian market, but throughout the Caribbean at prices which are less than the cost of production.

Broiler production in The Bahamas being technologically driven was the largest agribusiness, however, the demise of Gladstone Farms has been devastating to the growth and development of the sector overall.

The Bahamas as a result of its duty free concessions, proximity to the eastern seaboard of the US and outstanding sea transportation was an ideal locale for the production of winter vegetables, citrus and other orchard crops to the US market.

US agribusiness companies established farm operations on Abaco, North Andros and Grand Bahama. In 2004/5, the citrus groves in the Norman's Castle area of Abaco were let by the deadly citrus canker which caused the destruction of 3,000 acres of grapefruit. This was a blow to citrus exports from The Bahamas to the US.

In reviewing the agribusiness subsector, there is much concern about Market Access issues. The openness of the Bahamian economy has put agribusinesses at a disadvantage.

The Bahamas is the only Caribbean state which is not a member of the World Trade Organization (WTO) and does not abide by the rules and regulations of *The Agreement on Agriculture* (*AOA*). In many respects, the lack of adherence to the WTO, *AOA* has stifled the growth and development of agribusinesses and negatively impacted their competitiveness.

Contribution to GDP

The GDP of The Bahamas has been expanding. In 2005, the GDP was estimated to be $6 billion. This has resulted from the expansion in tourism and financial services.

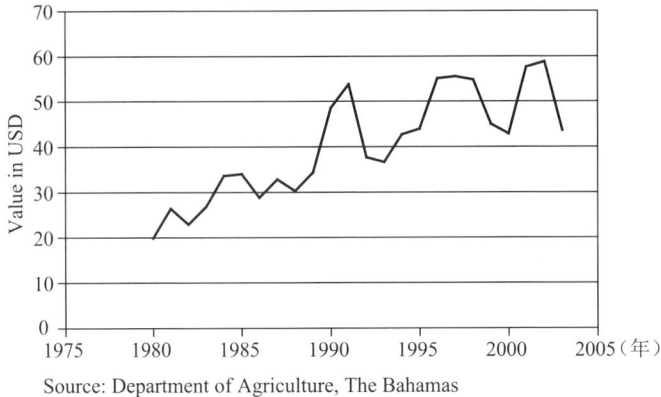

Source: Department of Agriculture, The Bahamas

Figure 2.4   National Output—Agribusiness and Small Farmer Subsectors in Million Dollars

Apart from fisheries, which significant in 2005, was a $100 million industry, has become a contributor to the GDP, while farming and forestry are either marginalized or in decline making little contribution to the GDP.

In the early 1950s, The Bahamas had a thriving lumber industry in the Pine Islands of Abaco, Andros and Grand Bahama. In recent years however, the industry has been non-existent. The pine in some of these areas is harvested for fence posts or burnt for charcoal.

Forestry experts have advised that The Bahamas needs a comprehensive policy to revive the forests, Pinus caribaea in order to enable the pine to be managed as a resource. The area under Pinus caribaea has been assessed to be about 500,000 acres or 2,023.44 sq. km. With the capacity to generate income while ensuring long-term sustainability.

In the southeastern Bahamas, particularly on the islands of Cat Island, Acklins and Crooked Islands, there are stands of Cascarilla bark, which has medicinal and liquor uses, is harvested and exported to Europe.

Farming's contribution to the GDP has dropped significantly to a lowly 1%. With the decline in poultry, citrus exports and challenges with market access for ornamental nurseries and food processors, the contributions from farming would fall below 1%.

Intermezzo: *The Eneas Files, The Bahama Journal*　50 Years of Economic Transformation

After World War II, Japan began its economic transformation and became one of the most advanced economies in the world.

In 1949, the economy of Taiwan (one of the provinces of China) was agricultural and it was competing with Cuba as the number one producer of sugar cane in the world. By the 1980s, Taiwan Province transformed its economy into an industrial one and had become a model. It legitimated the economic theory that it was conceivable to go from an agricultural economy to an industrial economy. It took the Taiwan Province less than four decades.

Development economists point to Japan and Taiwan, one of the provinces of China as glaring proof of economic transformation. Broadly speaking, the world economy has passed through two stages of development in the last 50 years and is now entering a third.

But, where does The Bahamas fit into the developmental pattern?

Prior to 1950, The Bahamas was a quiet "fishing village" type community. One minister in the early days of the former administration stated that he would rather see The Bahamas return to fishing village rather than have casino gambling. Well, that former minister is no longer with us, but there has been a proliferation of gambling casinos. Casino gambling is now a tourism development tool.

Sir Stafford Loftus Sands, as Chairman of The Bahamas Development Board, recognizes the fact that farming and fishing could not take The Bahamas to the economic heights which could project the economy to the level it has attained today. He redirected the economic emphasis of this archipelago by combining three elements, year-round tourism, real estate development and offshore banking.

By the 1990s, tourism in The Bahamas is generating 1 billion dollars in foreign exchange earnings. The Bahamas was transformed from an idyllic "fishing village" to a burgeoning service economy.

What is not appreciated is the fact that the model of development which was created by Sir Stafford is now being duplicated throughout the Caribbean. With the exception of Trinidad and Tobago, Guyana and Jamaica, the other countries now depend on tourism for their foreign exchange earnings. The marginalized economies like those of Dominica and St. Lucia are still tied to bananas.

The economic transformation, which The Bahamas went through over the past 45 years, brought with it certain social changes—some good and some bad.

One noted Caribbean academician in the field of education made the observation that the professional development in The Bahamas has been phenomenal. He pointed out that it took Jamaica 150 years and Trinidad and Tobago 100 years to achieve the professional depth and diversity that The Bahamas was able to accomplish in less than 50 years.

Further, the economy was able to generate per capita earnings which have been statistically calculated at $10,000 and this has enabled the country to enjoy a relatively high standard of living.

Socio-economic transformation is not a static condition; it is constantly changing. Fortunately for Bahamians, Sir Stafford had the foresight to formulate a viable economic model. PLP had the good-sense to build on those foundations and strengthened the model through various types of legislation infrastructural development, manpower training and development and maintained an environment which attracted investment for sustained development.

Apart from two or three periods of economic recession, the Bahamian economy has remained resilient during these latter years of the 20th century.

Like I mentioned earlier, the world passed two development stages. The three post-war decades can be best defined as the international stage. Commencing in the 1970s and accelerating in the 1980s, the world entered the second stage—globalization. At the end of the 1990s, the world has entered a stage which has been defined as the global borderless economy.

The question which faces The Bahamas is whether or not our country and its citizenry are being prepared to live, compete and function successfully in the economic atmosphere which the global borderless economy will bring. Like I said earlier, transformation is not static.

Economic Nationalism vs. Globalization

Let's not confuse economic nationalism with economic nationalization. Both concepts are distinct as one relates to the economy being owned by its nationals and the other refers to the state taking control of the economic activities, especially the acquisition of privately owned enterprises.

One of the cries during the colonial era and one which greatly influenced the drive to independence was the plea for economic nationalism—in essence Bahamians owning The Bahamas.

Apart from foreign owned entities like the hotels and the banks, the domestic economy of The Bahamas was essentially controlled by the merchants on Bay Street. This was essentially the manner in which UBP dominated life in colonial Bahamas.

When PLP came to power, the policy of joint ventures between Bahamians and foreigners was the mechanism to allow expansion of the economy and yet maintain some form of national involvement and control by encouraging and enabling the citizenry to participate directly in a variety of economic activities.

After the Cold War, the global economic landscape took a drastic twist. The European Economic Community (EEC) evolved into the European Union (EU). The North American Free Trade Area (NAFTA) comprising Canada, Mexico and USA was formed. In both of these bodies, the eradication of national tariffs was introduced as a means of expanding the markets for the countries involved. The concept of eradicating national boundaries as a barrier to trade had begun.

In conjunction with this, large companies in the industrial companies in the industrial countries, particularly those which had their genesis in colonialization were now perfecting and commercializing corporate multinationalism as a tool of commercial and economic domination.

With the backdrop of a geopolitical environment being based on the ideology of capitalism or communism, countries had to choose which "camp" they belonged to. With the elimination of ideological identities, economic development was able to proceed on more direct and open course. Countries were able to associate more freely without the concern as to whether or not their political philosophy was Capitalist or Marxist.

The atmosphere was further enhanced by the technology which ushered through advances in telecommunications and computerization. Information became globally available through satellite transmission via the telephone and the computer. Cyberspace was evolving to more powerful instrument that government controls. The path of economic nationalism would soon be doomed as a by-product of a bygone era. The realities of a new economic order was forcing governments and multinational corporations to change their mode of operation.

The countries of this region and this hemisphere were not immune to the transformation. In the bid to become relevant to the times, steps were taken to merge the economies of the Western Hemisphere into a single free trade area—Free Trade Area of the Americas (FTAA). The concept of globalization had become a reality for Caribbean countries like The Bahamas.

Since 1992, FNM government had embarked on a course which appears to be heavily skewed to the globalization approach of generating trade, investment and the creation of employment opportunities.

The globalization approach is based on liberalization but it also must take into consideration the different levels of development, specifically in human resources and sectoral development for it to maximize its benefits in The Bahamas.

The Bahamas is presently in the throes of this dilemma. In some sectors of the economy notably construction, financial services and the hotels in New Providence, there is the feeling of an economic boom. Yet, there are others who are experiencing a "boom deficiency" because of the deficiency in the level of human capital development.

The "boom deficiency" stems from the fact that there are shortcomings in economic integration, training, infrastructural development in some localities, financial resources, to name a few. Issues like these are crucial to the globalization concept as they are integral ingredients in the overall objective of sustainable development.

When economic variables are placed in juxtaposition to the social dimensions of crime, poor housing and high instability of the family unit, the road to economic and social reconstruction in The Bahamas is formidable. For globalization to work in this scenario, these considerations have to be borne in mind when pubic policies are being formulated.

At the political level, there must be clear understanding as to which path this country will take in its journey to improve the socio-economic lot of the average Bahamian. Far too often the message is garbled and confusing.

At the business level, many commercial entities are still gauging the Bahamian people as abuses are occurring in critical points in the business cycle—transportation is one of these are, particularly in the container business.

Because of stiff competition, retailers of food and merchandise seem to be giving the Bahamian consumer a better deal.

At the level of the man-on-the-street, globalization has created a new world with new challenges which require behavioral responses which are a departure from the days when economic nationalism dominated. Insecurity in the work place demands retraining program on an ongoing basis as skills become obsolete because of the changes in technology and the manner in which business is conducted.

The ground rules have changed and those who do not adjust will be left behind.

The Mechanism for Family Island Resettlement

Post World War II made The Bahamas essentially an urban society as thousands of Bahamians moved from the Family or Out Islands to Nassau for work, education and services. The development of Freeport, Grand Bahama further compounded the urbanization syndrome.

Recently, however, Marsh Harbour, Abaco, Spanish Wells, North Eleuthera and Clarence Town/Deadmans Cay, Long Island are emerging as attractive non-urban communities with the simplicity and friendliness of Nassau in the 1940s and 1950s.

The transformation of Nassau began in earnest with the development of Potter's Cay into the domestic shipping hub and the construction of the Paradise Island Bridge. In conjunction with this, Mr. Joseph Garfunkel developed Palmdale into a prime alternative business centre when he converted his Garfunkel Softball Field into the Palmdale Shopping Centre. This acted as a catalyst for converting Palmdale from a choice residential area to the commercial area which it has evolved into today.

As Palmdale expanded, it necessitated the destruction of Collins Wall to enable easy access for vehicular traffic to that area. Also, the late Sir Roland Symonette developed Blair Estates as the replacement residential area of the large numbers of people who were moving out of Palmdale. This gave rise to urban sprawl, as other locales like Nassau East, Seabreeze, Westward Villas and the Grove on West Bay Street came into prominence. South of the arch, the Grove and Golden Gates attracted the thousands who were pulling themselves up by their bootstraps as a result of a burgeoning tourism economy.

Public financed housing on a large scale began with Yellow Elder. The expansion continued with Elizabeth Estates, Flamingo Gardens and other communities in New Providence under government sponsorship.

In Grand Bahama, urbanization is expanding to Eight Mile Rock, where a modern multi-million dollar shopping centre is near completion and will set the tone there just as Joe Garfunkel's shopping centre did in Nassau. Urbanization brings many frustrations, alters the way man lives and society functions. The narrow streets of "Old Nassau" cannot adequately accommodate vehicular traffic. The pressures on real estate have caused the price of land for both residential and commercial use to soar.

Single dwelling ownership is now endangered and urban dwelling for many is now apartments and condominiums.

In New Providence the population per square mile is 2,152.5 persons and for The Bahamas in general it is 47.4 persons. This means that people live closer together in Nassau and with the average household size being about 4 persons, a lengthening life expectancy (68 years for men and 75 for women) and the bulk of the population being at the child-bearing level, population growth could explode to further exacerbate the urban syndrome.

Is there a solution on the horizon? Yes, we are beginning to experience it. The biggest change has been seen in the work place as it is no longer necessary for businesses to be located down town or in high commercial areas. The Information Era has made it possible for business via fax machines, cellular phones and the Internet to be conducted and to function almost with a minimal loss of work efficiency.

To enjoy a certain quality of life one does not have to reside in close proximity to the national capital to experience certain amenities. Videocassette recorders and satellite and cable television bring sport, news and entertainment from around the world to most distant locations. The family in Landrail Point, Acklins or Fox Town, Abaco is much attuned to Cable News Network (CNN) or Eentertainment Sports Programming Network (ESPN) as the fellows in Nassau, Miami or London.

With an efficient telecommunications system, Family Island residents can shop on TV and participate in the new world of electronic commerce or e-commerce.

Don King took boxing to the next level by his relationship with HBO on cable television which also has made it possible for National Basketball Association (NBA) to pay Michael Jordan millions and Major League Baseball to sign long-term contracts with the like of Sammy Sosa and others.

Planners in The Bahamas have not exploited these possibilities. Serious attention needs to be given to purposely initiating plans to make more Family Islands attractive to residential living. Andros is too large and well endowed with physical resources for human exploitation.

During the Sponging Era, Mangrove Cay was the second largest population centre in The Bahamas; today it is almost a ghost settlement. The same was the case of Long Cay prior to the construction of the Panama Canal when large numbers of Bahamian residents in the Crooked Island—Acklins area and laid adjacent to one of the world's important shipping lanes.

The Information Era has made it possible for population regeneration of localities like Mangrove Cay, Cat Island, Mayaguana, Acklins and Crooked Island. The possibilities, which this technology offers, are much in its embryonic phase of realization and acceptance in The Bahamas; yet its employment as a mechanism to induce the resettlement of many of our Family Islands seems to have been overlooked.

Urbanization

The world is going through a phenomenon called urbanization. From 1950 to 1980, the world's city or urban population went from 300 million to 1.8 billion and The Bahamas was no exception.

The urban population of The Bahamas in 1953 was around 46,000 and by 1980 it has risen to almost 120,000. This represented an increase of slightly less than 300% in 27 years. The 1990 census has not been released to gate but the figures should reflect a continuing increase.

Within the context of The Bahamas, this means that New Providence and Freeport are the urban centers with the high population numbers. Inhabitants on the Family Islands are a declining minority. The Bahamas over the last 30 years has had the majority of its population in its two cities.

Between 1901 and 1943 about 66% of the Bahamian population resided in the Family Islands. The change since 1953 has been dramatic.

In conjunction with the urban population increase, there has also been a greater concentration of people on New Providence and Grand Bahama, hence the population density on these islands has also expanded substantially. In 1980 the population density in New Providence was 1,693 people per square mile; in Grand Bahama it was 62.5.

These two factors of high urban population and high population densities have already altered the quality of life in The Bahamas, particularly in Nassau and Freeport.

The phenomenal upsurge in urban growth in The Bahamas stemmed from the process of economic growth and development, which started during the latter part of the 1940s. Nassau offered a concentration of infrastructure, both physical (electricity, roads, water supply) and social (schools, health facilities, entertainment).

This concentration of infrastructure in conjunction with economic growth and development (construction and tourism) lead to large numbers of individuals leaving the Family Islands for economic opportunities in Nassau. The search for work is the key force in urbanization.

There is also a downside to urbanization and Nassau, in particular, is facing aspects of these negative side effects. Traffic jams, intermittent electricity and water supply, environmental pollution, inadequate waste disposal, particularly in densely populated localities and increased crime rate.

The Bahamas has been fortunate to some extent in that there are no shanty towns or pockets of abject poverty, however there are areas where outdoor toilets still have to be used, residents are required to go the pump and garbage is uncollected.

There has been a Bahamian reaction to this urbanization process. Scores of Bahamians are returning to various Family Islands, simply because life in Nassau has become an intolerable situation.

Individuals who have attained retirement age, those who have availed themselves to job opportunities or those who wish to establish a new business base are the categories of individuals leaving urban life for the more slow paced, laid back Family Island existence.

The reversal of the urbanization trend is a difficult task as there is a huge cadre of individuals who are locked into the urbanized way of life because of the socialization process through which they have been reared.

The Bahamas is still in a unique position where its urban problems have not reached the point where they are unsolvable as is the case of several countries in our region.

The question of urbanization has to be addressed and requires planning and management. International planners have projected that by the year 2000, nearly 45%

of the 5.1 billion population of Third World countries will be living in urban areas. The Bahamas has already exceeded this percentage.

The reason for the burgeoning urban population in The Bahamas has to be attributed to the mass migration from the Family Islands. From 1901 to 1943, outside of New Providence, Andros, Cat Island and Eleuthera were the main population centers. At one point Mangrove Cay was second to Nassau in numbers of inhabitants.

Over the past 30 years, Cat Island has experienced a severe drop in residents; population growth on Andros and Eleuthera has not been outstanding, only steady.

Yes, urbanization is a fact of life and a phenomenon which is likely to accelerate. The answer, however, is through more balanced and effective development of the Family Islands in order that adequate employment opportunities may be created. Without this, the human drift to Nassau and Freeport will continue.

Chapter 3

Tourism: A New Dimension for Food Production

"Caribbean economies developed as extensions of the metropolitan economy; they were integral parts of the imperial system. Their contribution was essentially that of supplying raw materials."

—Anthony Hill, Jamaican, lecturer, University of Guyana, Jamaican High Commission, London, England

Growing up and living in a colonial Caribbean, one was led to believe that virtually everything came from the mother country. This misconception had its origin in the fact that colonies like The Bahamas and the other territories in the Caribbean were markets for the metropolitan country.

Sugar is a by-product of the sugar cane, yet we believe that sugar came from England. Coffee, a high value blending commodity, Blue Mountain Coffee of Jamaica, also came from England. On the other hand, a manufactured or processed commodity like lard was a cooking and baking staple and a very unhealthy food item, items like salt pork and salt beef were similar unhealthy by-products of British livestock industry. These and others were all significant contributors to the cardiovascular problems which are being reflected in Caribbean populations today.

In Jamaica today, codfish remains an important food item for people thousands of miles away. The same dependency exists for canned products like sardine, tuna and salmon. Health enthusiasts view these commodities as unhealthy foodstuffs.

Under the WTO rules and regulations, CARICOM countries lost their preferential market status with EU. When these states were colonies, UK was the market for raw materials like sugar cane and coffee beans which were processed and re-exported to the colonies. These commodities enjoyed a preferential duty status, meaning that commodities from the UK were charged a lower duty than for example, products from neighbouring Cuba, Haiti, Dominican Republic or even the US.

In 1968 when The Bahamas was still a British colony, steps were taken to secure a sugar quota from the UK. At the time the giant US lumber company—Owens-Illinois had some 20,000 acres of sugar cane under cultivation on the island of Abaco. Owens Illinois was able to secure a US quota, while the government of The Bahamas was attempting to qualify for a UK quota.

The commodity meetings were held at the International Sugar Organization's headquarters in London. It was the first time The Bahamas had been involved in this type of negotiation whereas the other British Caribbean colonies, often referred to as the Sugar Islands, had a long history of involvement with the International Sugar Organization. The UK, at one time, controlled the global sugar market through its various sugar producing colonies in the Caribbean, Africa, Asia and the Pacific. The UK was in the position to manipulate the buying price of sugar cane as well as the selling price through the commonwealth preferential duty system, hence the colonies were a secure market not only for sugar but for a range of other commodities, many of which contributed to unhealthy food preparations as the ingredients i.e. lard, salt beef and salt pork led to serious health problems.

Control of food was an important aspect of the colonial experience. With the development of tourism, food also became a control commodity through a changing consumption or dietary pattern.

Tourism and Regional Food Production

Annually 40 to 50 million visitors come to the Caribbean. The majority of these visitors are from the US and come by cruise ships. There is, however, a very high percentage of stopover visitors who come by air. The stopover American visitor feels comfortable when he or she is able to enjoy a slice of America in the Caribbean. This, nevertheless, does not take away from the Caribbean experience of trying things Caribbean i.e. exotic fruits and vegetables, cuisine, crafts, artifacts.

The Caribbean experience is constrained by the type of property and locale. Many properties have programmes which attempt to keep the visitor on property, i.e. the all inclusive property like Club Med or mega property like Atlantis with 38 restaurants and the largest casino in the Caribbean.

This slice of America has resulted in the introduction of the American fast food franchise. Throughout the Caribbean, possibility with the exception of Cuba, there has been a proliferation of fast food operations—American franchises under Caribbean ownership and some Caribbean fast food chains.

The American fast food franchises have influenced both food imports and the type of food eaten. Fast foods have negatively impacted the state of Caribbean health.

In The Bahamas for example, there is almost every variety of fast food outlet. There are American franchise operations specializing in pizzas (Dominos, Pizza Hut) and hamburgers (McDonald's, Burger King, Wendy's), to Subway, Quiznos, or gourmet establishments like Luciano and the very high end like Jean-Georges, Bobby Flay, Carmines and Nobu and Starbucks, the high end coffee house.

Local Caribbean chicken fast food operations have to compete with Kentucky Fried Chicken; Patti Take-outs have to compete with US hamburger franchises and Roti outlets with the pizza establishments.

Hotel and gourmet restaurants appeal to a Euro-American clientele. These restaurants require a range of high quality fruits, vegetables, meats, fish, cheeses and sausages. Some of these items, particularly fresh fruits, vegetables, some meats and fish can be supplied by local sources; however, the challenge has been consistency of supply, quality and reliability in meeting the demand throughout the year.

Table 3.1   Caribbean Visitor Arrival—2003

Destination	Cruise Passenger Arrivals	Stopover	Total
Anguilla		46,915	46,915
Antigua and Barbuda	385,686	224,030	609,716
Aruba	542,327	641,906	1,184,233
Bahamas	2,970,174	1,428,973	4,399,147
Barbados	559,122	531,211	1,090,333
Belize	575,196	220,574	795,770
Bermuda	226,097	256,563	482,660

(to be continued)

Destination	Cruise Passenger Arrivals	Stopover	Total
Bonaire	44,601	62,179	106,780
British Virgin Islands	304,338	278,114	582,452
Cayman Islands	1,818,979	293,515	2,112,494
Cuba		1,907,320	1,907,320
Curacao	279,378	221,390	500,768
Dominica	177,044	72,948	249,992
Dominican Republic	398,263	3,268,182	3,666,445
Grenada	146,925	142,333	289,258
Guyana		100,911	100,911
Jamaica	1,132,596	1,350,284	2,482,880
Martinique	268,542	453,160	721,702
Montserrat		8,375	8,375
Puerto Rico	1,234,992	1,321,846	2,556,838
Saba		10,260	10,260
St. Eustatius		10,788	10,788
St. Lucia	393,240	276,948	670,188
St. Maarten	1,171,734	427,587	1,599,321
St. Vincent and the Grenadines	64,965	78,535	143,500
Trinidad and Tobago	55,532	409,007	464,539
Turks and Caicos Islands		163,584	163,584
US Virgin Islands	1,773,948	618,703	2,392,651
Total: 38,352,342			

Source: Caribbean Tourism Organization (CTO)

Further, there are also specialty items. These specialty items are manufactured or processed for the convenience of the gourmet chef or in order to maintain a standard for the franchise operator. This sometimes places that specialty items outside of the production capacity of Caribbean agribusinesses.

A prime example is the table egg agribusiness. According to CPA, the table egg is a commodity in which most CARICOM states are self-sufficient or approaching self-sufficiency. Yet, there is no egg operation in the larger CARICOM states (Jamaica, Barbados, Trinidad and Tobago, The Bahamas) where specialty egg items like egg yoles, eggbeaters, powdered eggs, pasteurized eggs, frozen eggs or liquid eggs are processed. However, in hotels particularly mega properties, pastry and gourmet chefs require these items. This is adversely affecting table egg operators.

This has resulted in a two-tier market—one market for the fresh table eggs and the specialty items for the tourist market.

Tourism is no longer an isolated appendage of the economies of Caribbean states. The tourism food culture has become and is becoming intertwined with national food consumption. This means that more and more indigenous people are acquiring the taste and eating habits of the visitors whose presence is felt in every island state or dependency in this region.

This is also fueled by travel to North America and Europe by Caribbean people on business, shopping sprees, vacations or for training in the various disciplines.

This affinity to the tourists' cuisine has exacerbated an already health acute situation. The Caribbean Food Nutrition Institute (CFNI) has reported that,

> "Non-communicable diseases have gradually displaced communicable diseases as the main causes of mortality in the Caribbean. Nutrition-related Chronic Diseases such as obesity, diabetes and hypertension are major contributors to disability, illness and death in the sub-region. Hypertension and diabetes rank as the two leading chronic disorders among Caribbean populations and are also major risk factors for other diseases such as cardiovascular disease (stroke) and coronary heart disease."

The Caribbean is not alone in this dilemma. FAO in collaboration with the World Health Organization (WHO) has embarked on a programme to boost "the production, supply and consumption of fruit and vegetables."

FAO points out:

> "Research indicates that when consumed (fruits and vegetables) daily in sufficient amounts and is part of a balanced diet, fruits and vegetables help prevent serious diseases, including heart failure, stroke, diabetes and cancer and deficiencies of precious micronutrients and vitamins. WHO places low fruit and vegetable intake sixth among its 20th risk for global human mortality."

The situation has worsened because women comprise anywhere from 40% to 50% of the workforce in Caribbean states.

In The Bahamas, females dominate tourism. In 2005, there were 6,000 more female workers than males. (See Table 2.1)

With women representing a substantial element in the workforce, "convenience" foods will gain importance as the supermarket replaces the market as the prime outlet for food purchases and fast food outlets replace home-cooked meals.

Many of these convenience foods originate in North America and are replacing indigenous or traditional foods which are not available in a form which lend themselves to easy preparation for the working mother or professional woman who is more than likely a single mother or a wife and a mother.

With rising incomes, particularly in Caribbean states where the service sector like tourism are the chief sectors of the economy, small island states like The Bahamas, Barbados, Antigua and Barbuda will look to imports to meet their food demands.

In May, 2006 address by the Hon. Jarrette Narine, Minister of Agriculture, Lands and Marine Resources, Trinidad and Tobago at the 1st Caribbean Agri-Food Trade Convention, Mr. Narine stated the following:

> "Many of us here today are painfully aware of the fact that as a region the Caribbean imports approximately $1.5 billion in agricultural produce a year. As a region capable of producing much more agricultural produce than it is currently; this state of affairs is unacceptable. It has been estimated that in some Caribbean countries for every tourism dollar spent there is leakage in the form of food imports in the region of $0.60– $0.80."

In The Bahamas, it is about $0.85. It is this scenario which has placed most Caribbean states in the category of net food-importing countries.

FAO in a document titled, *Financing Normal Levels of Commercial Imports of Basic Foodstuffs* identified countries on the basis of the percentage spending of hard currency on food imports. The following Caribbean countries were highlighted based on 1995– 1998 data. (See Table 3.2)

This situation could become more acute. Based on the recent CTO figures on visitor arrivals, there are 110,000 to 137,000 visitors on any given day in the region. This is a high value market which will increase thereby increasing the demand for imported foodstuffs.

FAO has placed food imports in the region to be \$2.2 billion in 2004. (See Table 3.3)

Table 3.2   Caribbean Food Imports

% of Hard Currency	Country
10% plus of available hard currency (revenue from exports of goods and services minus debt service)	Barbados Dominican Republic Jamaica Trinidad and Tobago
10%–20%	St. Lucia
20% plus	Haiti
No data	Cuba Dominica St. Kitts and Nevis St. Vincent and the Grenadines

The Challenge: Feeding the Region

For centuries Caribbean agriculture was geared towards providing raw agricultural materials for industrial Europe; production to meet domestic demands did not come seriously into focus until the Independence Era. With the decline of preferential markets, upsurge in tourism and increased incomes resulting from the emergence of the service sectors, the capacity to meet the demands for food have been accentuated.

The Caribbean's existence was rooted in agricultural trade. Throughout the colonial years, export agriculture was the basis for the survival of the colonies as it was for many colonies, the only source of foreign exchange. As economies became more sophisticated, foreign exchange earning emanated from sources like tourism.

Agricultural trade has taken in the Independence Era a dimension which is very different and more complex as Caribbean states began to face the issues of globalization. Globalization has expressed itself via four trade regimes for most countries in the region. This is compounded by the limitations of small island states in matters of trade stemming from size and type of economies.

There are four trade regimes with which the majority of the states in the region have to contend. Since 1995, with the exception of The Bahamas, all of the independent

Table 3.3   Caribbean Food Imports Value in $1,000

Food Imports (Value in $1,000)	1990	1991	1992	1993	1994	1995	1996	1997	1998	1999	2000	2001	2002	2003	2004
Antigua and Barbuda	28,158	26,336	26,446	24,434	23,939	24,718	24,350	28,362	26,373	23,098	24,316	19,404	21,644	23,466	21,772
The Bahamas	179,109	195,970	170,534	161,772	178,882	205,563	220,156	215,182	213,914	226,570	320,220	282,429	204,469	168,353	197,765
Barbados	90,806	95,433	86,280	87,868	97,044	104,629	113,355	132,100	73,859	127,729	95,180	130,571	131,183	139,425	103,619
Belize	42,616	25,745	49,085	42,556	39,740	41,959	45,633	48,286	46,737	39,360	78,189	53,726	48,385	57,530	60,640
Dominica	18,984	19,054	18,340	16,099	17,108	21,566	24,832	24,717	23,393	19,867	23,256	21,310	20,503	21,320	22,468
Dominican Republic	219,370	243,457	248,461	305,394	326,710	394,092	438,566	491,681	478,736	410,961	429,581	415,181	515,919	466,250	490,610
Grenada	25,956	26,063	23,231	29,708	28,969	33,579	40,061	32,171	37,398	33,923	32,433	26,917	35,347	29,836	23,619
Guyana	33,280	31,929	37,440	42,240	37,825	51,930	52,888	77,426	79,669	107,213	72,067	74,959	74,087	65,956	68,085
Haiti	167,035	160,999	186,618	158,659	156,367	293,267	295,911	335,659	330,400	307,195	269,481	258,435	323,580	318,111	372,917
Jamaica	197,588	196,982	202,924	225,744	201,084	305,122	312,581	367,038	351,866	362,345	323,402	423,277	421,954	365,256	380,784
Saint Kitts and Nevis	15,764	15,319	14,061	15,050	15,827	19,382	22,629	20,472	20,149	18,954	28,039	25,464	24,872	26,568	18,832
Saint Lucia	44,773	53,326	55,903	56,855	60,639	64,875	63,626	69,381	68,829	65,414	68,988	61,839	58,457	69,625	41,366
Saint Vincent/ the Grenadines	25,235	25,795	26,540	28,348	27,499	29,247	31,279	36,723	37,623	29,819	22,740	25,029	37,324	36,005	30,472
Suriname	40,162	41,651	48,938	37,376	38,502	45,374	116,348	131,389	128,857	81,439	72,728	74,301	49,866	61,837	69,510
Trinidad and Tobago	196,804	205,029	204,512	172,008	165,761	221,764	229,637	243,580	263,649	255,116	257,594	290,132	276,688	293,634	316,019
CARIFORUM	1,325,640	1,363,088	1,399,313	1,404,111	1,415,896	1,857,067	2,031,852	2,254,167	2,181,452	2,109,003	2,118,214	2,182,974	2,244,278	2,143,172	2,218,478

Source: FAOSTAT, 2006

states have become members of WTO. In this regard, the WTO's *AOA* dictates global agricultural trade. At the hemispheric level, there is the proposed FTAA which, is essentially, WTO plus.

For the former colonies of EU states, there is the African, Caribbean and Pacific (ACP) arrangement. The Caribbean component of the ACP group comprises CARICOM and the Dominican Republic which operate as CARIFORUM.

Preferential arrangements into the EU for ACP states started with *LOME Convention*, which evolved into *The Contonou Agreement* and the successor *EU Partnership Agreement*.

At the regional level, there is CSME, which is the mechanism to integrate the economies of CARICOM states.

All of CARICOM with the exception of The Bahamas have to interface with these four trade regimes. From a technical expertise perspective, no CARICOM state has all of the manpower to effectively participate and monitor the various agreements and activities of all of these regimes. In this regard CARICOM created CRNM as the institution to devise trade policies strategies for CARICOM states.

The staffing of CRNM is drawn from the various CARICOM states and the policy decision of the CRNM reflects input from the various trade ministries and departments of the individual CARICOM states.

A prime example of the effectiveness of this arrangement with the CRNM, as the regional body, was demonstrated by working with individual states to safeguard a commodity which impacts food production in virtually every CARICOM state. The commodity in question is broiler, or chicken meat.

In 1990/1991, the Caribbean poultry agribusiness producing broiler meat was threatened by the importation of cheap chicken parts like wings, necks and backs, which were by-products of the US poultry industry. These parts were being sold at prices which were less than the cost of production.

Caribbean food importers took advantage of the availability of these low costs by-products to "push" them into Caribbean markets. This had the effect of destabilizing local production in CARICOM states.

Poultry production is an integrated agribusiness in the large CARICOM states of Jamaica, Barbados, Trinidad and Tobago, Guyana and Belize. This integration has married the small farmer to the feed manufacturer or poultry processor through a contractual arrangement.

CPA under the leadership of its Executive Director, Mr. Robert Best, has been able to unify this agribusiness thereby making the CPA the most effective commodity group in the region.

Poultry production has become a small farmer activity representing some 100,000 growers throughout the region. Broiler meat is now the chief source of protein in the region.

Apart from the dollar value of poultry as an agribusiness, poultry has cross cutting implications. In this regard, CARICOM governments have come to appreciate the all-encompassing role poultry production is playing in the agricultural sector of the various states.

As a result of the CPA activities at the national level and at the regional level through the CARICOM Secretariat and the CRNM, poultry has been projected in trade negotiations, especially in the FTAA, as a sensitive commodity.

Figure 3.1 Caribbean Nationals as Director Generals of IICA[1]

Trade and human development issues have sensitized Caribbean governments to the global agenda thereby causing them to sign on to global, hemispheric and regional mandates which have initiated policies and programmes to address hunger, poverty and food insecurity within the framework of food production.

The major global mandates are the following:

① Target 2015—Global Prosperity and Agriculture;

---

[1] Dr. Carlos E. Aquino, Dominican Republic (1992–2000); Dr. Chelston Brathwaite, Barbados (2001–2010).

② Target 2015—The Millennium Development Goals (UN);

③ Target 2015—The World Food Summit (FAO/Global);

④ Target 2015—The Agro Plan (FAO/ Hemispheric).

In view of these global mandates, sectoral contributions at the national and regional levels have to be aligned to meet the objectives and targets of these initiatives.

Global and hemisphere initiatives are fashioning Caribbean regional and national agricultural strategies. The instruments of these initiatives are agencies like FAO which has a sub-regional office in Barbados and representatives in Jamaica and Trinidad and Tobago and IICA which has representatives in all of the independent states in the region except Cuba.

Both FAO and IICA signed an accord to work together to provide coordinated technical assistance to national governments, particularly in areas which tie governments to the global mandates.

CARICOM has responded with Jagdeo Initiative which is implementing the Community Agricultural Policy whose main goal is to transform Caribbean agriculture to market-oriented, internationally competitive and environmentally sound producer of food products. In conjunction with this, there is also OECS Agricultural Policy and Strategic Plan. This plan is built around the premise that the states of the sub-region are best served in a collective approach.

Caribbean experts across the region have expressed major concerns regarding the manner in which Caribbean agriculture is being approached within realities of the challenges facing the region as a whole and states individually.

IICA's Caribbean Director, Dr. H. Arlington D. Chesney, a Guyanese, points out, "The region is in a food deficit situation, in terms of quantity and desired type, a situation usually exacerbated after natural disasters." Agriculture, as currently configured, cannot substantially, if at all, reduce these deficits, making food insecurity a threat to our sovereignty, social equity, stability and governance. Our efforts to enhance our own food security must be concentrated on developing a "new" agriculture.

Apart from developing a "new" agriculture, Dr. Winston Phillips, a Grenadian and former FAO employee looks at the continental Caribbean (Guyana, Suriname and Belize) vis-à-vis the small island states. His observations are as follows:

" ① It is difficult to speak of Caribbean agriculture as a regional unit today, as one could have done 20 or 30 years ago. The reality is that each country has witnessed tremendous political, economic, social, etc. changes, over the years that have shaped each country's agricultural sector in different ways.

② In almost every Caribbean country, macro policies have had a larger and more pervasive impact on the agricultural sector than sector policies themselves. This thought almost flies in the face of another comment: the need for strong commitment reflected through increased allocation of financial resources.

③ The potential of the agricultural sector is not the same in each country. While this is so, discussions at the regional level often give one the impression that the potential is the same for each country. Given this fact, the regional approach to the sector's development needs to adopt a different strategy. In this regard there will be some fallouts in various countries."

I believe that it is precisely because of the considerations above that we must speak of "Caribbean agriculture as a regional unit." I completely agree with Budram on the need to adopt different strategies—one such being, a cross-border private sector investment orientation. A few years ago, a regional colleague laughed when I stated that this was how we need to look at our regional agriculture. I agree that the agricultural sector has been affected by the way the countries have developed. Except for Trinidad were petroleum has always dominated, other countries' agriculture has been differently affected by tourism and other service sector growth. Yet, as Budhram correctly points out, our professionals continue to see the sector as being "same for each country." It is because of this that we focus so much on limitation rather than possibilities (too small farms, too little credit, no manufacturing outcomes, etc.).

The reality is that the agriculture of smaller countries, in addition to loss of traditional markets has been overtaken by service industries. The countries with larger land masses—Guyana, Suriname, Belize have remained predominantly agricultural. From figures that have been touted in recent years, it appears that Guyana produces the cheapest chicken, pineapples, sugar and rice; I would also hazard, beef and milk in the region.

Agriculturally, the smaller islands seem almost destined by topography to some kind of tree crop culture. On the face of it, fruit tree culture, and spices and essential oils production are worthy of serious consideration and examination. That the course and potential of the sector differ in each country adds an important point to the debate. Frankly, I was surprised that the author of the Jagdeo Initiative completely ignored the regional agricultural policy direction which highlights the potentials of countries with larger land masses to feed the Caribbean; and the potential for development trade by Guyana, Suriname or Belize inviting private sector investment, while the government financed infrastructure.

If, as my laughing colleague thought, this sounds too like the regional food plans, we should be reminded that the ideas then were rooted in governmental contributions to projects (I am not even sure we could call them investments). There are some signs of interest in increased intra-regional agricultural investments by the regional private sector. Whatever the substance of this, it is something to be encouraged by government preparing the way for cross border investments in the region. I would have thought that even out of specific national interest in this regard, and given what was happening with the sector in other countries, Guyana would have seen the benefits of actively promoting regional private sector investment in Guyana as a food producing/processing country; as would Belize and Suriname.

Whether we like it or not, the trend of private sector investment in the world today is to move where resources are available and cheaper; and where investments are encouraged. I do not think Caribbean investors are any different, or can afford to be any different in orientation. This is what underlined the move of manufacturing from Barbados to Trinidad in the early 2000s. Barbadians were not amused, but that's how things are happening today. Does anyone recall that when the telephone system in Trinidad was at its lowest ebb, Trinidadian businessmen would fly to Barbados to make their phone calls, and send their faxes? (One guy, even though he went to Barbados to make calls, reportedly was critical of Barbados because, unlike Trinidad, "everything worked" in Barbados.)

Smaller countries could position themselves agriculturally for more value added products, such as selected spices/spice processing, and other Chinese-American

BioMedical Association (Does it still exist?) oriented products. Maybe there is a huge lesson in Denis Noel's "Nutmed," which we all, professionals and governments are not seeing. It would be interesting to see how the CSME helps to facilitate these developments. Some of us will recall that Marcus DeFreitas was able to move agricultlural stuff out of St. Vincent to Miami, while we were struggling with the idea of a regional government shipping service for agricultural products!

The market aspect of Caribbean food production is sighted as having been a limitation. Mr. Martin Satney, Permanent Secretary in St. Lucia, argues that,

> "I've followed this debate/discussion with great interest, but whereas I can agree with many of the comments made to date. I think that unless we address the fundamental causal factors we will never be able to fully transform our regional agricultural sector and rural economy. The underpinning problems are structural in nature in relation to the management and ownership of the value created/generated within the production system (from farm to market, including value-addition). As has been noted in previous comments, the islands economies were all production driven, with the market end controlled, mastered and dominated by external business entities for several decades, until recently, i.e.—we hardly developed a business and entrepreneurial culture, and whatever little we did was conservatively limited to the lower end of the commodity's value chain. We learnt to be near experts at producing raw goods for a ready tailored market, in which we had a very limited role in shaping. When the market dramatically changed and continued to change, we totally misread the story. Why we went down that road for so long is for another debate on our relative 'satisfaction' with the modifications of the plantation system.
>
> Because we had so limited know—how about the market and marketing in general (from the practical business/value management standpoint), the existing opportunities that are presented today by the with alternative/nontraditional commodities even at the domestic level are difficult to capture, until some significant structural changes are effected

or a traditional 'banana-like' model re-emerges (which we all know is a fantasy, given the obvious irreversible changes in the trade environment).

The reality is, from a trade and export promotion standpoint, we still need to do what should have been done decades ago, with bananas or any other commodity, i.e.—develop a culture of entrepreneurship and promote innovation (a holistic strategy)—with focus on both backward and forward inter-sectoral linkages, taking into consideration the issues of food security and sustainable use and management of our natural resources. This strategic approach should not be limited to the national level, but extended to the regional level in the long term."

The Caribbean Agricultural scenario is summarized by Dr. Dowlat Budham, a Guyanese employed with IICA in these words.

" ① Caribbean agriculture has been on the decline (as in most other countries) for a long time. This is not new information. The real problem is that successive governments in all the countries adopted various policies and strategies over a long period that did not foster development of the agricultural sector. The slow demise of sugar and bananas (thru continued protection in the EU and US markets) actually prolonged the rate of decline of the sector. It is not surprising that after about 45 years of independence in several countries, one hears the same arguments about bananas and sugar.

② It is difficult to speak of Caribbean agriculture as a regional unit today, as one could have done 20 or 30 years ago. The reality is that each country has witnessed tremendous political, economic, social, etc. changes over the years that have shaped each country's agricultural sector in different ways. The only common thread that in the countries is guaranteed access to the protected markets for a few commodities (maybe there are a few others).

③ In almost every Caribbean country, macro policies have had a larger and more pervasive impact on the agricultural sector than sector policies themselves. When one adds to the type of agricultural policies pursued over the years, it is not surprising that stagnation and decline have been the result in the sector.

④ The potential of the agricultural sector is not the same in each country. While this is so, discussions at the regional level often give one the impression that the potential is the same for each country. Given this fact, the regional approach to the sector's development needs to adopt a different strategy. In this regard there will be some fallout in various countries.

⑤ Even with sound policies and strategies, agriculture (or any other sector for that matter) will not be developed unless there is a strong commitment that is reflected through the allocation of financial resources. The series of regional plans for the sector, starting with The Regional Food Plan in the 1970s through to the present Jagdeo Initiative (which is still in its infancy) have produced few or zero results in the sector, precisely because of the insufficient commitment of resources by the governments. The developments of US and EU agriculture have been due largely to huge financial commitments by those governments, sustained over many, many years.

The question is where the region's development priorities are and to what extent the governments are prepared to allocate the necessary resources to achieve these. The governments are still struggling to finance the regional development fund for agriculture being proposed under the Jagdeo Initiative."

Intermezzo: *The Eneas Files*   Do Bahamians Eat Healthy?

In my book, *Agriculture in The Bahamas: History Development (1492–2012)*, I pointed out that when Christopher Columbus and his men landed in this archipelago from Europe, they found a bountiful environment.

"The Europeans encountered a sub-tropical climate... a rich vegetation included edible fruits: guinep, sea grape, coco plum, pineapple, pine fruits and plums; ground provisions: cassava, sweet potato, peanut and flora with medicinal properties like the lignum vitae."

This environment had sustained the early inhabitants, i.e. Tainos, Arawaks and possible Seminoles from Florida, in pre-Columbian times. With virtually no trade in food, all of the inhabitants consumed the produce of these islands. Initially, the food crops sprung from natural vegetations and the eventual evolvement of cultivated crops like sweet potatoes and cassava.

In this sub-tropical environment unlike temperate Europe where storage crops had to be developed to sustain life over the long winter months, the inhabitants depended heavily on the seasonal fruits and vegetables which were generally of high nutritional value because of their freshness and had a tastiness resulting from the medium of cultivation and the harvesting methodology.

By the middle of the 19th century, The Bahamas was in the business of growing a substantial variety of food crops not only for itself but also for export. From the limited variety of food which Columbus and his men found growing in these islands, the expansion in the food production capability had greatly increased.

This variety and expansion was the food supply backbone which sustained life in this small British colony off the coast of Florida.

The diet of most Bahamians centered around a husbandry system which yielded crops and livestock along with an array of marine species to provide a healthy balanced diet based on freshness, excellent taste and in many cases, grown organically. This is seen in the nutritive content of fruits which were once important but today are endangered. Fruits like the tamarind which has high food value in its pulp which is rich in calcium, phosphorus, iron and vitamin B complex.

The sapodilla which many Bahamians seldom eat today is also extremely rich in calcium, phosphorus, iron, sodium, potassium, carotene as well as vitamins B1, B2, and vitamin C respectively.

This holds true for hog plums, scarlet plums, guinep and jujubes, yet these fruits have become lost food items in our diet.

The diet of The Bahamas today when compared to The Bahamas 50 years ago has become dominated by fast food i.e. chicken in the bag, chicken nuggets and wings, along with French fries in oil and covered with ketchup or imported foods which are canned and when fresh are tasteless and mechanically ripened. Most are grown with commercial fertilizers. In addition, more and more of this imported food will be genetically modified.

These genetically modified crops have been banned in European food stores because their effect on human health has not been determined.

During the second half of 20th century, there has been a dramatic change in the life expectancy of both men and women. The life expectancy of the male in 1990 was 68.32 years, and for females it was 76.528. In contrast to 1980 when it was 64.26 for men and 72.06 for women.

There are experts who attribute this change to improvements in medical technology, availability of health services and the wider use of health insurance programmes by a broad spectrum of the working population rather than to the type and quality of food which is being consumed by the average citizen.

This past week, *Time* Magazine came out with a new dietary food called low carb (carbohydrate) diets. How many Bahamians will be attempting this new fad? Your guess is as good as mine. One thing I know is that it will be tried. The big question is whether or not healthy eating can be found in these fad diets. Is eating like our forefathers the answer? Don't rule it out.

Serious consideration should be given to the introduction of initiatives which will ensure that the food supply of the country augers well for the health of our nation.

Genetically Modified Organisms

Bahamians need to acquaint themselves with the term Genetically Modified Organisms (GMOs). To average consumers, it may be new, but to scientists it is the way of the future.

In the next millennium, this term will have serious implications in the manner in which mankind develops. In science, it is the new age of biogenetics and impacts on all forms of organisms. Geneticists will be able, in the future, to customize human reproduction, boost agriculture and create other genetics industries.

In the upcoming WTO negotiations in Seattle, Washington next month, it will emerge as one of the most controversial topics. Its controversy stems from the fact that GMOs have raised serious concerns because of the perceived relationship to food safety and human health.

Presently, there is a three-pronged debate going on. Those pushing GMOs (the US, Argentina, Canada and Mexico) hold the view that genetically modified crops pose no greater threat to human health than unmodified crops and are against efforts to segregate modified and unmodified crops. Without labeling, consumers would be totally unaware as to whether or not they were eating modified or unmodified.

Developing countries in Latin America, Asian and the Pacific countries like Malaysia on the other side of the spectrum want to adopt a more cautious approach requiring extensive testing of GMOs to determine their risks to human health and the environment before commercialization.

EU, on the other hand, has maintained a middle of the road approach because European consumer groups are opposed to the use of GMOs, yet European policy makers and their scientific communities have not precluded the use of GMOs in its food production system.

For the past 18 months there has been a moratorium on the approval of GMOs in Europe; however, this past week the UK-based Astra Seneca was given the green light to market a genetically modified tomato.

A newspaper report on this approval stated that,

> "The decision received a cautious welcome from industry groups who have watched public and political opposition to genetically modified products soar in Europe, in stark contrast to the apparent apathy surrounding the issue in the US."

British consumers have been extremely active in blocking the introduction of GMOs in their food system. The British have gone through the mad cow disease crisis, hence their caution. The outcry of British consumers has been so loud and telling that genetically-modified-derived tomato paste was summarily removed from supermarket shelves. The public objection was based on the fact that the product lacked adequate testing thereby its effect on humans was undetermined.

Bahamian consumers, on the other hand, are disadvantaged. Firstly, The Bahamas is a net food-importing country where food importers determine, to a very high degree the type of foods Bahamians eat. Secondly, between 85% to 90% of our food is imported from the US, which is one of the leading countries engaged in the production of GMOs and supports non-labeling of products for classifying them into GMOs or non-GMOs. In this scenario, Bahamians will become, unknowingly, one of the largest consumers of

GMOs.

All of the questions have not been answered on GMOs. It is a relatively new field and the jury, both scientific and consumer is still out on this issue. For too long developing countries have been slow to act depending on the developed world to determine the course of action. We in The Bahamas should adopt a balanced position on GMOs because making a distinction on the basis of science does not mean that non-science concerns can simply be ignored.

In a recent report on this issue for CARICOM countries, the observation that

> "While the acceptance of genetically-engineered products has been generally slow in many countries, acceptance has been far slower for animal products than for crops. In this regard, the use of genetically altered crops for animal feed could lead to drastic segmentation of meat markets."

Many Bahamians have become in recent years quite knowledgeable about organically grown crops, crops grown with commercial fertilizers, meat products which may have growth hormones, and tree and vine ripened fruits and vegetables as opposed to gas ripened produce. Now, the new boy on the block is GMOs.

Over the years the incidence of diseases resulting from lifestyles and consumption habits has increased. Without a proper monitoring system through labeling, we could be opening ourselves to a new and different regime of health problems by indiscriminate consumption of GMOs based products.

There is an expression that you are what you eat.

Chapter 4

A New Sense of Self

"Each generation must, out of relative obscurity, discover its mission,
fulfill it, or betray it."
> —Frantz Fanon, Martinique, *The Wretched of the Earth*

The Caribbean will find it difficult to develop a sense of self unless the blackman is truly recognized. It is because of the African Diaspora that the Caribbean was able to exploit a resource and a commodity which had global importance.

In his book, *Seeds of Change*, Henry Hobhouse brings into the focus the role of the African in the Caribbean. Hobhouse puts it this way:

"How an unnecessary 'fool' became responsible for the Africanization of the Caribbean. It (the Caribbean) concerns only a very small part of the world, but one which, until 1800, was responsible for more than 80% of both sugar and the trade in slaves. As a direct result, this small region was simultaneously responsible for nearly half of all the seagoing effort, naval and civil, of the western European nations."

Did slavery in the New World leave a legacy of disrespect to the whole idea of manual labour? It is this association which has stigmatized the blackman in the New World and no matter his achievements this legacy may be the underlying reason for the failures in food production throughout the region.

As the major source of a highly valued commodity, sugar, and the market for the lucrative business of buying and selling Africans as chattel, it was in the interest of the Europeans to own a piece of the Caribbean, hence the influence of the Spanish, Dutch,

English and French in the region. The Caribbean became the sugar colonies of European nations. Later on, the Spanish-American War saw the incursion of the US into the region with Puerto Rico and the Virgin Islands.

Because of its colonial past, the Caribbean has never been a homogeneous region. In the north among the Greater Antilles, there are three languages: Spanish (Cuba, Dominican Republic and Puerto Rico), French (Haiti), and English (Jamaica). In the Lesser Antilles, there is Dutch (Curacao, Aruba, Bonaire), French (Martinique and Guadeloupe), and English (CARICOM states and the US Virgin Islands).

It is in the Lesser Antilles where the Anglophone influence has dominated. The former British colonies and Jamaica in 1958 formed the ill-fated West Indies Federation.

Despite the experiment with the Federation, there was recognition for the need of some kind of regional body and the Caribbean Free Trade Association (CARIFTA) came into existence; however in 1972, Caribbean leaders at the Seventh Heads of Government Conference decided to transform CARIFTA into a Common Market by creating a CARICOM of which a Common Market would be a significant component.

CARICOM has had its challenges and continues to have challenges, but has emerged as a key institution in the region and, perhaps more than any, has moved the region into defining its "sense of self."

In recent years this "sense of self" definition has come through CARICOM's initiatives on the free movement of people, CSME and the Caribbean Court of Justice (CCJ).

CARICOM has been able to widen its ambit of influence in the region by firstly accepting French speaking Haiti thereby breaking the Anglophone monopoly and secondly facilitating Associate Membership. Through CARIFORUM, the Dominican Republic has been included.

In total there are about twenty regional institutions falling under the ambit of the CARICOM Secretariat.

CARICOM has been able to distinguish itself in the international community, as it is a bloc in which all of its members adhere to democratic principles and where the rule of law is supreme. It is the hope of the region that this legacy of democracy would be adopted and practiced by its newest member, Haiti.

Christianity has left an indelible impression on the face of the Caribbean. In the former British colonies it was the Anglican Church. With independence, came the emergence of an indigenous church with "West Indian" leadership.

The Lord Archbishop, Metropolitan and Primate of the Church of the West Indies has become a leader in the global Anglican community. His Grace, Archbishop Drexel Gomez has become the spokesperson for the Third World on issues facing the Anglican Church.

The Province of the West Indies comprises the diocese of all the former colonies and now independent states. The Province has been unifying spiritual force in the region. This has been reflected in the liturgy of Anglican Church and the Provincial Seminary, Codrington College in Barbados has maintained academic standards for those entering the priesthood throughout the Anglican community in the region.

An indigenous Caribbean Anglican Church has given the Provincial Church a Caribbean perspective to the big issues facing Anglicanism globally.

In Cuba, Haiti, Dominican Republic and the US Virgin Islands there are Anglican or Episcopal communities. In Cuba, there is the Episcopal (Anglican) Church of Cuba, which is governed by the metropolitan Council of Cuba. This Council comprises the Archbishop of the West Indies, the Senior Bishop in the Province IX of the Episcopal Church of the USA and the Primate of the Anglican Church of Canada, who sits as the President of the Council.

Figure 4.1　His Grace, Drexel Gomez, Lord Archbishop, Metropolitan and Primate of the Church of the West Indies, Bishop of The Bahamas and Turks and Caicos Islands

The Bishop of the Episcopal Church of Cuba presides over the Episcopal Province of the Caribbean in Formation. This Province includes Haiti, Dominican Republic and Puerto Rico. Episcopalians in the US Virgin Islands fall under the Episcopal Church of the USA. Anglicanism is well established in the region.

Roman Catholicism dominates the Spanish and French speaking states as well as St. Lucia and Trinidad and Tobago. The Antilles Episcopal Conference is the Catholic body of archbishops and bishops of the region. In Haiti for example the liberation theology of Latin America was adopted by the former Catholic priest, Jean-Bertrand Aristide who eventually became Haiti's first democratically elected president.

Christianity pervades the region. Catholicism, Anglicanism and Baptists are the dominant denominations. Christianity is a characteristic of the Caribbean identity.

Sports play an important role in Caribbean identification. In CARICOM cricket unites all of the CARICOM states with the exception of Haiti. In the Greater Antilles (Cuba, Dominican Republic and Puerto Rico) and in Curacao, the US Virgin Islands, baseball dominates.

The West Indies Cricket Team is one of the best cricket teams in the cricket world. Caribbean cricket is so highly regarded that the Cricket World Cup was held in the region in 2007. This boosted tourism.

Caribbean baseball is a major force in Major League Baseball. Caribbean players represent anywhere 20%–25% of Major League players.

Track and field, however links all countries. In 1968 Olympics, the Caribbean with representatives from Cuba (Juan Taurean 400 and 800 meters), Jamaica (Don Quarry 400 meters) and Trinidad and Tobago (Halsey Crawford 100 meters) won gold medals from the 100 to 800 meters dominating these events. In subsequent Olympiads, Olympic medallists have come from Cuba, The Bahamas, Jamaica and the Dominican Republic. Recently, sportscasters identify athletes in many cases regionally thereby projecting the region to the sporting world.

Caribbean cultural icon, Professor Rex Nettleford coined the expression to define the Caribbean as the melody of Europe with "the rhythm of Africa." As Professor Nettleford puts it, the common cultural thread throughout the Caribbean is the link between Europe and Africa. Even though there has been the dominance of Europe through colonialism and the disconnect from Africa by design, the Caribbean culture is rooted in European and

African civilizations.

This dichotomous root structure has created a unique people. Out of the uniqueness of the people, there has evolved a way of life which is distinct from Europe or Africa. This is depicted in the music, cuisine, worship, lifestyle, general attitude to most things, architecture and the manner in which Caribbean people communicate.

As the region was embarking on the development of a new economic sector—tourism, steps were being taken to establish a regional tertiary institution—UWI. This was 1948.

Since 1948, UWI has played a pivotal role in training thousands in the Anglophone Caribbean. Throughout the region, however, there has been an expansion to tertiary education in every Caribbean state. The older independent states (Cuba, Haiti and Dominican Republic) have had universities and colleges for decades. In the newly independent states the development of tertiary education has taken place as a result of governmental and private sector action.

UWI remains the premier tertiary institution in CARICOM, however, recent figures of the Caribbean Knowledge and Learning Network (CKLN), indicated that there are approximately 150 tertiary institutions in the Caribbean.

UWI expanded its reach through its extramural programme. In this era of information and communications technology, CKLN will "connect the region's colleges and universities, fostering collaboration and the development of region-wide e-learning programmes." This will also facilitate the CARICOM objective to ensure that 30% of the population has tertiary education by 2010.

Some countries like Jamaica, have also enacted national targets to achieve the CARICOM 30% objective by 2015.

There is no doubt that UWI, in nearly 60 years of its existence, has been internationally acclaimed as the institution which projects the image of Caribbean academia. During this period UWI has become an authentic university with the capacity and reputation to hold its own with the older institutions around the globe.

Among the 150 tertiary level institutions, there are a cluster of offshore academic institutions of which there are 24 medical (and 1 veterinary) schools throughout the region. These institutions are a departure from the regular medical school as they are significantly less expensive and easier to establish an offshore medical school in the

Caribbean, where accreditation requirements do not include research programmes, full service universities or hospitals.

This departure from the norm has separated the offshore Caribbean medical institution from the traditional medical school which underwent reform in the US and Canada as a result of *The Flexner Report* which was published in 1910.

The basis of the report was that "there were too many schools, that many were sub-standard and that the pre-requisites for the study of medicine and the content of medical education needed to be defined." As a result of this evaluation, the report recommended that there should be minimum requirements for admission to medical schools and medical schools should be of four years duration (two years of basic science and the last two years of clinical work).

John Hopkins Medical School was the model used by Flexner who had surveyed the 155 medical schools in the US and Canada. At the time only "16 required two or more years of college work for entrance."

The offshore Caribbean medical institution has established the region as a centre for medical training. Overall there are 37 medical schools registered with WHO. There are med-schools in Trinidad and Tobago (1), Jamaica (1) and the Dominican Republic (9), one of the schools in Guyana, caters to domestic or regional students and several in the Eastern Caribbean States (Grenada, St. Lucia).

The World Bank Report states that,

> "70% of the international medical graduates entering the US between 1984 and 2004 have been from the offshore Caribbean medical schools. Currently there are an estimated 11,000 offshore students enrolled in these schools."

The Caribbean, a region of Third World states, is now providing the environment for the output of medical doctors to developed countries like the US and Canada.

CRNM is an important regional institution. More and more Caribbean countries look to services as the main earner of foreign exchange. Tourism, though referred to as a fickle industry, provides more foreign exchange to the economies of Caribbean states than any other service or commodity.

A prime example of a "new sense of self" was demonstrated in November, 2006 when the government of St. Kitts and Nevis established the Sugar Industry Diversification Foundation (SIDF). This decision stemmed from the fact that the government took the decision to get out of the business of growing sugar cane with its hundreds of small farmers and to embark on a programme to convert the economy of St. Kitts and Nevis to a service-based one.

The establishment of the SIDF reflects the confidence of the government of Prime Minister Dr. Denzil Douglas to put this twin-island state on a new economic development path. The government had the view that the SIDF is the best avenue "to meet the varied aspirations of the people of St. Kitts and Nevis."

CRNM has been able to create a common trade policy for much of the region with the exception of Cuba, the US dependencies of Puerto Rico and the Virgin Islands, the French Islands of Martinique and Guadeloupe as well as the Dutch "dependencies" Curacao, Aruba, Bonaire and Saba. Through a common trade policy, the Caribbean speaks with one voice on a range of trade regimes (WTO, FTAA and *EU Partnership Agreement*).

There are many facets to this region. As a tourism destination, CTO plays a strategic role in the promotion and development of the Caribbean region as a destination, distinct from any in the world.

The CTO is relatively new as it came into existence in January 1989. It is an amalgamation of CTO (founded in 1951) and the Caribbean Tourism Research and Development Centre (founded in 1974). CTO classifies itself as an international development agency.

The effectiveness of the CTO is determined by its ability to market the Caribbean and grow it, hence its membership comprises destination countries, each with its own peculiarities; however the commonalities, in my opinion, identify the region as one destination.

Caribbean institutions like CARICOM, UWI, CRNM, the Church, sports and culture are helping the region to develop a "sense of self" in order to bring a certain focus to the region by the potential visitor.

In Caribbean culture, for example, music stands out. Whether the music is reggae of Jamaica, Afro-Cuban, steel band of Trinidad, Calypso or Junkanoo of The Bahamas, the commonality of these sounds is "the rhythm of Africa." It is "the African rhythm" in

Caribbean music which distinguishes or identifies the sound of the region.

This rhythm is also found in Christian worship and liturgy. With the indigenization of the Catholic and Anglican clergy, the rhythm of worship has been transformed.

It is through this synchronization of institutions that the Caribbean has begun to develop a "sense of self."

Rum to the Caribbean is as wine to the Europe. Where sugar cane was grown in the Caribbean, a particular type or brand of rum was processed from that production locale. This has resulted in a range of rums being produced throughout the Caribbean. Some of these rums are internationally known, some regionally, and others are island specific.

One can always find a rum shop, which is usually frequented by men and where discussions on every topic takes place, where local foods are eaten and also where entertainment takes place.

Rum has many uses. It has gained the reputation of being an intoxicant while little work has been done on its medicinal properties or as an additive in cooking or baking. Despite these, rum is an important aspect of the socio-economic fabric of the Caribbean. It is one of the most distinguishing features of the Caribbean.

Over the past 500 years, sugar cane production has experienced many technological changes, particularly in plant genetics and breeding which has been reflected in improvements in maturation rates, sugar levels, responsiveness to soil types, etc. These factors have influenced the types of rums being produced on the various islands. In this era of globalization with its rules and regulations governing intellectual property rights, rum is a distinctive drink and specific rums should be protected as a product of the Caribbean as a protected designation of origin.

Australian Wine and Brandy Corporation signed an agreement with the EU in 1990s, and Canada in 2003 entered an agreement with the EU. CRNM should seek this arrangement for CARICOM rums.

The Caribbean has gone through two eras—slavery and colonialism, and is now in its third era—independence. The experiences of slavery and colonialism have left a psychological imprint on the minds of the people of the region and it is this imprint, which is being replaced with a new consciousness. It is this "sense of self" which is propelling the peoples of the region to new heights. Caribbean states are driving their own destinies.

Intermezzo: *The Eneas Files*, *The Bahama Journal*　CSME: Is The Bahamas In or Out?

Port of Spain, Trinidad—Three and a half decades ago, it was a chore getting to Trinidad. Today, it is a breeze—from Miami to Port of Spain in three and a half hours.

This twin-island state (Trinidad and Tobago) has undergone a lot of changes. There is a bustling economy and it is probably the most industrialized Anglophone state in the Caribbean.

The economy of Trinidad and Tobago has demonstrated a great deal of resiliency. After the bottom dropped out of the oil market, the economy received a violent shock, as its main source of foreign exchange was severely damaged—reserves fell, the country's infrastructure began to fall apart, unemployment began to soar and the drug trade flourished.

The economy is healthier now, as foreign investment has poured into several areas to build a highly diversified economy.

This week, the Caribbean spotlight is once again on Trinidad as the Caribbean Heads of Government meet in the region's 20th CARICOM Summit.

This Summit is pivotal to the future development of the region. Heading this Summit's agenda is the establishment of a single market economy. Moving in this direction will call for a drastic departure from the way in which CARICOM countries will operate, particularly for the development of a CARICOM currency, movement of capital among states, human resources utilization and trade. The implications for The Bahamas are substantial and will, no doubt, involve considerable debate.

The question of Caribbean integration and The Bahamas is a thorny one. Even though there are a number of issues which we share with the rest of the Anglophone Caribbean, the psychological barrier of total political and economic immersion still remains among Bahamians.

To develop a better understanding and appreciate, there needs to be more public education on this question. At the political, professional and public service levels, there is a deep understanding and appreciation for Bahamian involvement in Caribbean integration; however at the citizen and business levels, there is extreme discomfort.

CARICOM leaders are cognizant of this fact because the integration process is viewed with some suspicion resulting from memories of the failed West Indian

Federation. In order to address the uncertainty surrounding the implementation of a single market and economy, the Heads of Government have decided to undertake a region wide programme to sensitize people about the integration movement and its benefits.

There is a realization among CARICOM leaders that this integration concept is not an easy sell and is not something which should be fostered on a country. With this background, there is the acceptance that some countries will move slower than others.

In conjunction with the Heads of Government Summit, the agricultural sector of the Caribbean is also present in Trinidad and Tobago, as the Caribbean Week of Agriculture is being staged along with other agribusiness related activities.

Caribbean leaders who host these summits always like to "show off" the best of their countries. Trinidad's economy is on an upturn and one can see it and feel it.

There are the usual American fast food franchises like Kentucky Fried Chicken, Pizza Hut, Burger King and McDonald's here. Satellite and cable television transmission enables one to keep pace with the type of programming which one is accustomed. Men's and women's fashions are the same as in Nassau, Miami or New York. Cellular phones are plentiful, along with the latest information technology gadgets.

30 odd years ago, as a student in this island state, it seemed to be a distant land. With advances in technology, communication and transportation, Port of Spain does not seem to be so distant. The Caribbean and The Bahamas are coming closer; today there is more in common than there are differences.

Should The Bahamas Fear Caribbean Integration?

In 1992, international development experts saw the Caribbean's economic future as being precarious. The region was viewed as being fragmented, debt-ridden and increasingly bedeviled by high rates of crime and the destabilizing presence of drug-trafficking.

The future was viewed with so much trepidation in the Commonwealth Caribbean that the Heads of Government established the West Indian Commission to recommend ways to strengthen regional cooperation and integration. The Commission was chaired by Sir Shridath Ramphal who, incidentally, is heading the CARICOM negotiation team into FTAA.

It is my understanding that elements in The Bahamas Chamber of Commerce are opposed to CARICOM performing agency functions for The Bahamas in this negotiation process. The feeling is that The Bahamas should negotiate independently.

Several weeks ago, Mr. A. Leonard Archer, Bahamian Ambassador for the Caribbean, stated that it was time for The Bahamas to seriously consider Caribbean integration. The basis of his argument was that the economies of Caribbean countries were looking more and more alike—tourism, financial services, and other services, particularly those connected with information technology.

In the eyes of the international development institutions, agencies of the UN, and, of course, EU, the Caribbean is seen as a region in its own right. The US took this approach during the Regan Administration and launched the Caribbean Basin Initiative (CBI). This approach has caught on.

Bahamians have had a difficulty identifying with the rest of the Caribbean. Geographically the islands of the archipelago fall into two groups, each anchored to the mainland. The Greater Antilles, i.e. Cuba, Haiti and the Dominican Republic, Jamaica and Puerto Rico along with the Virgin Islands represent the northern ruin of the Caribbean Basin. The Lesser Antilles constitutes the Basin's eastern ruin. These comprise the islands from Anguilla to Grenada. Geographers believe that Trinidad and possibly Barbados may be geologically similar to Venezuela.

Lying to the north of the Greater Antilles, The Bahamas technically falls outside the Caribbean Basin. In the broader context, the Caribbean Sea defined the Caribbean region. However, it is within the broader context that The Bahamas is considered a part of the Caribbean. Owing to its British colonial background, the natural political affinity was drawn to the Anglophone countries of the Caribbean Basin, hence The Bahamas' alignment with CARICOM.

Prior to 1997, financial experts and analysts have often held up the countries and regions of South East Asia—Asian Tigers as models for Caribbean Basin countries to emulate. However, there has been some dramatic economic and financial reversals in Southeast Asia. Several of these countries were preferred as exemplary economic models for adoption.

Since 1992, the economies of CARICOM have been heading in a positive direction. In 1997, tourism remained the dominant sector in the region's economic performance with an increasing contribution to growth from the offshore financial sector. This supports Ambassador Archer's proposition that the economies of countries of CARICOM are looking more and more alike.

Recent statistics from CDB confirm the positive performance of the economies:

"The economy of Anguilla grew by about 6.5%, that of the Cayman Islands by 6%, the British Virgin Islands by 4.5% and the Turks and Caicos Islands by 4%. In Antigua and Barbuda, growth is estimated at 4.8%. For The Bahamas, expansion has been reported for the fifth successive year, with real GDP rising by 3.5%, a substantial increase from 1% of 1996.

Barbados also experienced a fifth successive year of economic growth, but its 4.3% did not match the 5.2% of the previous year. Growth of Belize reached 3% to double the 1996 performance of 1.5%, and in Grenada, it was 4.3% up from 3.4% the previous year. In Guyana, growth was estimated at 6.1%, well below the 7.9% recorded in 1996.

Jamaica's economy continued to stagnate, with perhaps the growth around 1%. In St. Kitts and Nevis the indication of an 8% rise in output, compared with 4.8% in 1996, and in St. Vincent and the Grenadines there has been marginal growth. Trinidad and Tobago's recovery continues with growth estimated at 3.2%. Decline seems to be taking place in Dominica and St. Lucia, as their economies are heavily dependent on banana exports."

From all indications CARICOM countries have made the right adjustments and are headed in the right direction. With such strong economies, it is in The Bahamas' interest to strengthen its relationship with CARICOM, particularly during the negotiation process on *LOME Convention* and FTAA.

Leonard Archer has hit the nail on the head. We need to study the implications of Caribbean integration more closely.

Caribbean Integration: Where Do We Stand?

The Anglophone Caribbean has defined itself as the primary initiators of Caribbean integration. The integration process has seen its ups and downs but over the past 40 years, particularly since the Independence Era, there has been steady progress. Throughout this period, however, The Bahamas has been partially committed to the process.

The most frequently expressed reason for Bahamian half-stepping has been that it has not been in our interest to go along with the integration process.

When UWI was started, the white oligarchical government held the position that a university education far exceeded the ambitions of the black majority, hence The Bahamas opted not to participate in the financing of the university. It was not until PLP government took over the reins of government that The Bahamas became a financed contributor to the UWI.

The Bahamas never saw itself as a part of the West Indies. The signature entry of West Indian integration as its cricket team embodied its identity internationally.

In the 1950s, West Indian track and field coaches were anxious to add Tommy Robinson to their team, especially the sprint relay; but they couldn't, because The Bahamas was not a member of the Caribbean grouping.

In the 1970s if Mr. Carlton Francis as Minister of Finance was not so insistent and farsighted The Bahamas wouldn't be sitting on the Board of Directors of CDB. The thinking at that time, as it is today, in some quarters that we could not benefit from the CDB and it was not in our interests to put our money in a Caribbean bank.

It took years, almost about five or six, that CARIFTA meet undertook the premier athletic events for our young in the region. Under Dr. B. J. Nottage's presidency of The Bahamas Amateur Athletic Association, it was decided that The Bahamas should participate in CARIFTA meet after viewing the meet in Barbados. Look at what The Bahamas has reaped athletically since participating in CARIFTA meet? It is the basis for the success of the Golden Girls.

International entities like EU, the Pan American Health Organization and FAO see The Bahamas within the context of the Caribbean.

With reference to the EU, there are a number of programmes from which funding can be obtained, however the regional headquarters of these funds are located in either Jamaica, Barbados or Trinidad as The Bahamas for administrative purposes is attached to one of these countries which are classified as the regional office. In far too many cases, The Bahamas does not benefit to the extent to which it is eligible or entitled because we are out of the regional "loop."

One of the most important challenges facing the Caribbean as a region is the question of globalization and the manner in which small economy states like most of the CARICOM countries will deal with this issue. Owing to the complexity of the issues facing participation in FTAA, the Caribbean has established a regional negotiation machinery where the technical expertise in trade has assembled in order to present a consolidated position.

This approach has already paid dividends. Just recently the Caribbean presented its position on *AOA* to WTO. The presentation was well received as critical areas of the document were accepted by the developed world, particularly the big players like the US and the EU.

In today's world for small countries like The Bahamas to go it alone is foolhardy. The tactics adopted by the government in dealing with the blacklisting of our financial services vis-à-vis CARICOM approach by taking the issue to the WTO will be evaluated and compared. The Bahamian public, at some point in time, will be able to judge the results of each approach.

The integration process has now reached to a very fundamental aspect of our civilization—the interpretation of our laws through a CCJ. The Bahamas has taken the position that it wishes for the Privy Council in Britain to continue performing that role. CARICOM says that its development is at the level where it can perform this aspect of governance within the region.

Many people see holding on the Privy Council as one of the last remnants of our colonial heritage. The British, on the other hand has already shown its hand by demonstrating on numerous occasions that its future is with the rest of Europe and it is integrating the fundamental components of its natural life into a monolithic entity in the form of EU.

In the not too distant future, we in The Bahamas will wake up to find out that the British will say that they are no longer interested in adjudicating our legal affairs. They did it physically through the independence process, the Commonwealth has become a talk shop and the list goes on.

The Bahamas at this juncture in our development and at this point in the 21st century still does not understand the importance of the Caribbean integration. It is paradoxical that all of the countries of the Caribbean, The Bahamas is perhaps the most cosmopolitan. Residing in the midst are natives of each Caribbean islands—Jamaicans, Haitians, Barbadians, Trinidadians, St. Lucians, Dominicans, St. Vincentians, Guyanese, Belizeans, Cubans, etc.

Chapter 5

9/11

> "No civilization was so little equipped to cope with the outside world; no country was so easily raided and plundered, and learned too little from its disasters."
>
> —V.S. Naipaul, Trinidadian, *India: A Wounded Civilization*

The events of September 11th, 2001 demonstrated the fickleness of tourism as a commodity and the vulnerability of economies with a heavy reliance on the tourism dollar. The Caribbean was hit by the air embargo as no flights could enter or leave the US.

The air embargo costs Caribbean tourism millions of dollars in earnings and put thousands temporarily out of work. 9/11 was a destabilizing event, economically, socially and politically. When the dust cleared, the implications were even more far-reaching. A new war in the form of the war on terror had become a reality, a war which would cause Caribbean governments to invest millions of dollars for security at airports, cruise ship terminals and specialized security training for a new cadre of workers.

For The Bahamas, 9/11 was expensive. On September 11th, the US Federal Aviation Administration halted all flight operations at US airports and flights would not resume until September 13th.

In 2001, there was an average of 4,211 visitors each day in The Bahamas and each spending at least $250 per day. For one day, the average expenditure was $1,052,750. With flights cancelled, The Bahamas was loosing more than 1 million per day.

No Caribbean state has as many airports as The Bahamas; there were 64 in 2005 of which 30 had paved runways. On some islands like Eleuthera, there are three (North Eleuthera, Governor's Harbor and Rock Sound) and each of these received international flights.

The installation of security equipment in the airport system would necessitate capital expenditure. In addition, the expenditure to recruit manpower was increased because of the security personnel who were needed throughout the archipelago.

In the budget address of 2002/3 by the Hon. Perry G. Christie, Prime Minister of The Bahamas and Minister of Finance, stated the following:

> "For the final quarter of 2001, available statistics show that total visitor arrivals contracted by 11%, reversing a 15.3% increase over the same period in 2000. Air arrivals were hardest hit, declining by 22.8% with a lesser drop of 5.1% for cruise visitors. It is estimated that total visitor expenditures declined during this period by some 28.5%.
>
> With post-September 11th average occupancy rates in hotels reported to be as low as 44% relative to a normal 57% level, properties responded with sharp price discounting and cost cutting measures, which included partial closures, temporary staff reductions and reduced working hours.
>
> Similarly, labour savings measures were implemented in many retail shops which depended heavily on tourism business, and financial institutions braced themselves for possible financial difficulties affecting workers, by providing opportunities for more manageable servicing arrangements for persons and household debt.
>
> As a result of the forth quarter losses, total visitor arrivals for 2001 contracted by 0.4% to 4.19 million persons. Air arrivals fell by 2.9% to 1.44 million and growth in sea arrivals slowed by 1.0% to 2.75 million. Consequent on general weakness in stopovers, who tend to stay longest and spend more, together with price discounting, estimated industry earnings fell by 3.5% to $1.75 billion in 2001.
>
> Corresponding hotel sector trends indicate that, although average room rates appreciated by 2.9% to $153.03 per night, the 4.4% reduction in the number of occupied rooms caused estimated room revenues to decline by 1.7%."

In the final analysis the government of The Bahamas had to borrow $125 million to complete the financing of the fiscal position of 2001/02 primarily resulting the aftermath of September 11th, losses of the private sector have been estimated to be in the hundreds of millions, particularly hotels and tourists related businesses.

The shorter workweek in the hotels adversely affected women, many of whom were single mothers and breadwinners in many households.

This summarizes the direct impact of 9/11 in The Bahamas.

The US government's Department of Homeland Security brought into force the Western Hemisphere Travel Initiative. This initiative requires that,

> "Americans as well as Canadians, Mexicans and Bermudans present a passport to enter the US when arriving by air or sea from any part of the Western Hemisphere."

Prior to this initiative, Americans coming to The Bahamas only needed some form of identification, i.e. driver's license or social security card were enough; 9/11 changed that arrangement.

Several of the 9/11 terrorists held student visas to US universities. In view of this fact that these visas were used to gain entrance to the US, there is a new policy by the US on the granting of the student visas. The process is stringent and highly selective causing many Caribbean students to be excluded from the process of obtaining student visas.

This is posing a serious difficulty for Caribbean students who now look to the region for tertiary education, thereby emphasizing the importance of a regional institution like UWI and universities and community colleges at the national level in conjunction with a number of foreign-owned and operated specialty universities/colleges in human and veterinary medicine. Training at the tertiary level in the region has deepened to the point where there are 150 tertiary level institutions.

Anti-terrorist efforts were also introduced at ports both in the US and the various ports of the Caribbean and cruise ship terminals. A major concern is underwater explosive devices or any mechanism which could endanger the security of a cruise ship.

Caribbean governments received another scare on Thursday 10th August 2006, when airports were put on a heightened security alert which came from the US Transportation Security Administration. This resulted from the uncovering of a terrorist plot to blow up airplanes traveling from London, England to the US. This alert covered aircraft flying to and from the US as well as aircraft to and from the UK.

UK carriers, British Airways and Virgin Atlantic, and Air Jamaica fly direct from the UK to the Caribbean. This alert temporarily disrupted travel as new security rules were introduced. A possible 9/11 was averted.

Prior to September 11th 2001, on any given day, the Caribbean region would have some 100,000 visitors who would spend from $100 to $250 per head. During the last four months of 2001, this inflow of visitors was disrupted. The daily revenue loss was from $10 to $25 million. In reviewing the Bahamian scenario, normalcy in the industry did not return for four to six months. For the region, the revenue loss approached 1 billion dollars.

9/11 was a major set back for the economies of these small island states in this region.

Intermezzo: *The Eneas Files*, *The Bahama Journal*   A Deepening Impact

With tourism decimated in the aftermath of the attacks on the World Trade Center and the Pentagon, Caribbean countries are bracing for a rough economic ride which may not end until mid or late 2002.

All of this week, Caribbean leaders in government and tourism have been in The Bahamas reviewing the situation in the hope that the commonality of the debacle may lead to an angle which may soften the fall or bring some sort of relief to hose experiencing shortfalls and declining financial indices.

Elsewhere in places like New York City, Orlando and Las Vegas, all sorts of gimmicks and measures are being employed to lure tourists back to the casino tables, beaches, theme parks, museum and shows. Hotels and airlines are playing big roles in these endeavors. How successful they are, is yet to be determined. "Price Sharing" is the name of the game and this is what it takes to survive financially.

This is the general scenario the tourism industry is facing. In the weeks since the attack, inquiries are increasing. For one property in Nassau it has inched up to 70% since the pre-attack days; bookings for Thanksgiving and Christmas appear to be strong and visits by travel writers are on the up-swing again. These are all positive signs.

This whole situation hinges on security. By now everyone should have recognized that the world is at war.

This is not far-fetched since earlier this week the Secretary General of the UN, Mr. Kofi Annan was concerned about Security Council memorandum from the US that other than Afghanistan there may be other eastern countries earmarked for bombing. This has enflamed an already high volatile scene.

This is the crisis today. Economic projections show a worsening state of affairs—one which may last as long as two years. If that is the case, this could mean economic devastation for a number of countries.

Global lending institutions assess that the terrorist attacks will negatively affect the dim forecast of global economic growth for the next two years—yes, the next two years. Further, the economic growth and development of the Third World or developing countries will be severely retarded.

It is projected that some 10 million people could be thrown into poverty which is having to live off less than one dollar per day.

Economists saw a slow down in growth in the industrialized countries like Europe, the US and Japan prior to the attacks. The attacks have resulted in a delay of the economic recovery which was anticipated.

Particularly hard hit has been tourism related trade. It is this perspective which has put the Caribbean and countries like The Bahamas in its present predicament of having suffered the cancellation of approximately 65% of the holidays booked.

During the 1990s, The Bahamas was in an extremely frustrated economic situation stemming from the heavy flows of foreign investment. This situation will not prevail as capital flows to developing countries will certainly slow down possibly to a trickle. Remember tourism dependent economies are no longer in vogue.

The Bahamas economic development policy based on the twin pillars of tourism and financial services would have to be adjusted and a macroeconomic policy would have to be introduced to reflect an improved investment climate and greater emphasis should be put not only on foreign investment but also on the encouragement of investment from indigenous sources.

No doubt the Emergency Session of the CARICOM Heads of Government Conference would have focused on the economic fallout emanating from the attacks, particularly in the tourism, aviation and financial service sectors.

For The Bahamas, the implications are grave. We have felt effects in tourism and financial services. With reference to aviation, it will mean a new role for our twenty airports scattered the length and breadth of our archipelago.

Stricter security rules will mandate new priorities for our Family Islands airports. Many of them will cease being ports of entry and on some islands where there are multiple airports only one may be designated for international flights—both private and commercial.

The longer the world remains in a war mode, the impact of the attacks will deepen.

Is Our World Safe?

Since March 2003, the US, Britain and a number of other countries had embarked on the invasion of Iraq. The initial reason given for the invasion was to rid the world of weapons of mass destruction believed to be in the possession of the Saddam Hussein Regime.

The overthrow of Saddam's Regime was relatively quick and without much loss of life. Once defeated, the liberators became occupiers. This occupancy has led to much civil strife in that country as every day newscasts are filled with account of people being killed by car bombs or just attacks by gunmen. In June of this year, the governance of that country was turned over to local people.

This past week, a US Senate report concluded that CIA provided false and unfounded assessments of the threat posed by Iraq that the Bush Administration relied on to convince Britain and the rest of the world to invade Iraq.

The report was repudiated, as the conclusion drawn was that the US Congress might not have approved the Iraqi War had the American lawmakers known the truth. The report had affected the credibility of Americans, its President and its Secretary of State, Colin Powell, who had to sell the idea of an invasion to the world through the UN' Security Council.

An aspect of this invasion was predicated on the elimination of terrorism and those countries which supported or harbored terrorists. Al Qaeda was also the common global terrorist enemy.

As a result of all of this, the world has been turned upside down and the impact is being felt in every nook and cranny of every country. The main element the world is feeling is the aspect of security—security at our seaports, our airports, our persons and the level of scrutiny of the individual person to travel among countries, particularly in North America and EU.

Let's look at what is taking place firstly in a country and secondly in our region.

There was a time when traveling was pleasurable, that is one did not experience the rigors of body searches by metal detectors and little old ladies who, one wonders, whether or not they know what they are looking for.

This whole security business has made Nassau International Airport a disaster case. One time ago, departure on a flight required one hour to check in. As a result of all the security procedures demanded by the US Department of Homeland Security, traveling has become security dominated.

Firstly you check in with the airline on which you are traveling. Then you walk behind the check-in area carrying or pulling your luggage. Depending on your departure, if it is after 4:00 p.m., then there is only one door to the US pre-clearance zone. This could mean standing in line with 100, 150 or 200 people depending on the flight which precedes yours.

When you get to the security machine, hopefully your luggage is not heavy. If there is a female ahead of you with a huge bag, between her and the female security, they have to strain to lift the bag on the security belt. All the security personnel are women; no men are around to offer assistance.

Think about the visitor who had just had four nights and five days in Paradise—he or she had an enjoyable relaxing vacation and was about to return home. The final encounter with Bahamian authorities is the security arrangements at the airport.

When you pass US Immigration and enter US Customs, you may have to undergo another search by a cadre of Bahamian security people before your bags are placed in the baggage belt. Then you go upstairs and your carry-on-bags are checked by another group of security people. Depending on the flight, time of day and destination, the drug enforcement people may bring in the dogs to sniff your hand luggage which had already been checked. If you are in transit through the US, then the whole security process has to be repeated. Security seems to be an endless undertaking.

Is Al Qaeda a threat to CARICOM? There may be a threat to US or British interests in CARICOM states, but not really to CARICOM governments. Why then is there all of the same type of security stipulations on flights between Nassau and Montego Bay or vice versa? Even more ridiculous, there are stringent security measures between Kingston and Bridgetown or Port of Spain. The whole region has been required to spend huge sums of money in establishing security apparatus at airports and seaports, just to satisfy Homeland Security.

The US has made this war on terrorism a global one. Small countries like The Bahamas face it everyday as a result of the security requirements of international trade and travel. In addition, security has impacted our cost of living as a substantial part of freight costs stems from security demands.

These security measures are wreaking havoc on general travel. For instance, attempt to obtain a visa to EU. Bahamians owing to historical ties can travel to Britain; getting to the continent is not an easy arrangement; it could take as long as two weeks to get a visa. Why? Because of security.

Despite all of these security initiatives, is our world any safer?

The Importance of Floridian Ports in Peace and War

Almost 50% of our visitors come by cruise ships. The cruise ship industry has become a major vehicle driving mass tourism in the Caribbean. For The Bahamas this 50% figure represent some 2 million tourists, mostly Americans.

Miami and Ft. Lauderdale have also become cruise ship hubs and gateway points to The Bahamas and the Caribbean. This is a huge business and generates substantial revenue and jobs for these two South Florida cities.

At both of these ports, security is a big issue. With the US at war, Miami and Ft. Lauderdale are viewed as sensitive security points and this has made the new Homeland Agency intensify its security involvement in that area because it is seen as being potentially vulnerable to terrorism attacks.

The measures contemplated range from shutting down these ports either totally or partially. Cruise ships entering these points are bordered and searched prior to arrival. In some circumstances, US Homeland Security Officials go to foreign ports to inspect ships bound to the US via Miami or Ft. Lauderdale.

At both Miami and Fort Lauderdale, officers are now employing high tech security equipment to check luggage in order to ensure that items like bio-chemicals or dirty bombs have not been planted in a passenger's bag.

For commercial vessels, shipping manifestos have to be submitted 24 hours in advance in order that the security people will have an idea of what is being loaded in the containers or ascertain knowledge of the contents of containers.

Miami, Fort Lauderdale, West Palm Beach, Fort Pierce, Jacksonville/ St. Augustine are the main east coast ports of Florida on the Atlantic Ocean. It is from there that most of the freight for The Bahamas is shipped. The Gulf of Mexico touches Florida's west coast ports of Sarasota, Tampa/St. Petersburg and Pensacola; however the freight originating from these ports to The Bahamas is small compared to the east coast Florida ports.

On both coasts, the ports are on alert; with a war, their status will change to high alert kicking in strict security measures, which will definitely influence the movement of cruise ship visitors and freight which, in the case of The Bahamas, represents 80%–85% of the food consumed by Bahamians. Other sectors of our economy like construction, particularly building materials will be impacted.

These security measures will affect visitor arrivals because cruise ship ports like Miami and Fort Lauderdale would be closed or may be operated at 50% capacity. This will have dramatic effect on the revenue of The Bahamas as income from visitor arrivals will decline. The impact on the destinations south of The Bahamas will be even more devastating.

The big three container companies, Tropical, Pioneer and Seaboard are the purveyors of most of our freight. In every likelihood, freight cost will be increased, as the security measures will have an element of expense, as demiurge will kick in thereby influencing overall freight rates.

Vessels like the Betty K, which is more orientated to palletize freight and operating out of Miami River, will also undergo severe scrutiny checks.

This is the scenario The Bahamas faces from the marine perspective. September 11th caused a great deal of focus on our air ports because of the manner in which Mohammed Atta and his gang utilized airplanes to wreak destruction. The security net has now been widened to include American sea ports, and this has reflected in the heightened security attention to Miami and Fort Lauderdale where any given weekend these ports combined could have twenty cruise ships in port awaiting to ferry thousands of Americans to The Bahamas and the Caribbean.

Tourism in the region has evolved to the point where more visitors come by cruise ships than by air. The cruise market is an extremely important factor in the tourism equation. If it is slowed or temporarily taken out of circulation, tourism business in this region will be devastated.

The implications for the freight business are just as economically far-reaching as all of the countries in the region, with the Dominican Republic as the exception, depends on the US agribusiness sector for food. Their situation is more acute as their agricultural export commodities have to be freighted to US. Back haul is a big factor in maintaining reasonably low freight rates for the far-flung Caribbean Islands, particularly the Leeward and Windward Islands chain of the Eastern Caribbean.

Floridian west coast ports play a pivotal role in the economic survival of The Bahamas and the Caribbean. The US War with Iraq will bring this fact home over the next few days and weeks.

War on Terrorism and The Bahamas

Are we in The Bahamas immune to terrorism acts? The answer is no. Terrorism is a major global concern and a threat to the national security of every country. The US has heightened its attention to this new tactic of warfare after September 11th 2001 by moving to create the new Homeland Security Department, giving it Cabinet status.

In conjunction with this concern for terrorism, the US Congress is being urged to pass the federal terrorism insurance bill, which is essentially a workers' compensation type of safety net. It will pay for medical care, replace lost wages, death benefits whatever the cause of workplace injury or death. September 11th has resulted in benefit payments of more than $3 billion to the spouse and children of those who were injured or lost their lives. This terrorism insurance is supposed to protect workers against another possible terrorism attack along the lines of September 11th.

One reason for this type of insurance stemmed from the fact that US insurance companies are reluctant to insure workplaces with high concentrations of workers like the World Trade Centre or in high-profile locations like the Pentagon.

Our powerful neighbour to the north has allocated tremendous resources—financial, legislative and governmental restructuring to insulate America, its people and economy from this war on terrorism.

For Third World or developing countries is the threat as real to them as to the developed, industrialized countries like the US, Canada and Western Europe? Perhaps the body which has done most to secure the world and small countries like The Bahamas is the UN through its Counter-Terrorism Committee.

This Committee's role is to strengthen global capacity in this field, through a coordinated programme of rules assessment and technical assistance. An important component of the UN programme is to achieve disarmament by strengthening global norms against the use or proliferation of weapons of mass destruction and by giving technical support to states seeking to curb the flow of arms, funds, and technology to terrorist cells. It is from this perspective that the US—Britain initiative to obtain UN ratification to search and destroy weapons of mass destruction in Iraq.

Among counter terrorist experts, there is a growing consensus that terrorists groups, notably Al-Qaida, are targeting western tourists. The attack on foreign visitors in Bali was only the latest and the most deadly on westerners in Asia. The fear is that this kind of terrorism may find itself in the Americas, possibly offshore tourism locales like The Bahamas and the Caribbean.

Our daily newscasts are filled with pronouncements about terror groups and their actions, mostly in the Middle East and other parts of Asia.

For The Bahamas the fear is international terrorism as domestic terrorism is not an issue here; at least not at this point in time. As a country we could become a victim of international terrorism because of the large numbers of Americans who can be found in The Bahamas any given day either on Bay Street, at our international airports, a property like Atlantis, the casinos and docks where the cruise ships berth. This is the threat to us, our visitors are targets and these are the types of venues that terrorists identify.

Small countries like The Bahamas do not have the financial resources to mount counter-terrorism campaigns nor can we afford to have an elaborate intelligence service to put us in a preventative mode. The solution to this situation is to align ourselves with international agencies which specialize in counter terrorism measures, the UN is one such body.

One of the linch-pins in the US policy against terrorism is to bolster the counter-terrorist capabilities of those countries that work with the US and require assistance. For The Bahamas, this is probably the best way to respond to international terrorism.

Since September 11th 2001, there are currently 69 nations supporting the global war on terrorism. Our government has never informed Bahamians, to my knowledge, as to whether or not we are one of the 69 nations. Further, 20 nations have deployed more than 16,000 troops to the US Central Command's region of responsibility. Have any members of our Defense Force been deployed or assigned to this unit? It is in our interest for our military to be exposed to these situations and obtain training from this type of international exposure.

The Bali incident sent shock waves throughout the world as it demonstrated the ruthlessness of international terrorism. A severe suffering was inflicted on hundreds of families. The damage to the economy and well being of Indonesia are probably incalculable. We in The Bahamas have to be vigilant in this war on terrorism.

The Post 9/11 World

Our World was turned upside down on September 11th, 2001. The acronym for this day, 9/11, has become a statement itself and it is recognized everywhere with great significance.

There are occasions which are so memorable in a nation's life, a community life and our lives as individuals. 9/11 is one of those occasions. Many older Bahamians can tell you where he or she was on January 10th 1967; the same can be said about the day when President John F. Kennedy was assassinated in Dallas, Texas. 9/11 is one of those events.

9/11, according to the leaders of the major powers, signaled that the world was at war. This time it was a war on terror. This was a very different war from the conventional war to which mankind has become accustomed.

In World War I, which featured trench warfare and bayonet charges, the enemy was there in face-to-face confrontation and hand to hand combat. In World War II, the atomic bomb was the instrument which was used to kill thousands in Japan as well as destroy the city of Nagasaki. This war on terror is different because it is impacting the global community in many ways.

The events of 9/11 have impacted the way we travel. For us in a mobile society like The Bahamas this is the most glaring. Every time we go to the airport whether at the domestic or international terminals respectively we are faced with security measures. Many of us can remember when this was not necessary. After 9/11, this scenario came into effect.

Security is one of the hallmarks of the post 9/11 world.

In conjunction with this aspect of security, there is personal security. Everybody needs a passport. Some governments are demanding their citizens to obtain passports if they wish to travel. Notable is the US. Americans at one time were not required to have a passport to travel to The Bahamas; 9/11 has caused this to be amended.

Students seeking admission to US colleges and universities have to be able to prove that he or she has the financial capacity to finance his or her education. This has become a very rigid undertaking. These guidelines apply to British universities. This stems from the fact that several of the 9/11 terrorists were in the US on student visas and this is the manner in which the US has responded.

Governments in western countries, particularly those in Europe, are vigilantly revising their immigration policies. At the community level, there is much concern about religious tolerance among certain ethnic groups and the notion of "Multiculturalism Versus Integration."

Leading the charge in this is Australia. The Australian government has stated that Australia was a country built on Christian principles and expected its citizens to function within that context. If they cannot then should leave the country. This is a very bold and deliberate position. Australia has felt the effects of war on terrorism when several hundred of its citizens were blown up by a terrorist bomb in Bali which is located in Indonesia.

Television has enabled us to view this war on a daily basis. We are aware of suicide bombers because we see it so often on television. Recently, the fighting in Lebanon between Israel and Hezbollah showed the suffering wrought by war.

9/11 created a new world. This state of affairs may be with us for a long time. Some people say the situation could worsen; only time will tell.

Chapter 6

A Residual Society

"Finally, the entire West Indian tradition is anti-intellectual. People's lives are bounded by the narrow materialistic considerations of the price of produce or the cost of living or the laziness of the workers or the growth of crime and delinquency or gambling or chasing after women (or men as the case may be) or just plain gluttony and imbibing."

—Dr. Eric Williams, Trinidadian, Former Prime Minister of Trinidad and Tobago, *Inward Hunger*

Every Caribbean state has gone through the experiences of slavery and colonialism, be it under the French, Spanish, British or Dutch. As colonies whose political and economic existence initially centered around slavery and then colonialism, a unique and different type of society—a residual society emerged.

The Caribbean is a region with a society which had to internalize the after-effects of the experiences stemming from slavery and colonialism and this has resulted in a behavioral pattern which, for centuries, was Eurocentric and disconnected from the roots of its African diaspora.

The descendants of African slaves have been emancipated in Haiti from France by revolution in 1804. In the Anglophone Caribbean, it has been for 172 years (1834) with the earliest tie being severed in 1962, 44 years ago when Jamaica attained its independence from Britain. The experience of sovereignty is relatively new for the former British colonies. The Great Antillean states of Cuba and Hispaniola (Haiti and the Dominican Republic) had been sovereign longer. (See Table 6.1)

Table 6.1 Dependencies and States of the Caribbean Region

British Colony	Independence Date	Dependency	Slavery Abolition Date	Slave Trade
Antigua and Barbuda	1981	Anguilla	1807	Trafficking in humans ended
Barbados	1966	British Virgin Islands, Cayman Islands	1834	Emancipated (4 yrs. apprenticeship)
Bahamas	1973	Turks and Caicos Islands		
Belize	1981	Montserrat		
Dominica	1978			
Grenada	1974			
Guyana	1966 (Republic 1970)			
Jamaica	1962			
St. Kitts and Nevis	1983			
St. Lucia	1979			
St. Vincent and the Grenadines	1962 (Republic 1976)			
French Colony	**Independence Date**	**Dependency**	**Slavery Abolition Date**	**Slave Trade**
Haiti	1804 (First Black Republic and 2nd oldest republic in Western Hemisphere)	Overseas Dept. of France: St. Martin, Guadeloupe, Martinique, Cayenne (French Guiana)	1848	Emancipation on colonies
			1830	End of slave trade
Dutch Colony	**Independence Date**	**Dependency**	**Slavery Abolition Date**	**Slave Trade**
Netherlands		Special overseas status: St. Martin, Curacao, Aruba, Bonaire, Saba, St. Eustatius	1863	Slavery abolished/ emancipation

(to be continued)

Dutch Colony	Independence Date	Dependency	Slavery Abolition Date	Slave Trade
Suriname	1975			

US Colony	Independence Date	Dependency	Slavery Abolition Date	Slave Trade
Puerto Rico		Internal self-government	1865	13th Amendment to US Constitution formalized abolition of "involuntary servitude"
US Virgin Islands		Territory of the US: St. Thomas, St. Croix, St. John		

Spanish Colony	Independence Date	Dependency	Slavery Abolition Date	Slave Trade
Cuba	1902		1820	Slave trade abolished
Dominican Republic	1844		1870	Emancipation in colonies

Even though the years between 1834 and 1838 were to be the apprentice period when the freed slaves would learn a trade, slavery unleashed on the individual island colonies, thousands of people whose basic training was the cultivation of the land. This grouping became the small farmers who abound throughout the region. The small farmer is a legacy of slavery.

Slavery developed a stratified society—master/slave relationship. Colonialism, on the other hand, featured political dominance and economic exploitation with very limited opportunities for the sons and daughters of former slaves. Independence brought social, political and economic transformation.

Through this transformation process, tourism emerged and evolved into a multi-billion dollar industry for the region.

After World War II, the economies of the Caribbean were agriculture-based; sugar cane was the leading export crop. With farm production as the main employer, these island colonies were dominated by rural populations of which the small farmer was the major category. By the end of 20th century the small farmer would become an endangered species as a result of the transformation of the economies during the post independence years. Even though Jamaica and Guyana have bauxite and Trinidad and Tobago has oil, the small farmer is still significant to the agricultural sector in those two countries.

Economic transformation for CARICOM states took place at an uneven pace. During the decade of the 1950s, Sir Stafford Sands as Chairman of The Bahamas Development Board commenced the economic transformation of The Bahamas from agriculture-based economy to a tourism dominated economy. Substantial foreign investment in hotel construction and governmental investment in infrastructural improvements took place.

The Bahamas would reach 1 million visitor arrival mark in 1968. By 1969, The Bahamas was attracting 1 million visitors, more than its nearest CARICOM destination competitor, Jamaica. For the other CARICOM states, in the decade of 1960–1970, tourism would emerge as a major sector in the economies of CARICOM states.

Table 6.2　CARICOM Tourist Arrivals 1969–1971

Country (Region)	Numbers		
	1969	1970	1971
Bahamas	1,332.4	1,298.3	1,463.6
Jamaica	279.9	309.1	359.3
Bermuda	281	302.7	319.3
Barbados	134.3	156.4	189
Trinidad and Tobago	117	117	136
Antigua	61.2	65.3	67.6
Dominica, Grenada Montserrat, St. Kitts-Nevis-Anguilla, St. Lucia, St. Vincent	97.7	115.5	123
British Virgin Island	29.5	33.1	46.1
Cayman Islands	19.4	23	24.3
British Honduras	28	31.5	45.6

Source: *The Stability of the Caribbean* (The Bahamas in millions; others in thousands)

The Caribbean provided the sun, sand and sea to nurture a burgeoning tourist industry. The source of investment to develop the industry came chiefly from the US, which is also the main market for visitors to the Caribbean.

The Caribbean, geopolitically, has been viewed as America's backyard and a region which falls under the US sphere of influence.

Over the years a symbiotic relationship has developed as the region has been a source of manpower, agricultural raw materials, bauxite, oil and natural gas. In return, the US has provided markets and foreign direct investments as remittances and funding for touristic and other projects.

The US census report of 2000 indicated that approximately 10% or 3 million of the

28 million immigrants came from the Caribbean primarily Cuba, Jamaica, Dominican Republic and Haiti. Remittances to the region from immigrants are substantial and, in the 1990s were $400 million. By 2002, they had climbed to $4 billion.

With reference to trade, 45% of all US imports from the Caribbean received preferential treatment in 2003. CBI was introduced during the Regan Administration. In 2002, *The Caribbean Basin Trade Partnership Act* came into existence.

The relative openness between the economies of the Caribbean and North America has fuelled Caribbean tourism which is responsible for stimulating the expansion of services in the region.

The Face of Caribbean Tourism

Tourism in the Caribbean has come to have a number of connotations. For Caribbean people it means employment. It is a chance for a career in a service industry, for some the most important industry on his or her island. To the visitor, it is the experience which may manifest itself in the sun, sand or sea. For the foreign entrepreneur it is the opportunity to invest and make a profit.

These three components are presented in various forms and differ from island to island. There is no monolithic view of tourism. There is an upside and downside to each approach.

The tourism culture in the Caribbean has been evolving over the past 50 years and it has influenced the socialization of Caribbean peoples who have to interface with the visitor who may be a cruise ship passenger, a hotel or bed and breakfast stopover, a second home winter resident or may be a student resident or spring-breaker. All of these types of visitors leave an impression on the islander and influences his or her outlook.

• Integrated Tourism

During the early years of tourism in The Bahamas, hotels were off limits to blacks as well as the gourmet restaurants, golf courses and an elite gaming house. The black Bahamian was principally a hotel worker—waiter, bartender, maid gardener or entertainer. Management was foreign and front desk clerks were either white or light skinned.

Nassau hyped its colonial architecture, British traditions and exclusive duty free shopping, making it a unique offshore colony. Nightlife for the visitor was in the black community—Over-The-Hill. It was in this locale where the nightlife of The Bahamas was centered. Native musicians playing calypso and goombay music with floor shows featuring native dancers flourished.

By the mid 1960s, the walls of segregation had broken down and by the end of the 1960s, Paradise Island opened as a second New Providence destination as gambling was introduced with the mega hotel facility.

The tourism culture of The Bahamas began to change. Bahamians began to frequent tourists establishments and nightlife in the Over-The-Hill community began to dry up as the hotels began to spotlight local entertainment as well as foreign.

By the early to mid 1970s, the tourism culture had become integrated into the Bahamian lifestyle. Political conventions, weddings, balls, parties, religious services, conventions and business meetings, were all taking place on hotel properties. The only aspect of tourist life in which Bahamians were denied participation was in the casinos where it was illegal for Bahamians to engage in casino gambling.

Tourism had also been instrumental in causing a dietary shift in the way Bahamians eat. There are a large number of American fast food franchises. The foods which are imported are processed and are high in sugar and saturated fats.

Through satellite transmission and radio broadcasts and proximity to the Florida mainland, The Bahamas is inundated with US advertising. This has influenced a range of purchases including food. Possibly only Puerto Rico and the US Virgin Islands are more integrated into the US economy and influenced by its advertising.

• Enclave Tourism

Enclave tourism has become an aspect of the tourism experience in The Caribbean. There are essentially two kinds—the all inclusive property (Club Med, Sandals and Breezes), the gated communities, which generally are the habitats for the winter or part-time resident and time sharing/condominium complex. All of these have an exclusionary connotation.

In Jamaica, for example, many of the all inclusive properties on the north coast have developed as a response to the prevalence of crime in some localities. For Club Med, Sandals and Breezes the all inclusive is a product and experience in itself.

In most cases, the general idea, even on mega Caribbean properties like Atlantis in The Bahamas, is to retain as much of the spending on property. There are subtle designs, in some circumstances, to discourage excursions into the island community.

• "Two Worlds"

Governments have to be careful that "two worlds" are not created as a result of developments in the tourism sector and the type of product or experience being introduced by the developers.

When there are "two worlds," the social pressure from such a scenario could have a negative impact as the disparity in lifestyles become glaring. With slavery as a background, tourism can be a reminder of a bygone era where essentially black people are providing service to white people and property ownership is foreign.

• Tourism Infrastructure

An important element in the development of a tourism sector is infrastructure. Since 9/11, security features at airports and cruise ship terminals have brought a new dimension to travel. New airports in the Caribbean would have to be 9/11 compatible.

Airports, cruise ship terminals, good roads, reliable utilities like telecommunications, electricity and water will not do it all; productivity and competitiveness will be the determining factors. These two components hinge on the ability of Caribbean states to provide cutting-edge technology for its manpower development and the expansion of the industry.

The challenge facing Caribbean states is the ability to position the region through technological advance to project it as a world-class destination.

The World Bank reported that the Caribbean has to be more responsive to the changing global environment. The lack of timely responsiveness has been reflected in the market decline which Caribbean tourism has been experiencing since 1995. This decline in competitiveness stems from "high and rising wages, inadequate skill formation and technology absorption."

For Caribbean tourism to survive in this global setting, the manpower has to be more productive if the industry is to remain internationally competitive.

Conclusion

The people of the Caribbean have had the experience of slavery and colonialism and it is very important to factor their perception of tourism into the development equation. For tourism to totally grow and expand in the region, the peoples of the various states and dependencies must identify with the product which is being presented to the global market and must be a part of its ownership—Sandals and Breezes are prime examples of world-class properties being created by Caribbean nationals.

Caribbean tourism must reflect the ethos of Caribbean society. This diverse and unique society born out of exploration, extinction and exploitation has a distinctiveness of its own. It is this distinctiveness which should form the centerpiece of the Caribbean tourism product and marketed to the global community.

Intermezzo: *The Eneas Files, The Bahama Journal* Fashioning a US/CARICOM Doctrine

This past Tuesday, the Secretary of State of USA, Dr. Condoleezza Rice, arrived in The Bahamas to meet with the Foreign Ministers of CARICOM. This event occurs annually. Several years ago, General Colin Powell, former US Secretary of State, also met with CARICOM Foreign Ministers.

During the Clinton years, President Bill Clinton met with CARICOM Prime Ministers on a number of occasions; on one occasion, he went to Barbados to hold discussions.

The Caribbean falls within the US sphere of influence and is seen as the US third border. The number one trading partner for most CARICOM states is the US.

In the case of The Bahamas the figure is 90%. Conversely, the US is a big market for CARICOM products. Most CARICOM states with the exception of Guyana and Trinidad and Tobago look to the US for tourists. Tourism has also replaced agriculture as the leading economic sector in virtually every state.

The Secretary's agenda with CARICOM comprised trade and competitiveness as well as other issues like immigration, drug trafficking and money laundering.

Putting this visit by Dr. Rice in true perspective, she came to talk about the issues confronting CARICOM. The Bahamas as a CARICOM state was the host. Based on reliable sources, The Bahamas is seen as one of the safest places in the region, hence the site for the meeting. Yes, Dr. Rice paid a courtesy call on the Prime Minister and his Cabinet; that was a CARICOM event.

Bahamians have been ambivalent about deepening our involvement with CARICOM. Last year, there was a national furor on the notion of The Bahamas signing onto *The Treaty of Chaguaramas* and becoming a member of CSME. There was a resounding rejection to the idea of involvement in CSME.

However, Bahamians have not either appreciated or understood the fact that this is the era of the geopolitical blocs. CARICOM is one of the oldest in the world. Bahamians at some point in time will have to decide whether or not we are in or out of CARICOM. Their position of partial membership where we cherry pick our issues will not always be an option for us. CARICOM leaders tolerate this attitude by us but as living standards and income levels rise in the region this avenue may be closed.

Last week the Privy Council ruled that the mandatory death sentence in The Bahamas was unconstitutional. CARICOM, on the other hand, has established a CCJ as the final Court of Appeal; most countries have opted not to refer its cases to the Privy Council. As the UK deepens its attachment to EU, Privy Council will itself be modified. The only door open to The Bahamas will be the Caribbean Court of Appeal. Further, in certain quarters of the Bahamian legal fraternity, there was a reluctance to use the Caribbean Court. Now that there is this ruling from the Privy Council, those who are pro-capital punishment will look at the Caribbean Court slightly different.

One feature which CARICOM states have developed an outstanding reputation is the sophistication of its democracy. Among CARICOM states, Barbados and The Bahamas have two of the oldest parliamentary traditions in this hemisphere. Representative democracy has been practiced from 1729 in The Bahamas. The Bush Administration has been touting the principle of democracy in Latin America, the Middle East and elsewhere, so CARICOM is a model for democracy in action. This is one of the issues on the agenda of the Secretary of State. Dr. Rice has praised the record of CARICOM states in its adherence to democratic principles.

Since the Independence Era, there has been one attempted coup in CARICOM and that was in Trinidad during the 1970s. All in all, CARICOM states with the exception of Haiti and to a lesser extent, Suriname, the ballot has been the mechanism for changing governments and this distinguishes CARICOM from Latin American states.

CARICOM comprises about 20 million inhabitants. There are also thousands of CARICOM descendants residing in the US and many of these people helped over the years to build the US. Many American black leaders, some in the Civil Rights Movement, have Caribbean heritage.

CARICOM forms a strategic part of the US border and it is in the best interest of CARICOM and the US to maintain a healthy relationship. Hopefully, Dr. Rice will fashion a doctrine for CARICOM to reflect the realities, which face those states in this Globalization Era and one, which will enhance the sustained economic growth and development of the states in CARICOM. This is essential as there are peculiarities in the manner in which the states in CARICOM were developed as all came out of the legacy of slavery. Most are not multiracial sophisticated societies with much developmental potential; however, it is the US with power to help in creating the framework for CARICOM states to attain or excel to new heights.

Haiti's CARICOM Admission: Bad Decision or Not?

At the recent Heads of Government Summit in Port of Spain, Trinidad and Tobage, Haiti was admitted into CARICOM. Criticism of that decision is mounting in the region as many see the decision as being hasty.

Haiti, since its independence from France has been dealt a difficult financial hand. The Western or colonial power of Europe made Haiti pay a huge price to France. At the time Haiti was the jewel of the Caribbean and an important overseas territory of France. Haiti's wealth stemmed from the financial rewards which resulted from its sugar production.

Today, Haiti is the poorest country in the Western Hemisphere with a government which is not functioning, a high illiteracy rate and unemployment. The country has been occupied by the Americans and other UN peacekeepers from the region including The Bahamas. Yet, political, social and economic stability evades the Haitian Republic.

It is this background which has many Caribbean people upset. The rationale being that some CARICOM states have problems which are similar but not as deeply rooted as Haiti. Many states in CARICOM are not meeting their financial commitments to Caribbean institutions like UWI and the CARICOM Secretariat. In the financial predicament which Haiti finds itself, can it meet its financial obligations? Many are dubious that Haiti will not meet its commitments and will become a drain on the limited financial resources of CARICOM. The question is, can Haiti pay its way?

There are those who believe the CARICOM should have followed the model which EU has used for the acceptance of new members. EEC, the EU's predecessor, established standards for admission. Some of the standards were a specific per capita income, the level of literacy, functioning democratic institutions and an impartial system of jurisprudence. Once a country was able to attain those standards, then it was allowed membership.

From all indications, CARICOM did not take this route and because of this, many people in the region are extremely skeptical about the decision. With Haiti's admission CARICOM has had the two poorest countries in the hemisphere—Guyana and Haiti.

The state of affairs in Haiti concerns every country in the region. After the Dominican Republic, Haiti's island neighbour, it poses the greatest threat to the socio-economic stability of The Bahamas as many Haitians seem to hold the view that they have some right to asylum in The Bahamas and either flaunt or ignore the laws of this land.

Many Bahamians see much of the Over-The-Hill areas of New Providence being occupied by newly arrived Haitians or first generation Bahamian-born Haitians. Socially these communities have degenerated to the degree where rehabilitative programmes in housing, sanitary facilities, greater access to health care and training and institutions are badly needed to resurrect these communities into socially acceptable locales for human habitation.

CARICOM is moving towards a single market and economy. With so many countries at the bottom end of the economic ladder, this goal seems a long way off. Further, the concept of the free movement of people within the region under the present environment will never be accepted by Bahamians.

The integration equation for The Bahamas is now further compounded with Haiti as a member of CARICOM. The tempo of life in Haiti is out of synchronization not only with The Bahamas but the region in general. Therefore, it is a foolhardy decision to admit Haiti at this time. Such a decision should be made when Haiti has displayed its ability to better manage its political, social and economic affairs.

CARICOM & Cuba: A Caribbean Initiative

During the Cold War Era, Caribbean states allowed US foreign policy to determine the manner in which those states reacted and co-existed with other countries, particularly those in this hemisphere and region.

This policy stood out in the way in which countries of this region dealt with Cuba;

The Bahamas was no exception.

After the overthrow of the Baptista Regime, Fidel Castor took control of Cuba and introduced Marxist Socialism. This was a political affront to the US as it defied the Monroe Doctrine which was the cornerstone of US foreign policy in this hemisphere.

Jamaica during the Norman Manley Administration conducted an open door policy to Cuba and began manpower and cultural exchange, as well as established trade relations. As a result of Jamaica's overtures to Cuba, US foreign aid was substantially reduced by the Regan Administration.

When Maurice Bishop's New Jewel Movement took over the government of Grenada from Eric Gary, Grenada established foreign relations with Cuba and this eventually led to the invasion of Grenada by the Americans.

It was also during this period when the Flamingo incident created tense relationship between The Bahamas and Cuba in the latter 1970s. Three Defense Force crewmen on the Flamingo were killed as a result of a Cuban attack. Cuba made reparations to the families of the slain crewmen and the government of The Bahamas.

Shortly after the Flamingo incident, FAO held a hemispheric meeting in Havana.

The Bahamas was represented by the then Minister of Agriculture and Fisheries, Hon. George A. Smith, the Permanent Secretary, Mr. Idris Reid and myself the Director of Agriculture.

At the time, the Ambassador for Grenada invited us to his home for dinner. During the course of the dinner, the Ambassador was able to explain the assistance which Cuba was giving to Grenada as it was just emerging from colonial status. The Cuban assistance was genuine as no strings were attached to the aid; it was an illuminating exchange for us from The Bahamas.

At the official reception for the delegates to the FAO Conference, President Castro requested a private meeting with Mr. Smith. It was during this meeting that Senor Castro expressed his regret for the Flamingo incident and indicated the desire of his government to deepen relations between Cuba and The Bahamas.

In meetings with Cuban officials, reference was made to former association between Cuba and The Bahamas, specifically to the free movement of people particularly from Inagua and Ragged Island and even parts of Andros.

There was a time in Bahamian commerce when Bahamians sought employment in

Cuba as workers in the sugar cane industry. As a boy, I can remember the Ragged Island vessels arriving at the Market Range with an assortment of Cuban products—rum, sugar, guava, cheese to name a few.

During the 1970s and 1980s, Dr. John McCartney and Lionel Carey along with others commenced frequent visits to Cuba to study Marxist Socialism. Their actions were viewed in officials circles as bordering on seditious and was frowned upon. Cuba was seen as a threat to export revolution.

This was the scenario under which the states of this region had to function. The environment has now changed.

This past week, CARICOM and Cuban officials met in Kingston, Jamaica to discuss Cuban's admission as a CARICOM member. It should be borne in mind that this is taking place even though the US embargo on Cuba is still in effect. CARICOM states are no longer prepared to have their relationship with neighbouring states dictated to by the US. This is a substantial departure from a bygone era.

Last year, CARICOM admitted Haiti to its ranks and gradually the old taboos are dying as the states of the region move closer together economically, socially and politically.

CARICOM is in the process of developing a single market and economy. With initiatives being taken on regional economic integration, the market of the Caribbean will expand substantially almost by 20 million people with Cuba's admission. Already Haiti and the Dominican Republic have opened new markets for CARICOM products and vice versa.

In view of the developments in the region, it is high time for The Bahamas to increase its profile with Cuba. It is one of our closest neighbours and through CARICOM that relationship will deepen. The geopolitical climate in the Caribbean region will offer a host of new challenges during our new century.

Christie's CARICOM Initiation

Two months after taking office, Prime Minister Christie will be attending the 23rd Meeting of the Conference of CARICOM Heads of Government in Georgetown, Guyana. The conference will take place on 2nd–3rd July.

For the past ten years, the former Prime Minister, Hon. Hubert A. Ingraham, was a force in CARICOM. He initiated several actions and held his own with the likes of Owen Arthur, Prime Minister of Barbados, P. J. Patterson of Jamaica and Basdeo Panday of Trinidad and Tobago, the heavyweights of CARICOM. In this regard, much will be expected of Mr. Christie to continue the leadership thrust which was started by the late Sir Lynden O. Pindling during his tenure as Prime Minister and carried on by Mr. Ingraham.

This will also be Mr. Christie's first encounter in international relations as Prime Minister. It is timely that this initial encounter is on the regional stage and at a level where he is among peers who are facing globalization and trade liberalization issues like The Bahamas.

In the context of The Bahamas, one will expect the Minister of Foreign Affairs and the Public Service, Hon. Fred Mitchell, to demonstrate a different slant in presenting a new Bahamian perspective in its relationship with CARICOM. During the previous administration, Mr. Ingraham's views seemed to dominate The Bahamas' position. With the then Minister of Foreign Affairs, Mrs. Janet Bostwick, there was more accommodation of Mr. Ingraham's perception of the Caribbean. There is every indication that Mr. Mitchell will play a strong hand in crafting a new policy position of The Bahamas with CARICOM, i.e. CSME.

The CARICOM Heads of Conference has adopted a new dimension to its agenda. There will be a civil society dialogue with the heads under the theme "Forward Together."

The CARICOM Secretariat has been urging member states to conduct national dialogues on the question of civil society. At the Forward Together Conference, member states will report to the Heads of Government the views of the citizenry on various themes relating to civil society.

Antigua and Barbuda as well as St. Lucia will be reporting on CSME. Obviously the citizens of those two states regard this a matter of major concern. To us in The Bahamas, this is a matter of low priority, as The Bahamas has no intention of joining the Single Market and Economy in the near future.

On the other hand, Haiti's theme is "The Role of Civil Society." In a country facing political turmoil and economic instability plus having a long tradition of military dictatorial rule comprehending the role of civil society is perhaps a central issue in that state's move to greater democratization of that society.

Most of the member states (two-thirds to be exact) have already indicated their themes. Based on recent CARICOM reports, The Bahamas has not submitted its theme even though the Ministry of Foreign Affairs held a meeting this past week with representatives of Bahamian Civil Society. From all indications, the feedback coming out of the meeting was that the members did not have adequate time to prepare for the meeting and the purpose lacked clarity.

At this conference, CARICOM will be celebrating its 30th Anniversary as a community. CARICOM is one of the oldest regional political organizations in the world. It has done a tremendous job in bringing the region together. It is difficult to imagine the region without CARICOM, that is the degree of impact it has had on the region. In recent years, a rival entity has come into being, the Association of Caribbean States, which is wider in membership scope as it includes all of the states which share a shoreline with Caribbean sea and includes the Central American States.

The substantive agenda items Mr. Christie and his delegation will have to face include the Single Market and Economy, Security and Crime and Haiti. There are the domestic or regional matters. For The Bahamas, the latter two are of fundamental importance, to our society. It will be interesting to see the manner in which these issues are addressed by our delegation before the region, particularly since Haiti is now a member of CARICOM.

On the international side of the agenda, CARICOM is grappling with the Free Trade issue, particularly the upcoming FTAA, which is supposed to be operational by the year 2005. This is sort of double jeopardy for The Bahamas that, unlike other member states, is not a member of WTO, therefore has to come to grips with both of these organizations. The FTAA is a major concern to CARICOM because it has the potential to wreak severe socio-economic damage to Caribbean agriculture, textiles and manufacturing industries thereby causing immense social dislocation and economic disruption.

The region has come to expect The Bahamas to play an expanding role in regional affairs. One would hope that Mr. Mitchell would find the mechanism to intertwine issues facing the various sectors in the Bahamian economy into the foreign policy thrust with CARICOM as well as find the way to project Bahamian professionals into leadership positions in CARICOM.

Caribbean integration is still an unresolved issue with Bahamians and should be given priority status in our foreign policy.

Tourism and the WTO: Are We Ready?

Tourism will not escape the rules of WTO. Whether we want it or not, tourism will have to face trade liberalization like every sector in our economy. The sooner we realize this and come to grips as best we can with the implications of WTO involvement, the better.

Tourism is the world's biggest industry. In terms of total global impact, it is worth $3.5 trillion of the GDP. This represents 11% of global GDP, 200 million jobs and 8% of total worldwide employment. Employment projections show where global tourism has the capacity to create 5.5 million new jobs annually until 2010.

Tourism is not only important to The Bahamas and the Caribbean, but also important to the world. However, the big players who dominate the industry are the tour operators, the hotel chains, the airlines and now the operators of computer reservation or global distribution systems in the developed countries. None of these are controlled by the Third World.

In the face of global advance, the world's tourism industry has grown at double the price of GDP for the past 30 years—with the share accounted for by developing countries rising to around one-third of the total.

Global tourism is dominated by the destinations of Europe, the US, Canada, China as the only Asian country and Mexico as the only Latin American country.

France attracts over 70 million tourists each year in comparison to the US' 50 million. Despite the 20 million plus differential, the US earns $70 billion annually to France's $30 billion.

When the figure of the top ten are compared to those figures generated by Bahamian tourism, The Bahamas is a small player on the world scene, and the Caribbean region when compared to other regions like Europe, Asia and Latin America is a big player.

Over the past 50 years, tourism has transformed The Bahamas from a fishing village to a thriving small archipelagic state. The journey to where The Bahamas is today was not easy. It took 20 years for The Bahamas to reach the first million visitors. The second million was achieved in 13 years and the third million only four years. Arriving at the fourth million has been illusive as we have been hovering at the 3.6 million level during the decade of the 1990s.

Visitor expenditure in The Bahamas reached the billion dollar level in the 1980s. Over the next 15 years, the highest total achievement has been $1.4 billion in 1998.

Looking at the arrival and expenditure figures, Bahamian tourism has every appearance of plateauing. The industry needs a new thrust—impetus.

Earlier this year, The Bahamas opted to seek observer status rather than outright full membership at the WTO. There are also many to believe that the WTO is only concerned at trade. Service is an important area hence the importance of tourism which is a service industry.

The Bahamas has displayed the syndrome of being left behind in many matters on the international stage. We all know what happened with the financial services vis-à-vis the actions of the Organization for Economic Cooperation and Development (OECD). Those engaged in international trade, are cognizant of the games the big players can play. Many of those countries in the top ten are members of the OECD. Already the OECD will attempt to put some parameters on investment in tourism and this will surely hurt developing countries like The Bahamas that depend on foreign investment to expand and improve the tourism plant. Restrictive business practices will be the watchwords.

The future scenario can be viewed through the bilateral arrangement between the US and China.

"For hotels and restaurants, equity limitations on commercial presence will be eliminated by the end of 2003. In the case of travel agency and tour operator services, foreign majority ownership will be permitted after January 1st 2003 and wholly-owned foreign subsidiaries after the end of 2005."

There are serious consequences for us if this evolves into a standard arrangement and the only differential is which year these aspects kick in depending on the terms a country like The Bahamas, negotiates its entry into full membership. The Bahamian people is owed an explanation.

CARICOM Tourism Today

In the 1960s while a student at UWI St. Augustine campus, Trinidad, most of the economies of the Caribbean states earned their foreign exchange mostly by exporting agricultural products. Sugar was the main stay of these former British colonies.

35 years later most of these economies have been virtually transformed. Like The Bahamas, the main earner of foreign exchange is now tourism. This fact came home to me this week, particularly after all of the fanfare surrounding the CARICOM Heads of Government Conference here.

It seems as if most of these CARICOM states have mimicked the Bahamian development model and not only jumped on the tourism train, but also have seen the merits of a financial service sector.

Back in the 1960s, the communication between The Bahamas and the southern Caribbean was very poor. Getting to Port of Spain, Trinidad from Nassau took almost 24 hours. In those days, British West Indian Airways, Ltd was the only carrier and it stopped to almost every island—Puerto Rico, Jamaica, Antigua, St. Lucia, Barbados and on to Trinidad. It seemed as if it took forever to arrive.

Telecommunications between the islands was poor. When my grandmother died, it took my mother and uncle almost two weeks to get in touch with me. My dormitory, Milner Hall, did not even have a telephone. Mrs. Innis, the lady who operated the dining hall, permitted me to use her office telephone to receive the call.

News by radio and television was out of the question. In order for me to listen to baseball, football and basketball games, I had to tune in to the US Armed Forces radio network.

The mail took forever; anywhere from two to four weeks to get a letter. My mother would send me issues of *The Tribune* and *Guardian* and it would seem as if The Bahamas was on another continent rather than in the same geographical region. Distance during those years impacted one differently—one felt far away. Today, the Internet enables one to correspond with colleagues and friends daily.

In today's Caribbean, tourism has made the difference. The life and times have been drastically altered, as everything has changed. One can get to any Caribbean island within hours. That 24-hour trip to Port of Spain, Trinidad is now three and a half hour plane ride from Miami to Piarco Airport, Trinidad; it's non-stop.

Satellite transmission has made it possible for one to watch the same television programmes down there that we watch up here.

Federal Express and DHL could bring mail and package delivery with 24 to 36 hours even to Guyana and Suriname.

The catalyst for most of these changes has stemmed from the need to be competitive in this highly lucrative tourism market which has made the Caribbean one of the hottest destinations on the globe.

During the Clinton years, Americans had a lot of disposable income which was spent on travel. It was chic to visit exotic tropical hideaways. Tourism developers took advantage of this and billions of dollars were spent on developing plush, elegant locales.

The concept of tourism was relative new to the southern Caribbean three or four decades ago. When I attempted to describe Bahamian tourism to my fellow classmates at UWI, they turned up their noses and said that Bahamians were waiting on the tables of rich Americans and Europeans. How demeaning!

The Bahamas recognized that tourism was more complex than that and by recognizing the complexity of the business, we were able to convert it from a seasonal economic activity to a thriving year-round business. Most of the Caribbean have not been able to duplicate the mechanics of this conversion. Herein lies the reason why Bahamian tourism professionals are in demand and are offered the top positions in the major Caribbean destinations. Jamaica hired Basil Smith, Jim Hepple is gone, Cliff Hamilton has headed Trinidad and Tobago tourism for years, Sandy Sands was in Guyana, and the list goes on.

Last week a friend of mine was in Martinique. The tourism industry there depended on one Air France flight per day from Paris. Antigua's industry is in trouble because of the reduced air arrivals mainly from Europe. St. Lucia is reverting to a winter season type industry because of adverse market and economic conditions; and Jamaica's industry is in big trouble as a result of the destabilizing effect of the West Kingston riots.

The newspaper headlines across the Caribbean do not indicate a region of tranquility and destinations where visitors can feel safe and secure.

Tuesday's headlines read: "Nine killed in Jamaica Violence" "Gunmen Kill Nurse in Bahamas Hospital" "Tourism Police Unit Coming to St. Vincent" "Antigua Hotels Closing Temporarily" "St. Lucia Economy Forcing Hotels to Close" "FAA Downgrade for Trinidad and Tobago" and "AIDS Emergency in the Caribbean."

It is no wonder that during the CARICOM Conference Mr. Ingraham called for a Tourism Summit next October. From every indication the Caribbean tourism product may be in serious problems. The Prime Minister is right; it requires regional attention because too much of today's Caribbean depends on it.

Bahamians and the Tourism Economy

Tourism in Third World countries differentiates itself from tourism in developed countries. The main aspect of the differentiation is that the indigenous people in Third World usually do not patronize the tourism economy of their countries. The local people who do are generally the elite of these societies or those with disposable incomes; the other portion of the populace is employees in some sphere of the tourism industry.

Several years ago, my family and I visited Kenya on a safari, which is really ecotourism in its purest states. An important feature of a safari is that you move from game reserve to game reserve and stay in a variety of accommodations. Throughout this trip, the Kenyans with whom we came into contact were workers—maids, waiters, guides or objects of curiosity.

In many parts of the Caribbean, specifically Jamaica and Cuba, separate enclaves have been built, almost isolated from the rest of society, for tourists. Both of these countries have highlighted the separation between locals and foreigners.

In Cuba, Varadero and Cayo CoCo are off-limits to Cubans. The only Cubans one sees at these destinations are the ones who work there. The Cuban government does not encourage fraternization by the Cubans with the visitors. Participation is confined to employment.

At a recent tourism conference in Jamaica, the Minister of Tourism of that country announced that his government intended to utilize soldiers at resorts in order to reduce crime against tourists and to halt the harassment of tourists by locals.

This surprising move was not initiated by the government but was requested by the Jamaica Hotel and Tourist Association. This deployment of troops has been viewed as a giant step against crime in the tourist resorts of Jamaica. Others see it as another indictment to separate the tourism economy from the bulk of the local people.

When one analyses the scenarios in Kenya, Cuba and Jamaica and compares them to The Bahamas, one can ascertain that the Bahamian scenario is completely different and dissimilar to the norm as it relates to other Third World countries.

In The Bahamas, Bahamians are in integral components of the tourism economy.

Bahamians not only work in the industry, but patronize it and do so heavily.

All of the local hotels have programmes dealing with on-island marketing and sales. Many of them look to the indigenous market to generate sufficient sales, particularly during slow periods, to improve their bottom lines.

Many of tourism statistics have failed to reflect the contribution of Bahamians to tourism earnings relative to the overall earnings of tourism in the national economy.

If you want proof, ask yourself these questions: Where are most wedding receptions held in New Providence? Who are the main patrons at Seagrapes for Sunday brunch? Where are the big social and charitable gala events held? What about political conventions?

In the tourism ancillary businesses, Bahamians charter the Yellow Birds for socializing and during the summer take their families to Blue Lagoon Island on holidays for picnics. Every element in the tourism industry benefits from Bahamian patronization.

Tourism in The Bahamas has been shaped to where it has features which are attractive to both the visitor and the resident. Both have been able to coexist and enjoy a product which has galvanized the economy of The Bahamas and catapulted The Bahamas to a level where the local inhabitants have interwoven their life into the fabric of the tourism economy.

Tourism is the golden egg, and the goose can be damaged to the point where its viability is seriously constrained. It is important to maintain the harmony which has evolved over the years. The secret to this harmony is to maintain an atmosphere which enables every Bahamian to enjoy the benefits of the tourism economy. The people's rights should not be trampled or disregarded. This intermingling has produced a unique product. It should be continually enhanced and not retarded by short-sighted policies and programmes.

Chapter 7

Haitians: A Resilient People

"It is in the method, not in the principle; that Toussaint failed."
—C. L. R. James, Trinidadian historian, journalist and
socialist, *The Black Jacobins*

Haiti's fragility is centered around the feature of widespread poverty and social inequality, economic decline, high unemployment, poor governance and violence. Haiti has been described as a fragile state. In its failure to maintain a stable social, economic and political country, Haiti has become the poorest state among the 34 states in this hemisphere. In the region it has been independent longer than any other island state and is the first independent black republic (1804).

With a population of 8.3 million people, a life expectancy of 52 years and a per capita income of $361, Haiti has remained mired in poverty.

Haiti's nearest neighbours (The Bahamas and the Dominican Republic) are battling with the influx of its nationals as illegal immigrants. This has resulted from a demographic situation where the population growth rate is 2.2% a year. With an existing population of 8.3 million, Haiti will become a country of more than 12 million people over the next quarter of a century. In 2003, 40% of Haitians lived in Port Au Prince, as the country increasingly became an urban society (Urban Centers: Gonaives, Port Au Prince, Cap Haitian) with a huge urban population approaching 4 million people. This situation prevails even though Haiti has the highest incidence of HIV/AIDS in the hemisphere and some 38,000 people die each year from the disease.

For the Haitian, migration is the mechanism to address the lack of opportunities and a source of income as "30% of all households and 44% of metropolitan households receive remittances from the Haiti diaspora." These remittances translate between $800 and 900 million annually and account for about 30% of household income. Haiti is second only to Barbados as the most densely populated country in the Americas.

Employment is primarily in the informal economy and the agricultural sector which is comprised of small subsistence farmers who represent 50% of the labour force.

There is a serious infrastructural problem. Half of the population in urban areas has no access to potable water, about a third of the population have inadequate sanitation, only 10% can obtain electricity and only 20% of the roads are useable.

The economy of Haiti, to put it mildly has been problematic. During the four decades (1960 to 2000), three of these decades have recorded negative growth. In those years (the decades of the 1970s and the second half of the 1990s) growth did take place. However, there was no sustainability and growth ceased.

One would have thought that the cessation of growth was rooted in political instability. This was not the case. The World Bank points out that,

> "The government increasingly intervened by employing fiscal and trade policies that were restrictive of the private sector and biased against exports, created monopolistic public enterprises and spent public funds without increasing the country's productive or absorptive capacity."

In essence, bad governmental policies were responsible for the retardation of economic growth.

Haitian Resilience

Haiti's arrival as an independent nation was like a breached birth. It was an occurrence which threatened the disruption of an important commercial commodity—sugar. It was an event which the colonial powers did not want to reoccur in the other colonial possessions in the Caribbean.

For the British, Haiti's independence in 1804 was three years before the abolition of the slave trade and the trafficking of humans from the West African principally and three decades before emancipation.

For this act of national defiance, the colonial powers penalized Haiti, making Haiti's arrival as independence a difficult process as it was achieved on the battlefield against Napoleon's Army.

(1) Governance in Haiti

When Haiti became an independent state in 1804, the European powers not only delayed international recognition of Haiti as a sovereign state and refused to trade by initiating an economic embargo similar to US embargo against Cuba, but also instituted an international diplomatic boycott. There would be no ambassadorial accreditation to Haiti. To make Haiti pay, the French government brought international pressure on this new republic and was able to have levied on Haiti an indemnity against the losses the French suffered.

There were years of political turmoil and social fending between the Mulatto elite and the newly freed African slaves. Africans in Haiti had a form of liberation; however for three decades after the Haitian Independence, slavery was the norm in the region.

Haiti for almost a century was experiencing political and economic instability and this led to the US occupancy of the country from 1915 to 1934. This period brought some stability; however on the departure of the US, the country fell into political chaos.

In 1957, Francois "Papa Doc" Duvalier, a country doctor, became President of Haiti. He would be succeeded by his, Jean-Claude "Baby Doc" Duvalier. The Duvalier Regime would rule Haiti for almost three decades (1957–1986).

The Duvalier Regime would be identified as the most repressive regime in Haitian history. After the overthrow of the Duvalier, Haiti would become engaged in political transformation into a democratic state. From 1905 to 1987, Haiti would have had 21 constitutions.

During the democratization phase, Haiti had fifteen different administrations from 1986 to 2005. (See Table 7.1) There were a number of presidents who served as president on several occasions (Namphy (2), Aristide (3) and Préval (2)).

Table 7.1   Haiti's Governments, 1986–2005

Adm.	Name and Position	Periods Served	Time Served
1	President Henri Namphy [military gov.]	2/1986 to 2/1988	2 years
2	President Leslie F. Manigat	2/1988 to 6/1988	4 months
3	President Henri Namphy [military gov.]	6/1988 to 9/1988	3 months
4	President Prosper Avril [military gov.]	9/1988 to 4/1990	20 months
5	President Hérard Abraham [military gov.]	4/1990	3 days

(to be continued)

Adm.	Name and Position	Periods Served	Time Served
6	President Ertha Pascal-Trouillo	4/1990 to 2/1991	10 months
7	President Jean-Bertrand Aristide	2/1991 to 9/1991	7 months
8	President Joseph C. Nérette	10/1991 to 5/1992	7 months
9	No de-facto president		
10	President Emile Jonassaint	6/1994 to 9/1994	3 months
11	President Jean-Bertrand Aristide	10/1994 to 2/1996	16 months
12	President René Préval	2/1996 to 2/2001	5 years
13	President Jean-Bertrand Aristide	2/2001 to 2/2004	3 years
14	President Boniface Alexandre	2/2004 to 5/2006	2 years
15	President René Préval	5/2006 to date	

Source: Based on World Bank (1998) and media

While the Caribbean in 1960s was emerging as a major tourism destination, Haiti's political repression under "Papa Doc" Duvalier had adversely affected its economic growth and development. From 1960 to 2000, Haiti's GDP per capita was negative. Only the decade of 1971–1980 was there positive growth. (See Table 7.2)

Table 7.2 Average Annual Real Growth Rates of GDP per Capita, 1961–2000 (in Percent)

	1961–1900	1961–1970	1971–1980	1981–1990	1991–2000
Haiti	−1.0	−1.4	2.6	−2.3	−2.3
LAC	1.7	2.6	3.1	−0.8	1.7
Sub-Saharan Africa	0.2	1.9	0.8	−1.3	−0.4
World	2.5	3.2	2.5	2.3	2.0

Source: World Bank

Agriculture continues to be an important sector in Haiti's economy. The leading sector is services. Tourism has been marginalized by political instability and turmoil.

(2) Haitian Coping Mechanism

Haitians have devised various mechanisms to cope with political instability and economic decline which have become the twin frustrations to building a quality lifestyle and a sustainable economy in Haiti. These twin frustrations have plagued Haiti immediately after gaining its independence from France.

Haiti's breached birth as a nation was met with an economic embargo and diplomatic isolation. Over the years, the Haitian people have acquired the skills to survive in this type of national atmosphere.

• Haitian Migration

World Bank estimates state that there are 75,000 Haitians in The Bahamas, 0.5 million in the Dominican Republic and some 2 million in the US and Canada. These overseas Haitians, through remittance now approaching 1 billion US dollars and representing 25% of the Haitian GDP, have been part of the coping mechanism for Haitians after World War II.

Haitians began in 1950 to leave Haiti in droves. This grouping represented technicians, skilled craftsmen and business people. Most of these people left for political reasons. By the 1960s it escalated during the Duvalier years and by the 1980s it began to include unskilled and peasant Haitians.

Migration became a refuge for the millions who resided outside of Haiti and a social safety net for those inside Haiti as the remittances from those outside were used to purchase basic necessities like food, education, healthcare and housing. (See Table 7.3 and Table 7.4)

Table 7.3   How Do Remittance Recipients Use the Money

Use of Remittances	%
Food	81
Education	74
Clothes	64
Savings	34
Healthcare	28
Housing	27
Business	14
Other	11
Repayment of debts	9
Payment of debts	7

Source: World Bank

Table 7.4   Amount of Remittances Received

Range	%
100 dollars or less	41
Between 101 and 300 dollars	42
Between 301 and 500 dollars	9
More than 500 dollars	8
NS/NR	1
Total	100.0

Source: World Bank

• Informal (Sector) Economy

Haiti attracted foreign direct investment to its manufacturing industry and services (tourism); however poor fiscal policies had adversely affected manufacturing and political turmoil made Haiti an unattractive tourism destination. This scenario resulted in the government being the primary employer. The private sector is relatively small as opportunities for private sector growth and development were stymied by the political climate in the country.

This environment has established in Haiti a huge informal sector employing, according to the World Bank, figures some 1 million self-employed people practicing "penny capitalism."

These "penny capitalists" engage in a wide variety of activities in micro enterprises (repair shops in rural areas, street side vendors of everyday items and of casual labourers in construction and farming in the rural areas).

• Cultural Life

Haiti has a vibrant cultural life which is reflected in its art and music. Though a poor country, there is a strong national will resulting from its entrance on the global scene as the first black republic. This fact has been a source of pride, particularly to those in the Haitian diaspora.

Investing in Children

The Episcopalians as the Domestic and Foreign Missionary Society have taken on the responsibility via the Parish of St. Dunstan's in Carmel Valley, California to develop the children of Hinche, Haiti by building and supporting Christian school, St. Andre's. (See Figure 7.1)

The environment in Hinche is as follows:

"The people of Hinche have not had municipal electric power since May (the photos were taken in September '06). The city is dark at night. Road conditions have deteriorated to the point that fuel tankers cannot travel to supply fuel to the municipal power system generators or to local retail stations. The trucks either breakdown from pounding on the poor roads, or get stuck in the mud. People then steal the fuel from the trucks.

The municipal water supply in Hinche has failed and the people must bathe and wash their clothes in the muddy, filthy water. The river is where they obtain drinking water."

St. Andre School is an oasis as it serves as a school and house of worship. It generates 24-hour supply of electricity, seven days per week to operate school, church and the equipment.

There are now 750 students. During the day there are more than 600 children from three years through 12th grade start arriving at 6:30 a.m. for classes which begin at 7:00 a.m. and also Saturday classes. A daily hot meal is provided to each student as well as the abandoned widows of the community while school is in session.

St. Dunstan's started this project when it was a lean-to structure with a concrete floor and a roof; it accommodated 33 students in 1993.

Figure 7.1   Children at Episcopal Funded School in Hinche, Haiti

Getting to America

For Haitians to get to America, they must pass through The Bahamas. The means of transportation are rickety crafts, often unfit for long sea voyages; yet the Haitian, in his desperation for a better life, takes the chance.

Thousands of Haitians take the sea route through The Bahamas and either use The Bahamas as a transfer point where he or she may stay temporarily or as a permanent abode. Whatever the eventual decision, he or she becomes an illegal immigrant.

The Bahamas is facing a huge illegal immigrant problem as a result of the large numbers of Haitians. The situation has had deep socio-economic implications. There is the language divide and illiteracy (47% of Haitians are illiterate). The affordability of housing for an illegal immigrant is a major concern causing thousands to seek alternative housing which is often at the shantytown level. Haitians have forced a serious strain on the Bahamian healthcare infrastructure as well as compromised the public education system as there are hundreds of Haitian children who are unable to speak English in addition to competing with Bahamians for spaces in certain school districts.

This has resulted in thousands of children being born to Haitians parents who entered the country illegally. These children know The Bahamas as their home; however obtaining Bahamian citizenship has become a bureaucratic nightmare.

This overall scenario has evolved into an emotional issue with The Bahamas. For many, the Haitian is seen as a threat to the ethnic composition of The Bahamas. To others, the Haitian is viewed as a source of labour both skilled and unskilled.

The big question facing The Bahamas and the illegal immigrant is the ability of the Haitian to be assimilated into a society which is rooted in Christianity, democratic institutions, jurisprudence based on British Common Law and a society which is sophisticated and cosmopolitan with a service-based economy anchored by tourism and financial services.

The Haitian issue is one of the constraints to The Bahamas' participation in CSME as Haiti is now a member of CARICOM. The CSME has a plank for the free movement of people.

Figure 7.2   Haitian Sloop With Illegal Immigrants Being Towed by Royal Bahamas Defense Force Vessel

Intermezzo: *The Eneas Files, The Bahama Journal*   Haiti and the 1790s

(Editor's Note: As Haiti celebrates 200 years as the first black independent state in the Americas, Godfrey Eneas introduces a different perspective on the Haitian Revolution and Haiti's march to independence.)

The decade of the 1790s centered around the activities on St. Domingue, which comprised the western third of Hispaniola. Hispaniola was significant. After Columbus landed on San Salvador in 1492, he sailed southeast for the larger island, to be named in honor of Spain, Spanish Island or Hispaniola.

St. Domingue's importance stemmed from two basic facts—firstly, it supplied two-thirds of the overseas trade of France, and secondly it was the largest individual market for the European slave trade. African slaves had become the basis for shaping the economic development much of the New World which included the US, Brazil and the other states in Central and South America, and, of course, the Caribbean. Activities in 1790s St. Domingue were pivotal to future political, social and economic events in the whole Caribbean region.

Caribbean islands from the mid 17th century began to establish themselves as wealth-generating colonies as the European nations saw the Caribbean as a locale for a New World based sugar industry.

The sugar industry became a remarkable source of wealth and material well-being for the Europeans, as it gave them the opportunity to gain much wealth. This bred European entrepreneurs in shipping, trading, merchandising, financing and substantial spin-off economic opportunities for the domestic economies of Spain, Portugal, The Netherlands, England and, of course, France.

The Caribbean became a focal point for European economic exploitation. Cuba and the Dominican Republic were Spanish colonies; the British had Jamaica, Barbados, Trinidad, much of the Leeward and Windward Islands; the Dutch controlled Curacao, St. Maarten and the French possessions were Martinique, Guadeloupe, St. Lucia and St. Domingue.

St. Domingue soon dominated French Caribbean interests. By the mid 18th century, St. Domingue's sugar industry, with coffee at the higher altitudes, posed a serous threat to Jamaica's claim to be the pre-eminent slave colony in the region. This was the economic framework in which St. Domingue entered the decade of the 1790s. It would become one of the essential factors in creating the state of Haiti—the land called Ayiti or "mountainous" island.

St. Domingue or Santo Domingo had another important element—black slaves from Africa. The slave population had reached an explosive level from 1763 to 1789 as the slave population had climbed from 206,000 to 465,429. There had never been such a large movement of Africans in so short a period into the American colonies, particularly those colonies in the Caribbean.

There was also a third dimension. In 1789, the French Revolution's ideas of liberty, equality and fraternity were instrumental in igniting the slave uprising in Santo Domingo.

The ethnic scenario in Santo Domingo was composed of a mixture of a huge African slave force, almost a half million, a colored or mulatto middle class, a French white Plutocracy and a colonial government administration in the hands of French officials. Political turmoil in France as a result of the French Revolution would lead to political turmoil in Santo Domingo. Squabbles ensued with colored and mulattoes against whites, middle class against upper middle class, French with colonials. As all of this was taking place, the African slaves seized the movement and revolted.

The rightness of the cause was fundamental in the debate of the day—racial equality and slave emancipation gave impetus to the movement. With the military brilliance of Toussaint L'Ouverture and his army of slaves, they not only defeated Napoleon's army, but also the Spanish and the British.

It was in Gonaives on January 1st 1804 that General Jean-Jacques Dessalines, L'Ouverture's successor, declared Haitian Independence. Today, a monument to the victorious general dominates the square where President Jean-Bertrand Aristide is due to preside over the official ceremony commemorating 200 years of Haitian Independence.

Haiti's declaration of independence was a telling moment, as it became the first black republic outside of Africa and the second post-colonial society in the modern era (after the USA). It demonstrated that ex-slaves organized into an army along with their guerillas or maroon squads under military leadership had the capacity to defeat the best European armies (French, British or Spanish).

The Haitian Revolution threatened the economic scene and the racial fundamental which dominated the Caribbean at the turn of the 19th century. The European masters had been defeated by their African slaves and this brought slave owners everywhere to realize and fear the implications of the events in Haiti, not only in other Caribbean islands, but also on plantations throughout the Americas, including the US.

The new leadership of the Haitian Republic established a constitution which embodied that any black man, woman or child who reached Haiti from any place in the New World would be granted citizenship in this new republic.

After 13 years of revolutionary activity, Haiti's Independence was officially realized on 1st January, 1804. However, with their freedom also came world isolation. It would take another 21 years (1825) before France recognized Haiti's Independence. After agreeing to pay France 90 million gold francs, Haiti's sovereignty was finally accepted. It would take another 37 years after the French recognition until the UN recognized Haiti as a sovereign republic in 1862. Haiti's status as a nation was grudgingly received by the European powers.

The Haitian Armada

The word Armada almost always conjures recollections of the famous Spanish fleet, which unsuccessfully attempted to invade England in 1588. The creation of the fleet stemmed from the fact that there were bad relations between Spain and England because of Spain's claim to the great wealth which had and was being exploited in the New World—the Americas were discovered as a result of Spanish financing for Christopher Columbus' voyage.

Spain decided to flex its military muscles and create the mightiest military force to attack England. This mighty fleet was dubbed the Spanish Armada.

Recent intelligence information from the US Coast Guard Service has indicated that south of The Bahamas on the western portion of the island of Hispaniola, another Armada is being assembled. At a recent count, some 600 sloops are built with others under construction for the mass transportation of humans from Haiti to the US through The Bahamas.

The creation of this Armada stems from a recent policy statement from President-elect Bill Clinton that Haitian nationals seeking asylum will not be denied entry into the US. The Armada is being readied to coincide with the Clinton Administration taking office on the 20th January, 1993.

The fallout from the implications of this policy on The Bahamas will be dramatic, far-reaching and will have significant effects on the socio-economic fabric of Bahamian life.

The Clinton Policy is directly opposite to the Bush Policy which intercepted Haitian sloops on the high seas and either forwarded them back to Haiti or deposited the Haitian refugees at Guantanamo Bay, Cuba for questioning and processing.

The Bush Administration was soundly criticized for this policy and claims were made that the policy was racist because the Haitians were black. On the other hand, the critics say, America was welcoming the Cubans by the thousands supposedly because they were mostly white and Cuban-Americans have a strong lobby in the US.

The Haitians claim that they are seeking a new home because of political oppression by the military junta. Bush Administration Policy was based on the position that the Haitians were leaving Haiti for economic reasons hence the policy of interdiction on the high seas.

Haiti has been a country where military rule has been the order of the day so this type of environment is not new. In conjunction with military oppression, economic conditions during the Duvalier Era were similarly bad and people were fleeing in large numbers. Owing to the hemispheric boycott, economic conditions are severe and extremely difficult presently.

By the time Mr. Clinton is sworn in as President of USA, there could possibly be a couple thousand Haitian sloops constructed and ready for the marine trek from its shores through The Bahamas to Florida, USA.

In the past these Haitian sloops have been known to accommodate numbers varying between 200 and 300 people. The first sailing of this Haitian Armada would bring a wave of 200 to 300,000 people. With January and February being the coldest months of the year and the seas are likely to be cold, choppy and rough, hundreds of these ships could run into serious difficulties in Bahamian waters thereby necessitating thousands of Haitians being offloaded on the Bahamian islands.

This could result in thousands of Haitians seeking refuge the length and breadth of this archipelago. This could emerge as a monumental problem for the government of The Bahamas and, perhaps, could represent the largest influx of men, women and children since the winds from Carolinas brought the Loyalists and their slaves to these islands.

In view of these possibilities, it would be expected that The Bahamas Defence Force would have all of its vessels in working condition in order to repel this human assault on our shores.

Further, one would expect that at the Organization of American States (OAS) and the UN, the nations of the hemisphere and the world would be sensitize to the problem The Bahamas may have to encounter early next year. Disaster could, literally, be on our eastern horizon.

The Exodus Continues

In recent weeks, The Bahamas has been inundated with illegal Haitian immigrants. It is believed that this mass smuggling of humans is executed by well-organized groups; many say either Bahamian or Haitian residents in The Bahamas comprise these groups.

From day one, the Christie Administration sought to aggressively attack this problem of illegally transporting Haitians to The Bahamas. In addition, the Minister of Foreign Affairs has been active on the international scene attending OAS and CARICOM fora dealing with the problems facing Haiti today and the impact this unresolved situation in Haiti is having on the region and countries like The Bahamas and the Dominican Republic, Haiti's closest neighbour.

On May 22nd and 23rd, the government of The Bahamas will resume discussions with Haiti, hoping to agree to a new treaty. An important aspect of this new treaty is, according to the Foreign Affairs Minister Mitchell, "The whole issue of intelligence gathering to see if we can get to the source of this problem."

This past week newspaper headlines in The Bahamas have carried stories on the mass influx of Haitian to our shores. The daily talk shows have also been bombarded with telephone calls from Bahamians expressing their sentiments on the fact that our health, educational and social services were being over-taxed from use by illegal Haitians. Even the Carmichael Road Detention Centre is at its capacity level as the number of illegal immigrants have mushroomed in the past few weeks.

The Bahamas lacks the resources to fix the challenge which our country faces from the onslaught of these illegal entrants. This is a scenario which is rooted in Haiti's advancement from a French colony to the first black independent state in the world.

As a French colony, Haiti was the pearl in the French colonial empire and the richest colony in the Caribbean. Haiti's fertile lands yielded substantial riches from the production of sugar cane and the by-products of sugar, molasses and rum. When Haiti liberated itself from France by defeating Napoleon's army to gain its independence;

France lost an important colonial possession.

The price of Haitian Independence would be a costly undertaking and to this day Haiti has not recovered. Western powers made generations of Haitians pay for their liberty. January 2004 marked 200 years of independence for the Haitian people.

Haiti's economic woes began soon after its declaration of independence and from the late 19th century Haiti began to suffer growing economic and political instability, some of which stemmed from reparation payments to France. These payments haunted Haiti through the US occupation years commencing 1915 will into the 1930s. Haiti has never been able to gain economic and political balance to enable the country to adequately address the monumental problems facing this impoverished country.

Haiti has become a problem country for the hemisphere. Those countries with the capacity to impact the Haitian situation seem to be paying little attention. In the Cold War Era, Haiti received much foreign aid from the US as it was seen as a potential beachhead for communist intrusion; hence the US was prepared to prop up dictators like Duvalier.

The world is in a new era fuelled by globalization, yet the international community is doing very little to pull Haiti out of its economic and political morass as it drags behind the rest of the hemisphere. It has gained the ignominious reputation as the poorest country in the hemisphere after once being the richest colony in the Caribbean.

Mr. Mitchell should be applauded for his foreign policy in addressing the challenge Haiti poses to The Bahamas and should consider direct aid to Haiti either in—expertise provision in healthcare, educational facilities or even agricultural inputs like seeds, planting material, farm implements and fertilizer. We must be more proactive rather than our usual reaction approach.

In 1950s, Kwame Nkramah opened the educational doors of Ghana to other Africans thereby enlightening many Africans as they sought independence. Dr. Eric Williams, former Prime Minister of Trinidad and Tobago, used that twin-island state huge oil revenues not only to assist other West Indians but also Africans. While a student in Trinidad during 1960s, there were Africans studying in Trinidad from scholarships awarded by Williams' government. Today Fidel Castro is doing the same. This proactive approach has dividends.

The Bahamas can use a proactive programme as a mechanism to assist in slowing the exodus to our shores.

Illegal Immigrants: Haiti's Labour Surplus Outlet

Despite the fact that dealing with Haiti is not an easy undertaking; the new government has made it a priority. This past Wednesday, Hon. Fred Mitchell, Minister of Foreign Affairs and Hon. Vincent Peet, Minister of Labour and Immigration made an official visit to Haiti. The central issue was the continuous influx of illegal immigrants from that impoverished country.

For months, there has been a steady stream of illegal immigrants entering The Bahamas and this has been an added strain to the country's defense force that also has to contend with drug traffickers who use The Bahamas as a corridor to the US. The whole southern border of The Bahamas is extremely vulnerable to movements by smugglers of illegal humans and drugs. In both instances, the final destination is generally the US with The Bahamas as a temporary stop.

The mission of the two Ministers was to sensitize the Haitian government to the fact that the patience of the Bahamian people had just about been exhausted on this issue as the tolerance level was reaching an all-time low.

For various reasons, Bahamians are a xenophobic people and extremely defensive about outsiders infringing on their national assets. The Bahamas homeland is seen as theirs with Bahamians being the recipients of the benefits which are generated by the homeland. Any intrusion into this national cocoon creates extreme uneasiness. It is this uneasiness which has prompted the government to send their ministerial emissaries to Haiti.

It is recognized that Haiti is the hemisphere's poorest nation. CARICOM has taken it into its political bosom knowing full well that its political structures are weak and also realizing that Haiti, unlike other CARICOM states, has not had a democratic tradition. The US, on the other hand, has suspended financial assistance to Haiti until it has put its governmental house in order. This has retarded Haiti's economic growth and development and the Bahamian delegation has promised to lobby to the US government to release these funds.

Bahamians are cognizant of all of these factors. The Bahamas Christian Church, despite the language differences, has demonstrated a keen sense of Christian brotherhood to the Haitian people in both The Bahamas and Haiti. Almost every Christian denomination has some sort of outreach programme for Haitian nationals; some denominations have even established Christian missions in Haiti.

Like the Church, the government of The Bahamas through its negotiators, Mr. Mitchell and Mr. Peet, have offered technical assistance in the form of manpower and equipment. In this regard, The Bahamas is providing Haiti with the means to undertake certain measures which will aid both countries in getting a better grip on the human cargo trade.

In conjunction with this, The Bahamas has taken a proactive stance by initiating measures to garner intelligence and take more aggressive steps to combat human smuggling.

From every indication, it appears that the Ministry of Foreign Affairs is coordinating this Bahamian initiative with CARICOM. Recently St. Lucia's Foreign Minister, the Hon. Julian Hunte, returned from Haiti on a joint mission with the Deputy Secretary-General of OAS. With hemispheric bodies and governments working in unison, solution to the problems facing Haiti may be found quicker, ultimately providing the foundation to uplift Haiti's political system and bring about a new political order.

This excursion into bilateralism between The Bahamas and Haiti—a country of 300,000 inhabitants providing assistance to a country of some 8 million people adds a new dimension to The Bahamas' approach in dealing with regional issues. The new government of the Hon. Perry G. Christie should be complimented and the introduction of this new policy approach by Ministry of Foreign Affairs should also be acknowledged. It is obvious that Mr. Mitchell has put a new stamp on Bahamian foreign policy.

We in The Bahamas must understand and appreciate that fact that Haiti has a labour surplus economy. On the other hand, many European countries are projecting labour shortages as the new phenomenon of "jobless growth" rears its head. This stems from a global economic environment which has radically shifted from natural resources, raw material based industrial development to knowledge-based industrial development. This renders the primary commodities of developing countries of marginal significance. Helping Haiti through this new economic reality will be difficult, particularly if Haiti does not comprehend the dynamics which are evolving around it.

Haiti Has to Build Credibility

The Bahamas and Haiti have been in regular discussions trying to address the problems of the mass migration of illegal Haitian immigrants to The Bahamas. From all indications, it is very obvious that the Minister of Foreign Affairs, Hon. Fred Mitchell, M.P. has developed an outstanding reputation through his efforts to find a solution to this rising problem for Bahamian authorities.

A major feature of Mr. Mitchell's thrust has been his sensitizing fellow CARICOM Ministers of Foreign Affairs about the problem and at the hemispheric level; he has been able to get attention of OAS. I presume his next step will be at the global level in the forum of the UN where more support needs to be garnered.

It is also apparent that in the global mega-organizations like the World Bank, the International Monetary Fund (IMF), hemispheric multilateral bodies like the Inter-American Development Bank (IDB), rhetoric is being directed to get them to make funding available for badly needed infrastructure upgrade.

This past week, *The Bahamas Journal* in a front-page article indicated that Mr. Mitchell stated that,

> "The IDB will now proceed to give them the development loans they require in order to develop various sectors in their economy which they couldn't qualify for before because the arrears and interest had not been paid."

This dilemma is nothing new to the Haitian economy. It did not just start with President Aristide; it has become a part of the economic and fiscal tapestry of Haiti; hence my skepticism about this situation and whether or not the IDB will be as generous as Mr. Mitchell asserts. For decades, Haiti has been its own worst enemy in matters of this sort and US Secretary of State, General Colin Powell is right when he reiterated several months ago on a visit to the Caribbean that there are really no tangible signs that the Haitian government is reforming its governmental structures in order to utilize millions of dollars either in grants, foreign aid or loans. All of these entities have adopted a tight-fisted attitude when it comes to dispensing funds to the Haitian government.

Haiti is one of these countries falling into the category of "millions of people around the world living in poverty because of Third World debt and its consequences." At every international conference, there is a clarion call for debt forgiveness by countries in Haiti's dilemma.

Both the World Bank and IMF have a programme called Highly Indebted Poor Countries Initiative and its purpose is to provide debt forgiveness for poor countries with good policies. It is from this perspective that Haiti is being denied assistance from some agencies and countries because there is very little evidence that "good policies" are being put into practice to alleviate the burden of poverty being faced by that country.

Haiti is in crisis and it seems as if donor countries like the US or organizations like the IMF and World Bank are unwilling to assist. This is not true. These institutions have been burnt on numerous occasions. Under the IMF stand-by loans, funding is granted to address critical situations, hopefully avoiding a re-occurrence. It has become a merry-go-round of crisis–IMF bailout–crisis–IMF bailout, and so on ad infinitum. Haiti has gone through this merry-go-round 22 times, more than Liberia (13), Ecuador (16) or Argentina (15).

This mass migration of illegal Haitians is affecting our quality of life in The Bahamas. In the most recent *Human Development Index Report*, The Bahamas remains in the top 50 countries in the world; however, our position has dropped from 43rd to 49th in 2003. The reason for the decline stems from the infusion of economically impoverished illegal immigrants from Haiti.

It is in our interest that steps is taken by the international community to provide funding to improve the situation in order to create employment opportunities for the Haitian people, particularly those in more rural areas of the country since these are the ones who seek our shores. Just last week, it was reported that 22 of those vessels sailed into Nassau Harbour. For most Bahamians, this is most upsetting.

Haiti has to begin by cleaning up its own act if it is to gain the confidence of the international agencies.

Haiti: Opportunity for a New Chapter

This past Sunday, Bahamians, the citizens of CARICOM and the rest of the world woke up to the culmination of a rebellion which saw the President of Haiti, Jean-Bertrand Aristide, flee his country. Some say he resigned; others say he was forced out. He said he left to avoid further bloodshed in his strife torn country of 8 million impoverished people.

It is ironic that a state, which prides itself on being the first black republic in the Western Hemisphere and celebrating 200 years of its independence from France, finds itself in a state of lawlessness and political chaos during the anniversary period.

In view of its present situation, has Haiti surrendered its sovereignty to the international community? It is apparent that Haiti lacks the capacity to govern itself during this particular point in time and now presents itself as a state which threatens the social and economic stability of the northern Caribbean. Haitians in The Bahamas represent almost 20% of our population, as large Haitian enclaves exist on Abaco, Grand Bahama, New Providence and Eleuthera.

For the past 40 years, Bahamians have experienced the impact of political instability in Haiti. One can easily remember the days of "Papa Doc" Duvalier and the dreaded Ton-Ton Macoutes, then there was Papa Doc's successor, "Baby Doc" with his flamboyant life style and was eventually overthrown. For almost three decades the Duvalier dynasty ruled Haitians as so-called President-for-life. This led to an exodus of Haitians to The Bahamas. After Baby Doc, there was military take-over along with the emergence of a priest preaching liberation philosophy and capturing the imagination of the Haitian people. This priest, Jean-Bertrand Aristide, would become Haiti's first democratically elected president in the 200-year life of that country after his expulsion from the Salesian Order in 1988.

The Haitian military has always played the role of power broker in Haiti. When Aristide was temporarily forced out, it was Raul Cédras, the military strong man, who emerged to take control of the country. Later, Cédras was forced into exile in Panama prior to Aristide's return to the Haitian presidency.

For the first time, however, satellite transmission has brought the Haitian crisis directly to our living rooms, as we are able to see like the carnage and chaos in our neighbouring and sister CARICOM state. The picture relayed the portrayal of a people who are willing to take political differences to the extreme. It is a horrifying scenario as it demonstrates the failure of the institutional underpinnings of a country.

The patience of the international community for countries like Haiti has worn thin. The situation has, in my lifetime, been a recurrent affair and many feel that it is time for the Haitian people to have some pride and remove itself from this state of constant dependence. The Caribbean and Latin America region is one of the more progressive regions on the global scene, yet Haiti languishes in almost a perpetual state of underdevelopment.

The political solution to Haiti may be another period of occupancy as a protectorate under the aegis of UN because it seems as if the political will among the Haitian people to govern themselves is absent. Haiti has to remove itself from the list of global socio-economic basket cases.

In its present state of affairs, Haiti is a threat to the northern Caribbean. It exports uneducated manpower. It is a health hazard as its medical infrastructure is in disrepair and has to be buoyed by Cuban professionals. Its economy is in shambles and the main source of revenue is remittances from abroad.

Whether we want to admit it or not, Haiti has been a dismal failure in governing itself. It will be in the interest of The Bahamas through CARICOM and OAS to insist that stringent measures are put in place to improve and upgrade the institutional structures needed to enhance a democracy in order to create a modern state.

Haiti is a "throw-back" country and its approach to governance is representative of a bygone era. Modern states in a globalized environment do not function in the same mode; Haiti has been left behind and the challenge of CARICOM, the OAS and the UN is to lift the level of governance in Haiti.

Aristide during his 14 years in the forefront of Haitian political power, never set the foundation for a participatory democracy in Haiti; his approach was very authoritarian despite his strong religious and theological background. It is this fact which created doubts about where he was taking Haiti among some of his closest supporters and allies (like the US and France).

Aristide was successful in destroying the military; however there is little else to point out as he has left Haiti possibly in the most deplorable state of any Haitian leader since World War II.

Development experts predict that it will take decades to restore some semblance of order and provide the institutional structures required for modern nation building. This will have to be conducted under the ambit of international bodies like the UN, OAS and to some extent, CARICOM. This is a long term effort and not a quick fix.

The Bahamas, however, needs to be at the table in some capacity as it is in our interest. After 200 years of independence and oldest black republic in the world, Haiti has to take this opportunity to open a new chapter in its national life.

Haiti—CARICOM's Newest Member

At last week's Caribbean Community Heads of Government Meeting in Montego Bay, Jamaica, the community accepted Haiti's application for membership.

This was a notable event for several reasons. One reason being, it represented a real step towards deepening regional integration because it marked the second entrant of a non-English speaking country and a country which was not a relic of the Community's British colonial past. The former Dutch colony of Suriname was the first non-English speaking country to join CARICOM. There is also another important reason which has its genesis in the black diaspora of the New World. Haiti being the first black republic in the world was a beacon of freedom for the black man in the New World. Immediately upon attaining its independence from France, this infant republic against all of international muscle of the world colonial powers who were engaging in the slave trade—the British, the Dutch, the Portuguese, the Spaniards, the French and the Americans—introduced a revolutionary immigration and citizenship policy.

The Republic of Haiti announced to the world that any black man who reached the shores of Haiti was a free man and, if he chose, would be made a citizen of that newly independent republic.

This was in 1804 and the slave trade was big business in the Caribbean. All of Haiti's neighbours had huge slave populations, especially Cuba, Puerto Rico, Jamaica and The Bahamas.

In the case of The Bahamas, Haiti's immigration and citizenship policy was in force for three decades before slavery was abolished in The Bahamas. It is very conceivable that slaves in The Bahamas took advantage of the offer for freedom and citizenship and fled to Haiti.

Haiti posed a threat to the lucrative slave trade and the metropolitan powers in Europe were determined to make her suffer financially for her transgressions against France.

Haiti was more important to France than her colony in Canada. The country's rich agricultural lands enabled it to become a major producer of sugar, coffee, spices and citrus, along with its mineral resources. The rich land was lost to France and the colonial powers punished Haiti by initially not recognizing its sovereignty. In order to gain sovereignty, it had to pay an exorbitant compensation price to France. The financial burden was crippling for the new republic and economic recovery remains to this day a difficult task for this country.

Almost two centuries after its independence, Haiti is now a member of a regional body with whom it can identify and with whom it can function in an atmosphere of genuineness and not skepticism and suspicion.

The CARICOM admission process is not a simple one. A working group from CARICOM Secretariat will conduct an investigation in consultation with Haitian officials to arrive at specific terms and conditions which must be met by Haiti before she is officially afforded CARICOM membership.

Jamaica's Prime Minister, Mr. P. J. Patterson, referred to Haiti's admissions by stating that, "It would greatly assist the process of building the democratic structures within Haiti by providing the outreach and contact with her sister nations of the Caribbean."

For us in The Bahamas, this CARICOM membership for Haiti will act as a catalyst to not only improve its "democratic structures," but also give it the institutional support to improve its economy thereby raising the quality of life of its citizens. In the long term, CARICOM's involvement will usher in initiatives to improve Haiti's educational institutions, health care system, allow for cross fertilization in cultural and sporting activities and create a large market for the regional and stem the tide of economic refugees to The Bahamas.

President Preval's government should be praised for moving in this direction. This marks a new beginning for the people of Haiti. This regional involvement may be the avenue through which Haiti's political existence is propelled in a positive direction. For too long, Haiti has been tagged as the poorest nation in the Western Hemisphere and hopefully CARICOM will provide the chemistry to remove this stigma from Haiti's international persona.

As Haiti helped those who were victims of the black diaspora almost two centuries ago, those of the diaspora who have been able to improve their socio-economic and political lot have offered a helping hand to Haiti.

The Informal Economy

It is amazing the manner in which economists arrive at a name for a particular economic factor, situation or even a theory. For the purpose of this article, economists have defined the informal economy or sector as all those forms of productive activity, both of goods and especially services, carried out on a small scale, while totally or partially evading institutional, fiscal or insurance obligations.

One would say that The Bahamas is a highly sophisticated economy with a Department of Statistics and a Central Bank which produce economic and financial statistics from the banking, manufacturing, tourism, construction and agricultural sectors of our economy as well as other important statistical data.

All of this information is published on a periodic basis and provides valuable economic data which is used to determine the rate of the economic growth—positive or negative, level of inflation, the balance of payments, etc.

Despite the sophistication of the economy, there is a burgeoning informal sector. One economist describes it as "the people's spontaneous and creative response to the state's incapacity to satisfy the basic needs of the impoverished masses." Other economists say that "the growth of this sector nowadays appears to respond to the pure logic of survival."

The informalization of economies is being viewed very closely by international organizations like the International Labour Organization (ILO), which has estimated that at least 70% of the new jobs which are created in developing countries like The Bahamas are currently in the informal sector.

This stems from the fact that, owing to downsizing of businesses in the private sector, privatization programmes by governments, decrease in employment opportunities in the public sector and the poor performances of economies, people are entering the informal sector because of the necessity to survive.

In his book, *The Planet of Castaways*, Serge Latouche projects a development model which originates from the spontaneous forces of the castaways of development. This view stems from the fact that the existence and the increasing growth of the informal sector are simply the economic manifestation of exclusion.

The Bahamas has not escaped this phenomenon of the existence of an expanding informal sector in our country. It has manifested itself in various forms.

① Small trades provided by a self-employed work force with virtually no formal training and no fixed work place—the shade tree mechanic, the proliferation of transportation "hackers" who frequent the Out-Patient Department of the Princess

Margaret Hospital and the various City Markets and Super Value Food Stores, conch, fruit and vegetable stalls throughout Nassau, operators of property and landscape maintenance concerns, vendors selling food on construction sites from the back trunks of cars, beer bottle collectors who sell them to the brewery, peanut and newspaper sellers, etc.

② Low skill level and the use of modicum of hire labour, particularly in the food take-away businesses; the 99¢ breakfast market which are springing up throughout Nassau. These types of entities require some amount of starting capital in order to get into business.

In many of the low income areas of New Providence there is a substantial amount of individuals operating 30 days establishments, selling sodas, tarts, and refrigerator-made icicles from Kool-Aid.

③ There is also the higher profile economic activity in which an individual engages but evades the institutional formalities of obtaining licenses, paying national insurance for employees, ignoring other regulatory guidelines which protect the employees and consumers and operate from home or a facility which cannot qualify for approval from the relevant government agencies.

These individuals may have sound professional training and expertise which was acquired from an entity in the formal sector, but has decided to operate in the informal sector in order to beat "the system."

Last week, the Minister of Finance stated that some 14,500 jobs were created in the formal sector under the FNM Administration since August, 1992. I wonder if anyone can tell us how many jobs were created in the informal sector resulting from measures like downsizing and the will of the man in the street to survive economically. As the labour market changes, employers demand a more adaptable employee as a result of new technologies begin developed hereby requiring a more knowledgeable and skilled employee. The informal sector will play a very important role in the economy of The Bahamas and, like ILO has estimated, will be responsible for creating more jobs than the figures of the Department of Statistics and the Central Bank will ever reflect.

The challenge with will face developing countries like The Bahamas is devising the appropriate mechanisms which will legitimate the economic activities which are taking place in the informal economy.

The informal economy may be an avenue which taps the real creative potential of

Third World peoples, particularly those who have been cast away and are now excluded from the formal economy. Those in our society who presently comprise the informal economy are possibly the real entrepreneurs of the nineties.

The Informal Economy: Investing in Human Capital

Last week this column defined the Informal Economy and gave examples of its existence in The Bahamas, particularly in our urban enclaves. The element which has been identified by economists to restrict the proliferation of this side of the economy is through a greater investment in human capital. In simple terms, human capital is a synonym for labour.

An overall economic policy framework must first be established in order for the investment in human capital to effective. This framework comprises the following:

① good governance, to ensure stability;

② economic management, to maximize resource mobilization and promote sustainable development;

③ human resource management, to support employment creation and income generation, and reduce poverty;

④ enterprise development, to increase the critical role of the private sector in over development;

⑤ science and technology to increase the efficiency of the population and facilitate infrastructural development.

In conjunction with this, there must also be the right structure of investment incentives and the proper functioning of capital, financial and labour markets.

Governments in The Bahamas have been relatively successful with ①. With ②, a great deal of emphasis has been placed on tourism and financial services and this has resulted in the establishment of institutions like The Bahamas Hotel Training College and various departments of the College of The Bahamas in order to support human resource development ③ in those areas. There has been failure in ④ and ⑤ and this has meant a great deal of dependence on the public sector to create jobs and hence the country's inability to keep abreast of the employment requirements of an expanding population. The Bahamas Technical and Vocational Institute has attempted to meet the manpower training needs of the trades and technology employment sectors of the economy, particularly the construction and light industries and manufacturing.

When these five points are viewed within this context, the deficiencies in human capital become more apparent, hence the need to invest in human resources becomes more critical. This aspect is the challenge which will face governments in the next century and the ability to address these issues will determine whether or not there is a real reduction in poverty and greater employment opportunities through the structure of the formal economy. Through this mechanism, sustainable increases could be generated, thereby improving the overall quality of life for a wider spectrum of the population.

The existence of the informal economy has demonstrated that there is a sector of our human capital where the only option for survival is through this avenue. The skills to compete in the informal economy are not in the possession of these people, plus the growth on this side is so insufficient to meet the needs of the employment requirements of the country.

The size of the formal and informal sectors will denote whether or not the national investment in human capital is headed in the right direction.

Chapter 8

The Bahamas, the Caribbean: Finding the Solution for Food Production

"Success in achieving a new social reality that is native-born and native bred cannot be accomplished by political decree alone, even though the rule of law can push-start and sustain the process. But it is the people who must invest in the two cultural facilities that are basically human, whatever one's cultural, racial or class origin. I refer to the intellect and the imagination."

—Professor Rex Nettleford, Jamaican and Caribbean Cultural Icon

There is great variance in the Caribbean from country to country; however when one views the region as monolithic entity, there is much diversity resulting from the variety of agricultural outputs with export capacity and the natural resource base as found in island and continental states.

The heterogeneous composition of Caribbean economies is reflected in the outputs which these countries export in order to earn foreign exchange.

In CARICOM, there are five sugar exporting states (Barbados, Belize, Guyana, Jamaica and St. Kitts and Nevis) in 1995–1999. Today only Belize, Guyana and Jamaica are engaged. Barbados and St. Kitts and Nevis have turned to services (tourism and financial services).

The Caribbean has lost its preferential arrangement with the EU and this has disrupted the banana industry in the eastern Caribbean states. In the sub-region of the eastern Caribbean, the economies of Dominica, St. Lucia and St. Vincent and the

Grenadines have been adversely affected as there are large numbers of small farmers engaged in banana production.

From the industrial perspective, the Caribbean exports a range of products: manufactured (electronic components, garments), industrial (chemicals, steel, machinery and transport) and mineral (oil and fuels, aragonite, salt, bauxite and alumina). (See Table 8.1)

EU has a trade surplus with the Caribbean and/or CARIFORUM. (See Table 8.2) Four out of the fifteen countries have a trade surplus with the EU (Jamaica, Guyana, Belize and Dominica) resulting from agricultural export. Ten countries (The Bahamas, Dominican Republic, Trinidad and Tobago, St. Vincent and the Grenadines, Antigua and Barbuda, Barbados, St. Lucia, Haiti, Grenada and St. Kitts and Nevis) have a trade deficit with the EU and one (Suriname) is in balance.

Most Caribbean countries, as a result of the changing global environment for sugar and bananas which have been traditional export commodities for most Caribbean states, have moved to services or have diversified their agricultural production to meet food security objectives and/or supply the tourism market with specific items.

Some island states have embarked on economic diversification strategies in order to decrease their dependencies on export agriculture and meet domestic demands in order to address food security concerns and satisfy the tourist market i.e. organic farming to meet the fresh vegetable market.

Some diversification strategies have been horizontal in order to develop new sectors. This was demonstrated as a result of CBI, which saw the introduction of free trade zones in Jamaica, Haiti and the Dominican Republic as well as other CARICOM states like Barbados.

In some sectors there have been vertical diversification as in the case of tourism where diversification takes place within the sector. In agriculture Jamaica and Belize are following the Brazilian example of produce ethanol from sugar cane.

This vertical diversification in tourism has been demonstrated in health spas (Jamaica, British Virgin Islands), medical education (Grenada, Dominica, Dominican Republic), eco-tourism and sports tourism. Mega properties like Atlantis have brought a new dimension to Caribbean tourism.

Table 8.1　Caribbean Exports Percent of Total Exports (Five Years' Average, 1995–1999)

CARICOM	Rum, Sugar, Molasses	Bananas	Citrus	Gold	Oil & Fuels	Chemicals	Bauxite & Alumina	Soap	Electronic Components	Machinery and Transport	Garments	Seafood	Spices	Cocoa	Timber & Lumber	Rice	Flour	Steel Products	Aragonite	Salt	Entertainment
Antigua & Barbuda①																					
The Bahamas②	x		x									x							x	x	x
Barbados	16.2	13.8				10.1			10.3												
Belize	26	13.8	18								9.6	9.9			1.1						
Dominica		32.3						30.1													
Grenada		5.4									4.8	13.7	22.0	11.9							
Guyana	24.6			22.1			15.6								2.2	14.5					
Jamaica	7.4						42.6				14.9										x
St. Kitts & Nevis	35.0									50.9											
St. Lucia		41.3									9.9										
St. Vincent & the Grenadines		35.3														11.6	15.0				
Suriname					3.6		76.9					7.8				7.1					
Trinidad & Tobago					46.2	24.3												7.8			

Source: IMF staff estimates

___

① 2003: Insufficient data.

② The Bahamas exports a range of citrus (limes, oranges and grapefruit) valued at $108 million, aragonite valued at $0.5 m.

2004: Salt valued at $12.4 m, rum at $31.3 m, Film Industry (studio on Grand Bahama).

1985–1993: The entertainment sector in Jamaica has expanded to include films ($50 m) and music (50 recording studios).

Table 8.2 Trade Profile of EU-Caribbean Trade, 2005

CARIFORUM	EU25 Exports (Million Euros)	EU25 Imports (Million Euros)	Trade Balance for EU (Million Euros)
The Bahamas	1,591	1,027	+ 564
Dominican Republic	793	474	+ 319
Jamaica	406	751	- 345
Trinidad & Tobago	536	507	+ 29
St. Vincent	286	263	+ 23
Antigua & Barbuda	219	121	+ 98
Barbados	157	88	+ 69
Surinam	192	192	0
Guyana	60	170	- 110
St Lucia	159	60	+ 99
Belize	99	114	- 15
Haiti	109	16	+ 93
Grenada	37	11	+ 26
Dominica	18	21	- 3
St. Kitts & Nevis	22	8	+ 14
			+ 861

Source: Agri-trade

Sun, sand and sea are not enough to attract visitors. Since 1995, the Caribbean has been losing market share. This is particularly true in CARICOM where tourists arrivals when compared globally was 0.91% in 1960 by 2002 it had declined to 0.69%. This has been impacted by the emerging Cuban product according to the World Bank.

In the World Bank Report, it points out that the slippage is a competitiveness issue i.e. high wages, inadequate skills in the labour force and poor technology adaptation.

Trinidad and Tobago, for example, has vertically diversified its petroleum sector. In the 1970s and 1980s almost all of its exports were in crude oil. Since the 1980s, the industry has been diversified into oil and gas refining, liquid natural gas production, and petrochemicals.

The advantage of vertical diversification is that there is less vulnerability to external market shocks.

Caribbean governments continue to find it a necessity to diversify their economies from the heavy dependence on export agriculture to other economic activities as the number of jobs needed to satisfy an expanding population was not being created. Like Haiti, migration was the response to population growth without jobs.

Jamaica, like Haiti, has been struggling with this challenge of job creation. The US 1990 Census indicated that 159,913 Jamaicans migrated to the US. This represented 15% of the Jamaican population.

The significance of this is the aspect of the brain drain from Jamaica. In this composition of immigrants, 23% had a secondary education while 67% had a post-secondary education.

Migration has become a symptom of the unemployment problem. The Caribbean has lost 10%–40% of its labour force to countries of OECD according to IMF. For some Caribbean states the situation is acute in that as many as 70% of people in the category with 12 years of completed schooling migrate. This high degree of migration has made the Caribbean the world's largest recipient of remittances as a percent of GDP. In 2002, it was 13% of the Regional GDP (IMF).

CSME provision for the free movement of people will go a long way in addressing the migration issue. Even though The Bahamas is not participant in the CSME, unofficial reports indicate that there are more CARICOM citizens in The Bahamas than any other CARICOM state. In Barbados, the demand for skilled construction workers has brought large numbers of Guyanese tradesmen to Barbados.

Over the past decades (1960s–1990s) there has been a transformation among three major sectors (agriculture, industry and services) of Caribbean states. The realities of globalization have had a dramatic affect on the restructuring of Caribbean economies. The greatest decline has been in the agricultural sector were GDP growth rates have not exceeded 1.4% and contribution to GDP has been neglible. Services GDP growth on the other hand, particularly tourism, has been outstanding.

To reverse the decline in Caribbean agriculture, CARICOM has responded with the Jagdeo Initiative. This is the most recent. There have been others. In 1975, there was the Regional Food Plan which was to increase domestic production. One of the reasons for the failure was the lack of commitment by CARICOM governments.

Then in 1983 there was the Regional Food and Nutrition Strategy, this encountered similar problem to those encountered by the Regional Food Plan. Six years later (1989), the Caribbean Community Programme for Agricultural Development was introduced as a replacement for Food and Nutrition Strategy.

In the same year, OECS devised its own Agricultural Diversification Programme.

CARICOM Programme for Agricultural Development was evaluated in 1995 and found to have certain deficiencies i.e. poor public and private sector awareness. By 1996, steps were made to devise the Regional Transformation Programme for Agriculture with the objective of correcting some of the limitations of the other regional plans.

Since 2002 the framework of the Regional Transformation Programme was based on six commodities (coconuts and oils and fats, small ruminants—sheep and goats, poultry, sweet potato, hot pepper and papaya). This programme came under the aegis of the CARICOM Secretariat in conjunction with representatives from member states so as to implement the programme at the national level.

When these initiatives are reviewed, the reasons for the decline of agriculture in the region are several. There has never been a successful regional programme as national governments are fearful of surrendering control of their sectors to regional bureaucrats.

Investing in Agriculture for Regional Food Security

Dr. Winston Phillips has suggested the following:

> "About 25 years ago, a suggestion was put to CARICOM governments

to earmark a portion of total food imports to originate from CARICOM sources. This idea was considered as imposing quantitative restrictions on governments, and most unceremoniously dumped, even though the reality was that with no-action expectations (no 'QRs'), intra-regional trade was almost non-existent relative to total food imports, and though the idea sought to stimulate action towards achievements of one of the CARICOM objectives. That was the occasion that the Agricultural Marketing Protocol met its death. I think it is time that CARICOM governments and our professionals face up to reality, and perhaps some CARICOM political incorrectness, and try to exploit the comparative advantages that certain countries have in agricultural production by (a) soliciting intra-regional private sector investment, on the one hand; and (b) encouraging private sector participative investment on the other. Guyana and Belize, for example, need to ramp up their agricultural infrastructure, and mount deliberate programmes to induce Caribbean investors in investing in their agricultural sectors, while other countries need to encourage their investors to participate. Investments from oil-rich Trinidad have potential for investment not only in agricultural production, but also in agro-processing. In the region, we have a long history of wooing investment in the tourism sector, and even in banking and internet services; why not the same approach for investment in agriculture. All the facilitating frameworks that the CARICOM might put in place, e.g. via the CSME, would be worthless unless governments and people take deliberate measures to exploit comparative advantage in the region. I know that there are arguments indicating that the concept of comparative advantage has changed in this knowledge-based world, but tell me, which countries in CARICOM are associated with relatively lower-cost (agricultural) production?"

Finding the Solution

Regional governments, agricultural professionals and academic agriculturists have failed the people of the region by their inability to develop a sustainable agricultural sector. This has been reflected in the declining GDP for the agricultural sector and negligible contribution of the agricultural sector to the economy of the region over the past four decades. (See Table 8.3)

Table 8.3   Sectoral GDP Growth Rates and Contribution to GDP Growth

	Agriculture	Industry	Services
Sectoral growth			
1960s	1.4	4.9	5.3
1970s	0.5	7.0	5.8
1980s	0.3	4.6	4.9
1990s	1.2	3.9	3.3
Contribution to GDP growth			
1960s	0.2	2.0	3.9
1970s	0.0	2.0	3.3
1980s	0.1	1.1	2.8
1990s	0.1	0.8	2.4

Source: World Bank (World Development Indicators)

Caribbean agriculture has been small farmer based and the political directorate, in order to garner votes, supported this non-competitive system of "welfare agriculture," particularly in the internal self-governing stage as well as in the Independence Era and did very little to bring innovative technologies to this grouping.

Agriculture has been used as the mechanism to keep rural people "employed" in order to avoid swelling the urban population. Despite this attempt, the rural youth has looked to urban centers for employment.

Vertical diversification in the agricultural sector would have averted the urban drift. Agro-industrialization would have provided agricultural connected employment in rural areas thereby developing new career opportunities for rural youth and women.

Finding the solution to Caribbean agriculture has to be viewed within the framework of three key components or aspects. They are the small farmer, sustainable agriculture, and trade.

When one looks at the performance of agricultural sectors across the region from the three key perspectives, the evidence is clear that regional agriculture, over the past four decades (1960–2000), has performed poorly and this has negatively impacted the growth and development of the countries in the Caribbean.

1. The Small Farmer

In his book, *An Economic Study of Small Farming in Jamaica*, Professor David Edwards, Agricultural Economist at UWI in the 1950s and 1960s, highlighted the condition of the small farmer and the state of small farming in Jamaica. Sir Arthur Lewis also pointed out the need to develop industries or services in order to siphon the surplus labour from the agricultural sector. Sir Arthur Lewis, St. Lucian and former Vice Chancellor of UWI and Director of the CDB was the winner of the 1979 Nobel Prize for Economics based on his Dual Sector and Terms of Trade Models respectively. In the Dual Sector development model, he deals with the migration of labour from the traditional sector (agriculture) to the modern sector (services i.e. tourism). In the Terms of Trade Model, he outlines the manner in which trade works between developed and developing countries. In The Bahamas, tourism growth and expansion was able to attract under-utilized labour in the Family Islands (rural) to the hotels as workers, women in particular. In Trinidad and Tobago, the petroleum sector has been a major employer.

For decades this did not occur. States like Barbados, Antigua, St. Kitts and Nevis and Trinidad and Tobago, to an extent, reduced their own reliance on sugar cane production.

A prime example of vertical diversification in agriculture has been in the poultry subsector. The poultry agribusiness is small farmer based in Jamaica, Barbados and Trinidad and Tobago and this has been facilitated through the system of contract farming with agribusinesses which are engaged in feed manufacturing, poultry processing or both.

Through the efforts of CPA, the industry has become one of the most competitive subsectors in regional agriculture. This has stemmed from the fact that the small poultry contract farmer has become an agribusiness person who is sensitive to the issues of food safety, technology, grades and standards and the rule of international trade as stipulated by the WTO.

Throughout the region, particularly in CARICOM, there are more than 100,000 small farmers engaged in the poultry agribusiness. The CPA has demonstrated through its programmes that the small farmer can become an agribusiness person and function competitively; however, the subsector must be structured to enhance the strengths with the larger agribusinesses thereby compensating for the deficiencies which the small farmer will not bring to the table i.e. economies of scale.

In this era of trade liberalization, the small poultry contract farmer has had to survive in an environment of market forces where imported poultry by-products from countries whose farmers are receiving subsidies under domestic support and export subsidies programmes and where market access rules are stringent. Through his competitiveness he has survived and poultry today is the major source of protein in the region.

In 2006, it is estimated that there are between 40 and 45 million people in the Caribbean. There are states like Haiti, Belize, Guyana, and to a lesser extent, Jamaica, where there are still large numbers of small farmers. This figure would easily range upward between 10% and 15% of the regional population being gainfully employed in agriculture. This is reflected in the high GDP contributor of agriculture and in low per capita incomes in countries whose economies are agriculture-based.

In the 1960s and 1970s, agriculture was responsible for 30% of employment in the region. (See Table 8.4) By the 1980s the situation showed dramatic change resulting principally from the realities of globalization whose impact was the loss of preferential markets in Europe.

Table 8.4   Agricultural Employment (1960s and 1970s)

Employment (%) Total Labour Force		
State	1960s	1970s
Barbados	26	16
Guyana	37	29
Jamaica	39	29
Trinidad and Tobago	21	16
OECS	46	32

Source: World Bank

As the economies of CARICOM began to move in the direction of tourism commencing in the 1970s, employment began to shift from the agricultural sector to the service sector.

To make this a reality, labour must be transferred to either industry or services and there has to be a higher degree of vertical diversification in the sector.

The second half of the 20th century has seen Caribbean agriculture loose its preeminent position as the sector which dominated the economies of these island states. The emergence or the ascendancy of tourism stemmed from the fact that a New World Order had come into existence. There was greater wealth, the mode of transportation had been changing, colonialism would crumble and people who were once subjugated were now stepping forward to take hold of the reigns of government in order to navigate a new and different development path for their countries.

The service sector, particularly tourism, has been a creature of the independence period for CARICOM and a post-war activity for Cuba and Dominican Republic. Even though there has been some level of tourism in Port-u-Prince, tourism has not had the impact on Haiti as it had throughout the Caribbean.

Even though Caribbean tourism has been generally successful, it is loosing ground on the global market from a regional perspective. In order for the region to grow as tourism destination, the role of CTO should be widened to include research, regional quality control by establishing standards and certification and an evaluation agency to ensure the competitiveness of the region as a destination. The Caribbean tourism establishment has realized that there must be initiatives in place to promote the Caribbean as a product. At the First Meeting of the Greater Caribbean Tourism Ministers Meeting in Havana, Cuba in November, 2006, an agreement called *The Final Declaration* was signed by the Ministers in attendance.

The Final Declaration is a strategic plan focusing on targeting visitors to the Caribbean as the UN World Tourism Organization has predicted that over the next four years, tourism travel will grow.

Even though *The Final Declaration* is a strategic programme it did not reflect food production and safety. Caribbean food commodities should be projected in order to provide a greater regional supply to the market in the tourism sector as well as ensure a food chain which is safe.

This should be a regional objective in which the CTO in conjunction with the relevant food monitoring authorities should stipulate for all member countries.

(1) Small Farmer: An Analytical Background

Edwards' *Economic Study of Small Farming in Jamaica* provides some interesting insights into the genesis of small farming in Jamaica and by extension in the Caribbean.

The study states the following:

> "Over a century ago, before the emancipation of the slaves, Jamaican agriculture was dominated by the plantation form of organization. Since then thousands of small farms have been created by the descendants

of the slaves… approximately 900,000 persons of a total population of 1,500,000 live on farms, and about 300,000 persons of a total gainfully employed occupied population of almost 615,000 are engaged in agricultural work. Thus agriculture provides employment for one-fifth of the island's population or almost one-third of the population over 14 years of age. Agriculture contributes to 19% of the total GDP."

This was the condition of small farming in Jamaica during the 1950s. Jamaica had a "per capita income of £78 (pounds sterling)" or less than $200 today.

Professor Edwards asserts that,

"The picture of small farming which emerges, although relating particularly to Jamaica, applies also to peasant-type farming in many other underdeveloped countries in the West Indies and beyond, where the essential features are similar though the settings differ."

The study was initiated by the Colonial Economic Research Committee which was made of economists from British universities and whose purpose was to advise the Secretary of State for the Colonies on economic research in the "colonies."

This initiative came along during a period when the government of Jamaica was considering the launch of a major agricultural development programme. Small farmers played an important role in the agricultural sector, hence the need for such a study. The study became a tripartite undertaking with the key players being Edwards from the Colonial Economic Research Committee, the government of Jamaica and the University (College) of the West Indies Institute of Social and Economic Research.

The Colonial Office was also concerned about migration. Between 1953 and 1955, 27,000 Jamaicans immigrated to England this did not include immigration from the anglophone colonies in the West Indies. This study was to assist in providing "an understanding of the economic and other relevant aspects of some of the more important small farming systems in Jamaica so that the possibility of bringing about improvements in them can be assessed."

While Jamaica was grappling with the challenges facing the small farmer community, The Bahamas was well on the way to restructuring its economy from an agriculture-based one to one based on services, namely tourism, which was being reoriented from a seasonal activity to a year-round business eventually evolving into the major sector in the economy of The Bahamas.

In conjunction with this reorientation, there was a massive movement of manpower from the field to hospitality industry. One of the beneficiaries of this transformation is women who are now the dominant gender in the hospitality industry.

In *The Theory of Economic Growth*, Sir Arthur Lewis points out the following with regard to the small farmer.

"In practice in most backward (developing) economies, the sector which responds least to growth in other sectors, and which therefore acts as a brake on all economic growth, is the agricultural sector producing food for home consumption. This is because when agriculture is in the hands of small farmers, the introduction of innovations depends more upon government initiative than upon the initiative of private entrepreneurs.[1]

To increase the output of peasants, however, requires a number of actions which are essentially in the government sphere; above all, considerable expenditure on agricultural research and extension as well as expenditures on roads, rural water supplies, agricultural credit facilities, etc."

Low investment in the sector continued into the 21st century. Among selected CARICOM countries, there has been relatively low expenditure by governments. As a percentage of GDP, expenditure ranged from 6.8% (2001) to as low as 0.6% (2002). (See Table 8.5)

Table 8.5 Govt. Expenditure on Agriculture and on Research in Selected Countries as % of GDP

Selected Countries	Year	
	2001	2002
Antigua and Barbuda	1.9	NA
The Bahamas	0.8	0.6
Barbados	2.7	2.6

(to be continued)

---

[1] It is this fact which has brought greater attention to agribusiness development which has been successful in poultry production in the region.

Selected Countries	Year	
	2001	2002
Grenada	6.3	5.7
Guyana	5.0	3.9
Jamaica	0.7	0.7
St. Lucia	6.8	6.0
Trinidad and Tobago	2.6	2.2

Source: IICA's Regional Director's address in The Bahamas, June, 2005

The picture of decline in investment continues into the new century.

Lewis further explained that,

"The experiences of Japan shows that appropriate expenditure by government in these spheres can have spectacular effects on output of peasants and that agriculture, far from lagging behind other sectors, and acting as a brake on the rest of the economy, can be turned into a leader, generating demand for other sectors and also providing them with capital. But most other governments in this situation have neglected peasant agriculture with the result that its failure to expand has kept down the rate of growth in other sectors."

This has been reflected in the Caribbean by the fact that Caribbean has become a food deficit region unable to produce enough for its nationals and millions of visitors. This has resulted from an inefficient agricultural sector which has been dominated by small farmers.

In the Caribbean, the level of innovation in the agricultural sector has been limited to agribusiness subsector and not widespread among small farmers. However, in tourism, innovation has been broad based. Lewis points out "innovation in one sector of the economy is checked unless other sectors expand appropriately." Even though tourism has grown, the agricultural output has not kept pace across the region. According to Lewis "smooth economic development requires that industry (and/or service) and agriculture should grow together." This has not happened, as agriculture has been a lagging sector.

Edwards' *An Economic Study of Small Farming in Jamaica* indicated that in the 1950s there were some 900,000 persons (possibly 1 million) were connected with small farming, this represented 60% of the Jamaican population. Lewis makes the comparison that France in the 1950s needed 25% of its population engaged in agriculture to feed itself whereas in other industrialized countries like the US and Canada, the figure was bordering on 10%.

For its survival, the small farmer sector in the Caribbean must become smaller, more efficient and improve its productivity through technology and greater investment in research. To achieve this, Caribbean governments have to increase the level of expenditure on the sector as many of the issues which faced this grouping a half century ago, as outlined in the Edwards' *An Economic Study of Small Farming in Jamaica*, still exists today. This is reflected in the poor contribution by agricultural sector to the GDP at the national and regional levels respectively.

(2) The Small Farmer: A Resource

The small farmer has not had a clearly defined role in Caribbean agriculture. He or she has been viewed, in some states, as a throw-back to a bygone era, a societal burden, a non-contributor or a drain on the public purse. This grouping has been villainized and has become the scapegoat for the failures in Caribbean agriculture.

Small farming has, in some quarters, been associated with failure and obsolesce. To many policy makers, it is a problematic area in which there are limited solutions. From epoch to epoch, the attention given to small farming has wavered. At the national level, its role in the agricultural sector of a respective country would sometimes be determined by the political climate, the attitude of donors or the agenda of international agencies rather than assisting this grouping in overcoming economic challenges like market forces or improving the capacity of stakeholders in the achievement of competitiveness.

Until a strategic role has been defined for small farmers at both the national and regional levels respectively, small farming will continue to decline and eventually disappear as an economic activity in the agricultural sectors of Caribbean states.

In the mid 1950s, 900,000 Jamaicans were tied or trapped to the land. Small farming became stigmatized as a dead end activity. At this time the hopes and aspirations of these people were centered around the ability of the Jamaican government to negotiate a good price and quota in the preferential Commonwealth market for their sugar cane, bananas, citrus or coffee. Today, the WTO's *AOA* has eliminated this preferential arrangement so millions of small farmers across the region are faced with economic uncertainty and social instability causing dislocation for thousands. Migration is no longer a reliable exit strategy as the industrialized countries are gradually closing the doors to this possibility.

It is this background which makes it mandatory for Caribbean governments to devise economically sustainable programmes for small farmers.

These programmes must be two dimensional. Firstly, to cut into the deficit which is being faced by all states due to their inability to meet the indigenous demand for food and secondly, to cut into the imports which are presently entering the region in order to meet the food demands of the millions of visitors who flock to the region by air and sea.

The small farmer is a legacy of slavery. When slavery unleashed this deluge of humanity in the Caribbean, these individuals farmed for subsistence purposes using a technology which they had adopted from their slave masters. Farming for them did not come out of the scientific tradition but from a tradition based on trial and error which evolved into an art form which was passed down from generation to generation, crop year to crop year and community to community.

Generally little notice is given to combining the art of farming with the science of farming or in the parlance of the technocrat, combining indigenous knowledge with scientific knowledge.

In the 1960s as a post graduate student at UWI in Trinidad, one's thesis was a study of the adoption farming practices in the Lopinot/La Pastora area of Trinidad. Lopinot/La Pastora was situated in a farming community in the northern range and located about eight miles from the Eastern Main Road. Cocoa and coffee were the main crops. The plantation was owned by a French man but worked by slaves who were responsible for establishing this cocoa and coffee estate. For the farming economy of Lopinot/La Pastora the guide to better farming was *The McDonald's Farmers Almanac*.

As an extension officer working in the islands of the southeastern Bahamas, the small farmers on these islands were descendants of slaves and still used the slash and burn technique on "pot hole" or coppice land, then in the 1960s to the present. Cultivation was based on low external inputs.

In the southeastern Bahamas, there are farming communities whose origin is based in the cultivation of cotton by Loyalists farmers who sought residence in The Bahamas around and during 1776 period when the US was fighting for its independence from Great Britain.

These Loyalists, mainly from the US south, brought their slaves and settled on various islands of the southeastern Bahamas. Their venture into cotton cultivation proved to be unsuccessful for various agronomic reasons causing them and their slaves to engage in a labour-intensive system of crop husbandry in conjunction with the production of small ruminants (sheep and goats).

In Lopinot/La Pastora and the southeastern Bahamas, the small farmers had to depend on indigenous knowledge with virtually no attention being given by government agencies to the scientific value of their techniques or the art of farming which were employed.

Despite the lack of resources, the small farmer has been a survivor. Their survival instincts should be crystallized into technologies which can be enhanced in order to improve their competitive capacity in small farming. Far too often, policy makers ignore the potential of the small farmer by excluding him or her from the decision-making process on policy issues and programmes. The private sectors, on the other hand, have adopted a different stance.

The success of the contract growers in the poultry agribusiness stems from the fact that private sector actors work with the small farmers stakeholders to achieve successful outcomes hence the survival of the poultry agribusiness in the Caribbean. The colonial legacy of the top-down approach still haunts the management psyche of government departments and agencies. It is this factor which may be one of the main contributors to the failure of agriculture in the region.

The small farmer plays a pivotal role in the multifuntionality of agriculture. It is he who interfaces directly with the environment; it is he who sustains local communities in the rural districts and it is he whose value system and work ethic provide the framework for nation building and good citizenry.

After years or even generations, small farmers have devised farming systems which are compatible with their environments and which have enabled them to produce a range of crops and livestock. Their challenge has been the adaptation of these farming systems to the market forces in which the small farmer has to function and compete with commodities which are supported by research, domestic support subsidies, export subsidies and economies of scale.

The Caribbean is a food deficit region where several states face food insecurity. Food deficiency has been exacerbated by growth in services, specifically tourism. Revenues from services are used to import food, a percentage of which could be supplied by small farmers.

Food deficiency is a recent phenomenon in some states as the small farmer community was able to provide several commodities for domestic consumption thereby enabling these states to enjoy a level of self-sufficiency. However, with the changing economies, the demand for more convenient foods is increasing. As urbanization set in and women began to become an important element in the workforce, the indigenous foods for domestic consumption lost dietary importance.

Policy makers in many states have ignored the role of the small farmer in the maintenance of self-sufficiency. In the case of St. Kitts and Nevis, for example, the government has decided to redirect its economy to service and direct its small farming community to other fields of employment.

Determining the number of small farmers and arriving at a definition for small farming have not been easy. Generally one can use the results of a census of agriculture; however censuses of agriculture are only conducted every ten years. In some states, Department of Agriculture maintain farm registers for various reasons i.e. to determine whether or not an operation is bona fide and eligible for subsidies, duty-free concession or assistance after natural disasters like hurricanes, droughts, fire or flooding. Another source is societies, cooperatives or commodity groupings. Agricultural societies in Jamaica, Barbados and Trinidad and Tobago are recognized by government as representatives of small farmers.

Table 8.6 shows the distribution of small farmers throughout the region. Small farmers are a special grouping requiring specific programmes to improve their competitiveness, yet some states do not differentiate the small farmer from the resource rich large farmer.

Table 8.6 Small Farmers (per Country)

Country	Year	Category	Number of Farmers	Number of Small Farmers	Source
Antigua and Barbuda	2005	Livestock	2,000	?	FAO registry: Control of Stay and Roaming Livestock TCP; this figure is also on the Internet

(to be continued)

Country	Year	Category	Number of Farmers	Number of Small Farmers	Source
Antigua and Barbuda			5,000	?	National Medium Term Investment Programme (NMTIP) document: 50% full time, 50% part-time
Barbados				?	NA; Ministry of Agriculture promised to send info but does not have it categorized as small or large; NMTIP document has no figures
		Registered	3,000	2,000	Barbados Agriculture Society is in process of creating a farmer register and project this figure for small farmers
Commonwealth of The Bahamas	2004	Registered	2,000	1,242	FAO registry: PS letter to H. Clarendon Sept 10, 2004; Department of Agriculture register of approved farmers; see Chapter Notes for more details
Belize	2004	Crop and livestock, mainly small farmers	12,000	12,000	Registry: Draft Project Document on Agricultural Sector Strategy /2004; NMTIP document: small farmers throughout but no figures
Dominica			?	?	NMTIP document: no figures
Dominican Republic			?	?	
Grenada	2004	At least 14,000 which is amount of small-scale holdings according to registry document		14,000	Registry: investment proposals for rehabilitation of the agricultural sector following hurricanes... August and Sept 2004; NMTIP document: no figures; see Chapter Notes for more details from Land Utilization Survey
	2006	nutmeg		10,000	NMTIP document
	2006	cocoa		3,500	NMTIP document: approx. 14,000 seems correct
Guyana				5,000	FAO registry: Draft Project Document on Emergency Assistance to Farmers; affected by floods/March 2005; NMTIP document: no figures
Haiti	2004				FAO registry: Investment proposals for rehabilitation of the agricultural sector following hurricanes... August and September 2004; no figures for Haiti

(to be continued)

Country	Year	Category	Number of Farmers	Number of Small Farmers	Source
Jamaica	2004		200,000	100,000	FAO registry: investment proposals for rehabilitation of the agricultural sector following hurricanes... August and September 2004; NMTIP document: no figures; see the memorandum by H.B. Bernard in Chapter Notes
St. Kitts and Nevis			3,084	?	St. Kitts and Nevis: NMTIP and Bankable Investment Profiles/ 2000 Agriculture and Fisheries Census; NMTIP document: crop, small ruminant, livestock, commercial; no figures
St. Lucia	2006		841	?	NMTIP document: "farmers"; no qualification or figures
St. Vincent	2006		1,000	?	NMTIP document: 1,000 farmers to be trained
Suriname					
Trinidad & Tobago			?	?	NMTIP document: 37.5% decline in farmers; no qualification of farmers, no amount mentioned

Source: FAO registry, NMTIP documents 2006, internet; FAOSTAT does not have figures

In Latin America, the differentiation goes deeper by separating small farmers from subsistence/landless farmers. In some Caribbean states, the subsistence/landless farmers may be squatters or may be operating as tenant farmers in a share cropping or other type arrangement. Whatever the scenario, the small farmer is an under-utilized resource.

In some states like Jamaica, there is the troubling question of the landless or those with more than a hectare of land but less than five hectares. This state of affairs has been addressed by the creation of land settlement schemes on government owned land or through the break-up of large estates in order to allocate economically viable parcels of land for the landless and those with little land.

In the absence of these type schemers, a high percentage of this grouping would either flock to the urban areas or immigrate somewhere, usually from the remittances from relatives who may be living abroad. Yallahs Valley Land Authority was one mechanism which was used by the government of Jamaica to address the landless or land marginality issue.

In the largest CARICOM state, Jamaica, there are 15,000 Jamaicans who do not own the land on which they farm and an additional 115,000 plus small farmers who seek a living from less than one hectare of land. These two groups comprise 130,000 smallholders.

When one reviews the composition of the agricultural sector in one of the smaller states, Grenada, in CARICOM, 71% of the farms are five acres or less. There is also a sizeable percentage (27%) of holdings of one and two acres.

With holdings as small as the ones in Jamaica and Grenada, it is virtually impossible for a small farmer to improve his or her lot in life from farming.

(3) Small Farming: A Reversal of Fortune

Selected countries and commodity groups in the region are recognizing the fact that steps must be taken to improve the lot of the small farmer and utilize this grouping as a vital element in their agricultural development programmes.

For years the small farmer was portrayed as a liability; today their fortunes are being reversed in a number of states.

• Cuba

Cuba is the largest state in the region. It has a population approaching 12 million. For the past four decades, it has been experiencing an economic blockade by the US, the wealthiest country in the hemisphere and the world.

Its political and economic ideology has identified it as a socialist state aligning itself with the Soviet Union and the Eastern European Bloc of States. With the ending of the Cold War and the collapse of the Soviet Union, it became necessary for Cuba to forge a new direction in its food production programme.

Cuban agriculture was industrialized with the use of tractors plus high input based manufactured fertilizers, specifically nitrogen fertilizers (192 kg/ha).[1] There was also the loss of preferential markets to the Soviet Union and Eastern Bloc countries from whom Cuba was paid three times the world market price for its sugar. The fall has caused Cuba to compete on the world market. In essence Cuba was experiencing the same type of scenario as those CARICOM states which also had preferential markets to EU withdrawn

---

① Wright, Julia. 2006. Cuba's Enforced Ecological Learning Experience. *LEISA*, Vol. 22.

as a result of WTO milling.

Cuba was now facing a food crisis as a result of the inability to buy the volumes of inputs to support the industrialized type of agriculture to produce food causing serious food shortages.

In order to reverse the slide into food shortage, the Cuban government took the decision to focus their food production systems on the following.

> "Technologies based on local knowledge, skills and resources instead of imported inputs... downsizing of farms reversals of the number of people leaving rural areas by improving rural conditions and opportunities."

Critical elements in this strategy were the expansion of research, greater emphasis on extension services and making land available to rural people.

This strategy proved to be successful as output increased to the point where "production and yields of staple foods doubled and continued to increase, while most importantly, food availability was restored to acceptable levels." The chief ingredient in all of this was the contribution of small farmer output.

• Guyana and Suriname

There are reports coming out of Guyana and Suriname that the Good Agricultural Practices (GAP)[1] concept is being pushed by IICA and is making an impact among small farmers. This is particularly evident among small farmers who are engaged in export agriculture.

Improvements have been seen in the quality and quantity of crops; water contamination and pest infestation have been reduced as well. This is seen in the area of integrated management and pesticide use.

GAP concept can be a vital instrument in the transformation of small farming. See Chapter Notes for more details.

• CARICOM Poultry

In CARICOM states, the main source of protein is poultry meat. With reference to table eggs, the region has a high percentage (between 90% and 95%) in self-sufficiency. The backbone of the agribusiness surrounding this commodity is the small farmer. CPA

---

[1] Chapter Notes provide outlines of the specifics about GAP.

has valued this regional agribusiness at $460 million employing 30,000 people in 14 states.

When the region was threatened with the possible outbreak of the Avian Influenza (Bird Flu), the livelihoods of thousands would have been affected. In Jamaica, the poultry agribusiness is small farmer dominated and is estimated to comprise about 10,000 individuals of whom some 2,000 are egg producers with capacities as small as 25 hens per holding.

The processing of broiler meat is small farmer related. In CARICOM there are three types of processors (large, small and cottage). Small farmers and/or the processing of less than 5,000 birds are placed in the cottage category and it is the cottage category which is reflected as follows. [1]

Table 8.7 Cottage Processors and Small Farmers

Cottage Processors' Market Share (per Country)		Small Farmers (per Country)
Barbados	30%	75
Belize	N.A.	380
Dominican Republic	80%	N.A.
Guyana	50%	100
Jamaica	30%	10,000
OECS	N.A.	380
Suriname	96% plus	25
Trinidad & Tobago	55%–60%	50

There are 3,000–4,000 cottage processors throughout the region and about 11,000 small farmers.

CPA has initiated activities to benefit the whole of the poultry sector regardless of membership and with no consideration to size of operation. This approach has been a tremendous asset to small farmers with many becoming contract growers in relationships with feed mills or processing plants.

Small farmers and cottage processors are making significant contribution to poultry production nationally and regionally. This has been demonstrated by the market share which is held as a result of the output from small farmers and cottage processors.

There is a role for the small farmers and the cottage processors; however, there must

---

[1] CPA, CARICOM Cottage Poultry Processors, Code of Practice.

be a deeper integration of them into the overall agribusiness subsector through deliberate initiatives. One such initiative is the tripartite arrangement where the CPA, national governmental agencies like Departments of Agriculture and local farmer associations work together to formulate strategies to advance the involvement of the small farmer and the cottage processor in this agribusiness so as to improve the competitiveness of this grouping in this globalization arena, and to encourage and facilitate the adoption of new technologies in order to achieve improved efficiencies and output.

The CPA has oriented its programmes to improve the competitiveness of all in this agribusiness be he or she small grower or cottage processor. This has taken place through the following initiatives.

① Regional schools and Training Seminars—2003–2005. CPA conducted six regional schools and ten national training seminars on various aspects of the poultry agribusiness (technology upgrade, disease prevention and management, preparation of on-farm and food safety manuals and devising industry strategies, etc.).

② Surveys. Various surveys on subsections of the poultry agribusiness have been undertaken in order to quantify the composition of the industry in the region and the value and contribution to GDP. This included national registration programmes.

③ Advocacy. The CPA has represented the industry at the Heads of Government and national levels respectively in order to express the concerns of the industry. There has also been cooperation at the national level with non-governmental organizations like agricultural societies, farmer groups and cooperatives.

④ Trade negotiations. The CPA has been very involved with CRNM in the negotiations with the WTO, FTAA and CSME and has sought to have poultry declared a sensitive commodity.

The CPA has been a force in aiding the small farmer who is engaged in one of the poultry subsectors, to survive in this era of globalization.

The three examples in this section are examples of where the future of the small farmer has been reversed from failure or marginalization to some form of economic viability. Initiatives like these can truly transform small farming into a national resource and assist in putting Caribbean agriculture on a sustainable basis.

2. Sustainable Agriculture

Caribbean through its production of sugar, bananas, coffee and citrus demonstrated its comparative advantage to produce these commodities for the global market. Caribbean tourism came into prominence because of its sun, sand and sea. In sectors, agriculture and tourism, the environment was the key factor.

Since all of the independent states of the region are members of the UN and its specialized agencies i.e. FAO, these states are signatories to the International Conventions (ICs), specifically those which relate to the environment and trade, respectively.

(1) What does this mean?

ICs on the environment comprise four Conventions, namely *The UN Framework on Climate Change (UNFCC)*, *The UN Conventions to Combat Desertification (UNCCD)*, *The UN Convention on Biological Diversity (UNCBD)* and The UN Forum on Forests which is essentially a process and actually not a convention.

These conventions are employed by the international community to bring focus to the actions which are required to address the global environmental and development issues which concern mankind. Many of these issues are environmental related as they affect farming, fishing, and forestry.

In some countries of the region, the governmental responsibilities for these issues are scattered among several ministries. In some cases i.e. The Bahamas they are located in three different ministries/departments; Agriculture (Ministry of Agriculture and Marine Resources), Forestry (Department of Lands and Services) and the Ministry of the Environment. The problem facing national government is the ability to create synergies among the various ministries/departments with responsibilities for specific aspects of the ICs.

Farming, fishing and forestry all interface with the environment. If there is deregulation to the land and soil, there is no farming (*UNCCD*). If there is the indiscriminate cutting of forests for firewood or the removal of forests for resort develop-ment, there will be loss of biodiversity (*UNCBD*) with implications on climatic and rainfall (*UNFCC*).

Caribbean governments must ensure that the environmental or ecosystems services (water, marine life, forests) are in place to ensure that both agriculture and tourism are sustained as they both depend on the environment.

In agriculture, there will be a growing competition though the diversification between agriculture for food consumption and/or agriculture to meet energy demands bio-fuels from sugar cane, corn and oil palms. Already land for food production is being lost to urbanization and resort development. There is an Australian Aborigine expression which says "If you take care of the land, the land will take care of you."

In a region where high quality land for food production is limited, steps have to be taken to preserve the food production capacity in the region.

(2) Why ICs?

ICs for Caribbean countries are new international commitments and offer new opportunities to point countries to national development goals and push them to new sustainable pathways, specifically in agriculture and tourism.

Countries which ratify ICs have reporting commitments which enable comparisons to be made. On the other hand, these are factors which point to the development of knowledge, technology, institutions, international relations and foreign findings and investments opportunities. The separation of the various ICs responsibilities in the various ministries/departments contributes to the inability of states to take advantage of the opportunities. It is through the synergy among the ICs that countries benefit, hence the need for more efficient coordination at the national level through the responsible ministries.

3. Trade

Trade has always been an important element in the economic life of the Caribbean. As colonies, the now independent states exported agricultural commodities to their European colonial markets. As independent states with the former European colonials establishing a union, these Caribbean states as members of the European supported group, ACP, enjoyed preferential market arrangements. This is the background for Lewis' Terms of Trade Model.

When preferential treatment came to an end, the Caribbean became subjected to WTO rules and regulations. At the hemispheric level, Free Trade Agreements (FTAs) were introduced. As a response to these globalization arrangements, CARICOM responded with CSME.

In this regard, trade has global dictates as agricultural trade is governed by *AOA*, which defines the rules and regulations under the WTO. *The Doha Ministerial Agreement* of 2001 covered the trade of goods and services. The FTAs also deal with the environment and agriculture.

Caribbean agriculture products have to be competitive in this trading atmosphere. They must be competitive on the global market as there are no longer any preferential markets. They must also be competitive in the regional market (inter and intra-island trade).

There is a demand for Caribbean products outside of the region and an expanding domestic food market for both the indigenous people and the visitors in the tourism sector. Caribbean governments have to provide the regulatory framework for competitive regional products to succeed against products, which are produced in the EU or the USA where farmers are heavily subsidized.

It should be noted that environmental and/or ecosystems services are important to the tourism sector as stated in *The Doha Ministerial Agreement*.

The Keys

The agricultural sector of national economies are evaluated on the basis of small farmers being converted to agribusiness men or women and whether or not their agribusinesses and farming systems are environmentally sustainable and able to function in a trade framework which enable them to succeed.

The keys offer the way forward for Caribbean agriculture.

Virtually all Caribbean states have tourism as a sector in their economies. However, only a few states in the region (The Bahamas, Barbados, Trinidad and Tobago) have transformed their economies from an agriculture-based one to either service (tourism) or industry-based economies respectively.

On the other hand, those which have remained agriculture-based have lacked competitiveness as they have depended on preferential trade arrangements to secure export markets. This lack of competitiveness has been one of the primary reasons for the failure of the agricultural sector over the past four decades (1960–2000) and the negative contribution to GDP growth in the region.

Tourism has revolutionized the Caribbean in terms of generating employment and foreign direct investment; however it has exacerbated food imports. Overall, tourism has changed the Caribbean.

During the Independence Era, Caribbean governments had to function against a background of globalization, trade liberalization and market forces. This has demanded a new approach to economic development and for agriculture-based economies it had been problematic as the non-competitiveness of small farming has been highlighted.

Economic transformation in this type of environment has been a challenge with which the states in the region are grappling—some have had success, others are struggling.

In the October 2006 Edition of the CTA's *Spore* Magazine, "Viewpoint", under "Agricultural Policy Article", "Small Is Still Beautiful," by Peter Hazel, denotes the changing face of agriculture in the following way.

> "Agriculture's role changes as a country develops. As people get richer, agriculture's share in national income and employment falls, small farms find it harder to compete with larger, more mechanized farms and consumers diversify their diets into higher value products and more processed and pre-cooked foods.
>
> Urbanization accentuates these patterns. In short, as countries become wealthier, farms become progressively larger, more commercial and more specialized in higher-value products. Many small farms disappear, while others adopt either by funding high value niches in which they can compete or by becoming part-time farmers. These changes are a normal part of the economic transformation of a country."

The Bahama Journal's Agribusiness Page

Agribusiness: The Hope for Regional Agriculture

There is a lively debate taking place among Caribbean stakeholders in the agricultural sector. The basis of the debate is to arrive at a position where stakeholders in the private sector can work in competition with the public sector and non-governmental organizations to secure the natural resources of the regional agricultural sectors and produce food products which are competitive in the global marketplace.

Regional Agricultural Sectoral Organizations

Several entities are seen as linchpins to the success of such objectives. On the one hand, there is the publicly funded CARDI. CARDI is the premier research body for CARICOM. Over the years, its role in CARICOM agriculture has constantly been questioned and, from time to time, there have been administrative re-organization exercises. Stakeholders are calling for a new look for CARDI.

The other entity is the Caribbean Agribusiness Association. This entity came into existence as a result of an initiative by IICA. IICA's view was that the way forward for Caribbean agriculture was for farming to be seen as a business, and not some part-time activity being performed by unskilled workers, hence the establishment of an association of various types of agribusinesses in the various CARICOM states. IICA through its representation office of the national level is proving to be a valuable tool.

There is FAO of the UN through its sub-regional office in Barbados. The sub-regional office has been a vehicle which has enabled a global organization like FAO to respond on a timely basis to challenge or address issues facing agriculture with national levels.

Agricultural Trade

Trade liberalization and globalization have caused Caribbean governments and agricultural stakeholders to view agriculture from a new perspective. This perspective was re-enforced when, in 1995, every CARICOM state with the exception of The Bahamas joined the WTO.

WTO rules and regulations forced governments and stakeholders to change the manner in which agriculture was being practiced. CARICOM responded by establishing a CSME whose objective was to introduce measures, at the regional level, to improve competitiveness and encourage greater inter-regional trade among CARICOM states.

The changing role of agricultural trade had just begun. The North American Free Trade Agreement comprising the countries of Canada, Mexico and the US would usher in the new era of free trade. This eventually led to discussions to create a hemispheric free trade body—FTAA. It is this hemispheric environment, along with the WTO, which pushed Caribbean governments and private sector stakeholders to come to grips with the fact that, if, the necessary stops were not taken to put Caribbean agriculture on a new level, the possibility of the sector becoming commercially extinct was a reality.

It is this background which has caused both the public and private sectors to take a new look at the institutions which are relevant for agribusiness growth and development in CARICOM states.

Agribusiness Thrust

The decision has been taken to establish a new CARDI. For this new CARDI to succeed, Robert Best, the Executive Director of CPA, is recommending that the new CARDI has "to work far more closely with us in the private sector. This is a great opportunity. Restructure the programme and make regional associations central."

In recent years, the CPA under Mr. Best's leadership has been and is an important force in shaping regional policies in the poultry industry both at the national and regional levels. The CPA has been particularly effective in sensitizing national governments and the Caribbean Regional Negotiation Machinery regarding the impact of imported poultry on domestic producers. The question of market access and the implications this has had and continues to have on local producers has been staggering.

One of the founding members of the CPA was Gladstone Farms. The whole idea of a CPA was started by the Gladstone Farm CEO, Bruce Hanson. Mr. Hanson while attending the annual poultry convention in Atlanta, Georgia pulled CARICOM producers together and this initial meeting gave birth to the CPA. Today, Gladstone Farms is no longer in existence as cheap, US subsidized poultry parts supported by shortsighted food importers caused the demise of the largest producer in the agricultural sector of The Bahamas.

The CPA has taught stakeholders among the various agribusinesses in the region that the basis for survival in a world driven by market forces is togetherness and solidarity.

Role of Agribusiness Organizations

Today, Caribbean stakeholders are represented through several types of organizations.

In Jamaica, Barbados and Trinidad and Tobago, small farmers lean towards agricultural societies. In Barbados for example, the Barbados Agricultural Society provides extension services for its members. This has virtually replaced the extension services in the Barbadian Ministry of Agriculture. In Trinidad and Tobago, the agricultural society has been fighting to secure the rights of poultry contract growers, whom the society feels are being exploited by the large poultry companies who provide growers with feed, baby chicks and market distribution.

The Jamaican Agricultural Society by representing mainly small farmers wields tremendous clout as a lobbying body with the government of Jamaica. In Jamaica, politicians listen to the Jamaican Agricultural Society.

The other entities are industry associations. Most Caribbean economies were agriculture-based and competing on the export market as well as securing export quotas with their former colonial masters. Certain commodities had a head start as they generated substantial foreign exchange for the local economies as well as employment, particularly in the rural areas. Commodities like sugar and coffee generated great wealth for the metropolitan economies of Europe.

Commodity associations for sugar, rice, citrus, bananas and coffee were export directed. With food security looming as an important issue, commodities orientated to meeting domestic food requirements have gained importance and this has led to the creation of commodity associations geared to the local market i.e. poultry, pork, vegetable and dairy.

Last year a workshop to encourage expansion of mutton production in the region was held in Barbados under the aegis of IICA. Mr. Arnold Dorsett, Assistant General Manager, BAIC and Edrin Symonette, an Eleuthera farmer, represented The Bahamas. Several important factors emerged.

① Edrin Symonette turned out to be the largest mutton producer in the region.

② The Bahamas is a major mutton producer in the region and offers a huge market for improved breeding stock from Jamaica and Barbados.

③ The Bahamas has the potential to diversify its production base into lamb meat and milk.

As a result of this workshop, Mr. Dorsett was selected to the membership of a regional committee on mutton production.

Other industry associations are springing up throughout the region namely in landscaping and ornamental horticulture and aquaculture (fish farming).

Impact of Agribusiness Stakeholders

Best makes an outstanding case for the stakeholders in agribusiness when he states that,

"① Who drives the lobbying to develop and defend the regional view of our major industries at the regional and international levels and pays for public sector representatives to go to international meetings to represent the region's interests?

② Who is actively investigating new business opportunities for the sector and ways to improve efficiency including agricultural health? Who owns and promotes substantial technical research stations for their industries?

③ Who battles with the public sector to urge them to change archaic laws and regulatory systems in keeping with the trade agreements we have signed?

④ Who bears the cost of the lack of these measures when our agricultural health and food safety systems fail?"

The answers to all of these questions are the stakeholders of the agribusiness sector.

The Caribbean is a relatively small region and its capacity to produce is limited. This makes it essential for industries to come together regionally to project concerns, which are common to all stakeholders, particularly at the global and hemispheric levels. No CARICOM state can do it alone and The Bahamas is no exception.

There is a role for Bahamian agribusiness to play at the regional level. For too long we have taken a back seat when, in fact, there are agribusinesses in The Bahamas which were comparable to those in the larger CARICOM states. The Bahamas has the third largest acreage in citrus among CARICOM states, only Belize and Jamaica have more. The Bahamas has the comparative advantage to grow a wider variety of vegetables on one Pine Island than any other CARICOM state. Already The Bahamas is a leader in mutton production. With more research, manpower training and funding this can be expanded to agro-industries.

Agribusiness is the hope for agriculture at the national and regional levels respectively. For agribusinesses to be competitive, the pubic and private sectors must be on one accord and work together in the best interest of the sector. National and regional groupings as associations, cooperatives or societies will ensure the survivability of agriculture as an economic activity.

Intermezzo: *The Eneas Files, The Bahama Journal* The Bahamas and CARICOM

It has been almost eight years since The Bahamas last hosted a Caribbean Heads of

Government Conference. Prior to this one, there were two others—July 1984 and July 1993.

During the decade of the 1990s, The Bahamas, owing to circumstances beyond its control has become intertwined in the affairs of CARICOM.

Being a Caribbean country, this is an inescapable fact, however, The Bahamas, despite the signs and circumstances refuse not only to acknowledge this fact but to accept it. What is the underlying reason for our inability to come to grips with the reality that The Bahamas is a small country with extremely limited resources?

When the global events of the past two decades are analyzed, the factors of globalization, WTO, FTAA, the OECD initiative against harmful tax practices, illegal immigration, the scourge of HIV/AIDS, drug trafficking and money laundering have all made it a matter of necessity to approach these issues not as a singular country but jointly with regional counterparts. To go it alone is a foolhardy exercise.

Before this deepening of involvement through the CARICOM arrangement, The Bahamas' position with the southern Caribbean islands or, as some would say, with West Indians was peripheral.

Academically, many Bahamians, prior to the era of universally free secondary education, obtained their secondary education at many of the prestigious private secondary boarding schools in Jamaica.

As UWI expanded and broadened its academic base, the government of The Bahamas recognized its value as a regional tertiary institution and decided to support it financially thereby guaranteeing places for Bahamians in the various academic and professional faculties.

The Anglican Church in The Bahamas has had a long relationship with academic life in the Caribbean through its association with Codrington College in Barbados where black Bahamians received their theological training for the Anglican priesthood. Today the link with Codrington has been intensified as almost 50% of the seminarians are Bahamians.

In the late 1960s, the then PLP administration took the decision to have The Bahamas become one of the founding members of CDB. By the 1970s, The Bahamas further extended its Caribbean involvement by participating in the CARIFTA Games. On several occasions The Bahamas hosted the games. Sporting participation now takes place in a variety of sports other than track and field with our Caribbean brothers and sisters.

At the dawn of the 21st century, Bahamian/CARICOM relationships are now at a crossroads. CARICOM governments have decided to go headlong into deepening the integration process. Some of the states are calling for the free movement of nationals between states and without passports or any sort of documentation. The Bahamas does not support this arrangement.

However, at this 22nd meeting of CARICOM Heads, two initiatives are being pushed—CSME and CCJ.

Members of The Bahamas Bar Association are already on record for being opposed to The Bahamas signing on to the CCJ. The view is that The Bahamas should stick with the Privy Council.

Most Bahamians are unfamiliar with CSME. In the Caribbean, however, this is not new because CARICOM states have been moving in this direction since the creation of CARICOM as a trading and political bloc.

Their inter-island trade along with the facilitation of a common tariff system has gradually pushed CARICOM in the direction of a single market and one Caribbean economy; much like the European Community.

Participation in this single market and economy will have serious implications for a Bahamas whose economy is open, depends on services and has a currency which is on par with that of the US dollar. In the Caribbean, currency value varies and great disparities exist from state to state.

In this region, trade is an important issue as most CARICOM states depend on earnings from exports as their major source of national revenue. With the exception of The Bahamas, all of the island states are members of WTO. With FTAA lurking in the background and scheduled to come on stream in 2005, CARICOM governments have agreed to negotiate its FTAA deal collectively through an entity called CRNM if which The Bahamas is an active participant.

Whether we Bahamians realize it or not, the ties to CARICOM are being grounded with each initiative. In his address at the opening ceremony, the Prime Minister of The Bahamas highlighted that he felt the Caribbean should be promoted in tourism circles with one identity with no national differentiation. He also called for a Regional Tourism Summit to be held here in The Bahamas sometime in October, 2002. Caribbean tourism will be under the spotlight.

As a people, I do not believe the average Bahamian is aware of the direction the political directorate is taking the country with respect to the Caribbean integration process. Whether most of us recognize it or not, The Bahamas institution by institution is being integrated into CARICOM.

It is a fact.

Our Region: Progress or Stagnation?

This past week, CDB held the annual meeting of its governors. It is interesting that 30 years ago, the late Carlton E. Francis, the then Minister of Finance in PLP was severely criticized for contributing to the capitalization of CDB. At the time, The Bahamas was one of the top three regional financiers of the bank.

During that period the skeptics felt that The Bahamas would never benefit from this investment and the funds would be squandered and misused by our "West Indian" cousins. Regionalism was a concept viewed with much suspicion.

Yet, earlier this week we learnt when The Bahamas Development Bank (BDB) borrowed $10 million dollars to fund its campaign to finance new entrepreneurs. The Minister of Finance was quick to add that the BDB had been reformed and was now geared to provide the venture capital which was badly needed to assist in the formation and development of our expanded business class.

For years regional institutions like CDB, CARICOM and UWI have not been completely understood and appreciated by Bahamians. A constant complaint is that there is too much talk and not enough action, hence the pace of growth and development have been slow when compared to other regions with similar institutions.

This criticism is not completely true as CARICOM, for example, has always practiced the big tent policy with allowed all of the countries in the region to join regardless of their level of development. This has been one of the main stumbling blocks to development.

A prime example has been Haiti's recent admission to CARICOM. Unlike EU which only admits members to the union when certain economic development standards have been attained, CARICOM granted Haiti membership despite the fact that it has the lowest per capita income in the region.

In his opening remarks at the CDB meeting, the Prime Minister of The Bahamas, the Hon. Hubert A. Ingraham stated The Bahamas was being "plagued by the seemingly unlimited flow of economic migrants."

For the past couple of weeks, The Bahamas has been inundated with Haitians attempting to escape the economic and political conditions in their homeland.

The political environment in Haiti has become volatile and this has led to an upsurge in violence which threatens their much delayed legislative and local government elections which have been scheduled for later this month.

The Haitian government was pressured by the US to set a new date for elections and warned that "failure to constitute a parliament by June 12th would risk isolating Haiti from the community of democracies and jeopardize future cooperation."

Like Haiti, there are other countries where large numbers of the populace is trapped in poverty. Here again Mr. Ingraham is calling for CDB

> "to develop more initiatives geared toward the reduction of poverty in order to stem the flow of economic migrants. In that vein, it is important for increased focus and attention to be given to the goal of poverty reduction and assistance to the poorest among us in the region."

The Bahamian economy has been buoyant through the influx of substantial foreign investment. This is likely to continue as the growth of the economy is projected to be 4% this year. The state of the economy will act as a magnet for those in the region where poverty is rampant.

The Bahamas is not alone in having a healthy economy. The Dominican Republic is urging investors to come to that country where in 1999 its economy grew 8.3% and is expected to continue on that path this year with a rate of 7%–7.5%.

The region, however, still heavily depends on the agricultural sector for employment, and agriculture today is market-driven and not production-led as in previous decades. Dietary habits have changed dramatically, particularly as the region becomes orientated more and more to tourism which, for some islands, has replaced agriculture as the major earner of foreign exchange.

Overall the region is still struggling to find itself economically. Socially, the problems abound, particularly in health, education and housing. Politically, the region is still fragmented and this, to a great extent, is rooted in the colonial past.

Our region's future in this new century will be largely determined by the choices we make in leadership, the path to economic development and the level of socialization we display in nurturing our environments.

Jamaica After 40 Years (Its First Female Prime Minister)

Kingston is the capital of Jamaica and a city of some 750,000 inhabitants. It is the largest city in the Anglophone Caribbean. One's first association with this city was at the early age of eight years old. That was more than a half century ago.

As the former centre of British colonialism in the Caribbean, Jamaica has been independent longer than any CARICOM state; it has been a sovereign nation for some four decades. In four decades a country passes through great socio-economic changes as it copes with the changing global environment.

International agencies like the World Bank have labeled Jamaica as a developing country. First world countries, or as some would say, the developed world, claim that Jamaica has lost ground developmentally over the past 40 years.

Development critics point out that its money has less value, its unemployment rate is perhaps the highest in the region, its deficits are too many and the country cannot service its debts to foreign lenders.

There is another perspective. The reason for this different point of view stems from the fact that countries in the developing world like Jamaica and The Bahamas have had their development agendas determined by others, chiefly those in the developed world who use their standards to determine where those of us in the developing countries should or should not be.

When one considers the fact that Jamaica is now a country of about 2 million people, there are several points which must be factored into the equation when making a developmental judgment. At independence, the population of Jamaica was under 1 million. Colonialism had created a wide disparity in income as it fostered less differentiation. Many Jamaicans emerged as the have-nots after independence. During the Manley Era, there was this desire to bring some equity to the socio-economic system, hence the unsuccessful experiment with socialism.

This experiment led to an exodus of Jamaicans out of the country as many of the professionals, the middle-class and siphoning of wealth out of the country by the business class. This dealt a heavy blow from which Jamaica has not fully recovered.

Despite this appearance of a setback, Jamaicans have a strong entrepreneurial spirit. There was serious economic transformation as the country moved from agriculture-based economy to tourism. Bauxite, which was one of Jamaica's main mineral exports on the world market, saw prices drop as aluminum became cheap. With the loss of preferential markets for its traditional agricultural products like sugar and bananas and shift in production activities along with low bauxite prices, the economy became a major issue.

Today, Jamaica has an extremely large informal economy. Some experts state that the informal economy is larger than the formal economy. What is the informal economy? Theoretically, an informal economy is that aspect of the economy which is not calculated into the national economic statistics.

Throughout Jamaica, one sees examples of what economists call "penny capitalism" where people are selling all sorts of things on roadsides, street corners, sidewalks, on horses, in vehicles and whatever. Thousands and thousands of people make a living in this manner everyday of the week, yet the World Bank and other agencies statistics would classify them as poor and unemployed and here lies the fallacy of the international system of economic classification.

The big element in the informal economy is the drug trade.

It is also said that there are more Jamaicans outside of Jamaica than in Jamaica. A big part of the national income is remittances from Jamaicans abroad.

Like most countries, Jamaica has been challenged by the provision of educational and healthcare facilities and services and infrastructure to facilitate national development. To provide these necessities, the country had to borrow huge sums of money. When a high percentage of your population is at the low tier of the income bracket, it hampers the revenue from taxation and that is why throughout the region, possibly with the exception of Trinidad and Tobago, which enjoys huge revenues from oil and gas, national governments are relatively poor.

Even a country like The Bahamas, which is considered a relatively wealthy place with a high per capita income, the government has earning capacity but operatesout of a deficit state because of the inability to collect revenue from taxes. Throughout CARICOM, this is a problem.

Since 1976, Jamaica has been experiencing exchange rate decline; however in some aspect this made their tourism product more attractive. In addition, Jamaica maximizes its tourism revenue through strong linkages with other sectors in the economy, thereby incorporating a substantial number of domestic items into their tourism product.

Jamaica is a vibrant and dynamic society as depicted in its music, cuisine and people.

Regional Sustainability

Developing countries undergo a great deal of criticism from the western press. But when one considers the level of economic development in many countries, it is amazing to see where some Third World leaders have brought their countries.

When many of these countries achieved their independence, the human resource was under developed; the infrastructure was centered on the natural resource of a country and the capacity of the owners to gain access to that resource thereby being able to exploit that natural resource. However, when one surveys the development scene of the Caribbean, specifically the CARICOM states of which Jamaica is the oldest at 43 years of independent status.

The CARICOM states, even though all of them have experienced economic uncertainties and difficulties, they have all managed to survive. The ups and downs in the Caribbean economic development process was in the hands of government, consequently it was the governmental process which drove development. With advent of globalization, all of that had to change, as the watchword in the globalization process became competitiveness.

Governments facilitate competitiveness whereas the private sector drives it. It is this re-orientation which has gradually shifted not only the reaction of governments but also the thinking of society—the private sector, the unions, non-governmental organizations, international bodies, funding agencies, etc.

The impact of this new approach has manifested itself in the Caribbean, and it can be seen and felt in every CARICOM state.

It has to borne in mind that there are really three component states comprising CARICOM. In the small island economies of Jamaica, Barbados, Trinidad and Tobago and The Bahamas, there is one type of development orientation. Then there is the sub-regional grouping—OECS, which is in the process of fashioning its own socio-economic development paradigm. The continental CARICOM states of Guyana, Suriname and Belize are huge landmasses with much potential in agribusiness, few people and are transforming their food production systems to become more competitive in the global market.

Haiti though a member of CARICOM remains a special case in my estimation because of its history and mode of development. All of the CARICOM states were former colonial possessions and whose development process was shaped by their colonial experience.

Within CARICOM, these are three distinct development scenarios now in place. Fundamental to all of them is the fact that they all must push their economies in the direction of achieving sustainable economic growth and development.

In all states, democratic principles are firmly entrenched and also in every state there is a stable government. The big question is the quality of governance in these states, specifically the decision-making process. There is a major concern regarding the manner in which social issues are tackled i.e. gender equality, socio-economic marginalization, human resource development, shelter, HIV/AIDS, poverty alleviation, etc. Most governments in CARICOM have been unsuccessful in finding sustainable solutions to these issues. The aftermath has been reflected in the proliferation of declining living standards in urban environments and the manifestation of this decline via the increase of crime, very often violent crime.

This is apparent in almost every state. In Jamaica, the murder rate has skyrocketed. Recently there have been a series of terrorist-type bombings in Port of Spain. In The Bahamas, violent crime has been and is being fueled by the drug trade.

For most of the second half of the 20th century, the Caribbean has been attempting to define itself as one of the premier tourism destinations in the world. Valiant strides have been made; the inability of governments to find solutions to these social issues will cause the strengths of the region i.e., sun, sand, sea to be minimized thereby retarding the capacity of the regional governments to attain sustained economic growth and development. For these islands and continental states comprising CARICOM are to become truly independent, the governments, civil society and the private sector have to work together to transform the region into a sea of sustainability in the social, economic, political and cultural life in the Caribbean Sea.

CSME: A Response to Globalization

One of the features of globalization is the adherence to international standards and regulations. Countries are expected to conform in a range of activities—some economic, some social, some political. For a state to be regarded as stable and a contributor to the global community, its national legislation and laws must line up with those of a globalized world. This is the environment in which we live and in which we have to compete.

This is globalization and experts have defined it as the following:

> "The integration and democratization of the world's culture, economy and infrastructure through transnational investment, rapid proliferation of information through communication technologies and the impact of free market forces on local, regional and national economies."

This is the interpretation or comprehension of the meaning of globalization. It is essential that we in this archipelago come to grip with the manner in which the world sees itself.

The seeds of globalization go as far back as the Industrial Revolution. It has been an evolving process. Unless we understand its genesis, it will be difficult for many of us to appreciate its impact on today's Bahamas.

The Industrial Revolution was the result of many fundamental, interrelated changes that transformed agricultural economies into industrial ones. The most immediate changes were in the nature of production: what was produced, as well as where and how. Productivity and technical efficiency grew dramatically, in part through the systematic application of scientific and practical knowledge of the manufacturing process. Efficiency was also enhanced when large groups of business enterprises were located in a defined area. The Industrial Revolution led to the growth of cities, as people moved from rural areas into urban communities to live and work.

These changes revolutionized the way people lived and worked. It was a decisive period in mankind's growth and development. It has not let up; globalization has only intensified what was started with the Industrial Revolution.

The Industrial Revolution caused economies to change and transformed societies.

Economic change accelerated far reaching social changes like in the area of the movement of people from rural areas to urban centers. Today, it is the movement of people from one country to another. The availability of a greater variety of material goods influenced people to move from rural locations to urban areas where amenities were more accessible and near at hand. Today 86% of Bahamians live between Grand Bahama and New Providence, the urban centers of our archipelago.

During the Industrial Revolution, science and technology come into greater focus and change the way houses was constructed. Information technology has done the same today as a borderless world has been created by the Internet.

The Industrial Revolution started in the second half of the 18th century; three centuries later we are in the Globalization Era, which is really a 20th/21st century version of the Industrial Revolution.

Europe and the US were the initial beneficiaries of the Industrial Revolution as their economies become highly industrialized. By the 20th century industrialization on a world scale extended to parts of Asia and the Pacific region as Japan, Korea and China emerged as industrial giants. Today mechanized production and more economic growth continues to elude much of the world, particularly those countries which provided the raw materials and manpower to fuel the Industrial Revolution and ultimately enriching the economies of Europe and the US.

For its benefits, Europe when shared its former colonial possessions create a block of countries called ACP States comprising the newly independent countries of the Caribbean, Africa and The Pacific. The US, on the other hand with geopolitical dominance, had the countries of Latin America and the Caribbean as its client markets. Despite the fact that the Industrial Revolution has been here for virtually three centuries, the states comprising the client markets are still struggling with the economic reality of underdevelopment.

To accelerate the situation, the beneficiary countries of the Industrial Revolution mainly EU, the US and Japan have thrust the globalization concept on these states, many of which are small economies, with limited human, physical and natural resources.

The main agent of globalization is the WTO and the mechanism for global economic integration has been the instrument of trade liberalization. The response to this new world economic order has been the establishment of economic blocs in order to take advantage of economies of scale. The smaller countries, particularly those comprising the client markets have utilized the economic integration approach as a response mechanism in order to achieve some semblance of economic scale.

It is out of this scenario that at the global level, the rules and regulations of trade are established by the WTO. To take advantage of economies of scale through economic integration, the Europeans established EU and the US set up NAFTA. By 2005 the intention is to further expand by creating FTAA, which will include the NAFTA countries (USA, Canada and Mexico) and the client market states of Latin American and the Caribbean.

Realizing its economic and political limitations, the Caribbean client market states of both Europe and US formed CARICOM. CARICOM initially was a political response to the international realities of states emerging from colonialism. The economic realities called for integration if they were to survive as sovereign states, hence the need for the establishment of a CSME as the response mechanism to globalization via trade liberalization.

At some point over the next decade, Bahamians will have to change and decide the mechanism of response to globalization of our country.

Epilogue: The New Caribbean

Every state and dependency in the Caribbean has passed through the three epochs of slavery, colonialism and internal self-government/independence to attain levels of sophistication in social, economic and political growth and development.

This has stemmed from a variety of reasons, natural resources, human resource base, geopolitical environment, trade routes and comparative advantages to its sister states and/ or dependencies. These reasons have also played a significant role in the integration of island peoples and the cross fertilization of culture and cuisine. Out of this has evolved a mix, which has produced characteristics which are common rather than differential in scope and appearance. It is this which has spawned uniqueness out of the diversity which is natural to each state, be it continental or island, or dependency.

In the 1950s, the Caribbean was portrayed by Hollywood with the movie *Island in the Sun*, which starred a Caribbean descendent, Harry Belafonte. One memorable scene in the movie was Belafonte and a group of small farmers loading bananas on to a freight ship as they sang *The Banana Boat Song*. The Independence Era has given birth to a new Caribbean and the Belafonte, *Island in the Sun* version is no longer on the radar.

The dissolution of the West Indies Federation in retrospect may have been a blessing in disguise. Its experience led to the creation of CARICOM which has come into its own as a regional bloc. It has steered the region in a number of areas, principally institutional strengthening, thereby enhancing the region's reputation as having a strong participatory democracy and solid foundation in democratic principles.

CARICOM's institutional response to WTO was the establishment of CRNM. CCJ will replace the Privy Council and become the region's Court of Final Appeal.

CARICOM has expanded to include Haiti. Through CARIFORUM, CARICOM has added the Dominican Republic and now needs to attract Cuba into its fold possibly by extending the CARIFORUM arrangement. Cuba is the largest island state in the region and its inclusion in the affairs of the region's premier political bloc would only enhance the importance of the region hemispherically and globally.

Cuba as a tourism destination is gaining momentum. In 2006, there were 2 million visitors. It is popular because of the safety to its visitors, its historic and cultural values and the enthusiasm of the Cuba people.

The Caribbean has become a major tourism destination attracting 40-50 million visitors annually by sea and air. This large number of people and the infrastructure to support this business has dramatically changed the landscape on virtually every island.

The Caribbean has become a centre for medical education. The Medical Faculty of UWI has become renowned for its scholarship in tropical medicine. Individuals from principally North America are being trained by the thousands in offshore medical schools in the Eastern Caribbean and the Dominican Republic.

Despite developmental advances, Caribbean people continue to migrate to the US and Canada. As the region matures, establishes its identity and develops a sense of self, leadership in the public and private sectors respectively will find new avenues to diversify our small island economies. The urge to migrate should decrease as greater opportunities come to fruition in the region, and with a single economy and market and the capacity of people to move freely about the region, the necessity to migrate would diminish substantially. There is already evidence of trend as thousands of CARICOM people have taken employment opportunities in The Bahamas. Likewise, hundreds of Guyanese are working in the Barbadian construction industry.

US Immigration and Census Bureau Statistics have revealed that since 2000, there are 8 million foreign-born US residents who came to the US for employment or education.

Among these 8 million, about 6% or 480,000 individuals were from the Caribbean. The median age was 27.6 years old of which some 240,000 pay 30% of their income or more for housing. Their incomes for men are $22,656 and for women $20,485. About 120,000 of these individuals live below the US poverty level.

The main field of employment is construction and followed closely by accommodation and food services and manufacturing.

When a comparison of this data, particularly per capita income and employment opportunities is made with Caribbean states, one can conclude that a number of Caribbean states offer comparable per capita incomes and employment opportunities thereby decreasing the need to immigrate.

With economic restructuring, the need to immigrate will decrease. The Dual Sector approach can do much to assist in realigning or right sizing Agriculture (small farmers) with Services (Tourism and Financial Services) in most states and Petroleum in Trinidad and Tobago.

The 2007 Cricket World Cup has already brought the region into the global spotlight as host for this global event. Even though it will take place in the Anglophone Caribbean, the region as a whole will receive substantial publicity and the event is expected to bring huge numbers of visitors from the cricketing countries of England, Australia, New Zealand, India, Pakistan, Sri Lanka and East and South Africa countries. This event will introduce a different grouping of visitors from the regular North American or European visitors.

Millions of dollars are being spent by CARICOM governments on training in hospitality as well as by the private sector in upgrading and refurbishing properties, particularly in the nine islands which will become venues for matches.

The promotional materials for this event will project the Caribbean as a region and not the individual venue sites. It is the region which is being presented to the world and not the individual states.

The post World War II Era ushered in the transformation of the Caribbean from economies which were agriculture-based to economies which are essentially service and/ or industry-based. For most Caribbean states this transformation started in the 1960s and today the region is a premier travel destination.

The economic thrust for the emergence of this new Caribbean was the region's proximity to North America, the relative political stability and the nurturing of social, religious and educational institutions resulting from its colonial ties to Europe. These combined with factors like the climatic conditions (sun, sand and sea), the enthusiastic people, the cultural diversity, democratic principles and a capitalistic environment made the region an ideal locale for investment in tourism developments and the establishment of offshore financial organizations. These pushed governments to provide the necessary infrastructure to enhance this new development path.

This scenario has improved both the standard of living and the quality of life in the region. This has been reflected in the rise of per capita income and burgeoning GDPs in most economies.

The Caribbean in the Independence Era is a very different place from the Colonial Caribbean. It has become a sophisticated domain as a result of second home owners who have developed enclaves on most islands. Where Financial Services is a component of the economy, offshore bankers, accountants, lawyers and other financial professionals have created a market for expensive residential accommodations as well as for schools and social amenities. On islands with a mature financial service sector, indigenous professionals have become a part of this lifestyle.

The Caribbean has become one of the global centers for professional education in medicine, both human and veterinary. These institutes can be found on almost every island and this has created a demand for accommodation for lecturers, students and administrative staffs along with the regional infrastructure for teaching, administration and other facilities.

This overall scenario has created a new Caribbean.

Chapter Notes

Chapter 1

CIA *World Factbook*

CARICOM Website

Sources of History

The Stability of the Caribbean

Geopolitics of the Caribbean

Chapter 2

Bahamian Handbook

Bahamas Dept. of Statistics

Agriculture in The Bahamas

History of The Bahamas

Chapter 3

Agri View, vol. 11, No. 2 and vol. 12, No. 1

IICA Background: Target 2015, The Jagdeo Initiative

FAO Magazine *Spotlight*: More Fruits and Vegetables

Caribbean Food and Nutrition Institute

Protocol for the Nutritional Management of Obesity, Diabetes and Hypertension in the Caribbean

Caribbean FAO List, Barbados

Chapter 4

World Bank Report: *A Time to Choose: Caribbean Development in the 21st Century*

Flexner Report, Wikipedia, the Free Encyclopedia

Chapter 5

Budget Address 2002

Chapter 6

Anthony Hill—*Development of Tourism* (Page 46−48) Economic Stability in the Mini States, The Stability of the Caribbean

Table 6.2   CARICOM Tourist Arrivals 1969−1971

Chapter 7

World Bank—Haiti	Options and Opportunities for Inclusive Growth Trends, Determinants and Constraints of Haiti's Economic Growth
World Bank—Haiti	Social Resilience and State Fragility World Bank Report No. 36069—HT April 27, 2006—Caribbean Country Management Unit

Chapter 8

Carstens, Agustin (2006, May 1)	*Regional Integration in a Globalizing World: Priorities for the Caribbean* Biennial International Conference on Business, Banking and Finance, Port of Spain, Trinidad and Tobago http://www.imf.org/external
World Bank Report	*Caribbean Countries Must Improve Productivity and Competitiveness to Accelerate Growth*
Anstey, Caroline	*A Time to Choose: Caribbean Development in the 21st Century* http://web.worldbank.org
Lewis, W.A	*Theory of Economic Growth*

Mr. Michael Griffin,

In response to the above, please note that for the purposes of our surveys here at the Ministry of Agriculture and Lands, historically, we defined "small farmers" as persons who operate less than 5 acres (2 ha) of land. According to the 1996 Census of Agriculture, there were 158,795 such persons in Jamaica. The composition was as follows:

Landless	14,980
Under 1 ha	115,267
1 ha–2 ha	28,548
Total	158,795

There is an overlap in the next category which is 2–5 ha. This consists of 22,332 farmers, but as you will notice it would include some of the farmers in our definition and some which would exceed the definition. I think the difficulty arose because in our context, 5 acres is a reasonably manageable farm size for a small farmer, and that was the farm size that we most often encountered in our surveys among this group. The lines became somewhat blurred when we went metric. Another Agricultural Census is to start in February, so we hope to be able to update the above information soon.

In the Agricultural Census conducted in 1996 holding/farm was defined as "The land being utilized in full or part for agricultural purposes..."

To distinguish kitchen gardens and backyard farms from genuine holdings, the following distinctions were made.

A holding or farm is any agricultural enterprise with a minimum of at least one of the following:

① one square chain (0.41 ha.) of cultivation crops including flowers whether in a greenhouse/shade house or not. Where the farmer has nothing else but a greenhouse/shade house it must not be less than 4,400 sq .ft. in area;

② 12 economic trees i.e. citrus, mangoes, breadfruit, etc.;

③ one head of cattle;

④ two pigs, two goats, or two sheep;

⑤ one dozen poultry including ducks, turkeys etc.;

⑥ six beehives;

⑦ a fish pond of any size.

Economic Units engaged solely in the following economic activities were not considered agricultural holdings:

—hunting, trapping, and game propagation;

—forestry and logging;

—marine fishing.

Activities related solely to the operation of plant nurseries were also not to be included.

As I have said the information is somewhat dated, the Agricultural Census from 1996 did point out that the area in agricultural lands was declining even then, and recent developments indicate that it has declined even further, but the information should provide some indication of what we had. We are putting systems in place to keep the information more current.

Regards,

H.D. Bernard

Information from the Agency for Reconstruction and Developmant Inc. (ARD) Land Utilization Survey, Grenada. Grenada's farmers may be aging, but six out of ten farmers believe that when they retire there is someone in the family who will continue operating the family farm.

This is one of several indications emanating from the Land Utilization Survey, conducted in November 2005 by ARD, in collaboration with the Ministry of Agriculture, Lands, Forestry and Fisheries.

The survey revealed that the mean age for farmers is 53.7 years, which is approximately two years older that it was when the Agricultural Census was conducted in 1995.

However, even though the mean age of farmers has increased, 62% say they can identify a relative as a successor.

The survey, which was geographically stratified from 100 Enumeration Districts, included face to face interviews with 1,016 randomly selected farmers. The questionnaire contained 104 questions under the following headings:

① Land status;

② Labour information;

③ Land utilization;

④ Nutmeg and cocoa;

⑤ Other crops;

⑥ Future intentions;

⑦ Praedial larceny;

⑧ Financial and technical assistance;

⑨ Farm associations and marketing;

⑩ Attractiveness of labour pool and land bank;

⑪ Farm contribution to income.

Here are some highlight about the state of Grenada's farms and the composition of the farming population, as gleaned from the survey:

① 73% of respondents were male;

② 62% were between the age of 41 and 70 years;

③ 77% indicated primary school as the highest level of education;

④ 68% indicated farming as their main occupation;

⑤ 71% of farms are less than 5 acres;

⑥ 27% of farms are between 1 and 2 acres;

⑦ 24% of farms are between 2 and 5 acres;

⑧ 89% of farmers own their farms and posses the Title Deed;

⑨ 77% do not have access to irrigation;

⑩ 69% use chemical fertilizer;

⑪ 40% use pen manure.

The land survey results were released to stakeholders during a formal presentation at the ARD Board Room on January 19 at which Minister of Agriculture, Lands, Forestry and Fisheries Gregory Bowen said the Government of Grenada generally and the Ministry of Agriculture, Lands, Forestry and Fisheries in particular will be guided by the survey results.

Minister Bowen said that,

> "We will do whatever we can—given our limited resources—in collaboration with the ARD, the commodity boards, the farming community and all other stakeholders involved in agriculture to further advance and modernize the sector."

January 23, 2006

Agency for Reconstruction and Development Inc.

Botanical Gardens, St. George's, Grenada

Tel: 473-439-5606/07/08

Fax: 473-439-5609

Email: mail@ardgrenada.org

Spore Magazine—"Viewpoint"

Summary of Registered Farmers by Island as of May 18th, 2005—Bahamas

Island	# Of Registered Farmers
Abaco	64
Acklins	4
Andros	182
Andros—south	7
Cat Island	245
Crooked Island	2
Eleuthera—central	90
Eleuthera—north	60
Eleuthera—south	121
Exumas	71
Grand Bahama	20
Inagua	1
Long Island	182
Mayaguana	7
New Providence	184
San Salvador	2
Total	1,242

Source: GAP

An Introduction

World agriculture in the 21st century is faced with three main challenges: ① to improve food security, rural livelihoods and income; ② to satisfy the increasing and diversified demands for safe food and other products; and, ③ to conserve and protect natural resources. These challenges have been articulated by the international community through the World Food Summit Plan of Action and the Millennium Development Goals with specific targets to be met by 2015.

Agriculture is expected to assure food security in a range of settings, now and in the future, and is increasingly called upon to produce positive environmental, social and economic benefits. While agriculture is a key contributor to sustainable development and to meeting these challenges, the paradigm is dramatically shifting for its primary producers in the context of a rapidly changing food economy and globalization.

These challenges can be tackled in part through a GAP approach—a means to concretely contribute to environmental, economic and social sustainability of on-farm production resulting in safe and healthy food and non-food agricultural products. A GAP approach can address the demand-side priorities of consumers and retailers, the supply-side priorities of producers and labourers, and those institutions and services that are bridging supply and demand. While a GAP approach may respond to the growing demands of increasingly globalized and integrated agricultural sectors, it can have important implications for local and national markets.

The development of a GAP approach by FAO emerges against an expanding backdrop of codes, standards and schemes relating to agricultural practices and products. In this context, the term GAP has many different meanings. For example, it is used to refer to private, voluntary and non-regulatory applications that are being developed in a number of forms by the private sector, civil society organizations and governments to meet farmers' and consumers' needs and specific requirements in the food production chain. It is also formally recognized in international regulatory framework and associated codes of practice to minimize or prevent the contamination of food.

Given the trend in development and adoption of codes and standards by different actors, and cognizant of the challenges of, and commitments to, world agriculture, FAO initiated a process of consultation to seek understanding and consensus on the principles, indicators and means of applying GAP. Following on two initial electronic conferences and elaboration of GAP concepts in the context of Sustainable Agriculture and Rural Development, the 17th Session of the Committee on Agriculture (COAG) in April 2003 recommended that FAO continue its initial work on a GAP approach.

This could include awareness raising, information exchange, economic analysis, pilot projects, technical assistance and capacity building, with a special focus on the needs of developing countries.

As follow up to the COAG discussions, an Expert Consultation on a GAP approach was held from November 10th to 12th, 2003. It aimed to review and confirm the overall concept, provide guidance on addressing concerns, identify strategies for implementation and recommend actions for FAO in the development and implementation of a GAP approach. Experts representing various disciplines and the private, public and civil society sectors from Argentina, Canada, Croatia, Ethiopia, France, Germany, India, Namibia, New Zealand, Malaysia, the Philippines, Uganda, UK, and US, as well as selected experts from FAO, participated in the consultation.

The Expert Consultation consisted of a mix of chaired presentations, facilitated dialogue, working groups, and opportunities for general comments. Three background documents[①] were provided to participants: an overall concept paper on developing a GAP approach was supported by two papers focusing on the following two aspects.

① A summary analysis of the types of existing codes, standards and guidelines related to agricultural practices.

② Incentives for adoption of GAP by farmers and other actors in the agricultural sector.

These documents were designed to serve a starting point for the discussions.

The consultation provided a wealth of insights and suggestions, the most significant of which is that a GAP approach should be seen as a means to an end (i.e. to achieve environmental, economic and social sustainability of on-farm production resulting in safe and healthy food and non-food agricultural products), rather than an end itself. The preliminary recommendations for FAO included the following aspects.

---

① The three documents are development of a GAP approach; summary analysis of relevant codes, guidelines, and standards related to GAPs; and incentives for the adoption of GAPs.

① Describe and define the concept of GAP that includes the following aspects:

three pillars of sustainability: GAP should be economically viable, environmentally sustainable, and socially acceptable; inclusive of food safety and quality dimensions;

with a focus on primary production;

taking into account existing voluntary and mandatory codes of practices and guidelines in agriculture;

within a given incentives and institutional context.

② Identify and compare existing GAP related schemes (for consistency) along with drivers and motivation and identify experience of countries practicing GAP in different formats.

③ Elaborate global principles as well as guidelines for developing and tailoring GAPs within a given context (based on menu of possible applications and the outcome desired).

④ Organize multi-stakeholder national and regional workshops for networking and promoting mechanisms to enable the development of agreed GAPs in local contexts.

⑤ Create capacity through:

awareness creation and education of actors in the market chain (including consumers);

awareness creation among policy makers;

information sharing through databases, portal, web (ecosystem, commodity, etc.);

pilot projects at the national and regional level—training of trainers and farmer leaders.

⑥ Mobilize resources for development and application of a GAP approach.